WORLD BEER

WORLD BEER

TIM HAMPSON

with **Stan Hieronymus**, **Sylvia Kopp**, and **Adrian Tierney-Jones**

LONDON • NEW YORK
MELBOURNE • MUNICH • DELHI

DK LONDON

Project Editor Becky Shackleton
Senior Designer Collette Sadler
Design Assistant Kate Fenton
Managing Editor Dawn Henderson
Managing Art Editor Christine Keilty
Senior Jackets Creative Nicola Powling
Jacket Design Assistant Rosie Levine
Senior Production Editor Andy Hilliard
Senior Production Controller Oliver Jeffreys
Creative Technical Support Sonia Charbonnier
Publisher Peggy Vance
Art Director Peter Luff

Editor Nicola Hodgson
Original Photography Peter Anderson

DK INDIA

Senior Art Editor Anchal Kaushal
Art Editors Prashant Kumar, Swati Katyal
Editor Divya Chandhok
Assistant Editor Neha Samuel
Managing Art Editor Navidita Thapa
Deputy Managing Editor Chitra Subramanyam
Pre-Production Manager Sunil Sharma
DTP Designers Manish Chandra Upreti, Neeraj Bhatia,
Nityanand Kumar
Production Manager Pankaj Sharma

First published in Great Britain in 2013 by
Dorling Kindersley Limited
80 Strand, London WC2R 0RL
Penguin Group (UK)

Copyright © 2013 Dorling Kindersley Limited

2 4 6 8 10 9 7 5 3 1
001-187276-Oct/2013

A CIP catalogue record for this book is available from the British
Library.
ISBN 978-1-4093-2160-6

Printed and bound in China by South China

Discover more at
www.dk.com

CONTENTS

FOREWORD

"Vive la différence! Viva la revolución." Not my words, but those of the late great beer writer Michael Jackson (1942–2007). Michael was one of the most influential and passionate advocates of beer the world has ever seen – he would marvel today at how the brave new world of craft beer has continued to evolve

SINCE MICHAEL JACKSON started writing about beer in the 1970s, beer culture in the US has undergone a revolution that has now spread worldwide. Some predicted that by the end of the last century there would be only five brewers in the US – now there are more than 2,000, and numbers are on the rise in many other countries as well. Around the world, new microbreweries and brewpubs are opening on an almost daily basis. Aspirant, ambitious brewers are sharing the stage with older brewers of great eminence, with roots and traditions reaching back, in some cases, hundreds of years. The old beer world of Europe has embraced this new revolution, and countries that once seemed awash with industrialized beers have been reinvigorated.

ACROSS THE PLANET there is a growing interest in innovative beer styles, some once lost and now revived, and others that are wonderful new creations. Through these pages the reader can visit Belgium and read about the marvels of Trappist breweries and sour beers like gueuze and faro; take a trip to Germany – once the home of ubiquitous lagers – and find beers that are heavy with aromatic US hops or deliciously smoked; or tour Italy, once famed for its wine and now renowned for having some of the world's most creative brewers. Turn a page and you can be in Australia, Argentina, Brazil, the Czech Republic, or Japan. Each country has some outstanding beers on offer – and thanks to the craft beer movement's spirit of collaboration, beer has few geographic or cultural barriers any more.

BREWING IS AN INDUSTRY whose roots can be traced back to our earliest times and its positive influences weave like a golden, sparkling thread through human history. But as well as being a rich part of our past, the craft brewing industry also provides a beacon of hope for the future – at its cutting edge is a new wave of entrepreneurs, running hundreds of microbreweries, many of whom are champions of localism. This book celebrates the quality, choice, experimentalism, and individualism of these craft brewers. It tells the stories of these innovative brewers and lifts the lid on their philosophies, technical set-up, and most outstanding beers.

THIS BOOK CELEBRATES the fact that beer has just as much variety and complexity as the finest wines, and through its tasting notes and food pairing suggestions, aims to aid the reader on their quest to find exceptional beer. In this book I hope to demonstrate the diversity and nobility of beer. Once journalists talked about beer, drank beer, and then wrote about wine. Today we can celebrate beer with great pride and embark on this world tour in pursuit of outstanding beer.

INTRODUCTION

A BRIEF HISTORY OF BEER

What made our ancestors hit on the idea that grains of grass mixed with water and touched by the magic of yeast could become a vivacious, enriching drink?

We'll never know for sure, but possibly some 9,000 or 10,000 years ago in the sweeping fertile plains of Mesopotamia, or somewhere in China, nomadic hunter gatherers started to grow and harvest an ancient type of grain and make an early form of beer. Archaeological evidence suggests that humans have been creating alcohol for millennia. And what a journey it has been. Over the centuries, our relationship with beer has affected our history, laws, culture, science, and technology. And beer has changed and evolved as we have. It is the journey beer has taken – through purity laws and Prohibition via the thrill of home-brewing – that has resulted in the rich proliferation of styles today.

1587

THE FIRST CORN-BASED BEER was brewed by colonists in Virginia, but that didn't stop them from sending back to England for more, as raw materials were scarce in the New World. The building of brewhouses became a priority as the colonists became settled, and in the early days many used birch and spruce in their beers. The first North American commercial brewery was started by the Dutch West India Company in lower Manhattan in 1632.

THE BREWER, A 16TH-CENTURY WOODCUT BY J AMMON, DEPICTS EARLY BREWING SCENES

4300bce

BABYLONIAN clay tablets detail recipes for an alcoholic drink made with grain – as well as being a thirst-quencher, it may also have been used as an offering to the gods.

FACT OR FICTION?

FICTION? In the year 1520, King Henry VI banned the use of hops in England.
FACT The story is simply not true, says beer historian Martyn Cornell. Hops were forbidden for use in ale, but this is because at the time, ale was classified as an unhopped drink.

7000bce

FICTION? Arthur Guinness took out a 9,000-year lease on the Guinness brewery in 1759.
FACT True. But according to beer historian Martyn Cornell, this was likely to have been a legal dodge, not overconfidence.

FACT OR FICTION?

ARCHAEOLOGISTS have recently discovered a 3,000-year-old rice and millet drink that was preserved inside sealed bronze vessels in a tomb at the Shang Dynasty capital of Anyang in the Yellow River Basin in China.

1000bce

IN BAVARIA, the so-called Beer Purity law – the *Reinheitsgebot* – was established. It states that barley, hops, and pure water are the only ingredients to be allowed in the brewing process. It didn't extend to the rest of Germany until 1906 but is still used today worldwide.

STAMPS CIRCA 1983 DEPICT A BREWER'S SYMBOL AND CELEBRATE OVER 450 YEARS OF BEER PURITY

IN MUNICH, a festival is held to celebrate the marriage of Crown Prince Ludwig – it puts German beer on the map and goes on to become the Oktoberfest beer festival.

A STAMP CELEBRATES THE FESTIVAL'S CENTENNIAL IN 1910

1810

POTTERY found in a Neolithic village at the Jiahu site in the Yellow River Valley in China contains traces of compounds found in alcoholic drinks.

7000bce

1516

FICTION? In 1772, a London brewer created porter, to replace a style pulled from a trio of casks called "three threads".
FACT It's a nice story, but porter was certainly drunk in London before this date.

FACT OR FICTION?

1842

THE FIRST GOLDEN LAGER

is produced in Plzeň, in the modern-day Czech Republic, and is an immediate hit. It is a renowned style that has been emulated worldwide.

THIS POSTCARD AND BEER MAT, MADE AROUND 1910 AND 1842, PROUDLY ADVERTISE THE WORLD-FAMOUS, PATENTED PILSNER URQUELL

1919

PROHIBITION, in the form of the 18th Amendment and the Volstead Act, restricted the manufacture and sale of alcohol in the US. The sale and distribution of beer fell into the hands of criminals and many breweries were forced to close. By 1932, Prohibition had become much derided and many people took to the streets to demand its end. Anheuser-Busch survived Prohibition by producing corn syrup, ice cream, malt extract, and root beer. Prohibition was repealed in most states in 1933 but continued in Mississippi until 1966.

SHEET MUSIC WAS WRITTEN THAT MOCKED PROHIBITION

FACT OR FICTION?

FICTION? Lager was first brewed in the UK in 1965.
FACT Absolutely wrong, lager started to become popular in the late 1960s and took off in the 1970s. It now accounts for three out of every four beers drunk in the UK, but it was certainly brewed in Britain as early as the 1870s.

FACT OR FICTION?

FICTION? US beer should be served ice-cold for best flavour.
FACT The success of the craft beer revolution has helped dispel this myth. Beer's flavour diminishes the colder it gets.

1976

FICTION? Refrigerated railcars helped create the first national brand in the US.
FACT It's true. By 1876, Anheuser-Busch owned a fleet of 40 refrigerated railroad cars that it used to transport bottled beer across the US.

FACT OR FICTION?

LOUIS PASTEUR published his seminal book *Études sur la Bière*, soon translated into English as *Studies on Fermentation*. For the first time, the mysterious world of yeast and its role in brewing was described scientifically. Modern brewing techniques were replacing the dark ages of empiricalism, and refrigeration and automatic bottling were becoming widespread.

1876

FOUR ENGLISH JOURNALISTS, Michael Hardman, Graham Lees, Bill Mellor, and Jim Makin, discuss setting up a consumer organization for beer drinkers. It goes on to become the Campaign for Real Ale (CAMRA) and is one of the world's most successful consumer organizations. CAMRA's membership is rapidly approaching 150,000 and its campaigning work has led to a resurgence of cask ale in the UK and a renewed interest in locally brewed beers worldwide.

CAMRA ORGANIZES BEER FESTIVALS ALL YEAR ROUND ACROSS THE UNITED KINGDOM

1971

HOME-BREWER Jack McAuliffe turned his hobby of home-brewing into a business, opening the New Albion Brewing Co in Sonoma, California. It helped kickstart a craft brewing revolution that would change the face of beer forever (see more overleaf).

JACK MCAULIFFE AT WORK AT THE NEW ALBION BREWING CO IN CALIFORNIA

NEW ALBION ALE & STOUT LABELS

1976

THE CRAFT BEER REVOLUTION

The craft beer revolution, which started in the US and has since taken off worldwide, had its roots in the Prohibition era, when the 18th Amendment placed restrictions on the manufacture and sale of alcohol in the US. By the time it was repealed in the 1930s, hundreds of local breweries had been lost, and those that remained only brewed a limited range. Over the years, many of the breweries were taken over by large companies, all brewing pale, bland beers.

CALIFORNIA SHERIFFS DUMPING ILLEGAL ALCOHOL DURING PROHIBITION

BUT CHANGE WAS ON ITS WAY. Californian Jack McAuliffe is widely regarded as the forefather of the US craft beer revolution. A naval technician, he worked on a Scottish nuclear submarine base in the 1970s. On his return to the US, he took up home-brewing in an attempt to recreate the ales he had developed a taste for while overseas. In 1976, he turned his hobby into a business, and opened the New Albion Brewing Co in Sonoma, California. He transformed equipment from a former dairy and soft drink factory into a brewery. It was California's first new brewery since Prohibition and the story of how McAuliffe's pale ale, stout, and porter were taking on the might of Budweiser and Miller became a national news story. Sadly, New Albion closed in 1982, but it was not the only brewery breaking new ground.

HAVING BEEN FOUNDED IN 1896, Anchor Brewing (see p.147) was well established when the New Albion Brewery opened, but it had suffered greatly during Prohibition. However, its fortunes changed following a buy-out in 1965 by Fritz Maytag, a Stanford graduate and heir to a washing machine company, which enabled the brewery to invigorate

ANCHOR BREWING WAS FOUNDED IN SAN FRANCISCO, CALIFORNIA, IN 1896

NEW ALBION BEGAN LIFE AS A DAIRY, USING EQUIPMENT FROM A SOFT DRINK FACTORY

its production and introduce US beer lovers to porter, barley wine, wheat ale, and, of course, its legendary Steam Beer. The brewery also experimented with exciting US hop varieties, such as Cascade. Breweries such as these were brought to the attention of the world with the help of the influential British beer writer and author Michael Jackson, who died in 2007. His vivid writing, public appearances, and TV documentaries fostered and encouraged a worldwide craft beer industry – the landscape of craft beer would look very different today were it not for his influence. Another figure at the forefront of the revolution was Charlie Papazian, who founded the American Homebrewers Association in 1978. It's an organization that has inspired thousands of brews. Meanwhile, across the Atlantic, the foundation of the UK's Campaign for Real Ale (CAMRA) in 1971 was another key moment in the craft beer movement. Consumers now had a forum in which to talk critically about the beers that they wanted to drink, and a rise in home-brewing meant that creating their own businesses became a very real possibility. Beer was being taken out of the hands of industrialists and given back to the people.

KEY LANDMARKS IN CRAFT BREWING

1920
With the adoption of the 18th Amendment, Prohibition comes into force, placing strict regulations on how alcohol is produced and sold. Prior to Prohibition, there were more than 3,200 breweries in the US. This drops to an all-time low of 80 US breweries in 1983.

1930
Prohibition is repealed in stages throughout the 1930s, but it is left to the individual states to dictate their own legislation. Until 2013, it was illegal to home-brew in Mississippi, which became the 49th state to legalize the hobby; the practice is still illegal in Alabama.

1971
The Campaign for Real Ale (CAMRA) is founded in the UK, followed later by the American Homebrewers Association in 1978. There is a surge in home-brewing on both sides of the Atlantic, and a palpable thirst for creative, exciting beers.

1977
British author Michael Jackson publishes the hugely influential *World Guide to Beer.* He was one of the first to publicize the few good beers available, and his writing, public appearances, and TV documentaries fostered and encouraged a worldwide craft beer industry.

SINCE THEN, innovation and experimentation have been watchwords of the US craft brewing movement, especially in creative, off-the-wall breweries such as Dogfish Head (see pp.154–155). One of its most unusual limited brews, Chicha, was a recreation of a South American drink called *chichi*, which is made with locally grown maize, peppercorns, and fruit. To make the beer, a portion of the maize was ground, chewed up and mixed with saliva, and then spat out and made into small flat cakes, which were dried in the sun. Enzymes in the saliva broke down the starch in the maize to release the sugars necessary for fermentation. Head brewer Sam Calagione said it took six people all day to chew and spit their way through 3kg (6½lb) of Peruvian blue corn. Indeed, US craft brewers alone now produce in the range of 140 different beer styles and the number is growing each year. Some of these beers are brand new – like American-style "brett beer", a US take on a Belgian lambic. The collaboration between Lost Abbey (see p.171) and New Belgium (p.166) has resulted in the "all Brettanomyces" beer, Mo' Betta Bretta, a blonde ale, produced using wild fermentation. Other breweries have also taken their cue from Belgium, such as Alaskan (see p.145), whose Raspberry wheat beer "follows an American take on this Old World style". Other beer styles, like adambier – a strong, sour, dark beer – and grätzer – a top-fermented, smoked wheat beer are reborn historic beers that were traditionally brewed in Germany and Poland.

MO' BETTA BRETTA
LOST ABBEY AND
NEW BELGIUM'S
BRETT BEER

HOWEVER, THE CRAFT BREWING REVOLUTION has now spread from the US to the rest of the world, and innovative and exceptional beers can now be found in every corner of the globe. One of the key ideals of the craft beer revolution has always been a willingness to share ideas and enthusiasms. Initially, brewers might have collaborated with other brewers from the same town, then it became common for brewers from Europe to create a series of collaborative brews with a US counterpart. But now this sharing is truly international. Craft brewers will travel from brewery to brewery and continent to continent, looking for new ideas and offering up their own in exchange. From South Africa and Australia to Japan and Argentina, a robust trade of philosophies and opinions is under way on how to brew great beers. Belgians are talking to Germans, Hungarians are sharing with Poles, and the Italians are leading the way. This worldwide conversation now knows no boundaries, as evidenced by collaborative developments in India, New Zealand, and Brazil, where experienced brewers are offering up their time and talents. Brewers are seeking out historical and long-forgotten recipes, trying to use locally available ingredients, or trying to create new beers – the only rule is that they must be interesting and have exceptional flavour. One such successful collaboration beer is the Anglo-American Pale Ale Twin Peaks (5% ABV), brewed by California's Sierra Nevada Brewery (see pp.176–177) and the Thornbridge Brewery (see p.41) in the UK. Sierra Nevada's brewer Steve Grossman describes the fruity pale ale as "a real collaboration between the Old Country and the New Wave of brewing".

TWIN PEAKS BEER
COLLABORATION
BEER PUMP CLIP

> ❝ **FROM SOUTH AFRICA AND AUSTRALIA TO JAPAN AND ARGENTINA, A ROBUST TRADE OF PHILOSOPHIES AND OPINIONS IS UNDER WAY ON HOW TO BREW GREAT BEERS.** ❞

1982

The first brewpub, Yakima Brewing and Malting Co in Washington, goes into business, founded by Bert Grant. For the first time, US law allows a company to sell beer it has produced along with food. Yakima established a successful model for this type of business.

1984

Charles Papazian publishes *The Complete Joy of Home Brewing*, a book that has gone on to sell more than 900,000 copies and inspire countless brewers. He had previously founded the Brewers Association and created the Great American Beer Festival in 1982.

1990

Sierra Nevada Brewery (see pp.176–177) of Chico, California, becomes the first microbrewery to produce over 50,700hl (31,000 barrels) of beer – an amount so large that the brewery exceeds the "micro" classification of 29,000hl (18,000 barrels).

2013

There are more than 2,400 craft brewers in the US, with one new brewery opening every day; on average, most Americans live within ten miles of a brewery. The industry employs more than 108,000 people and sells more than 15 million hl (9.2 million barrels) a year.

THE BREWING PROCESS

Brewing is a simple, natural process that produces drinks of great complexity. Fermentable sugars are extracted from grain using hot water. The liquid is brought to boiling point and hops are added for flavour, bitterness, and to ward off bacteria. It is then cooled, yeast is added, and the fermentation process begins – converting the sugar into carbon dioxide and the alcohol we call beer.

Mixing
the grist in the mash tun

1 MALTING

Before the grain gets to the brewery, it goes through a process known as malting. The sugar within the grain, which will feed the yeast during fermentation, is locked away in complex molecules of starch. To begin the process of releasing the sugars the maltster soaks, or steeps, the grains and then gently heats them to encourage them to germinate. As the seed starts to grow, the starch is broken down into simpler compounds. After a few days, germination is stopped and the malt is dried and heated in a kiln. The more intense the kilning, the darker the malt.

Germinated
malt is gradually dried in a kiln

Malted grains
are cracked in a calibrated mill

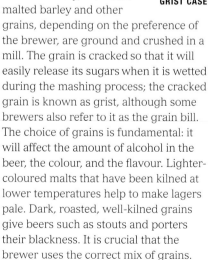

GRIST CASE

2 MILLING

At the brewery, the whole malted barley and other grains, depending on the preference of the brewer, are ground and crushed in a mill. The grain is cracked so that it will easily release its sugars when it is wetted during the mashing process; the cracked grain is known as grist, although some brewers also refer to it as the grain bill. The choice of grains is fundamental: it will affect the amount of alcohol in the beer, the colour, and the flavour. Lighter-coloured malts that have been kilned at lower temperatures help to make lagers pale. Dark, roasted, well-kilned grains give beers such as stouts and porters their blackness. It is crucial that the brewer uses the correct mix of grains.

The sugar-rich
water is strained from the mash

MASH TUN

3 MASHING

The grist is mixed with hot water in a vessel known as a mash tun in order to produce a sweet-smelling mash. The porridge-like mash is then left to stand. The heat of the water draws the sugars out of the malt. This is known as single infusion mashing. Some brewers take off some of the liquid, run it off into another vessel, heat it to a higher temperature, and put it back into the tun, once, twice, or even three times. This is known as decoction mashing. The higher temperatures draw out sweeter, more complex sugars from the malt. It is a traditional method that is commonly found in many European breweries.

Hops
are added at different times for flavouring

The boiled wort
is quickly cooled in a heat converter

The wort
is brought to the boil in a brew kettle

5 FERMENTING

The wort is then strained to remove the residue from the hops and any other ingredients before it is passed through a heat exchanger and rapidly cooled. The cooled wort will now be transferred into a fermenting vessel. Temperature is key at this stage of the process: if it is too warm the yeast will die, too cold and the yeast will take a long time to do its work. With the addition of the yeast, the real magic of brewing begins. The yeast feeds on the sugar, producing carbon dioxide, alcohol, and millions more yeast cells. There is a vast number of different yeast strains – but most breweries will have their own that they reuse many times.

The type of yeast
selected by the brewer will help determine the flavour

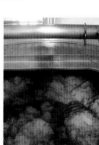

FERMENTING TANK

In the fermenting tank, *yeast creates alcohol from sugar*

4 BOILING

After mashing, the sugar-rich, sweet wort is either strained through the bottom of the spent grains, or passed into a large sieve called a lauter tun. As the sweet wort runs off, the grain is rinsed with more hot water to release its final sugars. The wort then passes into a brew kettle, or copper, and is brought to boiling point. Hops are added at different times for aroma, bitterness, and to stop unwanted bacterial activity. Some brewers "dry hop" by adding extra handfuls of hops towards the end of the process; some brewers also add other herbs and spices at this stage.

The beer
is racked so its flavours can evolve

❝ BREWING IS A SIMPLE, NATURAL PROCESS THAT PRODUCES DRINKS OF GREAT COMPLEXITY. ❞

6 CONDITIONING

Once fermentation is finished, the liquid is referred to as "green beer". It is removed from most of the yeast and transferred, or racked, into another vessel. It is then given time to condition and mature, and during this time a secondary fermentation will take place with the remaining yeast – all the while, the flavours of the beer are maturing and evolving. This stage can vary greatly in length. The beer is then put into a cask, keg, bottle, or can – although keller beers are served from the conditioning tank straight into the glass. Some beers are clarified, but others are served unfiltered. Some are pasteurized, while others are not.

CONDITIONING TANK

BEER STYLES

The family of beers is large and growing – some estimate that the total is now more than 80 different styles, many with extensive sub-divisions. Here are some of the broader styles that a "beer traveller" will encounter – but of course, the fun is finding them not just in this book but also in bars and shops worldwide.

Black beauty
As dark as night, porters and stouts can be dry or sweet

Smooth operator
The dense head gives a smooth, creamy start to a tripel beer

Copper colours
Ales and bitters have a distinctive, rich colour

Golden delicious
Light, golden, and an easy-drinking refresher

PORTER & STOUT

Porter was developed in London and was the first beer to be widely sold commercially, in the early 18th century. During the industrial revolution, "plain porter" was the drink of the working classes. The stronger versions were called stout porter, or stout for short.

FLAVOUR PROFILE
As maltsters and brewers learned how to roast barley to higher temperatures, porters became darker black and full of coffee and chocolate flavours. Lots of hops are usually added for bitterness.

ABV
Typically ranging from 4–8%, but stronger types can be found.

DUBBEL & TRIPEL

Belgium might be a small country, but it has probably given the world the biggest range of beer styles. "Dubbel" and "tripel" are terms used to denote the alcoholic strength of ales and are used – although not exclusively – by Trappist breweries.

FLAVOUR PROFILE
Dubbels are rich, malty brown beers with mild bitterness and some fruit character. Tripels are strong, sweet, malty golden ales with a dense creamy head.

ABV
A dubbel is likely to be between 6–8% ABV; tripels can range up to around 10% ABV.

ALE & BITTER

Ale and bitter are essentially the same beer. Bitter was first brewed in Victorian England and part of its appeal was that it could be served quickly, on draught, after a few days of conditioning. Many regard cask-conditioned ales – unpasteurized living beers – as the pinnacle of the brewer's skill.

FLAVOUR PROFILE
Ales and bitter are usually deep bronze or copper due to the use of dark malts such as Crystal; golden ales are not uncommon.

ABV
Most ales and bitters are under 4% ABV, but stronger versions are also available.

HELLES

A bright, light, golden-yellow beer often brewed near Munich in Germany, this is a style that has been mimicked worldwide. The flavours are far subtler than those of a pilsner-style beer, even though they look similar. Kellerbier versions are likely to be heavily hopped and unfiltered, and may be a little cloudy.

FLAVOUR PROFILE
Ideally, there should be a pronounced hop bitterness from the presence of noble hops, along with some malt presence.

ABV
ABVs range from 5–7%; a bock is a stronger version of the style.

Head start
Expect a wheat beer to have a big, foaming, flavoursome head

Brilliant bubbles
Fizzy pilsners have a bubbly head and a sublime flavour

Flavour complex
These gorgeously dark beers contain an explosion of complex flavours

Rainbow brew
Hoppy American ales vary in colour, from red and black to blonde

WHEAT

German weiss (white) or weizen (wheat) beers are made with 40 per cent wheat mixed with barley malt. Unfiltered types are called hefeweiss or hefeweizen; filtered versions are called kristal. The Belgian and Dutch versions, known as witte or bières blanche, are usually made with herbs such as coriander and orange peel.

FLAVOUR PROFILE
In some, the yeast gives strong banana, clove, and bubblegum flavours. Wheat beers are crisp, refreshing, and usually turbid.

ABV
Wheat beers generally range between 3–7% ABV.

PILSNER

Bohemian or Czech pilsners are examples of a beer style that has swept the world. Some versions of this beer are lagered – stored at a cool temperature – for three months, but many are lagered for a much shorter time.

FLAVOUR PROFILE
The flavour of spicy, herbal hops should be in harmony with the sweetness of the pilsner malt. Pilsners can be golden to pale amber in colour and should be medium- to light-bodied, with a malty, biscuity aroma and flavour.

ABV
Serve with a full, white head. ABVs are generally about 4–6%.

IMPERIAL STOUT

The first versions were often exported from Britain to Tsarist Russia, where in St Petersburg Catherine the Great gave them their imperial designation.

FLAVOUR PROFILE
A big, bold giant of a beer, the imperial stout's colour can range from dark copper to black. It is a stronger version of a stout, is high in alcohol, and is likely to be rich and malty – in some cases very sweet. Many flavours can be detected, including Christmas pudding-like burnt fruit.

ABV
Strong enough to keep for years – typical ABVs are above 8%.

AMERICAN ALE

The ale style has been reinvented by the US craft beer movement. American ales are characterized by floral, citrussy US hops like Cascade – although hops from other countries can be used – to produce high hop bitterness, flavour, and aroma.

FLAVOUR PROFILE
American ales range from deep, rich golden to dark copper in colour. They are generally very highly bittered through the use of citrus-flavoured hops, which are balanced with rich, juicy malt.

ABV
Strengths of more than 8% ABV are not uncommon.

TASTING BEER

Beer is probably the most democratic alcoholic drink in the world and it doesn't demand that you sip and swill every pint. However, being aware of all your senses when drinking can greatly enhance the experience.

We drink with our eyes: read the label or beer menu, what does it say about the beer? What colour is the beer, and is it cloudy? Looking at the beer whets the appetite and gets the tastebuds tingling. Touch the glass and note the temperature. Some beers, especially those that are lagered, are best chilled, while others need the warmth of a room to release soaring fruity aromas and esters. As you lift the glass, the work of the nose begins – a wheat beer might have bubblegum or clove notes; a highly hopped IPA could soar with tangerine or other citrus notes. Then sip and let the liquid caress your tongue. Is it sweet? Are there notes of bitterness? Can you detect dark fruits? What impact does the malt make? Then swallow. Is the finish long or short? Can notes of warmth from the alcohol be detected? Do the flavours from the hops linger on and on? You might want to record your notes for exceptional finds and old favourites so that you can compare them.

Scent-sational
The head is not only attractive, it also releases the beer's aromas

1 ANGLE THE GLASS

Good pouring is an art, and one that adds to the beer experience. Use a squeaky clean glass and hold it at an angle of 45 degrees. With most beers, don't be afraid to boldly pour so that a foaming head starts to form. As the glass starts to fill, bring it up to the vertical by the time the bottle is half empty.

TASTING NOTE ICONS

Throughout the book, each featured beer is given a set of tasting notes, food pairing suggestions, and is rated on a scale of one to three for hoppiness and for sweetness – two key flavours to note when sampling any beer. You can use this information to help you assess and enjoy any of the beers you sample.

 HOPPINESS
Hops can give a beer earthy, bitter, grassy, or citrussy flavours, depending on the variety used.

SWEETNESS
Sweetness can range from rich, malty caramel and toffee-like dark sugar tones to fruity flavours.

2 POUR

Continue to pour into the centre of the glass when the glass is vertical. This will help the formation of a perfect head – beer is the only alcoholic drink that has a naturally foaming head. If the beer has been bottle conditioned and has some yeast sediment in it, you will have to decide whether to stop pouring and keep the yeast in the bottle, or whether to empty it into the beer.

3 LOOK

Look at the beer: are there lines of carbonation rising up the glass? Does it sparkle and dance in the glass? What colour is it? A good beer should be enticing and intriguing. As you drink, a fine lacing of foam should be left on the glass – that's a sign not just of a good beer but a clean glass.

4 SWIRL

Our noses can detect more than 1,000 different aromas, and most beers contain a complex mixture of different scents. Swirling the beer in the glass will encourage its aromas to leap out.

5 SMELL

Take a good long sniff. Can you detect floral or citrus notes? Perhaps there are coffee or resin aromas? Esters add to the chorus in stronger beers, while wild lambic or gueuze beers should have strong, earthy notes of sweet and sour.

Glass aware
A careful choice of glassware can add to the enjoyment of a beer tasting

6 SAVOUR

Taste the beer and let it roll across your tongue, where your tastebuds for sweet, sour, salt, bitter, and umami are found. How does the beer feel and what can you detect? Is it grainy or fruity? The greatest beers are balanced, with the flavours working in harmony with each other.

FLAVOUR PAIRINGS

Beer and food pairing is meant to be a bit of fun that can add to the enjoyment of a glass of suds. Get it right and the ordinary can become sublime, but just remember – there are no right answers. Use these food and beer pairing suggestions to get you started.

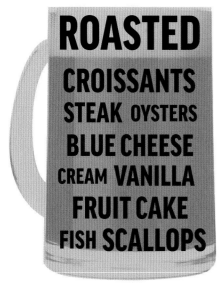

ROASTED
CROISSANTS
STEAK OYSTERS
BLUE CHEESE
CREAM VANILLA
FRUIT CAKE
FISH SCALLOPS

SOUR
ASPARAGUS
BLACK PUDDING
CHARCUTERIE
CREAM CHEESE
FRUIT
SEAFOOD
CREAM

SMOKEY
BARBECUED MEAT
CHOCOLATE
SMOKED CHEESE
BEEF **FISH**
CURED BACON
HAM DUCK
SMOKED SAUSAGE

HOPPY
PULLED PORK
BARBECUED MEAT
STEAK **GAME**
VANILLA ICE CREAM
CURED BACON
BLUE CHEESE
RIBS TACOS
CREAM
STRONG CHEESE

ROASTED BEERS

Many Irish-style stouts, dark lagers, and porters are full of roasted malt and rich chocolate flavours, underpinned by luscious coffee notes. Often, there are hints of vanilla and orange fruits.

BEER TYPES
Oatmeal Stout
    (see Beer Geek Breakfast, p.109)
Porter
    (see Edmund Fitzgerald, p.163)
Schwarzbier
    (see Schwarz-Bier, p.64)
Stout
    (see Export Stout, p.35)

FOOD PAIRINGS
Sweeter stouts pair well with a sweet, creamy dessert. Very dry stouts are better with dark, bitter chocolate desserts.

SOUR BEERS

Sour is a description that makes many people cringe. However, within the family of beers there are some that are sour. Many are a cocktail of a fresh stock ale and an older beer that has been infected with wild yeast and conditioned – they are a sweet and sour blend in a bottle.

BEER TYPES
Faro
    (see Faro Boon, p.83)
Gose
    (see Helle Gose, p.55)
Red Ale
    (see Grand Cru, p.88)

FOOD PAIRINGS
These complex beers pair well with salty, fatty foods, such as a plate of charcuterie or olives.

SMOKEY BEERS

The smoke flavour is derived from malt dried over an open flame – the different flavours depend on which wood is being burned.

BEER TYPES
Rauchbier
    (see Rauch, p.237)
Smoked Bock
    (see Urbock, p.60)
Smoked Doppelbock
    (see Eiche, p.60)
Smoked Porter
    (see Smoked Porter, p.145)

FOOD PAIRINGS
Smokey-flavoured beers pair well with smokey-flavoured foods, as they enhance and lift the flavour. Why not match with hot-from-the-barbecue meats, rich smoked cheeses, or smoked fish?

HOPPY BEERS

Many US-inspired beers are heavily hopped, which gives them a pleasant bitterness, and aromatic, spicy, or grassy flavours.

BEER TYPES
Barley Wine
    (see Hog Heaven, p.148)
Imperial IPA
    (see Hop Stoopid, p.165)
IPA
    (see IPA (Citra), p.35)

FOOD PAIRINGS
Strong, powerful hoppy beers demand either a strong-tasting food pairing such as strong cheeses and barbecued meats, or flavours that will balance them out – try matching them with sweet, simple desserts such as vanilla ice cream.

FRUITY
PÂTÉ CHICKEN
SALTED MEATS
ASIAN CUISINE
MATURE CHEESE
SHELLFISH
GAME
OYSTERS
SUSHI
MUSSELS
PORK
PICKLED FISH

CRISP
SEAFOOD
STRONG CHEESE
ASPARAGUS
CHICKEN KORMA
SCALLOPS
SPICY SAUSAGE
BARBECUED MEAT
FISH CREAM
MUSSELS
PORK
ICE CREAM
OYSTERS

BITTER
SWEET PICKLE
APPLE PORK
BREAD AND BUTTER
GAME HAM
STRONG CHEESE
SALTY CRISPS
LAMB BEEF

MALTY
SALTY CRISPS
HAM STEAK
CHILLI
ROAST MEATS
FRENCH ONION SOUP
CHOCOLATE
FRUIT CAKE
STRONG CHEESE
MUSSELS

FRUITY BEERS

The family of beers has some wonderfully fruity and tart brews. On their own, lambic and gueuze beers with their primeval earthy notes are unlike any other tastes in the beer world, or indeed in the wider world of alcoholic drinks.

BEER TYPES
Gueuze
    (see Vintage, p.88)
Kriek
    (see Kriek Boon, p.82)
Saison
    (see Hennepin, p.151)

FOOD PAIRINGS
They make great aperitifs with a plate of oysters, shellfish, and sweet pâtés. Lambic can also work with salty meats and home-cured pickled fish.

CRISP BEERS

A crisp beer, such as a well-attenuated pilsner, has much of the sugar fermented out, creating a light sparkling beer that dances dry on the tongue.

BEER TYPES
Pale Ale
    (see Wizard Smith's Ale, p.247)
Pilsner
    (see Pilsner Urquell, p.99)
Wheat Beer
    (see Hefe Weissbier, p.65)

FOOD PAIRINGS
The delicate, bitter flavours work well with mild seafood dishes. They also have the ability to cut through the fat of some meat dishes, allowing the flavour of the meat to come to the fore, so try with bacon or spicy sausages.

BITTER BEERS

A smooth bitterness is a key component of many British and American ales. Hoppy bitterness is often accompanied by fruity aromas and caramel flavours.

BEER TYPES
Ale
    (see Southwold Bitter, p.27)
Extra Special Bitter
    (see ESB, p.31)
Strong Ale
    (see Palo Santo Marron, p.155)

FOOD PAIRINGS
Such beers pair marvellously well with good unpasteurized cheese, fresh bread, and salted butter. They will also work equally well with the sweetness of roast and braised dishes of beef, lamb, or pork.

MALTY BEERS

Normally full of fruity flavours, malty beers often offer a balance of sweet malt and spicy aromatic hops. Some have flavours of caramel and toffee, while others bring nutty toast to the glass.

BEER TYPES
Belgian Ale
    (see Raison d'Être, p.154)
Doppelbock
    (see Loaded Canon Ale, p.273)
Schwarzbier
    (see Black Lager, p.175)

FOOD PAIRINGS
Light and easy to drink, these wide-ranging beers pair well with salty dishes. Why not try a plate of mature cheddar cheese or a crumbly Wensleydale, a bowl of crisps, and slices of ham?

BEER FESTIVALS

If you want to enjoy the culture of a country, town, or region, and sample unusual and exciting beers from the local area, get along to a beer festival. Some festivals are huge celebrations on a national scale, featuring bands, brewing classes, and beers from breweries in far-flung countries. However, many others are locally organized and far more intimate – some will have music, carnival parades, and rides on a Ferris wheel – but they all offer the chance to enjoy great beer in the company of like-minded beer lovers.

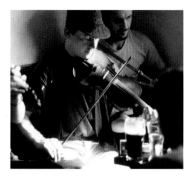

MANY IRISH BEER FESTIVALS CELEBRATE LOCAL BEER AND TRADITIONAL MUSIC

GOOD BEER AND GOOD COMPANY are ideal companions. And beer festivals organized by local communities are often the best places for the beer traveller to experience new, unusual, and rare beers. In the UK, the Campaign for Real Ale (CAMRA) organizes hundreds of festivals throughout the year, providing a fantastic opportunity for people to experience great beers, many of which will have been brewed in their local town or city. With more than 50,000 pubs in the UK, some say every day is a beer festival. Sheffield claims to be England's "beer city" due to the number of beers on sale, and should be a must-visit for any beer traveller. Beer and music come together for one weekend in July with the Tramlines Music Festival. Regarded as the country's best metropolitan festival, the event gets bigger each year as more venues, including pubs, join in. Later on in the year, CAMRA's biggest annual festival is the Great British Beer Festival (see below), a six-day extravaganza that welcomes tens of thousands of beer lovers and is normally held in London during August.

THE US HAS AN OUTSTANDING CULTURE of beer festivals, with more than 1,300 held each year nationwide. These are not just places to drink beer – many also feature local bands and food. The biggest festival in the US is the Great American Beer Festival, which was started by the US Brewers Association, and is attended by more than 50,000 people. Held in Denver, Colorado, organizers claim it "brings together the brewers and beers that make the US the world's greatest brewing nation". Meanwhile, to the east in Philadelphia, America's largest "beer celebration" – Philly Beer Week – takes place. A hugely popular city-wide event, it is held in May and features "hundreds of festivals, dinners, tours, pub crawls, tastings, and meet-the-brewer nights". Its local breweries include Dogfish Head (see pp.154–155), Samuel Adams (see pp.174–175), and Victory (see p.180). Across the border in Canada, Montreal's Mondial de la Bière has been established for over 20 years and attracts upwards of 80,000 visitors. It holds educational workshops as well as "meet the brewer" events.

THE GREAT BRITISH BEER FESTIVAL, ORGANIZED BY CAMRA

MONTREAL'S MONDIAL DE LA BIÈRE FESTIVAL, ESTABLISHED IN 1994

KEY WORLD BEER FESTIVALS

ZYTHOS
www.zbf.be

BELGIUM has some great beer festivals, but for the discerning beer traveller Zythos, run by the country's largest beer consumers' group in April, is probably the best. It features beer from many small and unusual brewers.

ØLFESTIVAL
www.beerfestival.dk

HELD IN COPENHAGEN, DENMARK, and organized by the Danish beer consumers' group Danol, Ølfestival was founded in 2000. Held in May, there are upwards of 70 brewers present and more than 700 beers can be sampled.

ČESKÝ PIVNÍ FESTIVAL
www.ceskypivnifestival.cz

THE ČESKÝ PIVNÍ FESTIVAL is a three-week celebration of Czech beer and food that is held in Prague each May. Traditional costumes are worn and beers from more than 70 brewers are served.

GREAT BRITISH BEER FESTIVAL
www.camra.org.uk

ORGANIZED BY THE CAMPAIGN for Real Ale, this is the world's greatest celebration of cask-conditioned beers. It is held in London for five days during August and is attended by more than 40,000 people.

WHEREVER YOU GO IN THE WORLD, you are likely to find a beer festival that will introduce you to some exciting local brews – many of which are organized by beer-loving local craft beer associations. The Japan Craft Beer Association established the Great Japan Beer Festival – the largest of its kind in Japan – in 1998, and has since held it every year. In China, the city of Qingdao has a 14-day festival that starts in August. With more than four million visitors, it is the largest in the country.

The Great Australian Beer Festival Geelong is a vibrant, interactive event, featuring not only beer tasting, but also live music and talks on home-brewing; Canberra also hosts its own craft beer festival in April. In New Zealand, one of the best festivals is Beervana – held in Wellington during August. Meanwhile, a growing interest in craft beers in South Africa has led to the start of a number of festivals, including the Jozi Craft Beer Festival and Clarens Beer Festival. Visit Stockholm, Sweden, in October for the annual Beer and Whisky Festival, which it claims is the biggest of its kind in Europe, or visit Belgium: for many years, Brussels has held a Beer Weekend in early September on the Grand Place, with more than 50 breweries taking part. And of course there are plenty of good times to be had in Ireland, too.

BUT THE WORLD'S BIGGEST and most influential festival is Munich's Oktoberfest. With roots stretching back to 1810, Oktoberfest is known not only for its vast beer halls and spirit of celebration, but also for the traditional dress many patrons and beer sellers wear: lederhosen for men and dirndl dresses for women. Welcoming upwards of 6 million people, who consume more than 6 million litres (37,000 barrels) of beer over the course of about three weeks, this festival has spawned imitators worldwide. Argentina's largest festival – a ten-day party in the mountains – is held in October in the small village of Villa General Belgrano, which was founded by German immigrants in the 1930s. The Brazilian city of Blumenau has held its own Oktoberfest since 1984 – the festival lasts three weeks, and is the biggest beer festival in the country. Hong Kong also has its own Oktoberfest, organized by the Marco Polo Hong Kong Hotel, it claims to be the oldest beer festival in Asia. And for Canadians and visitors who like a Germanic knees-up, the Kitchener-Waterloo Oktoberfest, founded in 1969, is held in Ontario. It is the largest Bavarian festival in Canada, with nine days of beer, oompah bands, dancing, and the largest Thanksgiving parade in Canada.

" BEER FESTIVALS ORGANIZED BY LOCAL COMMUNITIES ARE OFTEN THE BEST PLACES FOR THE BEER TRAVELLER TO EXPERIENCE NEW, UNUSUAL, AND RARE BEERS. "

NAGOYA BEER FESTIVAL, ORGANIZED BY THE JAPAN CRAFT BEER ASSOCIATION

OKTOBERFEST, THE LARGEST AND BEST-KNOWN FESTIVAL IN THE WORLD

BEERVANA
www.beervana.co.nz

NEW ZEALAND'S annual celebration of heavenly beer features upwards of 200 beers from New Zealand and Australia. It is held in Wellington – New Zealand's so-called "craft beer capital" – over two days each August.

GREAT AMERICAN BEER FESTIVAL
www.greatamericanbeerfestival.com

MORE THAN 2,800 American beers can be sampled in small 1oz (20ml) servings. Held in Denver, Colorado, the festival normally lasts for three days during September or October.

GREAT CANADIAN BEER FESTIVAL
www.gcbf.com

CANADA'S annual tribute to beer is held every September in Victoria, British Columbia. Held over one weekend in September, it features beers from more than 50 Canadian breweries.

OKTOBERFEST
www.oktoberfest.de

MUNICH'S thigh-slapping celebration of beers brewed by the German city's six breweries is a world-renowned and much emulated festival. Held for three weeks during September and October, it's a once-in-a-lifetime experience for beer drinkers.

EUROPE

UNITED KINGDOM

Fancy a Yakima Red, a Cornish pilsner, or a Chalky's Bite? The chances are you won't have to go far to find one because a beer revolution is sweeping the UK and a new generation of brewers is dedicating itself to transforming and challenging people's beer-drinking experiences. Forget the idea that UK beer just means bitter, mild, and milk stout – in every corner of the UK, brewers are re-discovering long-lost beer styles, experimenting with herbs and spices, and proving that they can brew a pint as exciting, innovative, and just as delicious as anything found on the Continent or in the US. There are wheat beers, blonde beers, sour beers, fruit beers, whoppingly hopped US-style beers, and even some crafted to a high strength for sipping. And with this increase in experimentation has come a rise in the number of breweries. Research by the Campaign for Real Ale finds that there are now more than 1,000 breweries across the UK, the highest number for over 70 years.

Of course, as well as its bright future, the UK brewing industry can also take pride in its role in the history of beer. Many of the great technological advances in brewing were first pioneered in the UK, and the nation has given the world some of its greatest styles, including ale and stout – it is also the spiritual home of cask-conditioned ale, marvellous "living beers" that continue to mature once they've left the brewery. Brewers are amply proving that beer is a versatile and varied drink – from beers heavy in roasted notes and spirit flavours to those with light, refreshing swirls of citrus – and many are pairing these wide-ranging flavours with food. If you want to match a beer to your meal, there are types that will complement everything, from sharp blue cheese to freshly made vanilla ice cream.

ADNAMS

Adnams may be more than 140 years old, but this is no old-fashioned company – it has some great green credentials, brews some fabulous beers, and is introducing a new generation to malt and hops.

THE FACTS...

OWNER Adnams PLC
FOUNDED 1872
ADDRESS Sole Bay Brewery, East Green, Southwold, Suffolk IP18 6JW
WEBSITE www.adnams.co.uk
PHILOSOPHY Doing the right thing

A PIER, A LIGHTHOUSE, SOME BEACH HUTS, and a few fabulously intimate pubs all make the town of Southwold on England's east coast stand out from the crowd. However, it is the brewery that stands in the shadow of the lighthouse – where in 1345 the "ale-wives" of the town used to make beer – that makes it truly remarkable. In 1872, two brothers, George and Ernest Adnams, bought the brewery with an inheritance from their father. Today, the Adnams family still own the bustling brewery, which has the reputation for making some of the finest quintessential English ales. The production of its "beers from the coast" is overseen by Fergus Fitzgerald. As the head brewer, he has turned his hand to many things, including the introduction of eco-friendly technology, which has made this the "greenest" brewery in Europe.

However, Fitzgerald's passion is not just for brewing traditional ale – he is revelling in exploring the limits to which styles can be pushed, be it low-strength or higher alcohol beers. American hops,

champagne yeast, and spices can all be found in the brewhouse. Cinnamon and a touch of juniper were added to a spiced winter beer and, drawing inspiration from other great brewing cultures, he has produced a Belgian-style wheat beer, a Dutch bock, and a New Zealand ale. However, it is not just champagne yeast that can be found in the brewery – there are champagne bottles too, which, when filled, are helping bring beer to a new audience. And as the brewery also has its own boutique distillery, we can perhaps look forward to some wood-aged beers in the future.

ADNAMS
SOLE BAY CELEBRATORY

TASTING NOTES

SOLE BAY CELEBRATORY ALE, 10% ABV
This beer pours like liquid gold, as bright and sparkling as the early morning sun dappling the waves of Sole Bay. Malt, sugars, and the white wine fruitiness of Nelson Sauvin hops are transformed with the introduction of champagne yeast. Sole Bay Celebratory soars and caresses the tongue like a vintage sparkling wine, but better – it's a beer.

FOOD PAIRING: Drink from a fluted glass with friends – it's the perfect apéritif for a party and will work perfectly with most pre-dinner appetisers.

SOUTHWOLD BITTER ALE, 4.1% ABV
There is nothing simple about a classic English bitter. Complex caramel and toffee aromas vie for attention, with hints of apple and perhaps even sulphur, before giving way to a long, lingering, hop bitterness. It's so good you'll have to have two.

FOOD PAIRING: Good hard English cheese, home-made sweet pickle, and some slices of apple are the perfect partners for this beer – or try it with fresh cuts of cold ham or beef.

BROADSIDE ALE, 6.3% ABV
With a bold mouthfeel, the taste is dominated by blackberries and other dark fruits, which vie for attention with the rich, roasted, sweet caramel malt. It's rich but not overwhelming. There are lots of hops and spice on the nose.

FOOD PAIRING: Good meat pies and hearty stews are made to eat with this beer, while its sweet fruitiness works well with strong, gamey meats.

ADNAMS
SOUTHWOLD BITTER

ADNAMS
BROADSIDE

BREWDOG

Big, bold, brash, and bright, BrewDog is part of a growing movement of new brewers who are making beer relevant to a new generation of drinkers. Based in Aberdeenshire, the company has grown fast and now sells worldwide.

THE FACTS...

OWNER BrewDog PLC
FOUNDED 2007
ADDRESS Balmacassie Industrial Estate, Ellon, Aberdeenshire AB41 8BX
WEBSITE www.brewdog.com
PHILOSOPHY Kicking sand in the face of convention

LOVE THEM OR HATE THEM, you cannot ignore them. When two 24-year-olds, James Watt and Martin Dickie, founded BrewDog in 2007, they were at the forefront of a movement to change the "traditional" image of beer. Drawing inspiration from the boldness and brashness of some US craft brewers, and with a punk ethos, they fearlessly plotted how to achieve their goal.

Brazenness, humour, and the brewing of good beer have all contributed to BrewDog's swift rise from being just another microbrewer to one known around the world. From day one they invested in "bass-ass" marketing and punk rock imagery. If there was a headline to be grabbed, they'd grab

it and if there was an argument to be had with a "man in a suit", they'd have it. And on their way they have made many people smile and others sit up and listen. On a quest to brew the world's strongest beer, they created – after a trip to a local ice cream-maker who helped with some cold distillation – Tactical Nuclear Penguin (32% ABV), Sink the Bismarck! (41% ABV), and The End of History (55% ABV). In a feat of outlandish marketing, they put 12 bottles of The End Of History inside seven dead stoats, four squirrels, and one hare and sold them – an unusual mix of art, beer, and taxidermy.

However, beneath the marketing hype, BrewDog's passion and ability translates into some great beers. BrewDog co-founder James Watt says it all: "We are committed to making the highest quality beers. Our beers are in no way commercial or mainstream. We take classic beer styles and give them a contemporary spin and the customary BrewDog bite." With beers such as the hop-smacking Dead Pony Club and 5am Saint and the smooth, sweet Dogma, BrewDog is here to stay.

BREWDOG
LIBERTINE BLACK ALE

BREWDOG
PUNK IPA

BREWDOG
TOKYO*

TASTING NOTES

LIBERTINE BLACK ALE 7.2% ABV
Lift the cap off and the potent aromas from the Simcoe hops leap out like demons from Pandora's box, which dance with the dark devils of the roasted malts.

FOOD PAIRING: Try with an assertive bowl of chilli con carne or a spicy sausage jambalaya. The rich flavours will also pair well with chocolate fudge.

PUNK IPA 5.6% ABV
Punk IPA is a beer of complexity and contradiction. Its will-o'-the-wisp appearance belies the power of the Chinook and Moteka hops and passionfruit flavours. This is a powerful beer made with Maris Otter malt.

FOOD PAIRING: Good food companions would be a platter of spicy meats, chilli salsa, and strong cheeses with wholemeal and rye breads.

TOKYO* IMPERIAL STOUT, 18.2% ABV
A strong, dark Imperial stout, Tokyo* is the ideal late-night sipping beer. It oozes the juices of dark fruits, roasted coffee beans, and the swirl of smoke from a lit cigar. The finish is as warm as a glass of cognac.

FOOD PAIRING: Bold beers deserve an adventurous food combination; pour a little over your favourite vanilla ice cream.

CAMDEN TOWN

London is burning with a new brewing energy, and one of the hottest stars is Camden Town, which is in the vanguard of a new wave of craft breweries in the capital. Since it opened in 2010, the brewery has enjoyed huge success.

Yankee twist
USA Hells is an English lager with an American drawl. It might be hazy in the glass, but is, in fact, pretty sharp

CAMDEN TOWN USA HELLS

CAMDEN TOWN'S STORY BEGAN in Australia in the 1960s when Patricia McLaughlin inherited McLaughlin's – or Mac's – brewery in Rockhampton, Australia, from her father Laurie McLaughlin. Not wanting to be a brewing mogul, she sold it. However, brewing and pubs were in her family's blood. Many years later one of her children, Jasper Cuppaidge, moved to London where he eventually took over the running of a pub, the Horseshoe, in Hampstead. He began to brew beer in the basement, and for his mother's 50th birthday recreated some of Mac's beer.

Jasper soon realized that there was a commercial demand for his beers, not just in his own pub but across the capital. So with the help of some friends and a bank loan, he moved out of the pub cellar and into seven derelict Victorian railway arches, where he installed a brand-new brewery.

Originally, the brewery was going to be called Mac's, but the name was already taken. When Jasper found that the internet address www.camdentownbrewery.com was available, the Camden resident knew he'd found the right name. Unfiltered versions of the beers, including a number of one-offs, can be consumed in the brewery's on-site bar.

TASTING NOTES

USA HELLS UNFILTERED LAGER, 4.6% ABV
Camden's USA Hells Lager is given an American drawl with the addition of American hops – Cascade, Centennial, Columbus, Citra, Simcoe – which add pineapple, mango, and swirls of lime to this slightly hazy, unfiltered, malty beer.
FOOD PAIRING: Seek out hot dogs with mustard, ribs, or cheese-topped burgers to enjoy with USA Hells.

HELLS LAGER, 4.6% ABV
With its gentle, lemony aroma from Perle and Hallertauer hops, Hells is an easy-drinking, crisp, refreshing beer, which exudes subtlety and complexity. The name is a corruption of the Pils and Helles beers that inspired it.
FOOD PAIRING: Hells partners with many foods especially meat. It's particularly good with chicken, ribs, and burgers.

INK STOUT, 4.4% ABV
Ink follows in the footsteps of some of London's great dry stouts – it is full of dark chocolate and roasted flavours, with a burst of dark red fruit from the Pacific Gem hops.
FOOD PAIRING: Stout can be paired well with chocolate, most types of meat, and oysters.

THE FACTS...

OWNER Camden Town
FOUNDED 2010
ADDRESS 55–59 Wilkin Street Mews, Kentish Town, London NW5 3NN
WEBSITE www.camdentownbrewery.com
PHILOSOPHY Reviving London's brewing heritage

CAMDEN TOWN HELLS

CAMDEN TOWN INK

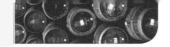

FULLER'S

London's longest-established, family-owned brewery is located at the Griffin Brewery in Chiswick, West London, where brewing began 350 years ago. Never one to stand still, it continues to push the boundaries of brewing.

THE FACTS...

OWNER Fuller, Smith & Turner PLC
FOUNDED 1845
ADDRESS Griffin Brewery, Chiswick Lane South, London W4 2QB
WEBSITE www.fullers.co.uk
PHILOSOPHY Brewing with pride

FULLER, SMITH & TURNER is an exemplar of the craft of brewing real ale. It's the only brewer to have won the Campaign for Real Ale (CAMRA) Champion Beer of Britain award four times with three different beers – ESB, Chiswick Bitter, and London Pride.

The brewery's first CAMRA Champion Beer of Britain winner, Extra Special Bitter, was launched in 1971. With ESB, Fuller's followed in the tradition of many British brewers and produced a stronger, richer beer for drinking during the winter months. However, it quickly became established as a bottled beer available all year around and was exported to the US with some success. In the States, ESB gained cult status with the new wave of US craft brewers, who were bowled over that so much taste could come out of a beer bottle. Many started to mimic its assertive style, using American hops rather than English. Now, in the US, Extra Special Bitter has come to denote a class of beer in its own right.

Fuller's current brewer, John Keeling, is a man who refuses to accept that the word "vintage" can only be used by wine-makers. The notion of vintage beer may have been conceived in 1995 when the Prince of Wales visited the brewery and threw a handful of hops into a copper of the brewery's 150th anniversary brew. The resulting beer, devised by John's predecessor Reg Drury, was the bottle-conditioned 1845. Seeing how well 1845 matured in the bottle, Reg created Vintage Ale in 1997, a limited-edition strong beer that is released annually, and is vintage-dated. It is a practice John has continued. Each year, a new vintage is brewed with different varieties of malt and hops, but always to the same strength. Like good wines, they can be kept for many years.

John Keeling also went on to create a range of beers with spirit-like flavours. In 2008, Brewer's Reserve No.1 was released – it had been matured for more than 500 days in casks previously used to store 30 year-old Scottish single malt whisky. It is now a much sought-after collector's item.

FULLER'S
GALE'S PRIZE OLD ALE

FULLER'S
VINTAGE ALE

FULLER'S
BREWER'S RESERVE NO.4

TASTING NOTES

GALE'S PRIZE OLD ALE BARLEY WINE, 9% ABV
A true vintage, each batch of Prize Old Ale is stored for 12 months in an oak vat. Dark red, it is full of tart, vinous flavours. Depending on its age there are hints of brandy or whisky. Some say it's best drunk when 20 years old.

FOOD PAIRING: This full-bodied beer pairs well with strong hard cheeses and Christmas pudding.

VINTAGE ALE 8.5% ABV
Each year the taste and texture of Vintage Ale varies. Even after four years, the orange notes of the Northdown and Challenger hops are discernible, and the alcohol is long and warming.

FOOD PAIRING: Some beers deserve to be treated like a fine whisky, on their own at the end of a meal in a cut-glass tumbler.

BREWER'S RESERVE NO.4 ALE, 8.5% ABV
Brewer's Reserve No.4 is a wood-aged ale with a full, spicy flavour of prunes, orange, and cinnamon. It matures for a year in vintage Comte de Lauvia Armagnac casks – the oak casks give a spirit-like flavour to the beer.

FOOD PAIRING: The swirl of Armagnac flavours helps it pair with a hard cheese or a rich pâté.

PAST MASTERS DOUBLE STOUT
7.4% ABV

Double Stout is brewed using a recipe from 1893. Its signature ingredient is Plumage Archer barley, carefully malted and kilned using 19th-century methods. Dark brown and creamy, this beer balances a rich fruity aroma with smoky, bittersweet, chocolate notes.

FOOD PAIRING: The beer's dark roasted malt melds well with the sweetness and creaminess of a cheesecake.

Epic Ales
Past Masters is a range of historic beers styles derived from the company brewing records, which date back to 1845

ESB ALE, 5.5% ABV

Deep tan in colour, with a rich hop nose, ESB has a complex taste, dominated by a breakfast marmalade, sweet citrus flavour, which is softened by a hint of honeyed fudge. Tongue-warming, it is full in alcohol.

FOOD PAIRING: The sweetness and strength of the beer make it a willing partner to game and other flavour-rich meat dishes.

LONDON PRIDE ALE, 4.1% ABV

This award-winning beer is the brewery's most famous, and they claim that it is "the classic English pint". Like a perfectly cut diamond, this well-balanced beer has no obvious flaws. The orange notes are balanced by soft toffee tones, which give way to a warm, resonating bitter finish.

FOOD PAIRING: This full-bodied beer would pair well with a warm steak pie.

FULLER'S ESB

FULLER'S LONDON PRIDE

FULLER'S PAST MASTERS DOUBLE STOUT

WITH MORE THAN 50,000 PUBS TO CHOOSE FROM, NO ONE IN THE UNITED KINGDOM IS EVER FAR FROM A WELCOMING PLACE TO ENJOY A BEER.

IN THE UNITED KINGDOM, A TRADITIONAL, DIMPLED BEER GLASS – OFTEN CALLED A TANKARD – CAN HELP KEEP ALE COOL ON A SUMMER'S DAY

HARVEYS

In the ancient town of Lewes, on the banks of the river Ouse, is one of the most picturesque breweries in England, Harveys, which was designed by one of the world's greatest brewery architects – William Bradford.

HARVEYS
CHRISTMAS ALE

HARVEYS
IMPERIAL EXTRA DOUBLE STOUT

THE "NEW" BREWERY was built in 1881 to a design that was a classic of Victorian ingenuity. Dubbed Lewes' cathedral, the brewery's tower used gravity to move raw materials around the site. These days, sadly, not many visitors get to see inside the brewery as it has a legendarily long waiting list.

The brewer Miles Jenner is immensely proud of his beers. In some circles he is revered for his recreation of one of the world's greatest beers – Albert Le Coq's legendary Imperial Extra Double Stout. Jenner was asked by an American importer to recreate the beer – last brewed in 1921 – and after much research, a recipe was compiled and a beer was brewed. It was stored for nine months before being readied to export to America, where it should have been sold in corked bottles, like the original.

However, disaster struck, and an undetected Brettanomyces yeast strain sprang into life. The beer had a dramatic secondary fermentation that forced the corks from the bottles – the beer needed more time to condition before it was ready to sell. Jenner learned the hard way why the original Georgian brewers stored the beer for 12 months before releasing it. Today when the beer is brewed, a metal crown cap replaces the cork, and it is conditioned for 12 months before bottling to avoid explosions.

TASTING NOTES

CHRISTMAS ALE BARLEY WINE, 7.5% ABV
A mouth-tingling array of molasses and cinnamon. Heavily hopped, it's a winter warmer of a beer with the strength to last several years in its bottle; it is for sipping and not swigging.

FOOD PAIRING: The sweetness of the beer will complement and enhance a sweet Christmas pudding laced with rum butter.

IMPERIAL EXTRA DOUBLE STOUT 9% ABV
As black as the darkest night, its aroma is an ecstasy of vinous flavours. The roasted malts interlay with dark fruit flavours, a hint of wild yeast sourness, and even some tantalising traces of blue cheese. There are overlays of coffee, prunes, and liquorice.

FOOD PAIRING: Try drizzling over creamy vanilla ice cream.

ARMADA ALE 4.5% ABV
Light to the eye, this heavily hopped, light copper-coloured pale ale has a rich fruity palate with soft dark berries and raisin flavours. The hops add a spicy pepperiness to the beer, which gives way to a sweet orangey finish.

FOOD PAIRING: It pairs well with dark orange chocolate.

Victory brew
This beer was originally commissioned by the National Maritime Museum to celebrate the 400th Anniversary of the defeat of the Spanish Armada

HARVEYS ARMADA ALE

THE KERNEL

In double-quick time, what started as a small idea has grown into a brewery that has had a huge influence on craft brewers around the world – The Kernel's minimalist packaging and independent spirit set it apart from the crowd.

THE FACTS...

OWNER The Kernel Brewery

FOUNDED 2010

ADDRESS Arch 11, Dockley Road Industrial Estate, London SE16 3SF

WEBSITE www.thekernelbrewery.com

PHILOSOPHY Collaboration and generosity of spirit

ONE OF THE STARRING ROLES in beer's renaissance has been played by Evin O'Riordain, who in 2010 founded The Kernel Brewery at Tower Bridge, London, under a railway arch. In only a few years, the man from Waterford in Ireland had won so many plaudits and awards for his big, bold beers that in March 2012 he had to move to a bigger site to keep up with ferocious demand.

O'Riordain's success is built upon his dedication to quality – taste and creativity, not the watchwords of an accountant or a marketing executive intent only on profit, decide what is put into the Kernel mash tun. He developed his cultured palate when learning about the art of cheese-making. This journey took him to New York, where he came across the work of pioneering US craft brewers, and he returned to London determined to learn how to brew. He set to with great enthusiasm, and the rest is history. His love of American beers has strongly shaped his own output; their use of big, bold, fruit-flavoured hops is a strong influence, and one he manages with exquisite skill. With

innate precision he understands how these flavours will meld, mingle, and co-operate in his own thought-provoking creations.

When it comes to brewing, The Kernel Brewery's focus is on innovation, not 21st-century industrial marketing. For example, each batch of Kernel's India Pale Ales is different, and is likely to use a different hop. O'Riordain also has a heartfelt desire to collaborate with other brewers to produce new and innovative beers of importance, as well as historical recreations. Add to this the trendy, minimalist packaging, and The Kernel is as exciting as a new powerful force in indie music.

TASTING NOTES

PALE ALE (AMARILLO) 5.7% ABV

Crisp, clean, and sharp, it's almost a palate-cleansing beer. The signature flavours of late-addition Amarillo hops bring aromas of summer flowers, orange zest, and there is some pepper and spice. It finishes with a long hoppy burst.

FOOD PAIRING: The orange zest in the hop partners well with a green Thai curry or contrasts with a pungent Roquefort or Danish Blue cheese.

IPA (CITRA) 8.1% ABV

American hops and British malt really do form a special relationship. A powerful burnished gold malt is strong and bold enough to support the clamour from the hops, which soar with tropical fruit, grass flavours, and some citrus. There is a long bitter hop finish.

FOOD PAIRING: It will take a big flavoured dish to stand up to the tropical fruit and high bitterness of the beer – try salted bacon, barbecued ribs, or strong hard cheese.

EXPORT STOUT 7.8% ABV

It's a symphony of flavours. Plums, prunes, and other dark dried fruits mingle with rum and coffee flavours. Then comes a long, lingering herbal hop bitterness which intertwines with espresso, leather, chocolate, and vanilla flavours.

FOOD PAIRING: Seek out well-flavoured blue cheese, robust meats, or even sweet Christmas cake.

THE KERNEL
PALE ALE

THE KERNEL
INDIA PALE ALE

THE KERNEL
EXPORT STOUT

MARSTON'S

Marston's is one of England's greatest real ale brewers. It is based in Burton upon Trent, the spiritual home to a beer style that is renowned around the world and the home of a once-vast brewing industry.

THE FACTS...

OWNER Marston's PLC
FOUNDED 1834
ADDRESS Marston's Brewery, Shobnall Road, Burton upon Trent, Staffordshire DE14 2BG
WEBSITE www.marstons.co.uk
PHILOSOPHY The home of good beer

Hip hops
A classic English IPA with an American edge – Cascade hops add a citrus zing

IN ITS 19TH CENTURY HEYDAY more than 40 breweries took advantage of Burton's supply of hard water, which is naturally suited to the brewing of ale-style beer. High in magnesium and calcium sulphates, it allows ale yeast to thrive and English hops to prosper. It generates a sparkling light-coloured beer – the colour of sherry and the condition of champagne – the venerated Burton pale ale. The water also gives fresh Burton beers a sulphurous aroma known as the "snatch".

One of the town's greatest brewers is Marston's, which was founded in 1834. In 1898, the company moved to the Albion Brewery, where it remains till today. Marston's innovative Victorian Burton Union fermentation system is still in use, as is the fermentation room, with its high vaulted ceiling, lines of interlinked wooden barrels, and the fermenters that give Marston's its greatest brew, Pedigree. The vibrant movement of the fermenting beer, passing from the barrel to the trough and back again, helps to create the complexity of Pedigree. As the beer moves through the linked barrels, its taste grows in intensity. Marston's is now part of Marston's PLC, which also owns the Banks's, Brakspear (see p.43), Jennings (see p.47), and Ringwood (see p.49) breweries.

TASTING NOTES

STRONG PALE ALE 6.2% ABV
The classic English combination of Maris Otter barley and Fuggles and Goldings whole hops produces a robust beer of great intensity and complexity. Initial caramel sweetness gives way to a long hop bitterness.
FOOD PAIRING: The strength and hoppiness of the beer enable it to cut through fatty foods, releasing new flavours.

PEDIGREE ALE, 4.5% ABV
Clear, bright, and sparkling, the malt sweetness is balanced by a hop bitterness, making it easily drinkable. On top of the complexity of tastes and aromas is a slight sulphur aroma.
FOOD PAIRING: Pair this classic beer with a steak and ale pie.

OLD EMPIRE INDIA PALE ALE, 5.7% ABV
A near perfect, copper-coloured English IPA. The initial pronounced biscuit maltiness gives way to a fruity sweetness that fades to a dry, lingering, bitter finish. It is made with Maris Otter barley and Fuggles, Goldings, and Cascade hops.
FOOD PAIRING: It pairs well with sweet-flavoured meats and good hard English cheeses.

MARSTON'S	MARSTON'S	MARSTON'S
STRONG PALE ALE	PEDIGREE	OLD EMPIRE

MEANTIME

It wasn't just brewing in London that took a turn for the better when Meantime opened in 2000; the high standards it set are now being emulated worldwide. Never compromising on quality, Meantime's beer has won numerous awards.

THE FACTS...

OWNER Meantime Brewing Company Ltd

FOUNDED 2000

ADDRESS Units 4&5 Lawrence Trading Estate, Blackwall Lane, London SE10 0AR

FOUNDED 2000

WEBSITE www.meantimebrewing.com

PHILOSOPHY A brewery built by people with ideas

Best of British
Is this the perfect English lager? English malt and hops embrace in this classic, long matured, continental favourite

MEANTIME FOUNDER AND MASTER BREWER Alastair Hook's mission in setting up the brewery was to mobilize people's tastebuds so that they could come to appreciate the full breadth of flavours, aromas, and colours that different styles of beer can have.

Hook trained as a brewer in Germany and has imposed the high standards he was taught there at Meantime. He uses only the best raw materials and treats them with respect.

A keen student of the history of beer and its cultural significance, Hook recreated several beers – including London porter and India pale ale – at a time when these styles were in danger of being forgotten in the UK. Meantime's extensive portfolio also includes a helles, a kölsch, a mocha coffee-flavoured beer, and some fruit beers.

In 2010 he took the step of opening a second brewery – the Old Brewery Bar and Restaurant – in the original 1836 Brewhouse of the Old Royal Naval College in Greenwich. Once a brewhouse for retired seamen living in the hospital, who had an allowance of two quarts of ale a day, the restaurant's shiny microbrewery – which is housed tall and proud in the restaurant – is now creating historical and modern beers including a zesty, fresh kellerbier.

TASTING NOTES

INDIA PALE ALE 7.4% ABV
Rich orange and marmalade flavours dance with grassy, hoppy, and some earthy aromas to conjure a beer of some complexity. Plenty of Kent Fuggles and Goldings hops help to recreate the flavours of the world's first great pale beer style.

FOOD PAIRING: Brewer Alastair Hook recommends trying it with an Indian curry or strong cheeses.

YAKIMA RED 4.1% ABV
German and British malts combine to produce a full-bodied, deep red ale. Five American hop varieties from the Yakima valley in Washington State add soaring fruit and citrus flavours.

FOOD PAIRING: Try it with sweeter meats such as veal, crispy roast pork, ham hock, or charcuterie.

LONDON LAGER 4.5% ABV
A clean-tasting lager, which is simply made but full of complexities. Long-conditioned, both the East Anglian malt and the Kentish hops come to the fore in a good balance.

FOOD PAIRING: With a good level of hops, this beer pairs with mature cheeses, hams and smoked meats, or oily fish.

MEANTIME
INDIA PALE ALE

MEANTIME
YAKIMA RED

MEANTIME
LONDON LAGER

ST AUSTELL

A proudly independent family brewer, St Austell has long been regarded as one of England's finest ale producers. Over the last few decades, the brewery's creativity has resulted in a stream of exciting beers and a host of awards.

THE FACTS...

OWNER St Austell Brewery Co. Ltd

FOUNDED 1851

ADDRESS 63 Trevarthian Road, St Austell, Cornwall PL25 4BY

WEBSITE www.staustellbrewery.co.uk

PHILOSOPHY An unrivalled commitment to Cornwall and Cornish suppliers

ENGLAND IN THE 1850s was a vibrant time for entrepreneurs. One such was Walter Hicks, who mortgaged his farm and home for £1,500 to set up a maltings. He bought one pub and then another, and finally the decision was taken to build a brewery. His vision was of a vertically integrated company – from the farm to the glass, the whole process was under his control. As this area of Cornwall prospered, so did the brewery. Generations of miners toiled, quarrying Cornwall's "white gold", china clay – and what better to quench their thirst than Hicks' beers?

These days, one of the brewery's best-known beers is Tribute. It was first brewed as a seasonal beer in 1999 to mark the total eclipse of the sun at 11am on 11th August and was called Daylight Robbery. It was brewed by the company's then new brewer Roger Ryman. Unlike many brewers of his time, he saw beyond the beers brewed within the British Isles and sought inspiration from brewers across the Atlantic in the USA. Rather than demure English hops, handfuls of tangy, citrussy hops from Washington and Oregon were thrown into the copper. And so Daylight Robbery went on sale, but unlike the clouds that disappointingly masked the eclipse, the beer was a shining success. The two-month sale period became three, then four, and so it went on. The company had a success on its hands, and decided in 2001 to rename the beer Tribute and make it a permanent feature.

ST AUSTELL CLOUDED YELLOW

ST AUSTELL KOREV

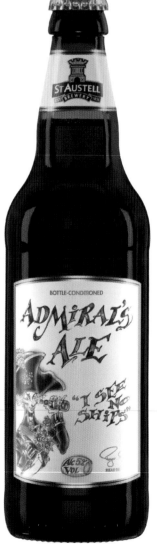

ST AUSTELL TRIBUTE   **ST AUSTELL** PROPER JOB   **ST AUSTELL** ADMIRAL'S ALE

Ryman and his team continue to develop new beers. Many of these are available at the St Austell's Celtic beer festival that takes place in a labyrinth of cellars under the brewery for one weekend in November. Every year there is something different. It could be a barrel of Tribute that has been aged for two months in a cask that once contained bourbon, producing high-flying wine and spirit notes. There have been strawberry-flavoured lagers and beers fermented with Belgian Trappist yeast – the creativity just goes on and on. One of the early graduates from this academy of beer was Clouded Yellow. Who would have thought that one of England's traditional ale brewers, who once had a reputation for conservatism and playing safe, would have produced a German-style wheat beer, full of spice, apple, and banana flavours?

Creamy head
The dense, smooth, long-lasting white head is a comforting feature of HSD

ST AUSTELL HSD

TASTING NOTES

CLOUDED YELLOW WHEAT BEER, 4.8% ABV

The colour of newly harvested hay, this bottle-conditioned wheat beer has hints of coriander hiding behind sweet banana notes. Pour it carefully to keep the sediment in the bottle, or pour it with a flourish so that the living yeast clouds the beer.

FOOD PAIRING: The harmony of sweetness and fragrant spices makes this an ideal partner for Asian cuisine, particularly Thai.

KOREV LAGER, 4.8% ABV

A new beer from St Austell, Korev lager takes its name from the Cornish word for beer. The use of soft, flavoursome Saaz hops, essential for the best continental lagers, brings a tantalizing but sometimes elusive grassy intensity to the beer.

FOOD PAIRING: It works very well with shellfish, and despite its delicate flavours, will cut through the sweetness of ham.

TRIBUTE ALE, 4.2% ABV

A modern British bitter with an American twist of zesty hops. The flavour is dominated by the citrus tang of the hops, which dance over the tongue along with elderflower and malt biscuit flavours. With a long, lingering finish, it's a great beer.

FOOD PAIRING: The freshness and zest of the beer means it pairs well with chicken, gammon, or fish.

PROPER JOB ALE, 5.5% ABV

Cornish Gold barley beats at the heart of this award-winning golden ale. Once a seasonal favourite, it is now brewed all year. A British beer with an American twist, the taste bursts and swirls with the citrus grapefruit intensity of the American Willamette, Cascade, and Chinook hops.

FOOD PAIRING: It works particularly well with both barbecue-style ribs or some lime-drizzled fish.

ADMIRAL'S ALE 5% ABV

This award-winning beer has been named the best bottle-conditioned beer in Britain and the world's best premium pale ale. It was first brewed in 2005 to mark the 200th anniversary of Nelson's victory at Trafalgar. This full-bodied beer has a rich mix of fruit cake, spice, and biscuit flavours.

FOOD PAIRING: It pairs marvellously with a hearty steak pie.

HSD ALE, 5% ABV

This is the most renowned of all St Austell's beers and was awarded a Silver medal at the International Beer Challenge 2012 and Gold at the European Beer Star competition 2009. Its colour is as striking as its flavour – it has a ruby red hue and deep, full flavours of toffee and raisins.

FOOD PAIRING: Ideal with steak or other red meats.

SHARP'S

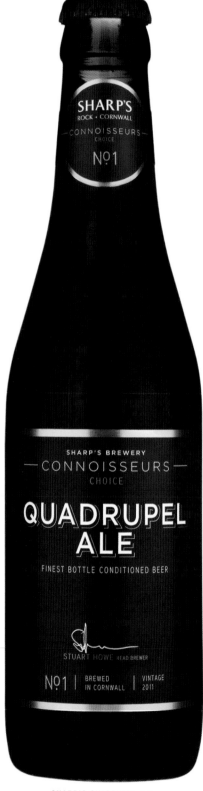

What started as a small "going nowhere" microbrewery in 1994 has been transformed into one of England's best-known ale brewers. Its head brewer Stuart Howe is fêted for his innovation and precision.

THE FACTS...

OWNER Molson Coors

FOUNDED 1994

ADDRESS Sharp's Brewery, Pityme Business Centre, Rock, Cornwall PL27 6NU

WEBSITE www.sharpsbrewery.co.uk

PHILOSOPHY Natural beers from Cornwall's Atlantic coast

SHARP'S
CORNISH PILSNER

SHARP'S
CHALKY'S BITE

WHEN SHARP'S, BASED IN ROCK, CORNWALL, was bought by global brewer Molson Coors for £20 million in 2011, there were fears that the brewery might close and production move elsewhere. Some thought that the global giant had only bought the brewery so it could get its hands on Doom Bar, one of the country's fastest growing ale brands.

However, Coors has made a major investment in the Rock plant and given head brewer Stuart Howe the scope to produce a range of new palate-challenging beers. He produced his first vintage of the Connoisseurs Choice range in 2011. The range includes bitter-sweet Quadrupel, dry, clean Single Brew Reserve, and rich, fruity Honey Spice Tripel. The range demonstrates Howe's skill and love of innovation. He says his beers are born out of a passion for beer and a love of aroma and flavour, balance, and precision. His ambition is to show the breadth of flavours available from beer.

Sharp's lower-strength beers are brewed with the same commitment to quality and taste as the stronger brews. "…it is very easy to brew big, bold strong beers with attention-grabbing attributes, but to make a lower strength beer with true character… poses a much greater challenge", says Stuart.

TASTING NOTES

CORNISH PILSNER 5.2 % ABV

A pale straw beer with a herbal lemon aroma, it is brewed using Pilsner malt, whole Saaz hops, and a Czech lager yeast. It is then layered with English thyme and more whole Saaz in a cold maturation vessel, before bottle conditioning.

FOOD PAIRING: Chill the beer before serving it with fish dishes or spicy food.

CHALKY'S BITE ALE, 6.8% ABV

Developed with celebrity chef Rick Stein to be as characterful as a strong Belgian beer, this delicate ale, named after Stein's dog, is overlaid with the flavour of wild Cornish fennel. Its three months of maturation give a beer of great depth.

FOOD PAIRING: Try it with freshly caught seafood.

QUADRUPEL ALE BOTTLE-CONDITIONED ALE, 10% ABV

It's a barley wine that thinks it's a port. The beer has been fermented with four different yeasts – saison, two types of English ale, and a Belgian Trappist. Transcending beer styles, its bitter sweetness gives way to warming alcohol.

FOOD PAIRING: Pair it with mature cheeses or rich, dark chocolate desserts.

SHARP'S QUADRUPEL ALE

THORNBRIDGE

Art and science work hand in hand at the Thornbridge Brewery in the heart of the Peak District National Park, Derbyshire, where some of the UK's most innovative beers are created by giving traditional ales a contemporary twist.

THE FACTS...

OWNER Thornbridge Brewery

FOUNDED 2005

ADDRESS Riverside Business Park, Buxton Road, Bakewell, Derbyshire DE45 1GS

WEBSITE www.thornbridgebrewery.co.uk

PHILOSOPHY Art and science working together

JIM HARRISON HAS A VERY BIG HOUSE in the country – Thornbridge Hall in Derbyshire. It was here that he decided to open a 16-hl (10-barrel) brewery in an old stonemason's and joiner's workshop in 2005.

As chairman of Sheffield Wednesday's football supporters club, the Owls Trust, Harrison was looking for ways to raise funds for the football club and he decided that it should have its own beer. He turned for help to the legendary brewer and pub owner Dave Wickett, who had founded Sheffield's Kelham Island Brewery. Wickett willingly got involved in the project, even though he was a supporter of arch rivals Sheffield United. This liaison led to the creation of the Thornbridge

Brewery, where the brewers were imbued with the ethos of brewing small batches of original beers using the finest raw materials. Some, like the heavily hopped Jaipur IPA and full-bodied Saint Petersburg Stout, are inspired by historical beers, but for others, fruits and herbs foraged from Thornbridge's grounds went into the beers. One beer, Bracia, uses an Italian honey made by bees that have feasted on chestnut blossom. Harrison and Wickett have also explored the boundaries of wood-ageing beer in barrels from different whisky distilleries.

In 2010, Thornbridge opened the state-of-the-art Riverside Brewery in Bakewell, Derbyshire, where the emphasis is on experimentation and exploring the boundaries of beer. Brewing also continues to take place at the old Hall, where a traditional infusion mash is used. While beer volumes have increased, the brewers are still looking for old recipes to which they can add a modern twist.

The image of Flora, the Goddess of Flowers, that features on some of the labels is taken from a statue within the grounds at Thornbridge Hall. With a string of awards, this relatively young brewery looks set to go from strength to strength with Flora's beery blessing.

THORNBRIDGE
SAINT PETERSBURG

THORNBRIDGE
BRACIA

THORNBRIDGE
JAIPUR

TASTING NOTES

SAINT PETERSBURG IMPERIAL RUSSIAN STOUT, 7.7% ABV
Saint Petersburg is smooth and, for a strong beer, easy to drink. Its flavours of dark bitter chocolate and raisins are easily discernible and give way to a coffee finish and lots of hops. It has a good warming finish.

FOOD PAIRING: A not-too-sweet dark, bitter chocolate dessert would bring out the best in the pudding and the beer.

BRACIA ALE, 10% ABV
Brewed four times a year, Bracia's distinctive flavour comes from the use of chestnut honey, which adds a rich, dark layer to the beer and conspires with the roasted and toasted notes of the malts to conjure a beer of smooth complexity.

FOOD PAIRING: Splash on top of vanilla ice cream.

JAIPUR INDIA PALE ALE, 5.9% ABV
Massive citrus hop flavours are smoothed and rounded by a honey sweetness in Jaipur. It's a beer that starts slowly, but on swallowing, the full intensity and complexity is realized as the warmth of the alcohol starts to work.

FOOD PAIRING: Delicious with bold food flavours, the beer works especially well with chilli and other spicy dishes.

ABBEY ALES

www.abbeyales.co.uk

BREWING RETURNED to the ancient City of Bath in 1997 when industry veteran Alan Morgan set up his own brewery, Abbey Ales. Morgan was one of a new wave of entrepreneurs who believed there was a market for beers from small local producers. His first beer, Bellringer, quickly became a favourite with locals and visitors. Made with Maris Otter barley, its colour is as yellow and golden as many of the city's historic buildings.

ABBEYDALE

www.abbeydalebrewery.co.uk

"WE JUST LIKE MAKING GOOD BEER", says Abbeydale founder Patrick Morton. Patrick cut his brewing teeth at Sheffield's Kelham Island brewery, the company that restored brewing pride to the steel city, before establishing Abbeydale in 1996 with his father, Hugh. A firm advocate of the philosophy that you don't make good beer by cutting corners, only 163 hl (130 barrels) are brewed a week. The company's best-known beer is Moonshine, a golden English ale, which is distinguished by a beguiling grapefruit hop aroma.

ACORN

www.acorn-brewery.co.uk

ACORN MIGHT BE a relatively new company – it was set up by former chef Dave Hughes in Barnsley, South Yorkshire in 2003 – but its yeast goes back a long way. All the company's beers are brewed on a 32-hl (20-barrel) plant, using a yeast strain that can traced back to the one used by the Barnsley Brewery in the 1850s. The yeast might be old, but the company's beers are thoroughly modern – two of its must-try beers are the award-winning Barnsley Bitter and Barnsley Gold.

ARKELL'S

www.arkells.com

ARKELL'S HAS BEEN a family business since it was founded by John Arkell in 1843. A traditional and independent company based in Swindon, Wiltshire, it is one of the few still to make a "boy's bitter". Once widely brewed, such beers are low strength and easy drinking. Arkell's 2B, at 3.2% ABV, is distinguished by tart, refreshing hops, while the popular ale Wiltshire Gold has a sweet malty taste and hoppy flavour.

ARKELL'S WILTSHIRE GOLD

ARRAN BLONDE

ARRAN

www.arranbrewery.com

LOCATED ON THE ISLE OF ARRAN in Scotland, this 164-hl-a-week (100-barrel) brewery stands in the shadow of the imposing Goatfell Mountain and overlooks the glories of Brodick Bay. Established in 2000, the company's beers are as crisp and clean as the Scottish air. One of its best beers is the clear and zesty, bottle-conditioned Arran Blonde, which, like all the company brews, is made without the use of artificial additives and preservatives.

B & T

www.banksandtaylor.com

ESTABLISHED IN 1994 in Shefford in Bedfordshire, when it was called Banks & Taylor, the company's mission statement was that it would brew traditional cask-conditioned ales using the best ingredients. It did then and it still does today. Its beers are made with pale, wheat, crystal, and roast malts, but the citrus-flavoured US Cascade hops are used in harmony with English Challenger and Goldings producing old-style beers with a 21st-century twist.

BATEMANS

www.bateman.co.uk

BEER WAS FIRST PRODUCED at the Salem Bridge brewery in 1874, and despite some trials and tribulations, Batemans is still owned by the Bateman family. It is built around an old windmill, and on most days a Union flag proudly flies above what is one of the UK's most picturesque breweries. Proud of its reputation for brewing "good honest ales", one of the brewery's latest bottled beers, Mocha, is brewed with Arabica coffee, Belgian chocolate, and barley grown in its home county of Lincolnshire.

BATH ALES

www.bathales.com

BATH ALES, known by its leaping hare symbol, was set up by Roger Jones and Richard Dempster in 1995. The pair had worked for the former Smiles Brewery in Bristol and they had a pint-sized dream to be a success. Now, their vision has become a 80-hl (50-barrel) brewery and they have created one of the most successful breweries in the south-west of England. The jewel in its brewing crown is Gem, a real ale with hints of butterscotch.

BATHAMS

www.bathams.com

TIM AND MATTHEW BATHAM are the fifth generation of the same family to run Bathams, a small, traditional brewery, housed in the Vine Inn, in Brierley Hill in the West Midlands. Founded in 1877, its best-known beer is Mild Ale – dark, fruity, and with a roasted malt sweetness, it is a recipe that has stood the test of time and is best enjoyed in one of the company's 10 idiosyncratic pubs.

BEAVERTOWN

www.beavertownbrewery.com

LOGAN PLANT, the son of Led Zeppelin's Robert Plant, is in the vanguard of a movement that is reviving brewing in East London, and he's hopping mad. He founded Beavertown in 2012, after a late-night drinking session led to an epiphany that brewing, rather than rock music, was his true calling. The company's best beer is Beavertown's rye IPA 8-Ball. Behind the 8-Ball are hops – lots of fragrant orange- and lemon-flavoured hops.

BLACK SHEEP

www.blacksheepbrewery.com

MASHAM IN NORTH YORKSHIRE is home to one of England's best-known brewing families, the Theakstons. Paul Theakston set up Black Sheep in 1992 after the village's other brewery, Theakston, founded by his family in 1827, was sold to a larger concern. Today, both companies are once again owned by members of the Theakston family. Lashings of Goldings and Fuggles hops give Black Sheep beers marvellous aromatic and floral fragrances.

BLUE ANCHOR

www.spingoales.com

BREWING HAS TAKEN PLACE in the Blue Anchor pub in Helston, Cornwall since the 15th century. In the 1970s, it was one of only four English pubs left brewing. And many thought the brewery, which once served as a monastery's hospice, was in terminal decline. But its survival has inspired a generation of new brewpubs. Its range of Spingo ales includes Bragget, an ancient recipe that could grace any US brewer of extreme beers – weighing in at 6% ABV, it is flavoured with honey and apples.

BLACK SHEEP RIGGWELTER

BRAKSPEAR

www.brakspear-beers.co.uk

THE JOURNEY FROM Brakspear Brewery's 17th-century spiritual home of Henley-on-Thames to Witney, Oxfordshire in 2004 has seen no diminishment of Brakspear's fine brews. The move followed the closure of the original brewery and the sale of its beer brands. The brewing equipment was bought, moved across the county, and reassembled. Brakspear still uses its famous double-drop fermentation system to brew its zesty bitters. Its marvellous bottled Triple is full of molasses and dark rum flavours.

BRECON BREWING

www.breconbrewing.co.uk

THE BOLDNESS of Brecon's brews is as big as the personality of the company's founder Buster Grant. Buster opened the brewery in 2011 and draws his inspiration from the surrounding Brecon Beacons, an uncompromising range of red sandstone peaks popular with walkers working up a thirst for his beers. One, Red Beacons, soars to zesty heights from the cocktail of Goldings, Sovereign, Pioneer, and First Gold hops.

BREWSTER'S

www.brewsters.co.uk

SARA BARTON founded Brewster's in 1998 and has worked hard to disabuse people of the idea that brewers only come from Mars. They can come from Venus too. Her hard work was rewarded in 2012 when she was named Brewer of the Year by the British Guild of Beer Writers. Renowned for collaborative brews with other women, she likes to develop new beers and put a twist on old styles by incorporating the latest hops.

BURTON BRIDGE

www.burtonbridgebrewery.co.uk

A RELATIVE NEWCOMER to England's spiritual home of brewing in Burton-upon-Trent, Burton Bridge was established in 1982 by Geoff Mumford and Bruce Wilkinson. The beers are brewed at the back of the idiosyncratic Bridge Inn pub and they often display the distinctive hallmark of locally brewed beers – the "Burton snatch" – marked by a whiff of sulphur when a beer is poured. The snatch is often detected in Burton's classic Golden Delicious ale, which is known for its crisp, apple fruitiness.

BUTCOMBE

www.butcombe.com

WHEN IT WAS FOUNDED in 1978, Butcombe was indeed a rarity, a new independent brewery. For many years its founder, the late Simon Whitmore, adhered to a principle of brewing only one beer – Bitter. A deeply satisfying beer, with a clean dry taste, derived from the use of Maris Otter malt.

The company was sold to Guy Newell in 2002 and now its range has expanded and includes Adam Henson's Rare Breed, named after a TV presenter and Cotswold farmer.

CALEDONIAN

www.caledonian-brewery.co.uk

FIRE HAS DONE NOTHING to diminish the reputation of the Caledonian Brewery in Edinburgh, now owned by Heineken. Infernos severely damaged the brewery twice in recent times, but phoenix-like, it has always reasserted itself as a brewer of fine ales. Its brewing copper is fired by a direct flame, which the brewer claims is the reason a hint of burnt caramel can be detected in its beer. It is best known for Deuchars, a zesty, hoppy beer that has a pleasant hint of butterscotch.

CASTLE ROCK

www.castlerockbrewery.co.uk

CASTLE ROCK WAS FOUNDED IN 1997 by pub owner Chris Holmes with the aim of creating high-quality beers to drink in a welcoming pub. Its best-known beer, Harvest Pale, was originally brewed for the 2003 Nottingham beer festival and it went on to be named Champion Beer of Britain by the Campaign for Real Ale (CAMRA) in 2010. A blond beer, it is brewed with an aromatic blend of US hops, giving it a gentle, lemon aftertaste.

CONISTON

www.conistonbrewery.com

TUCKED AWAY BEHIND the 400-year-old Black Bull pub in Coniston in the Lake District is the Coniston Brewing Company. Founded by Ian Bradley in 1995, its best-known beer is Bluebird Bitter, which was named CAMRA's Champion Beer of Britain in 1998. Made using the pure waters of the Coniston hills, the beer is named after the jet-propelled boat used by Donald Campbell during his fatal 1967 attempt to break the world water speed record on Coniston Water.

COTSWOLD

www.cotswoldlager.com

WHO SAYS THE ENGLISH DON'T BREW good lager? Richard and Emma Keene founded Cotswold Brewery in 2005, but rather than brewing ales "as everyone else was", they decided to show that hand-crafted lagers were beers of some distinction.

A range of unpasteurized beers is produced, including a Cotswold version of a German weissbier. Brewed with barley and wheat malt and flavoured with delicate Saaz hops, it has the authentic banana and tropical fruit flavours, and a large foaming head.

CROUCH VALE

www.crouchvale.co.uk

THE CROUCH VALE BREWERY in South Woodham Ferrers in Essex was founded in 1981 by two beer fans, Colin Bocking and Rob Walster. They had a dream that one day they could hold parties in their own brewery.

Since that day they have had many excuses for celebration and one of the biggest must have been in 2006 when its Brewers Gold was named Champion Beer of Britain, repeating its feat of the previous year. The pale, golden beer has a striking citrus nose.

DARK STAR

www.darkstarbrewing.co.uk

DARK STAR'S FIRMAMENT shines bright. Founded in the Evening Star pub in Brighton in 1994, with equipment little bigger than most home brewers have, it built its reputation on hops – lots of them. Its best-selling beer is Hophead, and with more than a passing nod to the vibrant US craft beer movement, it boldly uses lots of Cascade hops. However, serious beer-heads seek out Imperial, described as the "perfect going to bed beer".

DARTMOOR

www.dartmoorbrewery.co.uk

ENGLAND'S HIGHEST BREWERY, Dartmoor, is more than 420m (1,378ft) above sea level and it wants to reach new heights with its range of ales. Situated close to Dartmoor prison, the company's brews include Jail Ale and Dartmoor IPA – also known as Inmate's Pale Ale. Founded in 1994, when it was known as Princetown, its name changed in 2008, and its output now amounts to more than 490 hl (300 barrels) a week.

DONNINGTON

www.donnington-brewery.com

IS THIS ENGLAND'S most picturesque brewery? Donnington Brewery is housed in a working 13th-century honey-coloured Cotswold stone watermill, which was bought by Thomas Arkell in 1827. Very little seems to have changed since brewing started in 1865. The brewery was run for many years by the formidable Claude Arkell until his death in 2007, but with no children of his own, he left it to his cousins Peter and James Arkell, who also run Arkell's Brewery (see p.42).

DORSET PIDDLE

www.piddlebrewery.co.uk

LOCATED IN THE SMALL DORSET VILLAGE of Piddlehinton, the Dorset Piddle Brewery moved to an 13-hl (8-barrel) plant and new premises in 2011 after rising demand. Its best-known beer is the easy-drinking Jimmy Riddle, a complex, chestnut-coloured ale that has some spicy notes from the use of rye and oats. A seasonal favourite is a full-bodied 7% IPA, which is brewed in February, and at other times if the brewer fancies it.

ELGOOD'S

www.elgoods-brewery.co.uk

FOUNDED IN 1795, in Wisbech, Cambridgeshire, Elgood's was one of the first classic Georgian breweries to be built outside London and one of the few to have survived. The brewery has been in the hands of the Elgood family since 1878 and is now run by three sisters – fifth generation descendants of the man who bought it. Worth trying is the brewery's excellent Cambridge Bitter – a classic, complex English ale, made with Maris Otter barley and Fuggles and Challenger hops.

EVERARDS

www.everards.co.uk

WILLIAM EVERARD brewed his first pint in 1849 and his descendants still own the company. The firm's current Chairman, Richard Everard, says that the company successfully marries "tradition with ambition". This is exemplified by its best-known beer Tiger Best Bitter, which arguably achieves the ideal harmony between malt sweetness and hop bitterness. Crystal malt gives the beer its "rounded toffee character", which gives way to a long bittersweet finish.

GRAIN BLONDE ASH

HARVIESTOUN OLA DUBH

EXMOOR

www.exmoorales.co.uk

NOW MORE THAN 30 YEARS OLD, the Exmoor Brewery brought beer to the old brewing town of Wiveliscombe in Somerset. Its home is the former mash tun room of the Arnold & Hancock brewery, which closed in 1959. One of its best-known beers is Exmoor Beast, named after a wild cat said to roam local moors. It is an "exquisitely strong-willed, full-bodied dark porter" – a style first brewed in the 1700s.

GRAIN

www.grainbrewery.co.uk

FOUNDED IN 2006 by Geoff Wright and Phil Halls in a former dairy in the Waveney Valley, South Norfolk, Grain has quickly gained a reputation for complex and imaginative interpretations of older beer styles. Blonde Ash draws its inspiration from the Belgian witbier style. A cloudy wheat beer, it has the classic flavours of bubblegum, orange, and coriander, and pours with a large, appealing frothy white head. The brewery now owns the Plough pub in Norwich, where all its beers can be enjoyed.

GREENE KING

www.greeneking.co.uk

BIG IS BEAUTIFUL. Greene King in Bury St Edmunds in Suffolk can trace its roots back to 1799 when Benjamin Greene brewed his first pint. Ale has been a feature of this historic town since the 11th century. Today, the company vies for the accolade of being the UK's largest producer of ales. Much admired is its IPA Reserve: strong and full bodied, it is full of grapefruit and orange from the Styrian hops.

HALL & WOODHOUSE

www.hall-woodhouse.co.uk

FOUNDED IN 1777, Hall & Woodhouse is still run by seventh generation members of the Woodhouse family and they intend to keep it that way. Chairman and joint M.D., Mark Woodhouse, confidently asserts that the company is already planning for the 22nd century. A new brewhouse installed in 2012 has enabled head brewer Toby Heasman to trial a range of limited edition bottled beers including one that uses champagne yeast, continuing with the company's philosophy of brewing "Dorset ales with real character".

HAMBLETON

www.hambletonales.co.uk

NICK STAFFORD GAVE UP TEACHING to found the Hambleton Brewery in 1991. His masterly approach has seen the production of beers of some distinction. In addition to its core beers, which are distinguished by an imaginative use of hops, it produces two gluten-free bottled beers. Gluten Free Ale is flavoured with Cascade, Liberty, and Challenger hops, while Gluten Free Lager derives its citrus fruit character from East Kent Goldings and Continental Styrian hops.

HARDKNOTT

www.hardknott.com

DAVE BAILEY FOUNDED the small Hardknott Brewery in 2005, in a remote part of Cumbria. Uncompromising in his opinions, he says beer should not be confined to the narrow view of the masses. He wants drinkers to leave the safety of their favourite barstool and try something different. His brews are bold, challenging, and adventurous. One such is Queboid, a thoroughly modern, strong IPA that uses West Coast American hops and Belgian yeast. It is full of citrus and spicy banana flavours.

HARVIESTOUN

www.harviestoun.com

HARVIESTOUN IS A HEARTENING EXAMPLE of the success of Britain's new brewers. Life started with a 8-hl (five-barrel) plant in a barn on a farm in Dollar in 1985, but it has now moved to a purpose-built brewery in Alva, near Alloa in Scotland and is producing more than 16,365 hl (10,000 barrels) of beer a year. The company's ethos is to brew beer with flavour, aroma, and passion. Look out for Ola Dubh Ale, which is slowly matured in Highland Park whisky casks.

HAWKSHEAD

www.hawksheadbrewery.co.uk

FORMER BBC FOREIGN CORRESPONDENT Alex Brodie established Hawkshead in 2002, in a 17th-century barn, on a seven-barrel brew plant, in the Lake District. A life travelling the world and drinking in hundreds of bars had given Brodie a taste for good beer. Success came quickly as, in 2006 he had to move to Staveley, where a purpose-built brewery and visitor centre were built. Latest brews include some impressive oak-aged imperial stouts.

HEPWORTH & CO

www.hepworthbrewery.co.uk

WHEN KING & BARNES CLOSED its doors, head brewer Andy Hepworth and three other former employees continued the tradition of brewing in the Sussex town of Horsham by opening up their own brewery, Hepworth & Co. This was in 2001 and Hepworth's is now one of the county's largest producers. The firm is committed to using locally sourced barley and hop growers and is also licensed to produce organic beers by the Soil Association.

HESKET NEWMARKET

www.hesketbrewery.co.uk

POWER TO THE PEOPLE. Set up by Jim Fearnley in 1988, who at that time also ran the Old Crown pub in Hesket Newmarket in Cumbria, Hesket Newmarket's future looked bleak when he announced his retirement in 1999. However, a group of beer fans were determined that the brewery should continue. So the Hesket Newmarket Brewery Co-operative, a community enterprise with more than 60 members, was born. Most of the easy-drinking beers are named after local fells and are perfect after a day out walking on them.

HOBSONS

www.hobsons-brewery.co.uk

IT HAS BEEN QUITE A JOURNEY for Hobsons Brewery. Since 1993, father and son duo Jim and Nick Davis' home-brewing hobby has been converted into a thriving business that has gone from strength to strength. Despite their success, their founding principle of being a local brewer that serves its own community remains untarnished. The pair have shown that there is a market for artisanal beers, especially Hobsons Mild. Full of roasted nutty malt flavours, it is a delicious, smooth, flavourful beer.

HOGS BACK

www.hogsback.co.uk

ANYONE FOR TEA? Located in Tongham, Surrey, Hogs Back Brewery has a tradition of brewing well-crafted British beer. Its best-known beer is TEA (Traditional English Ale) – deep golden in colour, its aroma is full of dark berry flavours and orange zest. Founded in 1992,

the company quickly outgrew its original brewing equipment and is now brewing more than 284 hl (174 barrels) a week. Much sought after are bottled versions of its A Over T (Aromas Over Tongham) beer, a strong, rich, and sweetish barley wine.

HOLDEN'S

www.holdensbrewery.co.uk

AFTER 17 YEARS OF RUNNING many pubs together, Edwin and Lucy Holden's lives changed when they bought the Park Inn brewpub in Woodsetton, West Midlands, in 1915. The couple discovered that they enjoyed brewing and selling their own beer and Holden's brewery was born. One of their first beers, the Black Country Mild, was particularly popular with customers. As production expanded, they took over the adjoining building, which was formerly a malt store for the Atkinsons brewery.

Today, the company is run by third and fourth generation members of the Holden family, who own 20 pubs.

JOSEPH HOLT

www.joseph-holt.com

BUSINESS AT MANCHESTER'S Holt Brewery began in 1849 and it continues to be run by the same family today. The company is proudly and unashamedly old-fashioned, but that doesn't mean it lives in the past – it has steadily expanded its portfolio to include over 100 pubs and food houses.

These days it is run by Joseph Holt's great-great-grandson. The "new" brewery was built in 1860 and while little has changed in the brewing process, the fresh-tasting palate of the beer appeals to modern tastes.

HOOK NORTON

www.hooky.co.uk

FOUNDED IN 1849, Hook Norton's current brewhouse, built in 1899, is a near perfect example of a Victorian tower brewery. Its ingenious design uses gravity to propel ingredients around the brewery from the roof to the basement. The tower is home to one of the country's oldest working steam engines, which on special occasions is still fired up, entrancing all with its whirling belts, cogs, and shafts. The most beguiling beer from the brewery, where "progress is measured in pints", is the delightfully fruity Old Hooky.

HOGS BACK TEA

HOP BACK

www.hopback.co.uk

FROM HUMBLE BEGINNINGS in the cellar of the Wyndham Arms pub in Salisbury, the Hop Back Brewery, founded in 1986 by John Gilbert, has gone on to brew a beer at the forefront of a consumer revolution. In the early 1990s, John was one of the first to brew a golden beer designed to persuade a new generation of the merits of ale. Much emulated since that time but rarely bettered, Summer Lightning is an intensely bitter beer with a grassy, fresh hop aroma that bridges the gap between traditional British bitters and quality lagers.

HYDES

www.hydesbrewery.com

FOR GENERATIONS, HYDES HAS BEEN a favourite of Manchester drinkers. Family-owned and founded in 1863, the brewery has recently rationalized its production and moved to a new location in Salford away from its long-term home on Moss Side. As well as concentrating on its traditional ales, the new brewery now means the company is able to flex its brewing muscles by introducing a range of seasonal and specialist beers.

ICENI

www.icenibrewery.co.uk

INSPIRED BY THE ANCIENT QUEEN Boadicea who led a rebellion to keep the Roman invaders out of East Anglia in about 60 CE, Brendan Moore launched Iceni in 1995 with the intention of stopping industrial beers taking over the region. Many of Iceni's beers are influenced by the warrior queen, although Brendan doesn't advocate the destruction of London and St Albans as Boadicea did. Iceni has its own small hop garden where First Gold hops are grown.

INNIS & GUNN

www.innisandgunn.com

AN EXPERIMENT BY WHISKY PRODUCER William Grant in 2002 changed the life of brewer Dougal Sharp forever. The distiller wanted to produce a Scotch with beer flavours, so Sharp seasoned an empty bourbon cask for him by brewing beer in it. Once the beer had served its purpose, the plan was to throw it away, but the commercial possibilities of wood-aged beer bustling with soaring spirit flavours were quickly realized. Since then Innis & Gunn's 77-day matured Oak Aged Beer has been showered with awards and continues to go from strength to strength.

JENNINGS

www.jenningsbrewery.co.uk

JENNINGS BREWERY may be part of a bigger group today – it was bought by Marston's in 2005 – but there is still something fiercely independent about the Lake District-based company that was founded in 1874. One of its strongest beers is Sneck Lifter, a reddish dark ale. The dry, biscuit flavour of the Maris Otter malt gives way to chocolate and coffee notes, which work in harmony with the peppery, bittering sweetness of the Goldings and Fuggles hops.

KELHAM ISLAND

www.kelhambrewery.co.uk

KELHAM ISLAND WAS FOUNDED IN 1990 by a university lecturer turned pub owner, the legendary Dave Wickett, who died in 2012. Kelham was the first brewery to open in Sheffield in almost 100 years and for a while it was the city's only one. By 1999 Hope & Anchor, Whitbread, Stones, and Wards had all closed. However, Dave's passion for real beer inspired a generation of new start-up breweries, not just in Sheffield but worldwide. You might say he put steel back into the city.

LEES

www.jwlees.co.uk

THE LEES COMPANY was established by the visionary John Lees in 1828 and has been under the care of the legendary Lees family ever since. A former cotton maker, John recognized that Manchester's burgeoning workforce would like to drink beer, and lots of it, after a day's hard work. Now run by the sixth generation of the Lees family, the brewery's Moonraker, a strong barley wine, is much sought after. The brewery's maxim is "old-fashioned but cutting edge".

LOVIBONDS

www.lovibonds.com

THE BREWING BUG bit Lovibonds founder Jeff Rosenmeier in 1994 after trying a friend's home-made stout. In 2005, he gave up his job as a software engineer and decided that his hobby should become a business. Drawing on his American roots, one of his most creative brews is Lovibonds Gold Reserve. Dubbed a wheat wine, large amounts of local Oxfordshire honey is added to the mix, before it is fermented and then left to cold-condition for six months before bottling.

MARBLE

www.marblebeers.com

THERE IS MUCH MORE TO MANCHESTER'S BEER scene than breweries that were established in the 19th century. In 1997, owner of the Marble Arch pub, Vance Debechval, and manager Mark Dade had to make the choice between karaoke evenings or setting up their own brewery to secure the future of their pub.

Mark left in 2000, but his replacement James Campbell kept the brewing project going and draws inspiration from around the world. Beer became fun and fashionable and karaoke's loss was beer drinkers' gain.

MCMULLEN

www.mcmullens.co.uk

THERE CANNOT BE MANY COMPANIES that can trace their roots back to 1827. But during this time, life has not been without its ups and downs for McMullen's. The brewery came close to closure in 2002 – a family feud threatened the brewery with extinction when directors acrimoniously split over the future of the company. With the issues resolved, a new brewery was installed in 2006.

These days, brewer Chris Evans proudly states that he will only use whole hops and not pellets or extract to brew ale.

MOOR

www.moorbeer.co.uk

"WE MAKE NATURAL BEERS that are designed to be served with a haze", says native Californian brewer Justin Hawke.

Moor Brewery began in 1996 on a former dairy farm in the Levels and Moors area of Somerset. Success came quickly and the brewery won a number of awards, but then lost its way when it began to contract out its brewing. In 2007 Justin Hawke, who learnt to brew in a San Franciscan craft brewery, took over the company and began to work to improve the quality and flavour of the beer produced. Now, after much hard work, Moor's ground-breaking cloudy beers have an international reputation.

MOORHOUSE'S

www.moorhouses.co.uk

FOUNDER WILLIAM MOORHOUSE established his business in Burnley, in 1865. Originally Moorhouse's produced mineral waters and low-strength hop bitters for temperance bars, but in 1970, as times changed, the company began to brew full-strength beer. However, business went downhill, and in 1988 Manchester businessman Bill Parkinson bought the failing brewery because he "liked the beer". It was a challenge, but Bill's magic worked, and its Pendle Witches-themed brews are earning back the brewery's reputation.

MORDUE

www.morduebrewery.com

IN 1995 TWO TYNESIDE BROTHERS, Garry and Matthew Fawson, decided to set up a brewery that revived a famous local brewing name that had lain dormant since 1879 – Mordue. Although Mordue beers no longer quench the thirst of the thousands of dehydrated shipyard workers the brewery once served, the name is once again celebrated. Its best-known brew is Workie Ticket. Slang for workshy, it's not a description you would ever use for the Fawson brothers.

OAKHAM

www.oakhamales.com

HOPS PLAY A BIG PART in the brewing philosophy at Oakham. They love them, especially zesty American-grown varieties. Established in 1993, the company moved to Peterborough in 1998, where it now has two sites – a 123-hl (75-barrel) plant for its main brews and a 10-hl (six-barrel) toy in its brewpub where the brewers can create flavoursome brews just for the joy of it. Its Citra ale almost overwhelms the palate with its intense pink grapefruit and tropical fruit flavours.

OKELLS

www.okells.co.uk

SURGEON TURNED BREWER Dr William Okell founded the brewery on the Isle of Man in 1850. All of Okells' beers are brewed according to the Island's purity law – similar to the German *Reinheitsgebot* (see p.52). The law forbids the use of any additives as a substitute for the natural brewing ingredients of malt, sugar, and hops. It was amended in 1998 so that the brewery could use wheat and fruit in its beer.

ORKNEY DARK ISLAND

OTLEY O-GARDEN

ORKNEY

www.sinclairbreweries.co.uk

THE ECOLOGICALLY AWARE Orkney Brewery was founded in 1988 in a former school building in a remote part of Orkney, Scotland. Head Brewer Andrew Fulton says his favourite brew is Red MacGregor, an easy-drinking, tawny-coloured ale that blossoms with floral and fruity notes. Fans of wood-aged beer seek out the strong Dark Island Reserve. Matured in Orkney malt whisky casks for three months, it is redolent with fruit, spice, oak, and roast malt flavours.

OTLEY

www.otleybrewing.co.uk

FOUNDED IN 2005 by former professional photographer Nick Otley in Pontypridd, South Wales, Otley Brewery has become a destination for people seeking out beers with forthright floral and citrus hop flavours.

A big fan of American hops, Otley has used his visual skills to create a range of beers that look modern and appeal to a new generation. His award-winning O-Garden is a wheat beer flavoured with orange, coriander, and cloves.

OTTER

www.otterbrewery.com

SUSTAINABILITY IS PARAMOUNT to the McCaig family, who founded the Otter Brewery in 1990 at their home in the Blackdown Hills in Devon. The brewery boasts some serious green credentials: the beers are stored in an underground eco-cellar that is powered by solar panels; water used for brewing is taken from the brewery's own springs; and any effluent passes through a natural filtration system of willow beds, which have become a haven for wildlife, before being put back into the local water system.

PALMERS

www.palmersbrewery.com

FOUNDED IN 1794 in a former watermill, Palmers is the only brewery in Britain with a thatched roof. The Palmer family have been running the brewery since the 1890s and today they are fiercely proud of the brewery and its pubs' contribution to community life in Dorset. Its strongest beer is Tally Ho!, a complex dark ale, combining deep maltiness and a hint of bananas, balanced by spicy flavours from its Fuggles hops.

PITFIELD

www.pitfieldbeershop.co.uk

PITFIELD BREWERY'S RELOCATION from North London to a Soil Association-registered farm in rural Essex in 2006, where most of its barley is grown, strengthened the company's claim to be the UK's leading organic brewery.

Its beers are sold at farmers' and organic markets across south-east England. Much acclaimed is its 1792 Imperial Stout. Big, bold, and full of roasted barley character, it bursts with complex plum and cherry notes.

PURITY

www.puritybrewing.com

THIS ECO-FRIENDLY BREWERY, which opened in a converted barn in in 2005, is proud of its green credentials. There is even a waterlife sanctuary for cleansing the brewery's effluent.

The first beer to flow out of the conditioning tank was Pure UBU. Named after the brewery's dog, the cocktail of Challenger and Cascade hops creates a fragrant, fruity, almost spicy beer that is underpinned by the use of Maris Otter malt.

PURPLE MOOSE

www.purplemoose.co.uk

FOUNDED IN 2005 by former home brewer Lawrence Washington, Purple Moose is a thriving 16-hl (10-barrel) microbrewery in Porthmadog in North Wales that gives all its beers both English and Welsh names.

Best known is Cwrw Eryri/Snowdonia Ale, a golden, refreshing ale enhanced by the use of Central European hops – Savinjski Golding and Lubelski from Slovenia and Poland, which bring citrus and pine flavours to the beer and lead to a long throat-warming finish. Also noteworthy is the award-winning Cwrw Glaslyn/Glaslyn Ale – a golden, fruity bitter.

RAMSGATE

www.ramsgatebrewery.co.uk

RAMSGATE WAS FOUNDED by Eddie Gadd in 2002 at the back of a Ramsgate pub. He claims he learned to brew by numbers, but today he prefers to use passion rather than rote – "brewers not accountants should run breweries", he says. Gadd is an exponent of craft brewing and of encouraging brewers to collaborate on shared projects, such as getting brewers in Kent to brew new beers using new-season, locally grown green hops.

REDEMPTION

www.redemptionbrewing.co.uk

ONE OF LONDON'S NEW WAVE of craft breweries, the Redemption Brewery was founded in Tottenham in 2010 by Andy Moffat, a former banker, who reckons his new job is a step on the road to salvation from his previous career. The brewery might be small but its beers are big – hops, especially American, underpin many of the brews. His philosophies are that the brewer should respect time and patience, and that "automation is subservient to the skill of the craft brewer". The brewery has a strong environmental ethos, and all its power comes from renewable energy sources.

RINGWOOD

www.ringwoodbrewery.co.uk

RINGWOOD BREWERY should hold a special place for fans of today's craft beer revolution. It was founded in 1978 by Peter Austin, who brewed a thumping good pint, and is widely regarded as the inspiration for a generation of today's new wave of brewers.

Peter Austin is now in his 90s, and his company is owned by Marston's, but his Old Thumper is still a powerful beer with its rock and roll of malt tastes. This award-winning beer was originally brewed without a name in 1979 – the brewery ran a local competition to choose the winning name.

ROBINSONS

www.robinsonsbrewery.com

BREWING IN STOCKPORT, Cheshire, since 1838, the Robinsons Brewery is still owned by members of the Robinson family. In its spanking new brewery, the company claims to have the world's largest "hopnik", a giant strainer for getting flavours out of hop leaves.

Beer fans seek out its Old Tom, a dark, powerful beer full of dark fruit and chocolate flavours. A sister brew version contains bruised Chinese ginger root and botanical extracts.

ROOSTERS

www.roosters.co.uk

ROOSTERS BREWERY first strutted its stuff in 1993. Founder Sean Franklin was tired of brown British beers and wanted something lighter in colour but with a more adventurous hop. So beers such as Yankee were developed – a courageous harmony of soft Yorkshire water and American Cascade hops. Jump to the present day and the Fozard family now run the brewery. They too have a love of hops, and are filling the fermenter with flavours from Australia, New Zealand, Slovenia, and North America.

ST PETER'S

www.stpetersbrewery.co.uk

FOUNDED IN 1996, St Peter's Brewery is housed opposite a medieval, moated hall near Bungay in Suffolk. It brews a range of traditional bitters and milds, but often with a fruity twist. Blackcurrant, grapefruit, and gooseberry are added when in season, and at Christmas-time dried fruits, spices, and orange peel help create a special festival ale.

The bottled beers are known for their distinctive green packaging; the design is a copy of a flask-shaped bottle from Philadelphia in America, dating from 1770. Kegs and casks are also available to buy.

SAMUEL SMITH

www.samuelsmithbrewery.co.uk

THERE IS SOMETHING ENIGMATIC about the Samuel Smith Brewery. Family owned, and with one of the best-known names in brewing, it shuns publicity. The brewery's name has even been taken off its drays. The bottled beer range, which includes imperial and chocolate stouts, is regarded as the touchstone for the styles, and they have been widely emulated by many US brewers, but rarely bettered. Samuel Smith is Yorkshire's oldest brewery – the well in the Old Brewery was sunk in 1758.

SHEPHERD NEAME

www.shepherdneame.co.uk

MONKS IN THE 12TH CENTURY knew that the water in Faversham, Kent, was good for brewing – and so did the town's mayor. In 1698 he founded a brewery over an artesian well. Today, brewing still takes place on the site, which is the oldest brewery in Britain. Since 1864 it has been known as the Shepherd Neame Brewery.

Its range of well-hopped bitters includes the iconic Bishops Finger, a cocktail of dried fruits, pear, and banana flavours. Another popular and renowned beer, Spitfire, with its spicy, hoppy taste, was first brewed in 1990 to celebrate the 50th anniversary of the Battle of Britain, fought over Kent.

THEAKSTON

www.theakstons.co.uk

THE THEAKSTON FAMILY has been brewing in Masham in North Yorkshire since they bought a brewpub in the town in 1827 called the Black Bull. The family lost control of the company in the 1980s even though some still worked for it. However, in 2003 four Theakston brothers, whose great-great-grandfather started the firm 176 years earlier, bought it back. Its best-known beer is Old Peculier – a rich, full-bodied, smooth-tasting ale that is full of dark fruit flavours.

THWAITES

www.thwaites.co.uk

FOR MANY YEARS, Thwaites, which was founded in 1807 and is still family controlled, had a staid image. All that changed when the brewery installed a new craft brewery alongside its main plant. Named Crafty Dan, it will allow Thwaites Brewing Director Ian Bearpark to create short-run beers – as few as 41 to 49hl (25 to 30 barrels) – in new experimental flavours on a regular basis. In its first year of business it created 31 unique ales.

TIMOTHY TAYLOR

www.timothy-taylor.co.uk

THE TAYLOR FAMILY has been brewing beer under the Timothy Taylor name in the Yorkshire town of Keighley since 1858. The brewery has its own spring, supplying bountiful supplies of pure Pennine water, which is used to brew its beers.

Its best-known beer is the celebrated Landlord, which was first brewed in 1953. Made with Golden Promise malted barley, the Fuggles, Goldings, and Styrian Golding hops give a marvellous citrus and floral aroma.

TITANIC

www.titanicbrewery.co.uk

FOUNDED IN 1985 by brothers Dave and Keith Bott, the Titanic Brewery is named in honour of local boy Edward Smith, who had the misfortune to captain the ill-fated liner *Titanic*. Thankfully the fortunes of the Stoke-on-Trent brewers have been far more buoyant.

The brewery's refreshing Iceberg brew is a sparkling, golden beer. It is made with a combination of Maris Otter pale and wheat malt to which zesty, flowery Yakima Galena and Cascade hops are added.

TRAQUAIR

www.traquair.co.uk

BREWING BEGAN AT TRAQUAIR HOUSE in Scotland in the early part of the 18th century when beers were produced for the Traquair estate's workers. The brewery fell into disuse during the 1800s, although the vessels remained in place, gathering dust until 1965 when Peter Maxwell Stuart, 20th Laird of Traquair, decided to revive the tradition.

Traquair House Ale, its best-known beer, is fermented in unlined oak vessels and sings with soaring sweet sherry flavours.

TRIPLE FFF

www.triplefff.com

THE SMALL BREWERY IN ALTON, Hampshire was founded in 1997 by cabinet maker and home brewer Graham Trott, who said he wanted to brew "real ale that real ale drinkers drink". A fan of 1970s rock music, he named some of his beers after favourite record tracks. One such is Moondance – it's a golden ale that is hopped with handfuls of Cascade; another is Pressed Rat & Warthog, a complex ruby-coloured mild with hints of blackcurrant.

WADWORTH

www.wadworth.co.uk

THE WILTSHIRE TOWN OF DEVIZES is home to one of England's great real ale champions – Wadworth. Old it might be – it was founded in 1875 and beer is still delivered locally using a horse-drawn dray – but it is a brewery with its feet firmly rooted in the 21st century.

Its best-known brew is 6X, a tawny coloured, fruity ale that has been made for 90 years. Recently brewer Brian Yorston has started experimenting with a microbrewery to create some exciting one-off brews.

WELLS & YOUNG'S

www.wellsandyoungs.co.uk

TWO OF THE UK'S best-known brewing families came together in 2006 when Charles Wells and Young and Co. of Wandsworth in London merged, bringing together hundreds of years of brewing history. Wells founded his brewery in Bedford in 1876 and five generations later it is still family-owned. Young's had been on a site where brewing was first recorded in 1551, but is now based in Bedford. Their best-known beers include rich, juicy Wells Bombardier and light, crisp Wells Eagle IPA.

TRAQUAIR HOUSE ALE

WESTERHAM FREEDOM ALE

WESTERHAM

www.westerhambrewery.co.uk

ROBERT WICKS founded the Westerham Brewery in Westerham, Kent in 2004 in a former dairy. In so doing, he brought brewing back to a town that hadn't had a brewery since its Black Eagle Brewery closed in 1965.

A visit to the National Collection of Yeast Cultures helped Wicks track down the yeast that had been used in Black Eagle, which he then used to recreate the flavour of previous Westerham beers. Many of Wicks's beers are heavily and gloriously hopped with locally grown Kentish hops.

WHITE HORSE

www.breweryoxfordshire.co.uk

AFTER A 20-YEAR JOURNEYMAN CAREER in the brewing industry, Andy Smith decided that it was time he owned his own brewery and set up White Horse in 2004. The brewery is located in the Oxfordshire village of Stanford-in-the-Vale and, on a good day, Andy claims he can see the chalk carving of the white horse after which the brewery is named.

One of White Horse's most popular beers is Village Idiot, a blond assertive ale, flavoured with Challenger and Bramling Cross hops.

WILD BEER

www.wildbeerco.com

"DRINK WILDLY DIFFERENT" is the motto of the Wild Beer company, which was launched in 2012. Wild Beer is based just outside Bristol and aims to produce a very different breed of beers using flavour-complex wild yeasts and a range of unusual ingredients that are only limited by the imagination of the brewer.

The range of beers includes a number that are aged in oak barrels, adding soft vanilla and rich tannin flavours to the maturing beer, and others that use champagne yeast to give the beer an extra fizzy intensity.

WILLIAMS BROTHERS

www.williambrosbrew.com

ALLOA IN SCOTLAND was once a thriving brewing town, with many flourishing breweries. But over time the numbers dwindled, and if Scott and Bruce Williams hadn't taken over the old Forth Brewery in 2003 to set up Williams Brothers, none would

have been left. Their best-known brew is Fraoch, which is made with flowering heather instead of hops. The brewery's other beers use ingredients from the earliest days of brewing. Ingredients are foraged from hedgerows, woods, moors, and the seashore, while recipes are sourced from old manuscripts.

WILLIAM WORTHINGTON

www.nationalbrewerycentre.co.uk

OWNED BY INTERNATIONAL GIANT Molson Coors and located in the National Brewery Centre in Burton upon Trent, the William Worthington Brewery is home to the world's most authentic India Pale Ale. Worthington's White Shield is a survivor from the 1820s, when it was famed for its ability to survive the sea journey to India and arrive clear and sparkling. Production left Burton for many years, but in 2000 the brewer at the National Brewery Centre, Steve Wellington, persuaded the then-owner Bass to bring it back.

WOODFORDE'S

www.woodfordes.co.uk

WHERRY WAS THE FIRST commercial beer made by home brewers Ray Ashworth and Dr David Crease when they set up the Woodforde's brewery in 1981. The partners were part of a new wave of UK brewers inspired by stories of American home brewers who were beginning to push at the boundaries of traditional brewing. Like many of their American contemporaries, Ashworth and Crease wanted to rebel against what they saw as the "relentless blandness" of larger brewers' beers. The resulting zesty, refreshing Wherry is anything but bland.

WYE VALLEY

www.wyevalleybrewery.co.uk

WYE VALLEY WAS FOUNDED by former Guinness brewer Peter Amor in 1985. Inspired by his former employer, one of his first tasks was to create Dorothy Goodbody's Wholesome Stout. An instant classic, it is brewed with pale malt and roasted barley to create a smooth stout with a bitter edge. Originally brewed as a seasonal beer, it is now available all year round and has won many awards. Butty Bach, HPA, and Wye Valley Bitter are also produced by the company.

WILLIAMS BROTHERS FRAOCH

WYE VALLEY DOROTHY GOODBODY'S WHOLESOME STOUT

GERMANY

 **In every corner of the globe**, Germany is renowned for its beer culture. It is home to the world's most famous beer festival, Munich Oktoberfest, and it is responsible for the famed quality and purity laws, the *Reinheitsgebot*. These guidelines were set out in the 16th century to govern methods of beer production, and stated that beer should only be made with malted barley, hops, yeast, and water – with no other additions. Despite these laws being overturned by a European Court towards the end of the 20th century, they are still widely used, not just in Germany, but by many brewers worldwide.

Germany has an enormous wealth of traditional beers, boasting more than 15 classic beer styles, from the famed acidic, cloudy, banana- and clove-flavoured wheat beers of Bavaria, Leipzig, and Berlin to the smoky, mysterious dark beers of Bamberg. In southern Germany, brewers produce glorious pale golden helles, while in the north, along the banks of the Rhine, a range of alt beer varieties can be found.

Until recently, many German brewers were regarded as profoundly conventional and reluctant to try new ideas. But times have changed. Forward-thinking brewers have discovered flavoursome aromatic ales, and the fact that there is more to beer than the ubiquitous pilsner. Long-lost beer styles like the smoky adambier from Dortmund are being researched, while other brewers are experimenting with pale ales, well-hopped US IPAs, and wood-aged beers. And not to be outdone, the deeply conservative German hop industry is looking through its historical records to see if it can find hops that match the finest aromatics from the US and New Zealand. Beware, the sleeping beer giant of Germany has awoken.

CAMBA BAVARIA

Inspired by American craft beer, Camba Bavaria has won over the tastebuds of conservative Bavarian drinkers with hoppy ales and barrel-aged specialities. The brewpub offers a large selection of German and exotic styles.

THE FACTS...

OWNER Camba Bavaria GmbH
FOUNDED 2008
ADDRESS Mühlweg 2, 83376 Truchtlaching
WEBSITE www.cambabavaria.de
PHILOSOPHY Preserving the exceptional and combining it with contemporary variations from all over the world

CAMBA BAVARIA
INDIAN PALE ALE

CAMBA BAVARIA
HELL

BREWER MARKUS LOHNER founded Braukon, a company that provides brewhouse facilities, in 2003. Before that he worked as brewmaster at the Hofbräuhaus in Newport, Kentucky, in the US. The Whiskey State spoiled him with its barrel-aged beers, and he was exposed to more international beer styles than he had known in his native country. He returned to Germany full of ideas for exceptional beers. These were eventually put into effect when Braukon's technical centre also became the production site of Lohner's newly established Camba Bavaria. The first beers were classical Bavarian styles and later offerings were speciality brews. Camba Bavaria was among the first in Germany to introduce oak-aged beers. Bourbon Barrels, a dark bock aged in Woodford Reserve barrels came out in 2009. In 2012, the brewery released about 15 varieties, including such delicacies as oak-aged light bock in muscatel barrels.

Besides these rarities, the brewery offers a large selection: pale, amber, and brown ale, Christmas ale and IPA, you name it. Lohner claims that even the most conservative Bavarians are enthusiastic once they have tried the beers. It's no surprise that beer lovers from Munich drive for hours to pick up their load of Camba beers. Guests at the beautiful brewpub can choose from 40 varieties, 15 of which are on tap.

TASTING NOTES

INDIAN PALE ALE 8% ABV
Dark orange, hazy, and with a creamy head, it has fruity hop aromas and a creamy mouthfeel. A sweet, fruity first sip, with grapefruit, elderflower, and honey, leads to a long, bitter finish.
FOOD PAIRING: Goes well with steak, spicy Asian dishes, hot soups, stilton, and sweet and fruity desserts.

HELL HELLES, 4.7% ABV
Bronze-golden, with a shiny haze and a great white head. Hell offers a spicy, malty nose with a minty accent. After a sweet first sip it has a sparkling texture, medium body, and aromatic finish.
FOOD PAIRING: Great as a thirst-quencher or as a companion to roast beef, duck, spicy pizza, or alpine or parmesan cheese.

BOURBON BARRELS DOPPELBOCK, 8.5% ABV
Bourbon Barrels is chestnut-brown and aged for seven months in whiskey barrels. It has an aroma of dark cherries, whiskey, and vanilla, and is full-bodied with a dry and warming finish.
FOOD PAIRING: A great digestif and degustation beer, it is good with blue cheese, dark chocolate, or the occasional cigar.

Flavour complex
The soaring notes in Camba's wood-aged beers are introducing Germans to a new world of flavours

CAMBA BAVARIA BOURBON BARRELS

FAUST

Even though Faust caters predominantly to local markets in Lower Franconia, some beers in their portfolio have what it takes to gain international recognition. The history of the brewery also has many multi-national ties.

Dark fantasy
As its grand label and attractive swing-top cap might suggest – this is a beer of sumptuous complexity

BRAUHAUS FAUST has a tumultuous past – it was originally founded in 1654 by a Frenchman who had migrated to Germany after the Thirty Years War. A later owner, August Krug, was a persecuted leader of the liberal movement, who fled to the US and set up a brewery in Milwaukee, later known as Schlitz. Today, the Miltenberg brewery is run by Cornelius and Johannes Faust, whose family bought it in 1875.

Faust has a clear regional style even though head brewer and owner, Cornelius Faust, is strongly inspired by the international craft beer movement. As a regular on the jury of the World Beer Cup, he befriended US brewers and picked up their hopping techniques. This led to his own version of an Imperial IPA, which is heavily spiced with German and US hop varieties. He named it Auswanderer Bier 1849 (Expatriate Beer 1849) in reference to his predecessors.

The Eisbock is another interesting beer and has been highly decorated with international awards. The bock beer is frozen to extract the iced water and the resulting alcoholic concentrate is aged in oak for several months. After maturing, the beer is seductively smooth and complex, but not cloying. Faust has also released a vintage edition of their doppelbock and a malt-accented, strong Brewer's Reserve, made for keeping – not to mention the wonderful dark lager of the year-round range, spiced with a hint of smoked malt.

TASTING NOTES

EISBOCK BOCK, 11% ABV
Clear brown with a reddish hue, this oak-aged beer naturally has little carbonation. It is sweet and complex with intense malt aromas finishing with notes of sherry.

FOOD PAIRING: Try as a degustation beer or with tasty cheeses.

AUSWANDERERBIER 1849 IPA, 8% ABV
Amber-orange and opaque, this imperial IPA offers fruity and floral aromas reminiscent of apricots, roses, and herbs. It has caramel flavours, a hop-aromatic finish, and a juicy mouthfeel.

FOOD PAIRING: Pair with spicy dishes and sweet desserts.

SCHWARZVIERTLER DUNKEL DARK LAGER, 5.2% ABV
This mahogany-coloured lager has hints of toffee and chocolate; its sweetness merges into dark malt flavours with delicate smoked notes. It has medium body, a dry mouthfeel, and a velvety smoky finish.

FOOD PAIRING: Try with grilled or smoked meat or fish.

FAUST
EISBOCK

FAUST
AUSWANDERERBIER 1849

FAUST
SCHWARZVIERTLER DUNKEL

GOSLAR

At the age of 16, Odin Paul knew exactly what he wanted to be – an independent brewer. What he did not guess was that he would become an independent gose brewer. It is due to him that the lost style is back home in Germany again.

IN THE 1980S WHEN ODIN PAUL began his brewing apprenticeship, gose had almost disappeared from German beer culture. The top-fermented wheat beer style that originated in the Harz Mountains town of Goslar was very popular in the 16th and 17th centuries, but had fallen out of favour. It was only after the end of the German Democratic Republic that some brewers in Leipzig revived their version of the style and slowly it made a comeback.

When Paul moved to the town of Goslar in 2003 as a qualified brewmaster, he met a retired local brewmaster who had recreated a gose recipe from original sources and home-brewed the beer in small batches. He asked Paul to adopt the formula and keep the old style alive. Paul began to brew gose in a brewpub and it sold well – before long he was ready to build his own brewery in a heritage-protected 18th-century house in the centre of Goslar. In order to finance the enterprise, he founded a cooperative society – a project that won over 170 local shareholders who now pride themselves on owning a brewery. The renovated brewpub opened in 2009 and has become known as "the friendliest restaurant in town".

Paul offers three regular beers – a pilsner, a dark beer, and a light gose. He also runs specialities like märzen, a multi-grain harvest brew. Occasionally, he even pours a bock that has matured in whisky barrels. However, the light gose remains the most popular of the beers. Interestingly, it is not sour like the Leipzig version. "In former times it may have been that the gose went sour especially when exported to faraway places. But here in Goslar it never was", claims Paul. He does put more salt and coriander in his brew to give it a distinctive taste.

THE FACTS...

OWNER Odin Paul
FOUNDED 2009
ADDRESS Marktkirchhof 2, 38640 Goslar
WEBSITE www.brauhaus-goslar.de
PHILOSOPHY Make beer the cult drink that it used to be by offering a broad range of styles and sensory diversity

GOSLAR
HELLE GOSE

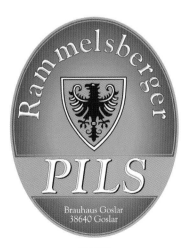

GOSLAR
RAMMELSBERGER PILS

TASTING NOTES

HELLE GOSE 4.8% ABV
Golden-orange with a fine haze and a creamy white head. Helle Gose offers slightly sulphurous spices along with some lactic and some salty notes. The drink is creamy, dry, and sparkling. Its spicy flavours are reminiscent of pine needles and herbs, while the fruity bitterness of orange peel appears to take it on to the finish. The slim body has a full flavour, supporting bitterness.

FOOD PAIRING: A thirst-quencher, it is good with cream cheese, asparagus, seafood and sweet German sausages such as black pudding and goose liverwurst.

RAMMELSBERGER PILS 4.7% ABV
This hazy, orange-golden pils has a creamy white head. It has a decent aroma reminiscent of hay, and a creamy first sip with pleasant hints of butterscotch. Its dry, slim body has an assertive bitterness and long finish.

FOOD PAIRING: It is especially good when paired with spicy dishes and grilled chicken or fish.

DUNKLE GOSE 4.8% ABV
The colour of dark honey with a shiny haze and thick cream-coloured head, Dunkle Gose offers a more fruity nose than the Helle variety. After a dry first sip, an assertive bitterness takes over and leads to a spicy finish with lingering grapefruit bitterness. It has a fluffy mouthfeel.

FOOD PAIRING: The perfect companion to sweet roasted meats such as honey-roasted duck breast.

Burnished copper
Dunkle Gose is unfiltered and has three malts added, which gives it its distinctive hazy, red-brown colour

GOSLAR
DUNKLE GOSE

BEER HAS PLAYED A KEY ROLE IN GERMAN LIFE FOR CENTURIES, AND DRINKERS ARE OFTEN FIERCELY LOYAL TO THEIR LOCAL BREWERY

IN RAIN OR SHINE, SIPPING A CHILLED BAVARIAN BEER IN A BAMBERG
BEER GARDEN IS THE PERFECT WAY TO PASS THE TIME

RIEGELE

With Sebastian Priller at the helm, a new generation has joined the management of Brauhaus Riegele, campaigning for the promotion of beer culture, the education of beer drinkers, and production of beers with character.

THE FACTS...

OWNER Dr Sebastian Priller
FOUNDED 1874
ADDRESS Fröhlichstraße 26, 86150 Augsburg
WEBSITE www.riegele.de
PHILOSOPHY To earn beer the status it deserves

SEBASTIAN PRILLER, head of Brauhaus Riegele, champions a higher appreciation of beer: "In light of the work behind every good beer, a new approach is needed, a new culture which celebrates beer drinking, from the serving temperature through to the appropriate glass", he claims. He is the fifth generation of his family to run the Riegele business and gets excited when he sees people rediscovering this "commonplace" drink in the brewery's own pub – whether as a result of being served an imperial stout at room temperature, or a wheat double bock in a Bordeaux glass. Priller claims that he especially enjoys hearing the pleasures of beer as the topic of conversation among his guests and loves the beer culture in general. But for many years it seemed that beer would not be his calling. After completing his studies in business management, he embarked on a career as an advisor for a renowned consulting agency. For four years he jetted around the world before he realized his destiny and joined his father in running the family business in 2006. At the time, Priller was 31 years old. He graduated as a beer sommelier with ease, and over the next few years became first Vice World Champion Beer Sommelier, then World Champion Beer Sommelier.

Priller values his brewmaster Frank Müller highly, saying: "It is enormously important that both owner and brewmaster strive in accordance with each other for the same goal". As an ambitious creator of beers, Müller has built a reputation for being an expert on yeast. He nurtures and works with more than 20 different kinds in his brewhouse and they are developed to be used in particular beers. For example, he has brewed a Belgian dubbel and an English imperial stout, each with a particular type of appropriate yeast. He has also used English Ale yeast in an unfiltered cellar beer – imbuing it with a unique structure. All in all, Müller brews 13 classic German-style beers and a couple of special editions, such as an IPA, as well as strong beers matured in oak and sherry barrels. All are made using traditional brewing methods and are unpasteurized or heated briefly to retain the benefits of the vitamins and healthy ingredients.

A visit to Augsburg is well worthwhile. The brewery offers a whole programme for beer enthusiasts, including well organized brewery tours, elaborate beer tastings, brewing classes, and beer expert seminars where participants learn all about the sensory evaluation of beer.

A wealth of choice
Riegele is at the forefront of a movement keen to celebrate beer's distinct character and demonstrate its variety

RIEGELE
KELLERBIER

RIEGELE
AUGSBURGER HERREN PILS

RIEGELE
COMMERZIENRAT RIEGELE PRIVAT

Classy glasses
*Dubbel has an attractive
frothy head that deserves
to be displayed in a great-
looking glass, such as this
long-stemmed type*

Lovingly labelled
*Labels are attached with
twine, which adds a touch
of vintage glamour and
means that they can be
removed and collected*

BIER

Sebastian Priller-Riegele

EDITION BY LOUIS PIANA

Stand-out style
*A range of distinctive,
attractive corked bottles are
used for the brewery's special
editions, such as Dubbel*

RIEGELE DUBBEL

TASTING NOTES

KELLERBIER 5% ABV
Light orange with fiery glints, this Kellerbier has
an opaque cloudy shimmer and a fine-pored head.
The ale is fermented with English Ale yeast and its
fragrance is both yeasty and fruity, with scents of
apricot and peach, beneath which there is a fine
roast aroma. The velvety, fruity initial sip is contrasted
by a distinct bitterness. It has a long, crisp finish and
a semi-dry mouthfeel.

FOOD PAIRING: Great with antipasti such as grilled
or pickled vegetables, dried meats, and ham. It is
very versatile with cheese – especially with brie or
camembert – and with grilled or roasted meat.

AUGSBURGER HERREN PILS 4.7% ABV
Straw-yellow, brilliant, with a great white head, this pils
is hop-accentuated. The aroma is dominated by herbal
and floral notes; the first sip is soft but dry, with an
assertive bitterness balanced by hop aromas of grass,
hay, and citrus. A sparkling, long, elegant hoppy finish.

FOOD PAIRING: A perfect aperitif, this goes with light
dishes such as goat's cheese, salads, spicy pâté and
terrines, and grilled fish.

COMMERZIENRAT RIEGELE LAGER, 5.2% ABV
This light golden lager has a fine foam. The nose offers
a biscuity maltiness and a decent fruity acidity, with
floral and citrussy moments. A creamy softness imbues
the palate and builds up to a medium body. Decent
sweetness dances with delicate acidity, mingling with
hoppy notes. It has a smooth finish.

FOOD PAIRING: This sophisticated thirst-quencher
works with cold platters, roast pork, stews, and
creamy cheeses.

DUBBEL 11% ABV
This strong ale is amber orange with a shiny haze and
creamy head. Bottle fermentation with honey seduces
with a fruity and herbal bouquet that also suggests
some alcoholic notes. A creamy sweet first sip changes
into a full body with honey, plums, and almonds bathing
in alcoholic warmth, lifted by herbal and fruity
bitterness. It has a medium bitter, warming finish.

FOOD PAIRING: Works well with strong flavours like
venison, spicy roast meat, and mushroom dishes.
Dubbel is a great-tasting beer and holds its own when
paired with chocolate, strong alpine cheeses like
gruyère, and the occasional cigar.

Schlenkerla SCHLENKERLA

Preserving old brewing traditions can make for exciting beer – Schlenkerla in Bamberg has not only preserved the ancient rauchbier – smoked beer – style for modern craft beer enthusiasts, but also brings out exciting new variations.

SCHLENKERLA BREWPUB IN BAMBERG is a landmark. The brewery dates back to at least the 15th century – their fabulous smoked märzen was first mentioned in documents dating to 1405. The current owner, Matthias Trum, is the sixth generation of his family to run the brewery and is eager to preserve their centuries-old brewing tradition. He still kilns his own malt over a beechwood fire as brewers used to do before modern firing installations were available – all beer used to have a smoky taste because of this.

Today the style only survives in the Bamberg region, where smoked beer is a common drink – a session beer. Outside the region, it is more or less considered a curiosity. The most famous rauchbier comes from Schlenkerla. As Trum claims, the recipe has been unchanged since the 15th century; only the equipment used has been modernized. Abroad, the beer is appreciated as the best example of rauchbier and serves as a reference for craft brewers who seek to experiment with smoked malts. It has also come to epitomize the German super speciality – even more than wheat beer. Being the only German lager made entirely of smoked malts, Schlenkerla's Märzen is rightly valued as an all-time classic.

However, Trum has not stopped with the success he achieved with Märzen – in 2009, he released a sensational doppelbock. Eiche, which means oak, is brewed with malt kilned over burning oakwood. The oak smoke lends the beer a much softer and more complex character than spicy beechwood does. Kilning with oak in the past was a rare luxury, since it served very well as timber. Trum, who says that he developed the recipe from old sources, has used it to create a delicious modern beer.

THE FACTS...

OWNER Heller-Bräu Trum GmbH

FOUNDED Circa 1405

ADDRESS Dominikanerstraße 6, 96049 Bamberg

WEBSITE www.schlenkerla.de

PHILOSOPHY Tradition means not preserving the ashes, but passing on the flame

Head-start
Märzen's very thick, creamy head makes a lip-smacking start to this complex, smoky-bitter beer

SCHLENKERLA MÄRZEN

TASTING NOTES

MÄRZEN 5.2% ABV
The brilliant chestnut colour of Märzen combines with a dense, thick, cream-coloured head. Smoke enters the nose and leather, ashes, and burnt wood mix with earthy notes like peat. The flavour of this smoked Märzen is like smoked ham with a base of solid roasted malt flavours, a hint of chocolate, and toffee – balanced by a brave bitterness. It has a velvety mouthfeel, medium body, and a dry and smoky-bitter finish.

FOOD PAIRING: This speciality goes well with roasted meats such as pork and beef. It is also good with tasty creamy dishes such as potato cream soup with bacon.

EICHE SMOKED DOPPELBOCK, 8% ABV
Amber brown with a red hue, the Eiche has a brillant white head. This smoked doppelbock has a pleasant smoky aroma of burnt wood with hints of vanilla and toasted notes. It has smooth flavours featuring toffee, honey, and hints of earthy notes, followed by a harmonious finish.

FOOD PAIRING: As for the Märzen, but most of all a great degustation beer. Great with chocolate and tasty cheeses.

URBOCK 6.5% ABV
Dark brown with red reflections, this dark smoked bock has a cream-coloured head and a smoky nose. Spicy smoke flavours of ham, ashes, and burnt wood are balanced by sweeter malt aromas of dried fruit, chocolate, and toffee. The bitterness remains in the background to support this full-bodied drink. It has a velvety mouthfeel and a smoky roasted finish.

FOOD PAIRING: Pair the Urbock with tasty meat: duck, roast goose, or spicy beef.

SCHLENKERLA
EICHE

SCHLENKERLA
URBOCK

SCHNEIDER WEISSE

Schneider Weisse has always been good at sustainable innovations. With collaboration brews, barrel-ageing, and dry-hopping, this traditional wheat beer specialist is one of the pioneers of the new German craft beer scene.

THE FACTS...

OWNER Weisses Bräuhaus G. Schneider & Sohn GmbH

FOUNDED 1872

ADDRESS Emil-Ott Straße 1-5 93309 Kelheim

WEBSITE www.schneider-weisse.de

PHILOSOPHY For more than 140 years we have devoted our entire knowledge, our skills, and our lifeblood to true enjoyment

IN A SENSE, SCHNEIDER WEISSE saved the wheat beer style for the 20th century. For about 200 years, the Bavarian sovereigns had monopolized the right to brew wheat. The dukedom ran several white brewhouses – Weiße Brauhäuser – and secured considerable earnings obliging landlords across the country to pour the royal brew. When wheat beer went out of fashion in the 18th century, the King leased the white brewhouses and sold the right to brew the style. Georg Schneider brewed for the principality. He believed in the style and was the first private person to acquire a licence, founding Schneider Weisse in 1872.

Today the brewery, run by the sixth-generation Schneider, Georg Schneider VI, is established as a renowned wheat beer specialist. They still brew their Original, an amber Bavarian wheat, according to their founder's formulation. Open fermentation vessels from which the brewers skim off the *kräusen*, the harsh, bitter-tasting foam, and a costly bottle fermentation to enhance the beers' texture, are the traditional features of their craft. Their Aventinus, created in 1907 as the first wheat doppelbock of Bavaria, has long since risen to celebrity status, consistently winning medals at international competitions.

However, Schneider Weisse is just as much a 21st-century brewery as a traditional one. In 2007 they were the first in Germany to brew a collaboration beer. Together with Garrett Oliver from Brooklyn Brewery in the US, Schneider brewmaster Hans-Peter Drexler created an unusual dry-hopped wheat doppelbock that has entered the year-round portfolio as Tap 5 – Meine Hopfenweisse. Schneider also experiments with barrel-ageing and releases limited editions regularly.

TASTING NOTES

TAP 7 – UNSER ORIGINAL WHEAT BEER, 5.4% ABV
The Original is an amber-coloured Bavarian wheat with a great head and aromas of ripe bananas, cloves, and nuts. After a sparkling first sip it is full-bodied with pleasant malt flavours balanced by spices, fruits, a hint of acidity, and a mild finish.

FOOD PAIRING: Great with roast meat, fried fish, camembert cheese, or fruity ice cream.

TAP 5 – MEINE HOPFENWEISSE DOPPELBOCK, 8.2% ABV
The yellow-orange wheat doppelbock offers intense floral and fruity aromas reminiscent of exotic fruits. The powerful bitterness is balanced by the yeast's fruitiness and the sweetness of the malt body. Spicy, hop-aromatic finish.

FOOD PAIRING: Pair with smoked fish, curries, chilli dishes, salsas, and chutneys.

TAP 6 – UNSER AVENTINUS DOPPELBOCK, 8.2% ABV
Ruby-dark, the dark wheat doppelbock is streaked with top-fermenting yeast, with a compact head, and offers fruity, tart aromas with hints of chocolate. A slightly sour palate combines with a fluffy mouthfeel, balanced by flavours of banana, pear, toffee, and dark chocolate, sliding into a dry, spicy clove finish.

FOOD PAIRING: Drink as a digestif. Try with intense flavours such as roast venison, blue cheese, and chocolate.

SCHNEIDER WEISSE
TAP 7 – UNSER ORIGINAL

SCHNEIDER WEISSE
TAP 5 – MEINE HOPFENWEISSE

SCHNEIDER WEISSE
TAP 6 – UNSER AVENTINUS

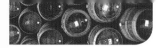

SCHÖNRAM

Run by the eighth generation of the same family, the long-established Bavarian brewery Schönram is at the forefront of the new German craft beer wave due to their quality-driven approach and an international brewmaster.

THE FACTS...

OWNER Alfred Oberlindober
FOUNDED 1780
ADDRESS Salzburger Straße 17, 83367 Petting/Schönram
WEBSITE www.brauerei-schoenram.de
PHILOSOPHY Making good things even better

THE PHILOSOPHY OF SCHÖNRAM has been explained by the current owner Alfred Oberlindober as the desire to "pursue one primary goal: brewing good beer – not for everybody but for those who appreciate it". As he emphasizes, volume production is the least of his concerns: "Quality has always been our highest priority. Quality not quantity".

However, Oberlindober's approach does not mean that the brewery does not plan to expand its production capacities. In fact, since Oberlindober took over the helm in 1994 at the age of 27, he has tripled the annual production of the family brewery from 17,000 to 55,000hl (10,400 to 33,600 barrels). He has been the chief instigator in kick-starting a hugely successful era for the Chiemgau-based company.

But the increase in output may also be due to another asset at Schönram. Shortly after taking over, Oberlindober appointed the US brewer Eric Toft as head of brewing. For this brewing artist, nothing is more abhorrent than beer with a commonplace taste, which goes some way to explaining why he played a key role in the US craft beer movement in the 1980s. Tired of the watery, mass-market beer that was widely available at the time, Toft and other beer enthusiasts like him, from all fields, set about brewing high-quality beers with character.

Toft was a geophysics student in Golden, Colorado, and began as a hobby brewer. He got the brewing bug and left for Europe to learn the art of brewing from scratch. He picked up valuable knowledge in Switzerland, Belgium, and Germany and now teaches German brewers. At Schönram, Toft has built up a reputation as a hop expert. While the majority of his German colleagues employ just one bittering hop plus a constant selection of one or two aroma varieties for their entire product range, he composes a unique hop profile for each of his beers. "Hops give the beer character", says Toft. No wonder his India Pale Ale was one of the first brewed in Germany. He also released the first single hop Bock. Meanwhile, he is dreaming of more. As a firm believer in the influence that location has on the hops and barley that he uses in his beers, his ambition is simple: "I want to show that terroir is important".

Top of the class
The brewery claims that Schonramer Hell is one of the most popular beers in the south-east part of Bavaria

Gold star
The barley used – chosen with care by Toft – gives the beer its characteristic golden colour

SCHÖNRAM HELL   **SCHÖNRAM** PILS

TASTING NOTES

HELL 5% ABV
Clear, light-gold with a white creamy head, Hell smells like herbs and honey with a hint of citrus. The texture is sparkling and the carbonation simply melts in the mouth. Hell has a slim to medium body, with grainy malts, grassy hop aromas, and a harmonious finish.

FOOD PAIRING: Makes a fine companion to cold platters with hearty German sausages, ham, and mild cheeses. It is also good with stews and fruity cream cakes.

PILS 5% ABV
Light-golden and brilliant with a great white head, Pils has a complex hop bouquet reminiscent of geranium, herbs, and citrus. It is crisp and dry with a trim body and an assertive bitterness. Floral and piney hop aromas round out the edges and add to the complexity. It has a long, bitter aromatic finish.

FOOD PAIRING: A great aperitif, it is good with light aromatic dishes such as wild herb salads with goat's cheese, or sautéed fish with herbs and buttered potatoes.

BAVARIAS BEST 10% ABV

Deep dark black-brown with ruby shades and an ochre-coloured creamy head, this imperial stout smells like dark chocolate with a hint of vanilla and cherries. After a spicy first sip there are complex aromas of dark malts, and a smooth texture, which are lifted by dark berry notes. Mint and lovage escort the drink to the finish.

FOOD PAIRING: Pair with rich beef dishes, creamy sponge cakes, such as Black Forest gateau, or matured cheeses like comté or cheddar.

ALTBAYRISCH DUNKEL 5% ABV

Deep brown with red tints and a cream-coloured head, this dark lager offers fragrant aromas of orange, herbs, and bread crust. The medium body seduces with toffee and chocolate, and brings cooling piney hop aromatics into play. Altbayrisch Dunkel has a bitter-aromatic finish.

FOOD PAIRING: This beer works well with smoky barbecued foods, fruity flavourful cheeses like gouda or cheddar, or sweet desserts such as pancakes with cream.

SAPHIR BOCK 8% ABV

This beer is golden-yellow with a fine white head. The scent is fruity-sour and evokes plums, melons, and lime. The initial sip is soft with an especially delicate effervescence. Flowery notes, reminiscent of geraniums, add to the strong bitter taste, which in the long finish displays a herby-peppery quality. It is dry with alcohol warming.

FOOD PAIRING: Excellent served in an elegant Bordeaux glass, this beer also works well with sharp alpine cheeses or spicy meats.

Dark arts
Worldwide, more and more brewers are wanting to show their mettle by brewing glorious imperial stouts such as the complex Bavarias Best

SCHÖNRAM BAVARIAS BEST

SCHÖNRAM
ALTBAYRISCH DUNKEL

SCHÖNRAM
SAPHIR BOCK

STÖRTEBEKER

THE FACTS...

OWNER Jürgen Nordmann

FOUNDED 1991

ADDRESS Greifswalder Chaussee 84–85, 18439 Stralsund

WEBSITE www.stoertebeker.com

PHILOSOPHY We don't brew mass market products but place value on distinguishing our beers by their taste

The former state-owned brewery, Störtebeker, was run-down when it was taken over by West German entrepreneurs, Nordmann, in 1991. They modernized the brewhouse and won over the locals with a strong emphasis on taste.

THE SITE OF STÖRTEBEKER BREWERY dates back to 1827. Over the course of the 19th century, the original brewery on the site, Stralsunder Brauerei, rose to become the main supplier to the Baltic seaside resorts. After World War II, East Germany nationalized the company; their beers acquired quite a reputation during the 1970s but the equipment slowly fell into disrepair. After reunification, the large West German wholesaler Nordmann bought the site and established its company headquarters there. They modernized the brewhouse and began by releasing three beers, two styles of the regional brand Stralsunder, and the premium Schwarz-Bier. Inspired by the gloomy legend of Germany's medieval buccaneer, Klaus Störtebeker, who fought the merchants of the Hanseatic League in the North and Baltic Sea in around 1400, the Stralsunder Brauerei called their black lager Störtebeker Schwarz-Bier. It was released in 1991 and soon became the best-seller of Stralsund Brewery. Subsequently, other beer styles with a distinct taste were released under the label Störtebeker, which eventually became the name of the company.

In 2012, the company re-branded itself as Störtebeker Braumanufaktur and created a large space for events at its brewery site with an emphasis on professionally hosted tastings and beer menus. Co-founder Jürgen Nordmann enjoys his position of being a brewery owner. He says, "It's very rewarding to do something that also bestows a cultural identity on the people in this region". Störtebeker aims to continue to challenge its customers. In 2012, it released Atlantik-Ale, a bone-dry, hop-aromatic, pale ale with a mighty taste, unlike anything ever brewed in this part of the Baltic shoreline.

TASTING NOTES

SCHWARZ-BIER BLACK LAGER, 5% ABV
Schwarz-Bier is coffee-brown and slightly hazy, with a cream-coloured head. It offers toffee and roasted aromas with hints of cocoa. The palate receives a smooth first taste building up to a medium body of coffee, chocolate, and roasted flavours, supported by a modest bitterness. It has a velvety finish with roasted notes.

FOOD PAIRING: Good with strong flavours such as grilled steak, smoked fish and meat, or nutty cheeses like emmental, as well as bittersweet chocolate desserts.

ATLANTIK-ALE PALE ALE, 5.1% ABV
Sunny-golden, opaque, and with a great head, Atlantik-Ale offers a decent bouquet of exotic and citrussy aromas with some flowery notes. A dry first sip leads over to a slim body dominated by a strong fruity bitterness. The mouthfeel offers a sparkling impression and some astringency. It has a long, bitter finish.

FOOD PAIRING: Try with grilled mackerel or deep-fried sardines, or spicy dishes like falafel or grilled chicken.

KELLER-BIER 1402 4.8% ABV
Light yellow with a haze and a firm white head, Keller-Bier offers floral and grassy aromas. It is fruity and hop-aromatic, and at the same time slightly sweet with an acid interplay of the yeast aroma. It has a medium body, which is hop-accented yet mild with an aromatic finish.

FOOD PAIRING: An excellent accompaniment to boiled beef, chicken, aparagus, vinegar-marinated meat, or seafood.

STÖRTEBEKER SCHWARZ-BIER   **STÖRTEBEKER** ATLANTIK-ALE   **STÖRTEBEKER** KELLER-BIER 1402

WEIHENSTEPHAN

Weihenstephan
THE WORLD'S OLDEST BREWERY

Weihenstephan is an institution in the world of beer. With its close links to the famous academy, the world's oldest existing brewery stands as much for tradition as for the highest technical expertise.

THE FACTS...

OWNER Freistaat Bayern
(State of Bavaria)

FOUNDED 1040

ADDRESS Alte Akademie 2,
85354 Freising

WEBSITE www.weihenstephaner.de

PHILOSOPHY To combine tradition
with the latest scientific and
technical expertise

THE FIRST REFERENCE to Weihenstephan is found in documents dating from 1040, attesting that the monastery on Weihenstephan mountain had the right to brew beer. Although the authenticity of the certificate is contested, what is known is that the monastery was founded in 725 and a hop garden, whose owner paid tithes to the monks, was cultivated nearby. All of this leads to the assumption that brewing at Weihenstephan dates back even earlier than the 11th century, making it the oldest functioning brewery in the world.

The monastery was closed in 1803 and its premises and rights were transferred to the state. By 1852, an agricultural school, which also held brewing classes, was established on the complex. Then in 1919 the school became an academy, and in 1930 the academy became part of the Technical University of Munich. It was only in 1921 that Weihenstephan was given the title Bayerische Staatsbrauerei (Bavarian State Brewery).

Weihenstephan Academy has educated generations of brewers and attracts students from all over the world who undertake practical studies there. In terms of research and development, the academy and the brewery cooperate closely, ensuring scientific knowledge is kept current in the brewhouse. Their elaborate system of quality control is not accidental – Premium Bavaricum, as they call it, is a multi-stage monitoring system operated by the brewers and university scientists with the latest technology at their disposal. Weihenstephan wheat beers and lagers are great examples of the style and are appreciated in more than 40 countries. A commitment to tradition means that most of the beers are German classics. One exception to this rule is a collaboration brew released in 2010 with the Boston Beer Company. Infinium is a strong ale, double-fermented with wine yeast – it makes for a complex drink with a pleasant texture.

TASTING NOTES

ORIGINAL PALE ALE, 5.1% ABV
This light-golden, brilliant helles has a nose that offers a decent sweet malt aroma. The sweet first sip is joined by elegant hop aromas with a moderate bitterness. It has fine carbonation and the finish is mild with a hint of acidity.
FOOD PAIRING: Try with sandwiches, stews, or sponge cake.

VITUS WEIZENBOCK, 7.7% ABV
This light-golden, cloudy wheat bock is bottle-fermented. Fruity aromas with hints of vanilla and traces of smoke from the yeast; the palate has a fluffy carbonation. The full body offers rich, fruity, spicy flavours before a mild finish.
FOOD PAIRING: Goes well with smoked or roasted meat, blue cheeses, and sweet and fruity desserts.

HEFE WEISSBIER WHEAT BEER, 5.4% ABV
Light-golden in colour and opaque with a huge white head, this wheat beer offers a sweet and pleasant aroma of bananas, cloves, and yeast. It has a sweet and fruity first sip, a rich body, fluffy mouthfeel, and a mild and dry finish.
FOOD PAIRING: Try with grilled chicken, seafood, ice cream, asparagus dishes, and, if you're in the region, weißwurst – a Bavarian white sausage made of veal.

WEIHENSTEPHAN ORIGINAL   **WEIHENSTEPHAN** VITUS   **WEIHENSTEPHAN** HEFE WEISSBIER

ALDERSBACH

www.aldersbacher.de

BEAUTIFULLY SITUATED in the south-eastern corner of Lower Bavaria, the baroque monastery complex of Aldersbach was bought in 1811 by Baron von Aretin. The Aretins have managed the premises since then, running a guesthouse, a renowned midsize brewery and a popular Bräustüberl – pub – where guests may bring their own food. Sticking to monastic brewing traditions with high-quality standards, the beer range covers the Bavarian classics from wheat beer to dark lager with the Urhell, a helles, being the most popular brew.

ALPIRSBACHER

www.alpirsbacher.de

SINCE 1877, THE GLAUNERS have cultivated the art of brewing in Alpirsbach, a small town in the Black Forest. It was the soft water from their own well that allowed them to brew good pils. Traditionalists, they always use whole hop cones. All of this contributes to the fine flavours of their beers and makes their pils an outstanding example of the style. Alpirsbacher offer a wide range of lagers and wheats, and recently released a powerful version of the Belgian abbey-style.

ANDECHS

www.andechs.de

BREWING AT ANDECHS Abbey Brewery dates back to 1455 and serves as its biggest source of income. The annual output from the modernized brewhouse – according to the monks – amounts to 100,000hl (84,000 barrels) and keeps growing; many attribute this to the strength and high quality of their distinctive beers. The brewery's most famous beer is the Andechser Doppelbock Dunkel: each year the black full-bodied beauty attracts one and a half million beer pilgrims to flock to Andechs monastery.

APOSTELBRÄU

www.apostelbraeu.de

INSPIRED BY A LOCAL female spelt grower, Rudolf Hirz of the Apostelbräu Brewery first brewed spelt beer (Dinkelbier) in 1989. This was pioneering in Germany at the time, taking place not long after the European court ruled that the *Reinheitsgebot* beer purity law (see p.52) was no longer legal. Since Hirz took over the family business in 2005 he has experimented with many styles and was among the first brewers in Germany to brew English-style pale ale. Most of his specialities are exported to Italy and the US, but it is only in his "Birreria" in Bavaria that you can taste them all – a worthwhile incentive to make the trip.

ARCOBRÄU

www.arcobraeu.de

THE CASTLE BREWERY OF MOOS has been in existence since 1567. Today, Holger Fichtel manages the brewery in Lower Bavarian Moos for the descendants of the noble family of Arco-Zinneberg. The brewery propagates its own yeast and prides itself on its pure cultivation – the brewers apply a fresh yeast to each brew of their unfiltered Zwickl; other production plants use the same yeast up to 15 times. According to Fichtel, this gives a distinct freshness to each brew.

ASGAARD BRAUEREI SCHLESWIG

www.asgaard.de

THE PAGAN GODS OF THE beer-drinking Vikings were the Æsirs, themselves beer lovers who, according to Nordic mythology, lived in a place called Asgaard. To Ronald T Carius, nothing was more obvious than to name his "heavenly beer" after the home of the Nordic gods when he opened his brewery and pub in 1994 in the town of Schleswig, an ancient area of Viking settlement. His malty The Divine amber lager is 4.8% ABV, with a fruity maltiness and a very strong, clear-cut bitterness.

AU-HALLERTAU

www.auer-bier.de

SINCE 1846, THE BARONS Beck von Peccoz have resided and brewed in the moated castle of Au-Hallertau, in the midst of Germany's largest area of hop cultivation. They offer the classical portfolio of helles and dunkles lagers. Yet, when asked about his favourite brew, Michael Beck von Peccoz points to their speciality Hallertauer Pale Ale, saying, "It is a family tradition to keep an eye on trends". No surprise then that in their ice cellar strong beers mature in oak barrels.

AUGUSTINER

www.augustiner.de

MUNICH'S OLDEST BREWERY, established in 1328, is Augustiner Bräu. Originally part of the Augustinian monastery connected with the city's cathedral, today it operates as a limited commercial partnership with 51 per cent belonging to a charitable foundation established by the last descendant of the former private owner, the Wagner family. Using the most up-to-date machinery, the water used in the brewery comes from the company's own well and the malt from their own maltings. The brewery survives and thrives despite not using marketing or advertisements. The beers have to speak for themselves, and they do it convincingly enough. Their star is the Lagerbier Hell, a malt-accentuated pale lager with an underlying hop bitterness in a supporting role. The beer is sold at the brewery's own tavern, the Bräustüberl.

AYINGER

www.ayinger.de

MUNICH SOCIETY is highly susceptible to a sophisticated beer culture. Ayinger Brewery, a 30-minute drive south-east of the city, aspires to meet these demands. Known for its fine Bavarian cuisine, the brewery's restaurant has become an attraction to urban *bon vivants* – and so have its beers. The over-130-year-old brewery has revised and updated some of its traditional recipes – the new Lager Hell is milder than previously, and if you are up to something stronger, try the world famous "Celebrator", a dark doppelbock, most of which is exported.

BARRE

www.barre.de

ACCORDING TO THE OWNER, Barre was the first brewery to produce pils in northern Germany. Founded in 1842, the largest privately owned brewery in East Westphalia is run by a sixth-generation member of the Barre family, Christoph Barre. He takes great pride in keeping the company's independence, in a world where so many other family-run breweries have gone under. Beers include Barre Pilsener and Barre Festbier. The Barre Brewery is also a visitor attraction, with more than 7,000 people visiting annually. They come to savour regional food in the restaurant and discover historic craft brewing in the ancient cellars that now house a museum.

BAUHÖFER

www.ulmer-bier.de

THE ORTENAU REGION in the Upper Rhine Valley, neighbouring the Alsace region in France, is blessed with many tasty pleasures, including food and wine. Ordinary beer with standard flavours would not meet the high expectations of the region. Gustav Bauhöfer, brewmaster and fourth-generation owner of the Bauhöfer family brewery, established in 1852, works hard to ensure that his brewery's beers meet the high standards. One of the region's renowned speciality beers is Bauhöfer's Ulmer Maibock, which has been made since 1893 and is named after its hometown Renchen-Ulm. The renowned golden bock combines light-heartedness with depth, and character with drinkability. The many medals and awards Bauhöfer wins every year prove that this brewery has the knack for brewing great beers.

BAYERISCHER BAHNHOF

www.bayerischer-bahnhof.de

THE BUILDINGS OF THE WORLD'S oldest remaining railway terminus (built in 1842) in Leipzig have been home to the large pub brewery Bayerischer Bahnhof since 2000. It has made a name for itself among beer aficionados, above all as a traditional pub serving its speciality, the Original Leipziger Gose beer. In addition to this sour beer style, master brewer Matthias Richter also brews Berliner Weiße, using the original recipe for export to the USA, as well as experimenting with pine needles and herbs for special brews served at festivals. Other beers available on tap include the Schaffner (conductor), a pilsner, the Kuppler (operator), a top-fermented wheat beer, and the Heizer (stoker), a light and sweet, velvety dark beer.

BERG BRAUEREI

www.bergbier.de

FAMILY-OWNED SINCE 1757, the Berg Brewery is led by Uli Zimmermann Jr and his wife, Beate. With the philosophy, "Small but powerful! Small is beautiful!" they use high-quality ingredients from the region and traditional brewing methods like a cold and pressureless fermentation and maturation process. Given the cult status their Ulrichsbier, a crisp brown lager, enjoys, they feel encouraged not to follow trends but to brew beers with character. Due to its individuality and unique nature, Berg Brauerei has become one of the most renowned in Upper Swabia.

BERGQUELL BRAUEREI LÖBAU

www.bergquell-loebau.de

THE LUSATIAN BREWERY Bergquell Brauerei Löbau is known throughout Germany for its top-fermented porters: lightly sweetened with malt sugar, they have a distinctly mellow taste. Different flavours including Lausitzer Porter, Cherry Porter, and Strawberry Porter have increased the fame of the brewery beyond the borders of its Saxony home, and increased sales significantly. Founded in 1846, Bergquell briefly stopped production after the demise of the German Democratic Republic (GDR). Then, in 1996, on its 150th anniversary, owner Steffen Dittmar opened a new building on a green field site. He is especially proud of the resource-saving brewhouse technology.

BISCHOFF

www.bischoff-bier.de

FOUNDED IN 1866, the Bischoff Brewery in the Palatinate community of Winnweiler is run by the fifth-generation member of the family, Sven Bischoff. To this day, they use the rock cellar constructed by the brewery's founder for storage. Bischoff offers a wide product range, from blond lager beers and wheat beers to specialities such as the Steinbrecher Original, an amber-coloured lager with a malt accent. The most popular beer remains Pils. However, the brewers also experiment with toasted wood barrels and wood chips that are added to the blond Bockbier when maturing.

BOLTEN

www.bolten-brauerei.de

THERE HAS BEEN A BREWERY on the site in Korschenbroich in the Lower Rhine area since 1266. Based on this, Bolten claims to be the oldest Altbier brewery in Germany. The Bolten family has brewed at Kraushof since 1753, finally selling the business in 2005. Michael Hollmann, a former boss of a large brewery group, bought it and turned it into an asset for the region. Bolten's delicious Ur-Alt is an unfiltered ale reminiscent of the brewery's roots.

BOLTEN UR-ALT

BÜRGERBRÄU BAD REICHENHALL

www.buergerbraeu.com

BAD REICHENHALL IS a city of saltworks, which has always made for a thirsty population. The Bürgerbräu was founded in 1633 and also comprises six alpine brewery pubs – including the Alte Post in the pilgrimage site of Altötting and the Berghof Schroffen in Bad Reichenhall. The portfolio includes blond and dark lagers, wheat, and Bockbier. The mild, gold-yellow lager sold under the name Alpenstoff has a trendy label and is specially designed to appeal to young people.

BÜRGERLICHES BRAUHAUS SAALFELD

www.brauhaus-saalfeld.de

MASTER BREWER AT SAALFELD, Ralf Hohmann, is rightly proud of his amber-coloured Ur-Saalfelder and blond Saalfelder Bock. Both beers have won European Beer Stars on several occasions. The family brewery dates back to 1892, becoming a joint stock brewery in 1925. From 1948–1991, it was a nationally owned company and after the end of the GDR private investors pumped seven million euros into it. The Bürgerliches Brauhaus primarily offers bottom-fermented beers, including three different pilsners.

CREW ALE WERKSTATT

www.crewale.de

MARIO HANEL and Timm Schnigula, two young business consultants, travelled the world, discovered pale ale, and decided: "That's what we want for Germany". They quit their jobs, researched brewing methods and ingredients, developed a recipe, and found a brewery to produce their own pale ale. It was released in 2011 and is sold as neither a pilsner, a lager, nor a wheat beer. Using three times the hops of a pilsner and a variety of aromatic varieties that are not usually found in Germany, the pale ale is only one of several beers made. The India Pale Ale (IPA) is another part of their portfolio. While the company chose Munich as their hometown, their contract brewer, Schlossbrauerei Hohentann, is a one-hour drive north-east of the capital of beer.

CREW ALE WERKSTATT IPA

DISTELHÄUSER FRÜHLINGSBOCK

DACHSBRÄU WEILHEIM

www.dachsbier.de

WHEN GEORG DACHS, a master brewer from Munich, came to Weilheim in 1879 he bought an agricultural property complete with a brewery, now known as the Dachsbräu. To this day his descendants, Ulrich Klose, daughter Ulrike, and son Günter, brew wheat beer according to a traditional recipe and method – including using laborious bottle fermentation methods. The family also still employs cool ship – a large cooling vessel and a shallow tray for cooling the wort after boiling. Besides wheat beer, the Dachsbräu offers typical Bavarian lager beers including blond, dark, bock, and festbier.

DINKELACKER-SCHWABENBRÄU

www.privatbrauerei-stuttgart.de

THE BREWERIES DINKELACKER and Schwabenbräu merged in 1994. From 2004 the company briefly belonged to the InBev group until Wolfgang Dinkelacker, the founder's great-grandson, bought it back in 2007. With 600 employees and the brands Dinkelacker, Schwabenbräu, Sanwald, Cluss, Haigerlocher, Sigel Kloster, and Wulle, it is one of Baden-Württemberg's largest private breweries. Highlights include the CD Pils, Stuttgart's first pilsner, bearing the initials of the founder, Carl Dinkelacker, and the Wulle-Bier, relaunched in 2008 and now a cult brand.

DISTELHÄUSER

www.distelhaeuser.de

THE BAUER FAMILY HAS RUN the Distelhäuser brewery in Distelhausen on the banks of the Tauber since 1876. They pride themselves on offering more than 18 different beer styles including seasonals such as Winterbock and Frühlingsbock. Among their year-round specialities are award-winning beers like their spelt ale and Kristall-Weizen (filtered wheat). In 2011 Distelhäuser began operating a microbrewhouse where they experiment with hops, yeasts, and malts to create even tastier characterful beers. While the regular portfolio is distributed widely throughout the region surrounding Tauberbischofsheim, the microbrews are only available to buy on-site.

DITHMARSCHER

www.dithmarscher.de

THE DITHMARSCHER PILSNER is a prime example of north German pils beer. It is crisply bitter with a light body. Straightforward bittering hops set the keynote, dispensing with any aromatic embellishment. Mild and spicy, it is full of natural freshness that comes from the soft local water and has a noble hop aroma and pleasant tart, fresh carbonation. Another offering, Dithmarscher Dark, is made using a 500-year-old recipe and contains dark malt for a full-bodied flavour. Founded in 1884 by Christian Hintz, Dithmarscher brewery has remained in family ownership to this day. While other breweries converted to crown caps, Dithmarscher never stopped filling swing-top bottles, and has found itself, completely unintentionally, at the beginning of a new fashion for the style.

DÖBLER

www.brauhaus-doebler.de

BRAUHAUS DÖBLER IN Bad Windsheim also houses a typical Franconian brewery pub, where guests can enjoy cold snacks of regional sausage or cheese. The family brewery produces four beers: pils, kellerbier, a wheat beer, and a seasonally changing beer. The product range, also available in bottles, includes the now rare Bavarian Märzen, an amber-coloured lager beer with a malt accent. Founded in 1867, Döbler is the last of 30 private breweries once active in the small Middle Franconian town.

DREI KRONEN

www.drei-kronen.de

AT THE HOTEL AND BREWPUB Drei Kronen (Three Crowns) in Memmelsdorf, a village in the Upper Franconian county of Bamberg, brewing is a matter for the boss. And since 2008 there have been two of them: Hans Ludwig-Straub and his eldest daughter, brewmaster Isabella. Together the two of them continue the 550-year-old tradition of brewing on the site with a range of unique Franconian beer styles and many tasty seasonals, rightly calling their business a "gourmet brewery". Beers include Balthasar, Bockla, bottle-tapped KellerPils, and Hefeweisen. Yet it is their prize-winning perennial dark, smoked malt lager Stöffla that remains the favourite for many of their customers. It can either be enjoyed on-site or taken home in bottles.

EINBECKER BRAUHAUS

www.einbeckerbrauhaus.de

WITHOUT EINBECK there would be no bock. In the 16th and 17th centuries, the beer from the hanse town of Einbeck was a European export hit. In Munich, the strong beer was so popular that the royal brewpub hired a brewmaster from Einbeck. The Bavarians spoofed Einbeck to "Oanpock" from which the name "bock" is derived. At one time there were over 700 brewhouses in Einbock; today this is the only one left that is privately owned. Acknowledging their history, they offer a variety of lagers with an emphasis on great bock beers.

ERDINGER

www.erdinger.de

THE BEGINNINGS of the site of Erdinger Brewery date back to 1886. After several changes of ownership, the manager of the brewery, Franz Brombach, bought it in 1935, later named it Erdinger Weißbräu and made his wheat beer one of the first to become popular outside Bavaria. His son and today's owner Werner Brombach have continued the success story. Currently exporting to 70 countries, Erdinger ranks as the world's largest wheat-beer-only brewery.

ERL

www.erl-braeu.de

IN LOWER BAVARIAN Gieselhörig, traditional brewing techniques are still employed. Fermented in open vats, unwanted harsh tannins and trub form a surface foam that can be removed manually. The beer is also conditioned in horizontal storage tanks whose greater area exerts less pressure, enabling the remaining yeast cells to continue fermenting under reduced stress. This all makes Erl beers especially harmonious. Founded in 1871, the brewery has been run by the fifth generation of the Erl family, Ludwig Erl, since 1998.

ETTAL

www.klosterbrauerei-ettal.de

THE BREWERY AND FARM at Ettal are the oldest of the Benedictine abbey's businesses and were founded in 1330. According to records, commercial brewing has been practised on the site since 1609, and the brewery was an important source of revenue for maintaining the monastery. The portfolio today includes Bavarian bottom-fermented classics such as helles, dunkles, and bock as well as a fruity wheat beer. Ettal is one of five monastery breweries in Bavaria still run by monks or nuns.

FÄSSLA

www.faessla.de

THE BREWERY PUB FÄSSLA IN Bamberg was founded in the 17th century following the Thirty Years War. The large gateway through which horse-drawn carriages once transported barrels now serves as a bar: pedestrians can order one of six lager beers at the window. Since 1986 the brewery, pub, and hotel have been run by the Kalb family. Two highlights are their Zwergla, a mahogany-coloured, malty, tart-tasting lager beer with 6% ABV, and their bottom-fermented Gold-Pils with 5.5% ABV; it has strong, thick foam and a flowery aroma.

FELSENBRÄU

www.sonnenstoff.com

THE MIDDLE FRANCONIAN Felsenbräu operates completely without fossil fuels, employing a wood-burning power plant and solar panels. Certified by the Technical University Munich-Weihenstephan in 2007, Felsenbräu's beers are the first to bear the official title "Solarbeer". Founded in 1927 and run in the third generation by the Gloßner family, the brewery still makes natural ice in winter to cool the rock cellar, where lager beers mature for a minimum of five weeks. The most popular of the 12 varieties produced today is the blond Felsentrunk.

FIEGE

www.moritz-fiege.de

FIEGE, FOUNDED IN 1876, originally brewed mainly for export outside Germany. This all changed in 1926 when the brewery first introduced pilsner to the Ruhr area. It was an innovation and a challenge to offer the lighter, hoppier lager to the region – the stronger, more full-bodied export style is what is traditionally considered to be symbolic of this area, and the drink of its coal miners and steel workers. Nevertheless, Fiege succeeded and built up a reputation for pils brewing. Today it offers a variety of styles from alt to lager, to wheat.

FLENSBURGER

www.flens.co.uk

FLENSBURGER BECAME a cult brand in the 1980s. Its rise was spurred by a German cartoon about an unemployed biker with a northern German accent named Werner, who drinks a lot of beer. Due to this boom, the private brewery, founded in 1888, began to distribute their pilsner nationally. What Werner fans thus discovered was an odd-looking brand with a surprisingly distinctive, typical north German character: "Flens", as it is lovingly called, is a bone-dry, straightforward, extra bitter pils.

FLÖTZINGER BRÄU

www.floetzinger.com

ROSENHEIM'S ONLY REMAINING privately run brewery, Flötzinger, dates back to 1543. Following numerous changes in ownership it was bought in 1864 by a forefather of the Steegmüller family, the third generation of which now runs the brewery. It offers 13 year-round and five seasonal beers, and also brews a wheat beer using a recipe from the Bierbichler Weißbierbrauerei, which it bought following its closure. Along with the Bierbichler wheat beer, the Flötzinger Hell is a cult beer in Rosenheim.

FORSTHAUS TEMPLIN

www.braumanufaktur.de

THE BREWMASTERS at Forsthaus Templin, Thomas Köhler and Jörg Kirchhoff, learned their craft at the nationally-owned VEB-Getränkekombinat Potsdam, then studied at the University of Technology in Berlin. They bought the brewery site on Lake Templin in 2002, remodelled the tavern, installed a brewhouse, and reopened it in December 2003. Their beers, mostly revivals of ancient regional styles, are all organic and unfiltered. Try their bottom-fermented Potsdamer Stange to which, at second fermentation, a Krausen is added to revive the yeast. The result is a fizzy, refreshing beer.

FRIEDENFELSER

www.friedenfelser.de

ON HEARING THE NAME Friedenfelser one thinks of the Schlossbrauerei. However, this is only one of many Friedenfelser businesses owned by the Baron zu Gemmingen-Hornberg family since 1886. These include an agricultural and forestry operation, a granite works, a sawmill, and a distillery. Of the 15 varieties of beer produced, two are termed "Zoigl". This refers to a communal brewing practice where the wort is brewed collectively in the parish brewhouse and then fermented and stored in individual family cellars.

FRITZALE

www.fritzale.de

FRITZ WÜLFING IS THE GERMAN counterpart of the American craft brewer. The search for well-hopped beers took this hobby brewer to the USA where he immersed himself in IPA, learning a few new hop techniques along the way. His first home-brew was so well received by friends that he founded FritzAle in 2010. Since then his beers, brewed according to the American style, have gone down a storm. This native of Bonn brews using the facilities of local breweries, previously Braustelle Köln, now Vormann in Hagen.

FÜCHSCHEN

www.fuechschen.de

WITHIN THE LAST DECADE, a lot of fuss has emerged around Brauerei "Im Füchschen". Having gained somewhat of a cult status among young consumers, the Düsseldorf brewpub's output has prospered. Its revitalization came with fourth-generation owner Peter König, a trained cook, brewer, and maltster. He took over the business in 1995, upgraded the menu with light meals, modernized the brewhouse, relaunched the brand and set up a new programme of events. Allegedly, his famous beer remained the same: a dry and smooth version of alt beer.

GUTMANN

www.brauerei-gutmann.de

OWNED SINCE 1855 by the Gutmann family, this brewhouse, farm, and malthouse are situated in a medieval complex that was once a moated castle. The Gutmanns specialized in wheat beer in the 1990s, with a focus on Bavarian craft tradition. After a first fermentation in open vessels, fresh yeast is added for a second fermentation in the bottles. The beer is neither flash-pasteurized nor filtered: only the fine haze of the living yeast shines through, bringing in delicious flavours, and winning this brewery more fans.

HACHENBURGER

www.hachenburger.de

OPERATING SINCE 1861 in the Westerwald area, Hachenburger has built a reputation on pils brewing. In fact, brewmaster Heinz Boßlet uses five different aromatic hop varieties for his pils. Being a proper hop-head he dedicated his first special edition to dry-hopping and created what can be called an "indo-germanic" version of pale ale. He used only the German aromatic variety Hallertauer Mittelfrüh, picked from the brewery's garden. It was a success. Boßlet continues developing his own styles.

HAMMERBRÄU

www.hammerbraeu.de

FOUNDED IN 1999, the Hammerbräu Pub Brewery is situated on an artificial hill in the grounds of the Mercure hotel in the Saxonian town of Riesa. The entire complex, including an American restaurant, belongs to Magnet Riesa GmbH, an operating company for leisure facilities and event gastronomy. This is why the Hammerbräu offers many events, such as schnitzel-Wednesday, litre-beer-day, dances in the brewery, and a mega-meal accompanied by three types of beer: an unfiltered blond lager, an amber-coloured märzen, and a schwarzbier.

HÄRLE

www.haerle.de

CLEMENS HÄRLE FOUNDED his eponymous brewery in the Allgäu village of Leutkirch in 1897. One of his first beers was a light brown unfiltered lager with a pronounced malty character. Gottfried Härle took over the business 90 years later. The fourth-generation owner decided to revive the foundation beer, and created Clemens Ohne Filter, an unfiltered lager with a fantastic orange hue – less malty than its predecessor and with a spicy, clean finish.

HERBSTHÄUSER

www.herbsthaeuser.de

THE HERBSTHÄUSER BREWERY, originally a pub brewery, dates back to 1581. It was bought in 1878 by the Wunderlich family, who steadily expanded brewing operations. Since 2006, the independent brewery has been run by a fifth-generation member of the family, Christian Wunderlich. Highlights include the

Herbsthäuser Pils and the light lager, both displaying especially aromatic hop notes. Like all Herbsthäuser beers, they are brewed using natural hop cones, generating complex hop aromas and pleasantly rounded bitter notes.

HESSISCHES LÖWENBIER

www.hessisches-Loewenbier.de

THE HESSISCHES LÖWENBIER brewery, founded in the late Middle Ages, has strong roots in its community. When the private brewery filed for bankruptcy in 2003, the residents of Malsfeld mounted a campaign for its preservation, with success. Frank Bettenhäuser, owner of the nearby Hütt Brewery in Baunatal, bought Hessisches Löwenbier and cooperated with the residents. They established a brewing museum in the filling plant – and the brewery is brewing again: a deserved prize-winner is their unusually full-bodied pils.

HIRSCHBRAUEREI SCHILLING

www.boehringer-biere.de

ORIGINALLY A PUB with a brewery and an agricultural operation, the Böhringer brewery has been in the hands of the Schilling family since 1874. In 1996, the fourth-generation Marianne Spitzer, née Schilling, took the helm. She now runs the small brewery in the Swabian Alb together with her husband, the master brewer Johann Spitzer, and their daughter Stephanie, who is making a name for herself as a beer sommelier. The Spitzers offer eight different beers under the Böhringer brand.

HOCHDORFER KRONENBRAUEREI

www.hochdorfer.de

ONE OF GERMANY'S most promising young brewers is Katharina Haizmann of the Hochdorfer Kronenbrauerei – a traditional brewery founded in 1654 at the edge of the Black Forest. A master brewer, Haizmann joined the company in 2010. On her arrival, an especially fruity IPA – the Hochdorfer Meistersud, a variation on the beer she created while studying, was launched. Other brews include export, pils, wheat beer, and seasonal beers such as the dark, malty "Barbara-Bock".

HOFBRÄU MÜNCHEN

www.hofbraeu-muenchen.de

SINCE ITS FOUNDING at the end of the 16th century, the Hofbräuhaus has been owned by Bavaria's rulers. In 1852, King Maximilian II bequeathed it to the Bavarian state, which owns it to this day. Until 1896, brewing was also conducted at the world-famous pub-restaurant in Munich's old town. Relocated as more space was needed, it subsequently moved to Munich-Riem in 1988. It regularly brews 11 beers, including a Munich Helles and its famous Oktoberfest beer. Its bright golden Hofbräu Original is emblematic of this famous brewery – the beer is malty and full-bodied, with 5.1% ABV.

HOPF WEISSBIERBRAUEREI

www.hopfweisse.de

FOUNDED IN 1892, and originally called Miesbach, the Hopf wheat beer brewery was owned by the Hopf family from 1921 until 2006 when it was taken over by the Paulaner group – itself part of the Heineken joint venture Schörghuber group. The brewery made its name with wheat beer innovations. In the 1980s it launched its first draught wheat beer. It was also one of the pioneers of light wheat beer. A unique pleasure is its red-gold Spezial Weisse with 6% ABV, produced solely in winter.

HÖVELS HAUSBRAUEREI

www.hoevels-hausbrauerei.de

IS IT A BITTER LAGER or a pilsy alt? The red and crispy Hövels Original seems to combine the qualities of many styles. It is perhaps the most elaborate creation of Germany's former "beer capital", Dortmund. Hövels was created in 1893 in order to answer a demand for more ambitious beers. Revived in 1984 using the original recipe, the beer has a mixture of four malts – wheat, light, and dark barley, and roasted malts. These are complemented by Hallertauer aroma hops.

Today the brewery produces three different beers based on original recipes and Hövels is produced in the Dortmunder Actien-Brauerei plant that belongs to the Radeberger group. Visitors to the brewery can eat in the associated restaurant and are invited to take the PinkusHövels' beer test with different beers alongside a menu of German dishes.

HOFBRÄU MÜNCHEN HOFBRÄU ORIGINAL

HUPPENDORFER

www.huppendorfer-bier.de

INITIALLY A PUB BREWERY, Huppendorfer has been owned by the Grasser family since 1750 and has steadily expanded to become a medium-sized business. Until 1982, the wort was cooled in a wooden cooling vessel but this has subsequently been replaced by a whirlpool and plate chiller. The Upper Franconian brewery is renowned for its lager beers – especially its amber-coloured Vollbier. A full-bodied wheat beer has also been brewed since 1999. On Sundays, their pub serves hot Franconian cuisine including roast pork with salad, dumplings, and lots of sauce.

HÜTT

www.huett.de

THE HÜTT BREWERY in Baunatal, owned by the descendants of founder Johann Friedrich Pierson, is deeply rooted in the culture of the nearby city of Kassel and the local area. Its centrepiece is the Knallhütte, where coachmen stopped for refreshment. It was here that Dorothea Viehmann, granddaughter of the founder, was born in 1755. She later recounted the yarns she had heard from guests to the Brothers Grimm – the basis for *Grimm's Fairy Tales*. Hütt's range of beers includes a remarkably robust Luxus Pils.

KARMELITEN

www.karmeliten-brauerei.de

THE KARMELITEN BREWERY was founded in Straubing in 1367 by the Carmelite mendicant order and has been owned by the Sturm family since 1879. In 1984, the Private Weißbierbrauerei Georg Schneider & Sohn bought a stake. Since 2008, Karmeliten has been run by Christoph Kämpf, whose long-term strategy includes promoting a greater diversity of flavours. In 2011, he introduced a classic märzen beer and in 2012 a high-priced character beer fermented using Belgian abbey and French champagne yeasts, which delights with a creamy mouthfeel and complex aromas.

KETTERER

www.kettererbier.de

THE INDEPENDENT KETTERER Brewery was founded in Hornberg in 1877 and is now run by Bärbel and Michael Ketterer. The elegant, hop-dominated pils is a product of the soft Black Forest water and fine Tettnanger aromatic hops. In contrast, the Ketterer Edel displays a gentle malt accent. Seasonal specialities include the golden Christmas beer and deep-dark Schützenbock, brewed using a yeast traditionally used for stout. The Ketterer Kellerbier and Ur-Weisse have even brought back World Beer Cup medals to Hornberg.

KNEIPE PUR

www.kneipepur.de

SINCE 1988, THE BRÄTZ FAMILY has run the Rock and Blues Pub in Brandenberg's Plaue, a venue for international music stars. Gernot Brätz sees himself as a "missionary in the cause of German beer", brewing sour fruit beers using raspberries and cherries, porter, rauchbier, wheat beer, oat beer, and new creations – accompanied by Karola Dröske's Cuisine à la Bière, which she prepares in the open show kitchen, attracting inquisitive star cooks and celebrities. Kneipe Pur is an institution in Brandenberg.

KNOBLACH

www.brauerei-knoblach.de

THE WHITSUN BEER FESTIVAL in Schammelsdorf is legendary – a village version of Oktoberfest. While the local football team plays neighbouring rivals, attracting a crowd of Bundesliga size, revellers enjoy beer from the Knoblach brewery. Founded in 1880, the pub and brewery are still in family hands. Their lager matures traditionally, without pressure, allowing some of the carbon dioxide to escape. This means there is less foam and it is not as crisp, but it is very agreeable. In contrast, their chestnut brown Räuschla, a märzen with malt accent, is much livelier.

KÖNIG LUDWIG SCHLOSSBRAUEREI

www.koenig-ludwig-brauerei.com

THE SCHLOSSBRAUEREI in Kaltenburg is owned by a descendant of the last Bavarian king, Ludwig III. Today's plant, opened in 1870, belonged for a time to the Munich Unionsbrauerei (today Löwenbräu, AB-InBev). It was bought back by the former royal family in 1955. In 1976, the present owner, Luitpold von Bayern, took over the management and established the brand's national reputation with König Ludwig Dunkel, a lighter version of the Bavarian Dunkel. In 2001, the Warsteiner group bought the national sales licence, with further licences for overseas production.

LANDSKRON BRAU-MANUFAKTUR

www.landskron.de

THE GÖRLITZ BREWERY has really been through every mode of enterprise. Founded in 1869 as a stock company, it was bought by Theodor Scheller in 1903. In 1945 it fell under Soviet control, before being nationalized during the GDR and afterwards bought back by the Scheller family. Acquired by Holsten AG (later Carlsberg-Germany) in 2003, it was transferred to Rolf and Heidrun Lohbeck's foundation by 2006. Landskron enlivens the region as a "culture brewery" with culinary and musical events, brewing blond lagers and special editions.

LÖWENBRÄU BUTTENHEIM

www.loewenbraeu-buttenheim.de

THE LÖWENBRÄU BREWPUB dates back to 1880. A fourth-generation descendant of the original owner, Johann Modschiedler, runs the family business and due to an excellent competitor, St Georgen Bräu, who brews just a short distance away, he must be inventive. With two seasonal festival beers in his portfolio he decided to offer a third as a year-round standard. Bartholomäus Festbier is a deep-golden delight, seducing with fruity-sweet, flowery aromas, a creamy body with hints of vanilla, and an elegant bitterness.

MAHRS BRÄU

www.mahrs.de

MAHRS IS ONE OF Bamberg's brilliant breweries. In the old brewpub they serve a beer called U from wooden kegs (U stands for Ungespundetes, a kellerbier), and on Ash Wednesday a select group, including Bamberg's mayor, gather to celebrate the release of Mahrs' Der Weisse Bock. Since its launch in 1994, this strong wheat ale has won loyal fans. Junior brewmaster and fourth-generation owner Stephan Michel uses dark wheat malts, as well as Munich and Pilsner malts in a classic two-step decoction mash to make the beer as full-flavoured as possible.

MAISEL

www.maisel.com

THE BROTHERS EBERHARDT and Hans Maisel opened the Maisel Brewery at the gates of Bayreuth in 1887. In 1955 their successors launched one of the first clear wheat beers, which they called Champagner-Weizen, laying the foundation for what was to become a nationally renowned wheat beer brewery. Fourth-generation Jeff Maisel now runs the company, launching characterful beers under the label "Maisel & Friends", created with brewer Marc Goebel and wine-grower Stefan Sattran. Beers include IPA, Weizenbock, and stout variations.

MAXLRAIN

www.maxlrain.com

THE 16TH-CENTURY Renaissance Maxlrain castle in Bavaria was bought by the Lobkowicz family in the 1980s and has blossomed into a popular event location – their medieval tournaments and open-air concerts attract numerous visitors. Brewing has been practised here since 1636 and the Lobkowicz family's claim is to brew Bavaria's most sophisticated beers. From their extensive portfolio, Schloss Gold, an export, is the most popular. The brewers are also experimenting with wooden barrels for ripening their dark doppelbock.

MECKATZER LÖWENBRÄU

www.meckatzer.de

THE ALLGÄU-BASED BREWERY, Meckatzer, dates back to the 18th century, has been family-owned since 1853, and is now run by Michael Weiß. Diversity and high standards are his core values and are at the heart of his business. A speciality of the brewery is Weiss-Gold, a blond lager characterized by a perfect harmony of malt and hops, which is easy on the palate while simultaneously developing an exciting complexity.

MEISSNER SCHWERTER

www.privatbrauerei-schwerter.de

FOUNDED IN 1460, Meissner Schwerter is the oldest brewery in Saxony. It was bought by the merchant Wilhelm Wohlers in 1953 and

PAULANER SALVATOR

was nationalized in 1972. From 1997 the brewery was run by a descendant of Wohlers who, due to financial difficulties, sold it to Eric Schäffer, owner of the mineral water company Oppacher Quellen. Its portfolio now includes a pils, an interesting red and dark lager, and a complex amber-coloured bock.

NEUMARKTER LAMMSBRÄU

www.lammsbraeu.de

FRANZ EHRNSPERGER, sixth-generation owner of Neumarkter Lammsbräu, was 25 when he took over the family brewery in 1971. He became one of Germany's first brewers to focus on organic ingredients, which were not readily available at the time – Ehrnsperger had to show some stamina to achive his ambitions, winning over farmers and shrugging off colleagues who called him insane. Eventually, the world's first all-organic beer was released in 1987. Today there are more than a dozen Lammsbräu styles, including Urstoff – a light lager – and several excellent weizens.

PAPIERMÜHLE

www.jenaer-bier.de

THE "PAPER MILL" IN JENA, which has served beer since 1737, was bought by the Kanz family in 1995. The new owners renovated the pub and added a brewhouse. Five beers: two bocks, two pilsners, and a schwarzbier, are available on tap. The Papiermühle also runs a distillery where two bock beers mature in oak barrels once used for whisky in the brewhouse cellar. The beer garden's ancient lime tree is protected as a natural monument.

PAULANER MÜNCHEN

www.paulaner-brauerei.de

THE ORDER OF PAULANER monks began brewing beer in Munich in 1634. The brewery was privatized in 1813 and today it is part of the Heineken joint venture with the Schörghuber group. The brands under this umbrella include Hacker-Pschorr, Auer-Bräu, Thurn & Taxis, and Hopf. It offers 15 beers under its own label including the famous Salvator – once drunk by monks to take the place of food during Lent and considered the founder of the doppelbock style. Paulaner yeast wheat beer is one of Germany's top-selling beers.

PINKUS MÜLLER

www.pinkus.de

THE PINKUS MÜLLER BREWERY has been a family-run business since 1816 and is the last remaining alt beer brewery out of more than 150 that used to operate in Münster, Westphalia. Head brewer, Hans Müller, works alongside his daughter Barbara and her husband Friedhelm Langfeld to produce ten regular beers. They are all brewed according to the strict German purity laws and use only organic products. Pinkus Spezial, a malt beer, uses hops, yeast, and premium brew water. Untreated with protein stabilizers, it is stored for three months at temperatures around 0°C (32°F) to produce a naturally clear unfiltered beer. Other regulars include Pinkus Alt, which has a refreshing wine-like character, and the spicy, herby Pinkus Pils.

PLANK

www.brauerei-plank.de

IN 2001 IN LAABER, a village near Regensburg, a party was held to celebrate the 50th birthday of Maria Plank, head of the Plank brewing family. Her son Michael had brewed a beer called Dunkler Weizenbock for the occasion, which was based on a recipe for an ale that the Plank brewery had sold until the 1980s. Today, the recreated version of this classic is admired worldwide, and has achieved a gold medal at the World Beer Cup – where the small brewery, founded in 1883, was also decorated for the light-coloured, less complex variation, Heller Weizenbock.

PYRASER LANDBRAUEREI

www.pyraser.de, www.pyraser-herzblut.de

PYRASER, FOUNDED IN 1870 in a Franconian village, may well be considered Germany's most adventurous brewery. Owner Marlies Bernreuther took over from her father in 2010 and together with her brewmaster Helmut Sauerhammer offers a range of specialities and seasonals. These include Hopfenpflücker Pils, a pils with fresh hops from the brewery's own hop garden, Rotbier (Vienna lager), three or four different weizens, and a unique 6-Korn-Bier that is made with wheat, barley, spelt (40 per cent), rye, ancient grain, emmer, and oats. A new series, Edition Pyraser Herzblut, is also daring, with sophisticated creations like an IPA and a bourbon-barrel aged Doppelbock.

PINKUS MÜLLER PINKUS PILS

PLANK-BIER DUNKLER WEIZENBOCK

RATSHERRN

www.ratsherrn.de

RATSHERRN, LAUNCHED by Hamburg's Elbschlossbrauerei in 1951, became one of the city's major pils brands in the 1980s. However, in 1994 the brewery was forced to close and the brand was taken over by Bavaria and neglected. In 2005, the Nordmann Group, primarily a drinks wholesaler, bought the rights and opened the new Ratsherrn brewery in the middle of Hamburg's lively Schanzenviertel, reactivating the brand with a craft-beer image. Today, brewers Thomas Art, Philip Boll Horn, and Nile Timmann challenge themselves to produce the most delicious beers in northern Germany. They look back on the long history of brewing in Hamburg as well as gaining inspiration from the international craft beer movement in the USA, Denmark, Italy, and Austria, to produce a pils, a rotbier, and a pale ale made using local ingredients as far as possible.

RIEDENBURGER BRAUHAUS

www.riedenburger.de

MARTHA AND MICHAEL KRIEGER, fourth-generation proprietors of Riedenburger Brauhäus – in operation since 1866 – discovered archaic einkorn and emmer wheat through their cooperation with the nearby monastery of Plankstetten. With it they created an emmer ale for a local historical festival. Not only did people love the beer so much that the Kriegers decided to include it in their portfolio, but they have also now been honoured for their contribution to the revival of ancient crops. Emmerbier is remarkably creamy.

RITTMAYER

www.rittmayer.de

OWNER AND MASTER BREWER of Rittmayer, Georg Rittmayer, has built the family business – founded in 1422 in Hallerndorf in Upper Franconia – into a successful, medium-sized concern. In addition to a filling plant, he opened a new resource-saving brewing facility in 2012 that dispenses with the use of fossil fuels. Furthermore, he has also made a name for himself as a creator of unusual beers. Alongside German classics such as a hefeweissbier, landbier, kellerbier, bock, and radler, he offers a Vintage Edition and a cask-matured Oak Reserve.

RATSHERRN ROTBIER

RITTMAYER HEFEWEISSBIER

ROSENBRAUEREI

www.rosenbrauerei.de

AFTER GERMAN REUNIFICATION, Nicolaus Wagner, great-grandson of the brewery's co-founder, bought the Rosenbrauerei, and has built it up into one of the most important independent breweries in Thuringia. Since 1938 the brewery has had its own spring and has benefited from the particularly soft water it produces, which is especially suited to pils production. Rosenbrauerei's portfolio boasts two pilsners as well as a helle, a bockbier, and a schwarzbier – a beer style with its origins in the region.

ROTHAUS

www.rothaus.de

ROTHAUS IS ONE OF the three state-owned breweries in Germany (the other ones being Weihenstephan and Hofbräu, both in Bavaria). Fortunately, the federal state Baden-Württemberg knows how to run it – while the German beer market may be losing volume overall, Rothaus has increased its business. Situated in the Black Forest, Rothaus brews with extremely soft water from sources in a protected area deep in the woods. Their Tannenzäpfle, a smooth, aromatic and harmonious pils, is a favourite among urban beer-lovers in Hamburg and Berlin.

SCHAUMBURGER

www.schaumburger-brauerei.de

THE SCHAUMBURGER brewery in Stadthagen offers 16 different types of beer, all bottom-fermented lagers: from the best-selling Pils and amber-coloured Landbier to the deep-dark Schwarzen Ritter. The brewery draws its water from the Bornau source, which is especially soft, lending the Schaumburger Pilsner a fine structure. Founded in 1873, the private brewery in Lower Saxony has been run by Friedrich W Lambrecht since 2003 and is now owned by a fifth-generation member of the family. It has a workforce of 20.

SCHEYERN

www.klosterbrauerei-scheyern.de

BENEDICTINE MONKS have been brewing in Scheyern monastery since 1119. In 1951, the brewery was leased to Augsburg's Hasen-Bräu (later the Tucher/Radeberger group), who transferred bottling and then production to Augsburg. The brewery fell into disrepair,

forcing the monastic community to take action. They terminated the lease, built a new brewhouse, hired master brewer Tobias Huber from Aichach and celebrated their reopening in 2006. The portfolio consists of blond and dark lagers, wheat beer, doppelbock, and pils. The Hopfazupfabier, a blond märzen, is served at hop harvest – after all Scheyern is in Hallertau.

SCHLOSSBRAUEREI HERRNGIERSDORF

www.schlossbrauerei-herrngiersdorf.de

IN 2010 THE SCHLOSSBRAUEREI launched the Hallertauer Hopfen-Cuvée, a pilsner seasoned with the aromatic hop varieties Hallertauer Perle, Tradition, Mittelfrüh, and Saphir. An elegant drink, it is part of a trend that uses hops to create a rich, characteristic aroma profile, not just the bitter notes. Founded by Benedictine monks, the brewery has been owned by the Pausinger family since 1899.

SCHMUCKER

www.schmucker-bier.de

SINCE ITS FOUNDING, the Schmucker Brewery in Odenwald has been in private ownership. It has continually increased production since the 1960s and invested in new facilities. In 2006 it was taken over by Brauholding International (BHI), a joint venture between Heineken and the German Schörghuber group. The medium-sized company's portfolio is impressive, featuring 16 beers including the highly unusual Rosé Bock, a reddish starkbier brewed with different types of malt, and refreshing bright-golden Meister Pils. A regional highlight is the Schmucker fête, held every year in July.

SCHNITZER

www.schnitzer-braeu.de

SCHNITZER WAS founded in 1968 by the dentist Dr Schnitzer and initially specialized in the manufacture of wholefoods and grain mills, later adding gluten-free organic products. A gluten-free beer brewed from millet and mung bean malt was introduced in 2006 and is brewed under licence and sold in Europe, Canada, and Australia under the name "Schnitzer Bräu German Premium". The company is located in the city of Offenburg in Baden-Württemberg, near the French border.

SPEZIAL

www.brauerei-spezial.de

SPEZIAL BREWERY was founded in 1536 and has been owned by the Merz family since 1898. It is one of the only two traditional rauchbier breweries in Bamberg that makes its own malt, kiln-dried over burning beech wood. Its rauchbier, lager, märzen, wheat beer, and bock are brewed using a quantity of smoked malt and have a discreet, smoky taste. Only the Ungespundete is brewed without smoked malt. It is cellar-matured without pressure so that some of the carbon dioxide can escape, giving it a smooth texture.

ST GEORGEN BRÄU

www.st.georgenbraeu.de

ST GEORGEN BRÄU IS renowned for its kellerbier. It claims to be the first brewery to bottle lager directly and unfiltered from the ripening tank in around 1900. In contrast to large breweries that have offered filtered, flash-pasteurized, or pasteurized kellerbiers with separately produced protein trub since the 1990s, St Georgen supplies its best-seller untreated. In addition to the standard range, the Buttenheim brewery also offers seasonal beers such as its Hopfenzupferbier, seasoned with freshly harvested hop cones from its own garden. Its Doppelbock Dunkel is a high-alcohol (7.3% ABV) beer with a sweet, plum-like aroma.

STAFFELBERG BRÄU

www.staffelberg-braeu.de

TOURISTS EAT AND DRINK well at the Staffelberg brewpub in the heart of Franconian Switzerland. Karl-Heinz Wehrfritz, brewer and butcher, is the sixth generation of his family to run this family business that started in 1856. His Staffelberg Märzen, produced here since 1951, is a bottom-fermented Franconian amber lager that seduces with a caramel body balanced with a proper bitterness. The beer is fairly strong (5.5% ABV) and rather sweet, which is the reason why most other breweries have abandoned the traditional style. Yet, Staffelberg has held on to the märzen and serves many enthusiasts with it. The brewery also produces Mai-Bock, Landbier Hell, Landbier Dunkel, Pils, Hefe-Weissbier, Festbier, and a heavily hopped, bright and spicy Doppel-Bock.

SPEZIAL RAUCHBIER

STERNQUELL

www.sternquell.de

THE SAXONIAN STERNQUELL brewery was founded in 1883 at Plauen. By 1910, annual production was impressive, and during the years when Germany was divided into East and West, Sternquell Pils had already made a name for itself. The brewery expanded to become the largest in the Chemnitz administrative region. Following reunification it was bought by Brauholding International (BHI), a Heineken-Schörghuber joint venture, and managed by the BHI's Kulmbacher Brauerei AG.

On its 150th anniversary in 2007, Sternquell launched its amber-coloured Kellerbier. Its flagship beer is the Sternquell Pils, a bottom-fermented lager with dominant hop flavour, which is characterized by its strong, aromatic odour. It has a sparkling freshness and an alcohol content of 4.9% ABV.

STRECK

www.streck-bier.de

THE PRIVATELY OWNED Streck Brewery was founded in 1718 in Ostheim by the brewer and butcher Peter Streck. It has been run by Axel Kochinki, a tenth-generation descendant of the family, since 2010. Master brewer Gerhard Felber is particularly proud of its Burgherren Pils, seasoned with Hallertauer and Spalter select hops and given a long maturing in the cool cellar. In 1996, a dunkel, the Ostheimer Dunkel, was produced for the first time in 50 years to celebrate the 500th anniversary of Ostheim. It contains a generous portion of Munich malt that gives it a rich, dark chestnut colour. Streck's Weizen is a naturally cloudy, top-fermented, light wheat beer that won a gold prize from the German Agricultural Society in 2011.

TALSCHÄNKE

www.talschaenke-woellnitz.de

THE WÖLLNITZ DISTRICT OF JENA was once renowned for its Berliner Weiße – no surprise then that the only beer produced by Kay Hoppe in his pub brewery is a wheat beer of the Berlin variety. He serves it pure, with raspberry or woodruff syrup and a caraway spirit called Strippe. Hoppe founded Talschänke shortly after the fall of the Berlin Wall and unveiled the self-built brewing facility in 1997. The house, with taproom and covered beer garden, provides plenty of room for guests.

TRUNK ALTE KLOSTERBRAUEREI

www.bierfranken.eu/brauerei-detail.php?id=31

THE PILGRIMAGE CHURCH Vierzehnheiligen near Bad Staffelstein was opened in 1772. The monastery brewery, directly behind the basilica, opened at the same time, with a pub and beer garden. Since 1803 the Trunk family has brewed here under the brand Nothelfer ("holy helpers"). Their output includes a pils, a lager, an organic wheat beer – and most popular of all, the dunkel. Bock, festbier, and erntebier (harvest beer) are served seasonally. Thanks to the quality of the beer and the brewery's location above the Obermain Valley, Trunk has achieved cult status in Upper Franconia.

UERIGE OBERGÄRIGE HAUSBRAUEREI

www.uerige.de

TWICE A YEAR, on the third Tuesday in January and October, Uerige brewpub is crammed full. This is when they serve Sticke, the famous altbier variant of the 6.5% ABV Uerige. Made with more malt and more hops than the regular Uerige, its name comes from the word "stickum", a dialect term for "gossiping" – the story goes that people used to gossip that the master brewer had been over-generous when weighing out the ingredients. The Uerige brewery was founded in 1862 and continues to brew the old way using a coolship and a drip cooler. Their regular Alt is the most bitter in Düsseldorf, the home of this ale style. For export only, they produce DoppelSticke (8.5% ABV). It pours almost like oil, bringing along a fruity-sweet, herbal-bitter complexity.

UNERTL

www.unertl.de

THE CLASSIC UNERTL weissbier pours amber with a copper hue and a yeasty haze, wearing its creamy head up high. The recipe is unchanged since the brewery opened in 1895. When other weissbier brewers began offering variations of the style, the family brewery stuck to its recipe. As third-generation owner Alois Unertl explains, they brew with 70 per cent instead of the customary 50 per cent of wheat malt, which brings a freshness to the beer.

WELDE WEIZENGRAPE

WALDHAUS

www.waldhaus-bier.de

THE BLACK FOREST BREWERS from Waldhaus pride themselves on a decades-long sequence of quality awards including World Beer Cup and European Beer Star medals for their main product, the Diplom Pils. It is a favourite with many connoisseurs due to its well-toned body, light-hearted malt character, and complex hop aromatic spirit. According to Dieter Schmid, fourth-generation owner, Waldhaus only put in natural hops stemming from Spalt, Hallertau, and Tettnang. Another important ingredient is the wonderfully soft water from local forest sources.

WELDE

www.welde.de

THE CURRENT OWNER of Welde Brewery, and fourth-generation family member, Dr Hans Spielmann, combines art and culture with his brewery in Plankstadt. He designed the "dancing bottle", the first designer bottle for beer, and in 1994 initiated the Welde art prize, held annually with participants from around the world. Each year he also labels a limited edition of his flagship beer Welde No 1 Premium Pils with artists' labels. Master brewer Stephan Dück annually brews a new vintage beer, seasoned with exotic aromatic hops. As well as a light and dark hefeweizen, the brewery produces WeizenGrape – a light, refreshing wheat beer flavoured with grapefruit juice.

WISMAR BRAUHAUS

www.brauhaus-wismar.de

BEER WAS FIRST BREWED in the Wismar Brewery opposite Wismar's old harbour in 1452. At the time there were over 100 breweries in the port city and Wismar beer was known throughout Europe. One such brew was Mumme, a dark top-fermented beer seasoned with herbs. In 1995, managing director Herbert Wenzel reopened the traditional brewery and since 2000 Stephan Beck has been its head brewer. For the 550th anniversary, he produced a Jubiläums-Mumme, a dark starkbier with 24.4% ABV – a milder version with 10% ABV now forms part of the regular product range. Other beers produced include a pilsner, the mild and aromatic Roter Erik, a malty Herbsfestbier, Weinachstbier, and Maibock.

BELGIUM

 **Witbier, Trappist, lambic, kriek**, and gueuze are among the amazing variations of up to 25 beer styles produced by Belgian brewers. Even though Belgium has borders with Germany and the Netherlands, many brewers and beer drinkers have done their best to resist what they view as the "pilsner invasion" – the onslaught of beer monoculture. For Belgium is rightly famed for the individuality of its beers – in Flanders, a region with a rich, creative brewing history, soaring pale ales, sour red-browns, and coriander-infused wheat beers can be found. In Wallonia, in southern Belgium, locals enjoy their tart and dry saisons – a style that has become a must-brew beer for brewers not just in the New World but also in many of the old beer-brewing countries, such as the UK. And indeed there are many Belgian styles that are becoming popular worldwide: much more Belgian-brewed lambic is probably drunk in New York City than in its spiritual home.

But the brave new world of taste exploration has not escaped Belgium's brewers. Seemingly exotic, flavoursome hops like Citra and Amarillo have been used in a number of breweries, and Belgium too is embracing the possibilities that these hops offer to those pairing food with beer as in and around Brussels there are many beer cuisine restaurants. Every visitor to the country's capital should find time to visit the Cantillon brewery (see p.86), which today is a working museum. It is arguably the most authentic gueuze brewery in Belgium. One of the great thrills as a "beer traveller" is to taste these intensely dry, uncompromising sour beers not just in the brewery where they were made, but with the brewer.

3 FONTEINEN

Armand Debelder preserves the tradition of blending lambic beers to create the traditional Belgian brews known as gueuze. He produces his own lambic, using wild fermentation to create his respected brews.

"YOU CAN'T MAKE A FORTUNE IN GUEUZE", says lambic brewer and blender Armand Debelder, "but I have my reasons to devote myself to lambics. I am extremely fascinated by the taste". A true artist, Debelder creates the beers he really loves. "Luckily, we have the possibility to brew these beers in the oldest way again", he says; the beers have gained widespread acclaim for using wild fermentation. However, his career as a brewer has been no picnic.

Armand's father bought the café and *geuzestekerij* – the location where lambic beers are blended – in 1953 and expanded the establishment with a restaurant, which today is run by Armand's brother Guido. Armand learned the art of blending from his father in the 1980s and took over the task after ten years of devoted practice. "You need experience to be able to do this, and it only comes over time", he says. A stickler for detail, he had long refused to brew his own sour beer. However, in 1998 a small brewhouse was installed and, again, Armand took his time to bring lambic brewing to perfection.

Disaster struck in 2009, when a faulty thermostat caused the temperature in Debelder's bottle storage area to rise from 16°C (61°F) to 60°C (140°F). Some of the fermenting bottles exploded, others started leaking. The gueuze of 80,000 intact bottles was spoiled. Many volunteers came to help uncork them, Debelder distilled the contents and sold it as Armand'Spirit but was forced to sell his brewing equipment. Luckily, many lambic supporters and other lambic breweries helped him out. His wife Lydie Hulpiau invented the exclusive vintage series Armand'4 with different blends of the last lambics before the disaster. To secure the continuation of 3 Fonteinen, Debelder has now partnered up with Michaël Blanckaert. Together they acquired a new brewing system and resumed brewing activities.

THE FACTS...

OWNER Armand Debelder
FOUNDED 1953
ADDRESS Hoogstraat 2a, 1650 Beersel
WEBSITE www.3fonteinen.be
PHILOSOPHY Ancient tradition combined with passion

3 FONTEINEN
OUDE KRIEK

3 FONTEINEN
OUDE GEUZE VINTAGE

TASTING NOTES

OUDE KRIEK 5% ABV
Ruby red, with a thin head and light lacing, Oude Kriek is made of young lambic matured with cherries for six to eight months in casks, followed by four months of bottle fermentation. It is an invigorating drink with a tart aroma of cherries and musk.

FOOD PAIRING: Excellent with rich, flavourful dishes such as duck and goose, venison with cherry sauce, and goat's cheese.

OUDE GEUZE VINTAGE 7% ABV
Vintage is Oude Geuze that, after its bottle-refermentation, is left to mature for several years. The tartness then transforms into complex, deep, and smooth flavours of citrus, fruits, and earthy flavours like wood and leather.

FOOD PAIRING: Try with oysters or steamed mussels with creamy sauces, pâtés and sausages, salads made with gueuze vinaigrette, or the earthy flavours of stilton.

BEERSEL BLOND PALE ALE, 7% ABV
This strong Belgian pale ale pours clear golden with a medium-sized white head. It offers a sweet fruity nose of yellow plums, mandarins, and bananas on a biscuity malt base spiced with floral and earthy hop aromas. The first sip is fruity and sweetish, balanced by a spicy bitterness. It has a medium body, and creamy texture, with a dry and fine hoppy finish.

FOOD PAIRING: Pair with appetizers like salty prosciutto or smoked salmon, pasta with pesto and parmesan, or grilled fish.

Light refreshment
Blond beers are ideal thirst quenchers

3 FONTEINEN
BEERSEL BLOND

ACHEL

The youngest and the smallest of the six approved Belgian Trappist breweries, Achel was set up in 1998, when after more than 80 years of abstinence the Abbey of Saint Benedict in Achel revived its brewing tradition.

THE FACTS...

OWNER St Benedict Monastery, Achel

FOUNDED 1998

ADDRESS 3930 Hamont-Achel

WEBSITE www.achelsekluis.org

PHILOSOPHY Monastic life is about simplicity, strength, and quality. Trappist beer is the ideal product to symbolize this

THE ORIGINS OF THE MONASTERY SITE at Achel date back to the 17th century, when Dutch monks established a chapel there that later became an abbey. The first beer brewed was the Patersvaatje beer in 1852, but it was only after the abbey was converted to a Trappist monastery in 1871 that brewing became a regular activity. This came to an end in World War I when the monks abandoned their monastery due to the German occupation. In 1917, the German military dismantled the brewhouse to take advantage of the copper from the kettles. After the war, the monks at Achel concentrated on agriculture and cattle breeding.

These days all monasteries, including Achel, have difficulties in recruiting brothers or nuns who are willing to share their way of life. As the average age of their fraternity rose they had to restructure their business and focus on easier jobs for the monks. They sold most of their lands to be able to invest in a new brewery, tavern, guest house, and shop. With the help of brothers from Westmalle and Rochefort they took up the brewing business again. They first started with lighter beers only poured at the tavern: their blond and their brown, both unfiltered with 5% ABV, are still only available from tap at the site. The two bottled 8°, also a blond and brown, as well as Achel Extra (a brown with 9.5% ABV), were released in 2001. Their latest, the Achel Extra Blond (9.5% ABV), is also only available in the abbey.

Angelic ales
The profits from the sale of Trappist beers support the charity work the monastery carries out

TASTING NOTES

BRUIN 5.5 BROWN ALE, 5.5% ABV
Hazy brown with a tan-coloured head, this brown ale has aromas of toffee, dark fruits, and has toasted notes. Its sweet first sip is followed by fruity, herbal, and caramel flavours balanced by hop bitterness. It has a malty finish.

FOOD PAIRING: Great with roast pork dishes or black bread sandwiches with cold cuts of meat.

BLOND 8 BELGIAN ALE, 8% ABV
With a firm white head and deep orange colour, this strong Belgian ale offers grainy and fruity aromas reminiscent of sweet apricots and pears. The fruity aromas translate into a complex fruity, malty flavour, which is accompanied by some spices. Blond 8 has a thick, full-bodied mouthfeel and a herbal, bitter finish.

FOOD PAIRING: Good with tasty and spicy sausage dishes like duck sausage in a cassoulet, or pork in a delicate sauerkraut, as well as with gamey hams and peppery steaks.

ACHEL BRUIN 5.5

ACHEL BLOND 8

ALVINNE

Alvinne is notorious for creating exaltation or dismay in the world of beer – it dares to experiment, often with surprising results. Yet in a short space of time, the brewery has grown from a tiny microbrewery to a thriving enterprise.

THE FACTS...

OWNER Davy Spiessens, Glenn Castelein, Marc De Keukeleire

FOUNDED 2004

ADDRESS Vaartstrat 4a, 8552 Moen/Zwevegem (West-Vlaanderen)

WEBSITE www.alvinne.be

PHILOSOPHY Innovative and creative brewing with respect for traditions

SINCE 2004, THE CO-FOUNDERS of Alvinne (which means "elf"), Glenn Castelein and Davy Spiessens, have been testing the limits of brewing. "We like to be experimental and innovative by using traditions in new ways", says Castelein. The two former home-brewers advanced quickly to the avant garde of the beer world. Alvinne was among the first to age beers in oak barrels, using new hop varieties as well as creating collaboration brews with European partners. With the recognition of the international craft beer scene, the "Picobrouwerij Alvinne", as they first called themselves, expanded quickly from a wooden shed in a private backyard to a bigger place in Heule near Kortrijk. Three years later, in 2010, Marc De Keukeleire gave new wings to the elf when he brought a new technological innovation to the brewery. The food engineer and home-brewer had bred his own yeast strain, Morpheus, after many years of tinkering.

Morpheus is a mix of ale strains and lactic acid bacteria that can be used for both sour and non-sour beers. It is perfect for the mixed fermentation styles typical of the West Flanders region: Oude Bruin or Vlaams Rood. With this new boost, Alvinne invested in a brewhouse with a capacity of 200hl (122 barrels), new fermenters, and a historic industrial building in nearby Moen. They moved there in 2011. The brewing enterprise now comprises a shop and brewhouse, which holds brewing classes, and a "Proefloft", or tasting loft.

The Alvinne Craft Beer Festival, held every other (even) year at the brewery is well received by international beer enthusiasts, and features notable craft brewers from all over the world.

TASTING NOTES

GASPAR 8% ABV
A strong-willed ale, Gaspar has an orange hue and tones of earth and hay on the nose. Heavily hopped, its citrus notes seem to jump out through the creamy white head. The hops add lots of herbal spice flavours.

FOOD PAIRING: The warmth of the alcohol and sugar flavours make it an ideal partner to a good burger, chips, and salad.

CUVÉE D'ERPIGNY 15.2% ABV
Amber-brown, this hazy barley wine has a tan-coloured head, and is aged in Monbazillac barrels. The aroma is an enchanting blend of honey, grapes, nuts, and vinous notes. The flavour is sweet and the mouthfeel creamy, reminiscent of plums, oak, wine, and earthy nuances. It has a warming finish.

FOOD PAIRING: A complex fireside drink, it should be savoured without rushing.

MORPHEUS WILD UNDRESSED 5.2% ABV
This deep red-brown sour ale has a tan-coloured head. It was the first beer brewed with the Morpheus yeast strain, exclusively for the US. It has a fruity and spicy nose with moments of wood, and a moderately sour taste with aromas of cherries, lemon, and earth. It has a tart finish.

FOOD PAIRING: This refreshing, easily drinkable sour ale is great with shellfish dishes, especially lobster. It also makes a good partner for omelette or eggs Benedict.

ALVINNE GASPAR

BOON

THE FACTS...

OWNER Frank Boon, joint venture with Palm Breweries

FOUNDED 1975

ADDRESS Fonteinstraat 65, 1502 Lembeek, Vlaams-Brabant

WEBSITE www.boon.be

PHILOSOPHY An award-winning brewery proud to produce GTS: "guaranteed traditional specialities"

In 1975, at a time when dozens of breweries and blenders gave up, Frank Boon took over an old gueuze and kriek plant. Against all the odds he has succeeded in establishing a successful brewery of excellent lambic beers.

BOON KRIEK BOON

IN 1975, SOUR BEERS were the style that 20-year-old Frank Boon loved most, and his favourite blender was the brewery's former owner, René De Vits. However, De Vits had no heir and when he told Boon that he was going to have to close down the brewery, Boon decided to step in and take over. Boon had grown up with beer. His grandmother and her brothers ran a lager brewery that had fallen on hard times and finally closed in 1970, and the family also brewed their own beer at home. Boon had originally promised them that he would never enter the brewing business. And yet, in his early twenties with a degree in social science in his pocket, he felt compelled to break his promise. Who else would take up the task?

Boon bought the site from De Vits and set out with the aim of producing traditional gueuze and kriek of excellent quality, knowing that no big brewer would be prepared to deal with the labour- and capital-intensive production of this ancient style of beer. In the beginning he only blended gueuze by using lambics from two other breweries. When these shut down their production, like many others in Payottenland, Boon began to brew his own lambic. That was in 1990.

Lambic has remained a small speciality, but Frank Boon has done well. He has saved his beloved cobweb-covered brewhouse and increased production 20-fold. When he wanted to expand, a partnership with Palm Breweries gave him the means to do so. Today there are about 230 large wooden vats filled with lambic in his cellar in Lembeek, which amounts to about 10,000hl (6,110 barrels) of lambic for use. Boon acknowledges that "it takes a lot of beer to make a little bit of nice gueuze". Unlike most of his conservative allies who strictly follow the "oude" (old) traditional recipes, Boon has modified some styles in making fruitier and less tart products by using "meerts", very young lambic, in his Kriek, for example.

Mix and match
The skill of making a kriek beer comes from the ability to masterfully blend lambics of different ages

TASTING NOTES

KRIEK BOON 4% ABV

This bright red kriek is a blend of lambics of different ages. After a year of cask fermentation, 400g of cherries per litre (14oz per 1¾ pints) are added to activate a second bottle fermentation. After two years in the bottle, refreshing sweet-sour notes of cherries evolve into adult port wine or sherry aromas.

FOOD PAIRING: The sourness of the beer will pair well with delicate seafood such as mussels and scallops.

KRIEK MARIAGE PARFAIT 8% ABV

Ruby red with a pink moist head, this gueuze is made of one-year-old strong lambic aged in oak barrels with 400g per litre (14oz per 1¾ pints) of ripe cherries. Bottle-fermented, it matures for two years. With an aroma of vanilla, moss, roses, and cloves, its full-bodied fruitiness is reminiscent of cherries, balanced by some sweetness.

FOOD PAIRING: Ideal with rich foods such as duck, goose, venison, foie gras, and pâtés.

FRAMBOISE BOON 5% ABV

Bright pinkish red with a rose-white head, Framboise Boon is made with 300g per litre (11oz per 1¾ pints) of fresh raspberries and a few wild cherries. It is light and effervescent with an assertive fruity nose. It has a moderate acidity and a long fruity finish with hints of almonds.

FOOD PAIRING: Tastes wonderful when paired with a chocolate mousse or a goat's cheese salad.

GEUZE MARIAGE PARFAIT 8% ABV

A blend of three-year-old lambic with younger varieties, it is filtered, then bottle aged for at least six months. It is smooth with a subtle sourness balanced by woody flavours, a vanilla body, and a bitter aftertaste of cloves, which becomes more intense as you drink.

FOOD PAIRING: Enjoy this sublime brew with rich, flavourful foods such as snails, smoked salmon, goat's cheeses, or oysters.

OUDE GEUZE BOON 7% ABV

Hazy bright golden with a white head, this gueuze is a blend of 90% mild 18-month-old lambic, 5% strong 3-year-old lambic, and 5% very young lambic, and is bottle fermented for several months. The flavours are grapefruit, ginger, and Muscat grapes supported by a smooth sourness. It has a smooth finish.

FOOD PAIRING: This sour, fruity beer will complement salty meats, such as charcuterie.

FARO BOON 5% ABV

Amber brown with a little head – Faro Boon is composed of old lambic with spices and candy sugar added to produce a lighter lambic with lower alcohol content. The sour-sweet aroma is reminiscent of balsamic vinegar, the mild vinegar-like sourness balancing the sweetness.

FOOD PAIRING: The sweet-and-sour flavour of this beer makes it a good match for fruit-based desserts.

BOON
KRIEK MARIAGE PARFAIT

BOON
FRAMBOISE BOON

BOON
GEUZE MARIAGE PARFAIT

BOON
OUDE GEUZE BOON

BOON
FARO BOON

BELGIUM IS NO SMALL COUNTRY WHEN IT COMES TO BEER: IT HAS MORE THAN 25 INDIGENOUS BEER STYLES WITH COUNTLESS REGIONAL VARIATIONS

BEER BRINGS TOGETHER THE ARTS OF BREWING AND DESIGN AT THE CANTILLON BREWERY'S GUEUZE MUSEUM IN THE HEART OF BRUSSELS (SEE P.86)

CANTILLON

"It takes passion and patience to make this beer", says Jean Van Roy, the owner of Cantillon – and obviously devotion, too: "As a lambic brewer you have to keep close contact with your beer. Only then can you get the feel of it".

THE FACTS...

OWNER Jean Van Roy

FOUNDED 1900

ADDRESS 56 Rue Gheude, 1070 Brussels

WEBSITE www.cantillon.be

PHILOSOPHY To brew purely in the traditional way with traditional equipment and natural ingredients, without sweeteners, preservatives, or juice instead of fruits

MAKING THIS CONNECTION WITH Jean Van Roy's brews can be difficult though, as every spontaneous fermentation develops differently. Every lambic cask, which matures for up to three years, is unique. "We cannot control the fermentation, we have to follow it", Van Roy explains. Wisely, he points out that lambic brewers can never be called masters. They have to rely on their senses. "This is more complex than brewing ale or lager. We have to taste the beer", he says. In fact, he tries lambics from up to ten casks, young and old, before he blends his gueuze.

Van Roy is the fourth generation of his family to run Cantillon. He grew up in the brewery, entered business in 1989, and since 1990 has worked to accomplish nearly every task of the brewing process himself. He admits that there have been many times that he has dreamt of travelling the world. Instead, though, the world seems to come to him. About 14,000 people visit Cantillon annually, and 90 per cent of them are foreigners. Some are enthusiasts on a gueuze pilgrimage, but most of the visitors are attracted by the "museum" Van Roy's father set up in 1978. He converted the brewery into a living exhibition where the Van Roy family can be seen working with the same equipment they used in 1900. The entrance fees have secured Cantillon's survival in the financially turbulent decades since.

While his father was known for his radical traditionalism, Jean Van Roy experiments here and there. Fou' Foune is brewed with apricots, while in Iris he uses 50 per cent dried and 50 per cent fresh hops, and then gives the brew a second fresh hopping before bottling. He has also fermented lambics in terracotta amphoras – a technique he learned from Sicilian winemaker Gabrio Bini.

CANTILLON
KRIEK

CANTILLON
GUEUZE 100% LAMBIC BIO

CANTILLON
GRAND CRU BRUOCSELLA

TASTING NOTES

KRIEK 5% ABV

Cloudy amber-red Kriek is a blend of six-month to one-year-old lambic matured with fresh cherries in oak or chestnut casks for several months, then bottle-fermented for up to five months. Kriek has an aroma of cherries and wood, with a tart but smooth flavour and a creamy mouthfeel. The brewery recommend that it is consumed within 12 months of bottling.

FOOD PAIRING: This thirst-quenching beer makes a great summer drink and is good with flavoursome snacks such as cheese, olives, and radishes.

GUEUZE 100% LAMBIC BIO 5% ABV

The light yellow, cloudy Gueuze is a blend of one-, two-, and three-year-old lambic beers. It has aromas of fruits and leather with quite a tart first sip. The beer has a sour flavour with notes of straw, cider, and leather, followed by a dry finish.

FOOD PAIRING: This versatile beer is good as an apéritif, great with steamed mussels, oysters, and shellfish dishes, and works well with fruity-sweet pâtés and spicy terrines.

GRAND CRU BRUOCSELLA LAMBIC, 5% ABV

This golden-yellow opaque lambic is a specially selected single-cask edition that has been matured for three years. It has an aroma of apples and honey and is dry with elegant acidity and hints of toasted bread.

FOOD PAIRING: It makes the perfect companion for seafood and delicate meat dishes like tarragon chicken.

DE LA SENNE

De la Senne enriches Belgian beer culture with a clear commitment to Brussels and the revival of lost styles. It could export all of its capacity, but prefers to sell most of it locally.

THE FACTS...

OWNER Yvan De Baets, Bernard Leboucq

FOUNDED 2006

ADDRESS Steenweg op Gent 565, 1080 Brussels

WEBSITE www.brasseriedelasenne.be

PHILOSOPHY To brew beers full of flavour, not full of alcohol

THIS NEWCOMER to Belgium's brewing scene turns recent trends in craft brewing as well as the dominant image of Belgian beer culture upside down. "Our basic idea is to create beers that offer a lot of flavour at as small an alcohol degree as necessary", says Yvan De Baets, co-founder and brewmaster of the De la Senne brewery in Brussels, adding, "We brew what we like to drink ourselves". When he and his business partner Bernard Leboucq finish a long working day, they would not choose to drink a strong beer like tripel, instead favouring "something easy-going, refreshing, and tasty". Thus, their Saison de la Senne (4.3% ABV), Stouterik (4.5% ABV), and blonde Taras Boulba (4.5% ABV) are fantastically balanced, complex, unique, and easy-to-drink beers – and, most surprising of all, they are inspired by Belgian beer tradition. "In the monasteries as well as for the people, the common drink used to be beer instead of water", says De Baets. When people consumed 11 pints (six litres) or more per day to balance their fluid levels, it was light beer they drank. As a book geek, De Baets has researched Belgian beer culture from the primary sources. He also listens to what old brewers tell him about former common styles of which the tafelbier might be the last remnant. De la Senne recreates some of the lower-alcohol styles and revives this lost culture.

However, there are also some strong beers in their portfolio – the dark winter ale Zwarte Piet (8% ABV), the tripel La Jambe-de-Bois (8% ABV), and the sold-out Flanders brown ale Crianza (7% ABV). De Baets comments, "In former times, the strong beers were reserved for special occasions like distinguished visitors or feasts". It is only right that De la Senne has a few of these, too.

TASTING NOTES

STOUTERIK STOUT, 4.5% ABV
Very dark brown with a tan-coloured head, this Belgian stout offers rich, sweet, and roasted aromas with hints of chocolate and coffee beans. The palate is light with a refreshing herbal bitterness balanced with roasted notes and a dry, bitter finish.

FOOD PAIRING: A good session beer. It goes well with a range of flavours, from black bread sandwiches, nutty cheeses like emmental, and grilled fish to roasted potatoes.

TARAS BOULBA ALE, 4.5% ABV
Pours deep golden with an orange hue, almost clear, has a fine white head and offers a fresh nose of lime, tangerines with underlying caramel, and toasted aromas. Crisp and dry first sip, assertive bitterness evolving into a fluffy centre of caramel and toasted bread. A slight sour interplay leads the beer into the finish of long lingering, aromatic bitterness.

FOOD PAIRING: This superb, thirst-quenching aperitif can be enjoyed with light but spicy dishes: goat's cheese salad, curried prawns, or lemon tart.

ZWARTE PIET STRONG DARK ALE, 8% ABV
This dark amber-brown brew with a creamy golden head offers rich malty aromas of toast, cocoa, and dried fruit, with some alcoholic notes and yeast. It has a rich palate of dried fruit and bitter chocolate, some vanilla with uplifting hop aromatics, and a moderate sweet finish.

FOOD PAIRING: This is a great fireside drink or degustation beer, with chocolates, cigars, or tasty matured cheeses.

DE LA SENNE STOUTERIK

DE LA SENNE TARAS BOULBA

DE LA SENNE ZWARTE PIET

RODENBACH

Rodenbach is one of the world's most unusual beer-makers, preserving and promoting the classic barrel-aged mixed-fermentation-style of production to make a range of traditional sour Flemish brown ales.

THE FACTS...

OWNER Palm Breweries

FOUNDED 1836

ADDRESS Spanjestraat 133–141, 8800 Roeselare, West-Vlaanderen

WEBSITE www.rodenbach.be

PHILOSOPHY Beers brewed with a deep respect for beer culture and craftsmanship

RODENBACH IS A FAMILY-OWNED BREWERY, opened by four brothers in 1821. In the 1870s one of the brothers, Eugène Rodenbach, travelled to the UK, where he learned how to make beer from a mix of old and young beers fermented in oak barrels – this has since become the brewery's speciality. By 1998 the company was in the hands of Palm Breweries. They converted the old brewhouse into a conference centre and built a new, state-of-the-art site.

The wooden vats in the cellars at Rodenbach, which are an indispensable part of the mixed-fermentation step of the beer-making process, have become a visitors' attraction in their own right. Endless brick-plastered aisles are lit by overhead spotlights and fringed by huge oak vats held together by red rings, each jacked up on brick-built piers under a dark wooden ceiling. This "cathedral of *foudres*" – French for "huge vats" – leaves visitors awestruck. "Without wooden vats, Rodenbach wouldn't exist", says brewery director Rudi Ghequire. As Ghequire explains, the beers undergo a primary fermentation pitched with

Rodenbach's own yeast culture in cylindro-conical tanks. The secondary fermentation takes place in horizontal tanks to sediment the yeast cells and develop the lactic acid bacteria although at least "two more years of maturation and patience" are required. During this time the beer rests in 300 huge oak vats (120–600hl/75–370 barrels each), where it takes on the wonderfully complex flavours from the wood and the micro-organisms living within it. Many of the vats are as old as the brewery, most of them are self-built, while some were purchased from other brewhouses in the area and rebuilt at the Rodenbach site. The brewery employs a team of coopers to maintain these precious containers.

RODENBACH
VINTAGE

TASTING NOTES

VINTAGE OAK-AGED GUEUZE, 7% ABV
A single-vat edition, Vintage is the beer tasters' choice. It is selected only from the bigger vats in which the beer matures more slowly due to having less surface-contact with wood. It has a complex aroma of pomegranate, vanilla-like oak, earthy notes, spices, and sherry. Its sweet and round first sip of caramelized malt flavours is balanced by a firm acidity. It has a long finish.

FOOD PAIRING: Good strong flavours such as game meats, gamey liver pâtés, and matured cheeses.

GRAND CRU FLEMISH RED ALE, 6% ABV
A ruby-brown Flemish red ale with a blend of two-thirds oak-aged to one-third young beer. It has aromas of red fruits, turmeric, and balsamic vinegar. Sweet and sour with moments of fruits and oak, it has a pleasantly dry finish.

FOOD PAIRING: A great aperitif, it works with olives, pickled vegetables, and fish – as well as with lobster and crab dishes.

CARACTÈRE ROUGE FRUIT ALE, 7% ABV
This limited-edition beer is oak-aged for two years with cherries, raspberries, and cranberries. Ruby-red, this cloudy ale offers a great nose of red fruits, with wine-like and woody notes. It has a creamy texture, and is uplifting, dry, and well balanced, with a refreshing fruity finish.

FOOD PAIRING: Works with goose liver and mild blue cheese.

RODENBACH
GRAND CRU

RODENBACH
CARACTÈRE ROUGE

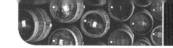

WESTVLETEREN

One of the most revered breweries in the world, Westvleteren produces some of the hardest beers to come by – perhaps their scarcity is one of the reasons for their popularity – and draws people from all over the world to visit.

ON THE PLAINS OF WEST FLANDERS there used to be a queue of cars visible from miles around, pushing slowly through the gates of Saint Sixtus Abbey in Westvleteren. Beer lovers lined up for a case or two of Westvleteren 12. The popular barley wine is only available on certain days and, like the two other beers of the monastic brewery, exclusively sold directly at the abbey. When traffic became a problem, the monks began to sell their beer to customers who had pre-ordered by telephone. But the phone lines are so busy they keep breaking down…

Westvleteren Brewery has become a pilgrimage site – a goblet full of their 12 represents the Holy Grail for beer enthusiasts as in many international rankings this dark strong ale is listed as the best beer in the world. As a result, even more busloads of beer tourists and individual travellers flock to the abbey's giant tavern to get a taste of Westvleteren's exclusive products, which are not normally available to purchase in other places. Hence it's no wonder that, on the back porch of the café superbly gilded by the afternoon sun, visitors feel privileged when they eventually savour Westvleteren's blond, the 8, and on rare occasions also the 12.

Despite this attention, the brothers of the Trappist monastery, of whom there are about twenty, remain unaffected. They stick to their remote lifestyle and to their modest brewing schedule. One beer writer per year is granted a tour of the brewery. As they say, they brew beer but their monastery is not a brewery. They brew to pray. Luckily they know their craft.

THE FACTS…

OWNER Saint Sixtus Trappistenabdij
FOUNDED 1839
ADDRESS Donkerstraat 12, 8640 Westvleteren, West-Vlaanderen
WEBSITE www.sintsixtus.be
PHILOSOPHY We brew to pray

TASTING NOTES

BLOND ALE, 5.8% ABV
Lucid golden and slightly hazy with a thick white head – this golden ale offers a nose of exotic fruits, hay, and spices. Initial sweetness evolves into a full body with a balancing bitterness, effervescent and fluffy mouthfeel, and a long dry finish.
FOOD PAIRING: This beer is great with hearty dishes like sauerkraut and sausages, fried beef, or fish.

8 DUBBEL, 8% ABV
This cloudy dark brown dubbel has a cream-coloured head and complex malty aromas reminiscent of raisins, cloves, and herbs. It has well-balanced flavours of sweet and soft roasted notes, which support its bitterness. Its mouthfeel is crisp and clean, with a long, tasty finish.
FOOD PAIRING: Try with grilled and smoked meats.

WESTVLETEREN BLOND

WESTVLETEREN 8

ABBAYE DES ROCS

www.abbaye-des-rocs.com

IN 1979, JEAN-PIERRE ELOIR started brewing in Montignies-sur-Roc as a hobby, but it soon grew to become a vocation. His daughter Nathalie studied brewing and took on the small family business. Abbaye des Rocs' beers are only made from water, hops, malt, yeast, and spices. Nathalie uses coriander, orange peel, cumin, or ground ginger and completely does away with sugar. The brewery was among the first to use malted oats in its beer, as in its Blanche des Honnelles (6% ABV), released in 1991.

ACHOUFFE

www.achouffe.be

THE ACHOUFFE BREWERY in Houffalize-Achouffe in the province of Luxembourg is a start-up success story and the paragon of Belgian craft beer. Home-brewers Pierre Gobron and Chris Bauweraerts founded their business in 1982, setting out to create high-quality specialities. Their first product, La Chouffe, a blonde ale of 8% ABV, found many fans at home as well as abroad, and quickly rose to become a Belgian classic. In 2006, Achouffe was bought by Duvel Moortgat.

AFFLIGEM

www.affligembeer.be

IN 1970, THE FAMILY BREWERY De Smedt in Opwijk acquired the licence to brew the beers in the town of Affligem's Benedictine monastery, whose site dates back to 1790. Due to their great success, Heineken bought De Smedt's brewery in 1999. Next to the Dubbel and Tripel, the Blond is the most famous. Affligem has also taken on the brewing of Postel abbey, through whom they offer the same three styles.

BELGOO

www.belgoobeer.be

BELGOO BEERS ARE CREATED and brewed by Jo Van Aert in the Brasserie La Binchoise in Binche. Van Aert founded the company in 2007. He makes bottle-conditioned ales using various types of grain: the blond Magus (6.6% ABV) contains barley and wheat malt as well as oats and spelt; the blond, dry-hopped Luppo (6.5% ABV) is made with barley and oats. The Saisonneke is a refreshingly dry-hopped Saison.

BELGOO SAISONNEKE

BOSTEELS DEUS BRUT DES FLANDRES

BLAUGIES

www.brasseriedeblaugies.com

FROM THE OUTSIDE, the brewhouse at Blaugies looks like a shed, but from this small system originate the finest effervescent saisons. Pierre-Alex Cartier and Marie-Noëlle Pourtois started the farmhouse-brewery in 1988 and passed it on to their sons. Cédric runs the attached restaurant and Kévin is the brewer. Their unique Saison d'Epeautre (6% ABV) is made with buckwheat. In 2013, they collaborated with the US brewery Hill Farmstead (see p.191) to produce Vermontoise (6% ABV), a spelt-saison spiced with Amarillo.

BOSTEELS

www.bestbelgianspecialbeers.be

BOSTEELS USED TO FOCUS on pils brewing, but since the 1990s they have turned to speciality ales. Pauwel Kwak (8% ABV) is on the sweet side and known for its unusual drinking glass, originally designed for coachmen. Tripel Karmeliet (8% ABV) is a fruity three-grain ale. The spicy Deus Brut des Flandres (see also Malheur, p.93) is a true innovation. The brewery, founded in 1791, is run by Ivo Bosteels and his son Antoine.

BROOTCOORENS

www.bierenaturelle.be

IN THE 1990S, ALAIN BROOTCOORENS began brewing and working on recipes in his garage. In December 2000, he opened his business in the small town of Erquelinnes as a part-time brewer. His passion is locally produced beers of high quality: for example a blonde and brown Angelus, both all-natural bottle-fermented ales. His place is open on Saturdays for visitors and offers the opportunity to use his equipment for customer brews on demand.

CARACOLE

www.brasserie-caracole.be

FRANÇOIS TONGLET STARTED Caracole in 1990. At first, the brewery was situated in a shed in Namur, later moving into a beautiful 18th-century brewery in Falmignoul, formerly the home of Brasserie Lamotte. Tonglet still works with the old vertical brewhouse with direct wood firing. Caracole offers four bottle-fermented beers: the amber ale Caracole (8% ABV), the rich brown Nostradamus (9.5% ABV), the dry golden Saxo (8% ABV) and the lightly spiced wheat Troublette (5% ABV).

CAZEAU

www.brasseriedecazeau.be

THE ORIGINS OF farmhouse brewery Cazeau go back to the 18th century. After 35 years of closure, Laurent Agache and Quentin Mariage, both descendants of the owning family, decided to revive the brewery in 2004. They renovated the building and bought used equipment in England. The cousins brew several bottle-fermented ales under the label Tournay, and a delicious annual limited edition called Saison Cazeau (5% ABV), spiced with fresh elderflowers.

CHIMAY

www.chimay.com

THE ABBEY OF NOTRE DAME de Scourmont is a pioneer of monastic brewing in Belgium: it was the first to sell its beer commercially in 1862 and the first to use the appellation "Trappist" after World War I. In 1992 they invested in a bigger brewhouse. Many ascribe a loss of spiciness in their beers – the Rouge (7% ABV), the Tripel (8% ABV), and the Bleue (9% ABV) – to the new facilities, but most agree that this quality is regained after ageing the bottles.

CNUDDE

www.eine.be/index.php/nl/brouwerij-cnudde

IN 1919, THE CNUDDE FAMILY bought a brewery in Eine, north of Oudenaarde, and gave it their family name. Their Flanders Brown Ale, first released in 1933, is brewed using open fermentation. Usually their Cnudde Bruin (5% ABV) is only available in kegs, but for special events they bottle at Strubbe in Ichtegem (see p.94). The brothers Lieven, Steven, and Piet Cnudde also have other occupations – they brew depending on the community's demand. Once a year they release Bizon (7% ABV), a kriek with cherries from their own garden.

DE CAM

www.decam.be

PALM BREWERY'S MANAGER Willem Van Herreweghen set up De Cam in the village of Gooik in the 1990s. At that time only two other gueuze blenders were active in Payottenland: 3 Fonteinen (see p.79) and Hanssens. De Cam's first blend was released in 1997. Today's director, Karel Goddeau, studied brewing in Ghent, but was disappointed with the little they taught about spontaneous fermentation.

DE GRAAL TRIPEL

Luckily this did not diminish his passion. He blends lambics from Lindemans (see p.93), Girardin (see p.92), and Boon (see pp.82–83) to create his gueuzes and krieks.

DE DOCHTER VAN DE KORENAAR

www.dedochtervandekorenaar.be

IN AROUND 1550 EMPEROR Charles V preferred the juice of the "daughter of the ear of corn" to wine, claims Ronald Mengerink, who started his brewery, De Dochter van de Korenaar, in 2007. And he does his best to convert today's gourmets to the Renaissance emperor's attitude. His blond Noblesse (5.5% ABV), the decently smoked Bravoure (6.5% ABV), and the rich, creamy, but crisp Embrasse (9% ABV) have been available in New York's restaurants since 2009. Several oak-aged editions are also produced.

DE DOLLE BROUWERS

www.dedollebrouwers.be

MAVERICK IN APPEARANCE, the beers of De Dolle Brouwers ("The Mad Brewers") have a truly individual character. Kris Herteleer, the founder and boss, breathed new life into Belgian beer culture: in 1980, this educated medic revived a run-down brewery in the village of Esen near Diksmuide and established one of the first microbreweries in the country. The beers are brewed with an intricate malt composition and hops from nearby Poperinge. Their first Oerbier, a reddish brown mixed-fermentation brew, develops in sourness as it ages.

DE GRAAL

www.degraal.be

FROM THE BEGINNING, the idea was to offer a wide range of quality beers. That is why De Graal Brewery produces classics such as the Blond (6.5% ABV), the Tripel (9% ABV), and the Dubbel (6.5% ABV), as well as some variations like Gember (8% ABV), a blond spiced with ginger, or Slock (6.5% ABV), a bitter blond brewed with US hops. Wim Saeyens, a graduate from Ghent brewing school with a PhD in pharmaceutical science, started the microbrewery in the Flemish Ardennes in 2002 and his business has enjoyed consistent growth ever since.

DE HALVE MAAN

www.halvemaan.be

DE HALVE MAAN ("The Half Moon") is the only remaining family-run brewery in the heart of Bruges. In 1856, the Maes family began brewing sour brown ale. The next generation made English-style stouts and pale ales, and in the 1980s Véronique Maes introduced an ale called Straffe Hendrik before the company ceased operations. In 2005, Véronique's son, Xavier Vanneste, revitalized the brewery, successfully launching Brugse Zot, and bringing back Straffe Hendrik.

DE KONINCK

www.dekoninck.be

THE FAMILY BREWERY De Koninck was bought by Duvel Moortgat in 2010, but is still run as an autonomous brand. De Koninck, whose origins date back to 1833, has influenced Belgian beer culture deeply: being the only city brewery in Antwerp, it has become an icon of the Flemish metropolis. De Koninck's main product, a Belgian pale ale (5% ABV), has become a benchmark of the style. It is served in a glass called a *bolleke*, a term also used for ordering beer.

DE RYCK

www.brouwerijderyck.be

IN 1886, FOUNDER OF DE RYCK, Gustaaf De Ryck, went to Bremen to learn brewing. Today's fourth-generation owner also went to Germany – and to Ghent – to learn the craft and is one of the few female brewers in Belgium. An De Ryck took over the family business in the 1970s. De Ryck's flagship beer is the Special (5% ABV), which An brews using a recipe from the 1920s. De Ryck also sells fruit beers and fine Belgian classics such as the award-winning Arend Tripel.

DUPONT

www.brasserie-dupont.com

IN 1986, THE "YEAR OF THE BEER" in Belgium, the small family-run brewery, Dupont, gained popularity beyond its region of Hainaut – it developed rapidly and became one of the world's most recognized Belgian breweries. Dupont still brews using direct firing and uses square fermentation vessels for a distinct flavour. Moinette (both blond and brown) was their regional best-seller before Saison Dupont became their flagship beer.

DE RYCK AREND TRIPEL

DUVEL MOORTGAT

www.duvelmoortgat.be

TO COMPETE WITH THE GREAT British ales that flooded Belgium, Moortgat (founded in 1871) introduced Duvel (8.5 ABV%) in 1923. The beer was recognized as the pinnacle of the golden ale style. The brewery, renamed Duvel Moortgat, went public in 1999 and invested in the speciality segment: breweries like the Czech Bernard (see p.104), the US brewery Ommegang (see p.151), and the Belgian Achouffe (see p.90) belong to the group, which after a share buy-back and a delisting from the stock exchange is still family-controlled.

GÉANTS

www.brasseriedesgeants.com

BREW-ENGINEER PIERRE DELCOIGNE restored a 13th-century castle in Irchonwelz, installed a brewhouse, and opened his Géants ("Giants") Brewery in 2000. He uses malted barley from the region and hops from Poperinge. His first and most popular beer is Gouyasse (6% ABV) – an unspiced, bottle-conditioned blonde. Delcoigne is also head of the nearby Brasserie Ellezelloise, known for its Quintine ales and the rich Hercule Stout (9% ABV). Both breweries are now sold under the label Brasserie des Légendes.

GIRARDIN

NO WEBSITE, NO E-MAIL, NO BREWERY visits – the largest of the authentic lambic brewers and gueuze blenders, Girardin, is also the most withdrawn, although it is open for beer sales on weekdays. Since 1882 the family has brewed on their farm at Sint-Ulriks-Kapelle. They grow their own wheat and barley. In winter they brew lambics, in summer a pils, the Ulricher Extra. Much praised is their Gueuze Girardin 1882 (5% ABV), also known as Black Label, for its moderate sourness and balanced complexity.

GLAZEN TOREN

www.glazentoren.be

GLAZEN TOREN BREWERY came into being when beer writer Jef van den Steen teamed up with beer enthusiast Dirk De Pauw to indulge their passion. They began with home-brewing but quickly realized that they would need to expand their knowledge of the brewing process. So they enrolled in a

three-year class at the Ghent brewing school to become qualified brewmasters. Together with Mark De Neef, they found a building in Erpe-Mere, East Flanders, and in 2004 the first beer was released: Saison d'Erpe Mere (6.5% ABV). Glazen Toren enjoyed success quickly, exporting to the US and Japan. Shortly afterwards in 2006 and then again in 2008 they had to expand their facilities.

HET ANKER

www.hetanker.be

IN 1990, CHARLES LECLEF, a descendant of the family who bought Het Anker ("The Anchor") Brewery in 1872, took over the business. After what had been a serious decline in the 1980s, Leclef reconstructed the historical buildings in the town of Mechelen, modernized the production system, revised the product line, opened a hotel, and installed a distillery. Next to their classic Gouden Carolus, a blond ale with 8.5% ABV, they introduced specialities like Cuvée van de Keizer (11% ABV).

HOEGAARDEN

www.hoegaarden.com

THE WITBIER STYLE (Belgian wheat) was almost extinct when Pierre Celis revived an old brewery in 1966 in Hoegaarden, a small place next to Leuven and a former boomtown of beer production. His refreshing witbier, seasoned with coriander and orange peel, became a success and is often regarded as the perfect summer beer. Today the brewery belongs to Anheuser-Busch InBev. Hoegaarden (4.9% ABV) is available around the world, but Hoegaarden Grand Cru (8.5% ABV) is not widely exported.

HOF TEN DORMAAL

www.hoftendormaal.com

WITHOUT THEIR FARM, the beers of the Hof ten Dormaal Brewery would not exist. The brewery, established in 2009, is entirely self-sustaining. The Janssens grow their own barley and hops, use water from their own well, and cultivate their own yeast. Their energy comes from the rapeseed oil from their fields. They brew various ales including a curious witloof (chicory) beer and have started a barrel-ageing project with casks from all over Europe. The first, a strong blond from a jenever barrel, was released in June 2012.

HUYGHE

www.delirium.be

IN 1906, LÉON HUYGHE, who came from the hops town of Poperinge, and his wife Delfina, a brewer's daughter, took over a brewery in Melle, East Flanders. Eighty years later, their granddaughter Any and her husband Jean De Laet developed the modest lager brewery into a site for speciality ales. Their breakthrough was Delirium Tremens, a blond ale (8.5% ABV) in a stoneware-look bottle with pink elephants on the label. In 2012, Huyghe opened a new plant, capable of producing 350,000hl (214,000 barrels). Most of their beer is exported.

JANDRAIN-JANDRENOUILLE

www.hesbayebrabanconne.be/spip.php?article555

THE WELL-MADE CREATIONS of two engineers who converted an old farmhouse into a brewery, Jandrain-Jandrenouille, in 2007, are IV Saison (a blond, 6.5% ABV), V Cense (an amber, 7% ABV) and VI Wheat (a Belgian wit without any spices added; 5% ABV). Nobody will ever know the truth about their unreleased brews I, II, and III, but many beer lovers wonder what style the VII is going to be. The brewers are hoping to increase their capacity, which is currently a mere 8,000 bottles a year.

LEFEBVRE

www.brasserielefebvre.be

FOUNDED IN 1876, the Lefebvre brasserie is run by Ann and Philippe and their children Paul and Céline, the fifth and sixth generations of the family to work there. In 1983, the Abbey of Floreffe gave them the licence to brew their beers, although Lefebvre also offers fruit beers, saisons, and witbiers. The tasty Barbãr (8% ABV), brewed with honey, was introduced in 1989. The research for the right hop formula for Hopus took about two years; the strong blonde and bitter ales (8.3% ABV) are brewed with five different varieties.

LINDEMANS

www.lindemans.be

THANKS TO THE FAMILY'S EXPERTISE, Lindemans, a former farm located west of Brussels where brewing was originally a side line, has now devoted itself to the brewing of lambic and gueuze for over 60 years. Bucking trends at the time, Lindemans revived their Faro beer in the 1970s – a lambic sweetened with rock sugar, and developed further fruit beers alongside the Kriek. The outstanding beers from this most successful lambic craft brewery are Gueuze and Kriek Cuvée René.

MALHEUR

www.malheur.be

MALHEUR OR BOSTEELS? In 2001–2002 both breweries in the small city of Buggenhout launched a world first. Bière brut: brewed in Belgium, bottle fermented using champagne yeast, shaken and turned throughout, and then finally freed from the yeast. The resulting beers were wonderfully foamy and dry-fruity. Manu De Landtsheer, head brewer at Malheur, produces several other fine ales in his family brewery, which he restored in 1997. However, no festivity is complete without his Dark Brut or other champagne beers.

MORT SUBITE

www.mort-subite.be

COUNTLESS PEOPLE TASTED their first sour beer when they tried Mort Subite ("Sudden Death") in the centre of Brussels. The café Cour Royale was renamed after the popular local dice game, and the brewery De Keersmaeker was renamed after the café when it took it over in the 1970s. Since then the brewery itself has been taken over and now belongs to the Heineken group. Its Lambic, Gueuze, Faro, and the remarkable Oude Kriek continue to be brewed in the idyllic village of Kobbegem near Brussels.

ORVAL

www.orval.be

ORVAL IS THE ONLY BEER of the Wallonian Trappist Abbey, which was rebuilt in 1926; the brewery opened in 1931 to help repay construction costs. Dry, complex, elegant, with an intriguing development during ageing, Orval (6.2% ABV) is fermented and conditioned with various yeast strains, dry-hopped with fresh hop cones, and bottled with Brettanomyces added. In the young beer, fresh floral and herbal hop aromas dominate but after a month of lagering these yield to the more earthy perfumes of the wild yeasts. The true goût d'Orval (taste of Orval) takes about a year before it emerges.

OUD BEERSEL

www.oudbeersel.com

THEORETICALLY, LAMBIC BEER can be brewed anywhere. However, it is only found in Belgium, primarily in a small area to the west of Brussels centred on the small town of Beersel. In 2005, courageous Beersel residents revitalized the disused Oud Beersel Brewery founded in 1882. Today Gert Christiaens and his father Jos produce both the excellent Oude Geuze and Oude Kriek, as well as two ales marketed under the Bersalis brand.

PALM

wwww.palm.be

IN AROUND 1920, unable to afford a refrigeration plant for the production of modern lager beers, the Steenhuffel village brewery began brewing a top-fermented Spéciale, a little stronger than pils both in terms of alcohol and taste. It became a huge success. Palm became a cult hit in the Netherlands, and following the 1958 World Fair became synonymous with Belgian beer. Fortunately, the family used this success to keep beer, such as Boon's Gueuze-Lambics (see pp.82–83; joint venture) or Rodenbach's Flemish Red Ales (see p.88; takeover), alive.

ROCHEFORT

www.abbaye-rochefort.be

THE TRAPPISTS IN ROCHEFORT brew three brown ales, all using the same recipe, differing only in strength: 7.5% ABV (6), 9.2% ABV (8), and 11.3% ABV (10). Visitors can spend the night at the Abbey Notre-Dame de Saint-Rémy, although the beers are not sold there. The two strongest are available throughout Belgium, although 6, which is brewed once a year, is hard to find. To buy 6 try Rochefort's small shop or its cafés.

ROMAN

www.roman.be

EVEN IN BELGIUM it is rare for a brewery to be run by the 14th generation of the same family. The first evidence of a brewer named Roman in the village of Mater, near the city of Oudenaarde, originates from the 16th century. Today, Carlo and Lode Roman run a medium-sized business brewing virtually all styles of beer prized in Belgium: from lager beers and witbier, to strong ales (Sloeber) and abbey beers (Ename). A regional speciality is the dark brown ale, Adriaen Brouwer.

RULLES

www.larulles.be

THE TOWN OF RULLES is situated close to Orval, which sets expectations high as it is close to the famous Orval Brewery (see p.93). However, what Grégory Verhelst has produced in his brewery, named after the town where it is located, deserves the greatest respect in its own right. His first ales (Blonde, Brune, Triple) were clean and well-balanced, but the 2005 creations were sensational: the fresh summer ale Estivale, rich in aromas, and the dark flavoursome Cuvée Meilleurs Vœux. Since then, Rulles has tripled production to 2,500hl (1,500 barrels) and in 2012 the brewery was expanded again to a capacity of 5,000hl (3,000 barrels).

SILENRIEUX

www.brasseriedesilenrieux.be

SILENRIEUX IS A VERY SPECIAL BREWERY. On his farm at the foot of the Ardennes, Eric Bedoret cultivates old varieties of grains such as spelt and the pseudo-grain buckwheat. Since the mid-1990s, together with scientists from the Centre for Malting and Brewing Science at the University of Leuven, he has developed a witbier from spelt (Joseph) and a dark buckwheat ale (Sara). Since then, further special beers have been added, including a gluten-free organic ale. Thanks to its success, Bedoret's harvest has long ceased to be sufficient to supply the brewery.

SILLY

www.silly-beer.com

THE NAME OF SILLY BREWERY is not meant as a joke, although it certainly helps to make it memorable. The family brewery, which began in 1850 and is now run by the sixth generation of the same family, is simply named after its location, which in turn is named after the river Sylle that winds through the heavily wooded province of Hainault. Half the brewery's production is bottom-fermented beers, while the traditional top-fermented programme includes a brown beer named Saison and the nutty Scotch, recently available in a barrel-aged version. In 1975, Silly took over the Tennstedt-de Croes Brewery's legendary range of beers under the name Double Enghien. In 1990, a white beer known as Titje was introduced, which has helped the business grow further. Other beers include Saison de Silly, Double Enghien, and Divine.

SINT BERNARDUS

www.sintbernardus.be

THE LITTLE TOWN OF WATOU profits from its location in the hop-growing region of Poperinge and its proximity to St Sixtus Abbey, Westvleteren (see p.89). Between 1946 and 1992 Watou was the production site for the monks' commercial beers. Abt 12 and Prior 8 are still brewed according to Trappist recipes using Westvleteren yeast, and thanks to the brewery's salesmanship, the excellent Tripel can be enjoyed as far afield as Israel or Kazakhstan. However, it tastes best in Watou's wonderful beer restaurant 't Hommelhof.

SINT CANARUS

www.sintcanarus.be

PIET MEIRHAEGHE, A FOOD ENGINEER, calls his brewery, founded in 2002, "Belgium's smallest". In fact, due to lack of capacity, his top-selling beer, the incredibly dark Sint Canarus Tripel, is brewed at the Proefbrouwerij in Lochristi. In the village of Gottem in East Flanders, idyllically situated on a neglected arm of the river Leie, Mierhaeghe brews the blond ale De Maeght van Gottem, which is supplied with a fresh hop cone in each bottle. In addition, he organizes entertaining beer seminars as Dr Canarus.

STRUBBE

www.brouwerij-strubbe.be

IN A TYPICALLY BELGIAN SCENE, in the small parish of Ichtegem in West Flanders two structures extend into the sky from the market square – the church tower and the brewery chimney. In 1854, the Strubbe family started brewing beer here for the villagers – and shortly thereafter, the entire region. The seventh generation of the same family is still here today. Since the mass closures of breweries in the 1970s, the Strubbes have gradually and intelligently improved their equipment and beer-making programme. Today it ranges from classic table beer to the remarkable Keyte Dobbel-Tripel.

TILQUIN

www.gueuzerietilquin.be

THE BEGINNINGS OF TILQUIN Brewery could not have been more auspicious. Shortly after Pierre Tilquin, an educated bioengineer, opened his lambic blendery in Bierghes in May 2011, his Oude Gueuze, in bottles and on draught, was sold simultaneously at two bars in Brussels – Moeder Lambic and Café Délirium, as well as in the Monk's Café in Philadelphia. Tilquin is celebrated as the only blendery in Wallonia. He buys young lambic, matures it in oak barrels for years, blends different ages, and conditions the blend after bottling for six months.

TIMMERMANS

www.brtimmermans.be

FOUNDED IN THE 18TH CENTURY, Timmermans brewery is renowned as the oldest existing producer of lambic. In Itterbeek, west of Brussels, it brews a broad palette of gueuze, lambic, and fruit beers, including new creations such as a pumpkin lambic or Blanche Lambicus, a witbier made like a lambic. From 1985–2013, they also brewed the dark sour beer speciality from Bruges, Bourgogne des Flandres. The brewery has been part of the John Martin group since 1993.

TRIEST

www.dentriest.be

MARC STRUYF BEGAN PRODUCING BEER in his small brewery, Triest, in Kapelle-op-den-Bos, 19km (12 miles) north of Brussels in 2009. Before that he had occasionally brewed his own beer in the kitchen of his pub restaurant. Since then, he has quickly earned respect with his clean cherry beers, and the Triest IPA – made with the new hop variety Mosaic – won the Public's Choice Award at the 2013 Bruges Beer festival.

TROUBADOUR (BROUWERIJ THE MUSKETEERS)

www.troubadourbeers.com

THE BREWERY'S ENGLISH NAME, "The Musketeers", is no accident – it was set up by a group of four brewing engineers who came together in 2000 (of whom only two remain at the brewery). They were interested in English beers. However, their creations, such as the mild, dark red stout (Troubadour Obscura) or the pale ale (Spéciale) are all refined with Belgian finesse. With Magma, the brewers have created a highly individual beer: a tripel with the vigorous hop accent of an IPA. The Musketeers brew in the Proefbrouwerij in Lochristi.

TROUBADOUR MAGMA

URTHEL

www.urthel.com

SINCE 2000, HILDEGARD VAN OSTADEN has been composing her exquisite beers in Koningshoeven, which is also home to the Trappist La Trappe beers. Her brewery, De Leyerth, now renamed Urthel, attempts to bring a fresh spirit to Belgian beer styles with exciting hop additions. One example of this is Hop-It, a Belgian-style IPA that has a thick foam and a rich, spicy-fruit flavour. The brewery also produces delicate, choice malty beers, such as the top-fermented, bottle-conditioned, bitter-hoppy and warming dubbel Parlus Magnificum. In 2011, van Ostaden established the Hoppeschuur in Ruiselede, West Flanders; an experimental brewery open to the public.

VAPEUR

www.vapeur.com

AT THE BRASSERIE À VAPEUR ("The Steam Brewery"), Belgian brewing tradition meets the craft beer movement. The brewery was founded in 1785 in the Wallonian village of Pipaix. It was forced to close in 1983, but then the ancient facility was bought and restored by a beer-loving couple, Jean-Louis Dits and his wife Sittelle. Jean-Louis' entire brewing expertise before setting up the brewery stemmed from home-brewing experiments and enthusiasm. He had visited the former Dupont factory in 1967 and had never forgotten the warmth and excitement he felt for the old brewery, so when his chance came to buy it he jumped at the opportunity. His complex Saison de Pipaix and the strong amber ale Cochonne, along with boldly seasoned lager beers, demonstrate his imaginative mastery of the craft.

VERHAEGHE

www.brouwerijverhaeghe.be

NORTH-WESTERN FLANDERS, along the river Leie between Kortrijk and Ghent, is the home of sour red-brown ales. The Verhaeghe family business, founded by Paul Verhaeghe in 1885 in the village of Vichte, is one of the few breweries in the area to have survived the boom in lager beers of recent times. Even its simple, sour-fruity Vichtenaar is stored in oak barrels for eight months; the complex Duchesse de Bourgogne is stored for one-and-a-half years. The Echt Kriekenbier is made from a red-brown ale and cherries matured in oak barrels.

CZECH REPUBLIC

It is impossible to write about the Czech Republic without using the words "beer" and "great". If the UK is famed for developing dark, ale-style beers, then this region can lay claim to a beer style that has swept the world – pilsner. It was here in the mid-19th century that a brewer in the town of Plzeň pioneered a new golden, bottom-fermented beer. Flavoured with the aromatic, locally grown and distinctively citrussy Žatec hops, it is a style that has been widely emulated but rarely bettered. Josef Grolle's creation also used the prized locally grown Moravian barley, which is still the sweet staple of most Czech beers today. Before this time, the local beer was likely to have been top-fermented and of variable quality, and many beers from the area were brown in colour. Grolle's clear, golden, cold-fermented beer was a revelation. Pleasing to the eye when poured, it became an instant success.

Czech breweries are proud of their heritage and there are many breweries with long and illustrious histories. The country boasts the oldest brewpubs in the world and companies like Budweiser Budvar are rightly prized far beyond the borders of the Czech Republic. But no country's brewing reputation can remain strong if its beer culture stands still, and today many new brewers are now joining the Czech beer scene. On the outskirts of Plzeň is the Hotel Purkmistr (see p.102), which opened in 2007. In an effort to challenge the conventional wisdom, the brewery's range includes an unfiltered pale lager, a cherry beer, and a cappuccino-flavoured beer. Once a year, in September, brewer Petr Míč hosts a beer festival in the yard of his brewery and the surrounding streets, which features more than 140 beers from the Czech Republic's new wave of brewers, where drinkers can discover that there is much more to Czech beer than just its glorious pilsners.

BUDWEISER BUDVAR

Southern Bohemia's most famous brewery, Budweiser Budvar, uses traditional brewing methods, high-quality raw materials, pristine water, and long lagering – resulting in one of the best beers in the Czech Republic.

IN 1895, THE SOUTHERN Bohemian city of Budweis was home to a sizeable German-speaking minority who ran the Budweiser brewery. The Czech-speaking community decided to band together and set up a rival brewery to cater to their own tastes, and Budvar was born. The beer they produced was rich golden Světlý Ležák, or pale lager beer, which has since gone on to become one of the world's best-known Bohemian beers.

Today, the brewery's home is a state-of-the-art brewhouse with gleaming copper domes, tiled floors, and large windows that let light in on the brewing process; the traditional double decoction process is used. Malted barley comes from Moravia and whole-leaf Saaz hops go into the boil, while the water comes from a well deep beneath the city. Budvar undergoes 90 days of cold-conditioning, or lagering, in which the beer "sleeps" to emerge fresh and vital. For many years, the brewery focused on its 12° plato Světlý Ležák and a 10° plato lager for draught taps in pubs. However, in 1997 it launched Premier Select, also known as Bud Super Strong. This was followed by Budvar Dark and a yeast beer. Budvar is known as Czechvar in the US due to a legal dispute over the use of the Budweiser name.

THE FACTS...

OWNER Czech Government
FOUNDED 1895
ADDRESS Budweiser Budvar, Karolíny Světlé 4, České Budějovice 370 21
WEBSITE www.budejovickybudvar.cz
PHILOSOPHY To use the best raw materials and have a stubborn commitment to traditional brewing practices and the highest quality control

Cool customer
A slow maturation of 90 days at a temperature close to freezing is key to Budvar's famed vitality

TASTING NOTES

PREMIER SELECT STRONG LAGER, 7.6% ABV
Bright gold in the glass, this beer has an elegant nose of honey and almonds, while the palate is drenched with fiery alcohol at first before being caressed by honey, almond, and cherry flavours, leading to a lasting dry and bittersweet finish.
FOOD PAIRING: Use this beer as an apéritif with tapas such as salami, prosciutto, or mild chorizo.

IMPORTED DARK LAGER 4.7% ABV
Known as a Tmavý Ležák in Czech, this is a midnight-dark beer that has coffee, light toffee, and smoke leading to an elegant and medium-bodied mouthfeel, with ground roast coffee beans and toffee-meets-vanilla sweetness before a dry finish.
FOOD PAIRING: This big-tasting beer is assertive enough to stand up to the classic Czech stew goulash, as the roast and smoke notes will cut through the richness of the sauce.

CZECH IMPORTED LAGER PALE LAGER, 5% ABV
Rich deep gold with a sweet, grainy nose and a hint of lemon and spice in the background. The palate is bittersweet and juicy, finishing with a dry, sweetish, and appetizing bitterness.
FOOD PAIRING: Try with grilled garlic prawns. The bitterness of the beer teases out the juicy sweetness of the shellfish.

BUDWEISER BUDVAR PREMIER SELECT

BUDWEISER BUDVAR IMPORTED DARK LAGER

BUDWEISER BUDVAR CZECH IMPORTED LAGER

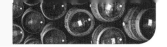

NA RYCHTĚ

The city of Ústí nad Labem is home to the major brewery Zlatopramen, which was bought by Heineken in 2008. In 2010, citizens who fancied a local beer got a boost with the opening of the brewpub Na Rychtě.

THE FACTS...

OWNER Pivovar Hotel Na Rychtě
FOUNDED 2010
ADDRESS Pivovar Hotel Na Rychtě, Klášterní 75/9, Ústí nad Labem 400 01
WEBSITE www.pivovarnarychte.cz
PHILOSOPHY Traditional Czech beer brewed in a lively brewpub and restaurant

THE HOME OF NA RYCHTĚ is a busy 19th-century beer hall and hotel just off the main square in the northern Bohemian city of Ústí nad Labem. Inside the hall it's all dark wood, individual booths, and a buzzy, boisterous atmosphere as waiters weave in and out of the drinkers, their arms full of plates of rich Czech cuisine and foaming glasses of the beer brewed on-site. At the back of the hall, there's a tiny, shiny, copper-faced kit, which blends into the space's general aesthetic. It's a small operation, capable of producing 1,000 litres (6 barrels) in one brew, using the classic double decoction mash, floor-malted barley, and the mighty Czech hop variety Saaz. Because of the double decoction process, the brewing day is 12 hours long. When the beer is ready it is pumped downstairs into a cellar where it ferments for 7–12 days, before spending at least a month lagering in closed vessels. There are no short cuts here.

Jaroslav Rottenborn is in charge of brewing. He is a highly experienced brewer who spent time with Zlatopramen before it was bought by Heineken, and Breznak, who make their beer over the river Labe in nearby Velké Březno. The selection of beers brewed includes the usual pale lager and, more unusually, a cranberry beer, in which cranberry juice is added after fermentation. Surprisingly, there is no dark beer produced, nor is there a wheat beer, as the brewmaster does not want a different, possibly tricky, yeast strain in the brewhouse. The hotel runs an annual beer fair in the spring, which features a selection of small local breweries.

TASTING NOTES

BRUSINKA FRUIT LAGER, 4.8% ABV
With cranberry juice added during the lagering process, the aim is to allow the sour-sweet notes of the fruit to come through, as opposed to just sweetness. The hop character is light, while the cranberry juice gives a hot summer's day quenching feel.

FOOD PAIRING: The tartness of the beer would lift the sweetness of grilled sausages served with potato pancakes.

MAZEL PALE LAGER, 5.2% ABV
The classic Světlý Ležák (otherwise known as pale lager) is a ghost of gold in the glass. The nose has sweet malt, toasted grain, and Saaz spiciness on the nose, while the medium body is bittersweet and has a caramel lightness before it finishes dry and bitter.

FOOD PAIRING: Try it with roast duck, gravy, and red onion cabbage, or similar meaty dishes, and see how the bitterness of the beer cuts through the sauce and lifts the sweetness of the meat.

VOJTĚCH AMBER, 4.8% ABV
Vojtěch pours a gleaming, sleek, amber-chestnut into the glass beneath an espresso-coloured head of foam. The nose is light sweet caramel and earthy hop, while the palate is at once sweet, bitter, earthy, dry, and medium in its fullness.

FOOD PAIRING: The caramelized malts suggest that it's time for a barbecue, with perhaps some grilled chicken, and if you're feeling virtuous, slap on some radicchio as well.

NA RYCHTĚ BRUSINKA

NA RYCHTĚ MAZEL

NA RYCHTĚ VOJTECH

PILSNER URQUELL

When the beer of Plzeň was considered undrinkable, a Bavarian brewer was called in to help and in 1842 Josef Groll came up with the world's first golden lager. Pilsner Urquell still remains a byword for good beer.

Worldwide wonder
Much emulated but rarely bettered, the Pilsner beer style is brewed on every continent

GOLDEN LAGER WAS BORN in the Bohemian city of Plzeň in 1842 when local worthies decided to do something about the bad reputation of the local beer. Bavarian brewer Josef Groll was hired and he produced a gold-coloured, bottom-fermented beer, which conquered Plzeň and Prague, before beginning its journey across Europe. So popular was the beer that all manner of similarly golden lagers were dubbed Pilsner, or later in Germany, Pilsener, and in 1898 the trademark Pilsner Urquell – meaning "Pilsner from the original source" – was registered to forestall this wave of imitators.

During the communist years, Pilsner Urquell, along with Budvar, were the two main Czech beers found in the west, but with the Velvet Revolution in 1989, the brewery left behind the old style of fermentation, in pitch-lined oak vessels in underground tunnels, and plumped for stainless steel conical fermentation and maturation tanks. Further change came in 1999 when the brewery was bought by global brewers SABMiller. All this is of little concern to the thousands who visit the tourist attractions of the site, which can be likened to a kind of Disneyland of brewing. The brewing process is resolutely unchanged. A triple decoction mash still takes place, using well-modified lager malt, while the brewing liquor is soft. Saaz hops go into the copper, and fermentation is for ten days, followed by 30 days' maturation. In Prague, unpasteurized Pilsner Urquell can be drunk, served from polyester-film sacks kept in vast steel tanks.

THE FACTS...

OWNER SAB-Miller
FOUNDED 1842
ADDRESS U Prazdroje 64/7, Východní Předměstí, 301 00 Plzeň
WEBSITE www.pilsner-urquell.com
PHILOSOPHY To brew the original golden lager

TASTING NOTES

PILSNER URQUELL PALE LAGER, 4.4% ABV
Pale gold in colour, the fragrance of this beer has a subtle, sweet-malty character with resiny hop, a hint of honey, and herbal aromas. The palate is gently grainy and herbal-tasting with a hint of light citrus. There is a pleasing bitterness and grainy dryness in the finish.
FOOD PAIRING: The dryness and maltiness of Pilsner Urquell makes it an excellent partner for naturally sweet meats such as pork, or grilled meats and barbecues.

GAMBRINUS PALE LAGER, 5% ABV
This excellent golden beer is an easy-drinking, full-bodied, pale lager with hints of lemon, a malty-sweet, citrussy palate, and a crisp, full finish.
FOOD PAIRING: As with Pilsner Urquell, sweet, mild-flavoured meats such as pork or chicken match well with the crispness of the beer and the full-bodied mouthfeel.

PILSNER URQUELL PILSNER URQUELL

PILSNER URQUELL GAMBRINUS

FOR ANY BEER TRAVELLER, THE CITY OF PRAGUE WITH ITS GREAT BARS AND OUTDOOR CAFÉS IS A MUST-VISIT DESTINATION

THE CZECH REPUBLIC IS HOME TO A CLASSIC AND WORLD-RENOWNED BEER STYLE – PILSNER – CREATED BY PILSNER URQUELL (SEE P.99)

PURKMISTR

Whether it's a classic Světlý Ležák, a dark lager, or a beer flavoured with cannabis or blueberry, Purkmistr has a brew for everyone – the brewery even has a beer spa, but that's not for drinking…

THE FACTS...

OWNER Lukrécius a.s.

FOUNDED 2007

ADDRESS Selská náves 2½, 32600 Plzeň

WEBSITE www.purkmistr.cz

PHILOSOPHY Beer, health and wellness, food, and sleep all on one site

IF YOU WANT A BATH IN BEER then you've come to the right place at Purkmistr, as a beer spa opened in the summer of 2012. Mind you, the same would be true if you wanted a bed for the night or something to eat. The brewery, which opened in 2007, is just one of the elements of this hotel/spa/restaurant complex, located on the outskirts of Plzeň about 90km (56 miles) west of Prague, and dating back to the 17th century. The brewery is housed in one of the dining areas; a well-burnished assembly of copper-covered vessels with a pleasing red-brick backdrop. Diners can tuck into such dishes as the Cooper's Skewer – a mammoth feast of pork fillet, pork tenderloin, and chicken breast grilled on a skewer – while enjoying a glass of the brewery's full-bodied 12° and watching the brewer do all the hard work.

As is usual for all punctilious Czech breweries, Purkmistr uses Moravian malt and Žatec hops and, like its bigger neighbour, Pilsner Urquell, several miles away, is blessed with very soft water, which is ideal for the beers it makes. Double or triple decoction is used, while lagers get three to four weeks for lagering and stronger beers receive seven to eight weeks. Two strains of yeast are used, one for cold-fermenting beers, another for the wheat beer Scribe. As well as making beers that fit the Czech-style spectrum, Purkmistr is known for adding unconventional flavours to its beers. These could mean beers flavoured with blueberry or blackberry fruit essence, though the more adventurous might be interested in Purkmistr's cannabis-flavoured beer. And after that a turn in the beer spa might do you a world of good.

TASTING NOTES

SVĚTLÝ LEŽÁK PALE LAGER, 4.8% ABV

This classic Czech pale lager is orange-gold in colour and sits beneath a meringue-white head of foam. Its nose offers notes of gently toasted grain and a pinch of aromatic grassiness; on the palate it has caramel, dryness, and a lingering bitter finish.

FOOD PAIRING: The crisp carbonation, grainy sweetness, and cutting bitterness of this classic Světlý Ležák provide an ideal foil for the bright, spicy flavours of Vietnamese, Thai, or even Mexican dishes.

PIVO WASABI SPICE LAGER, 4.8% ABV

No prizes for guessing the added ingredient in the brewery's Světlý Ležák – the wasabi gives the beer a ghostly greenish tinge while there is a slight trace on the nose. On the palate, the wasabi's heat is an intriguing counterpoint to the Světlý Ležák's malt sweetness and hop grassiness.

FOOD PAIRING: The top choice of food to accompany this beer is sushi. It will act as an extra source of heat.

POLOTMAVÝ LEŽÁK AMBER LAGER, 4.8% ABV

This is described as an "English-style beer", but in reality it's a classic Czech amber with a dark chestnut hue, caramelized malt, and Saaz herbal aromatics on the nose and a slightly toasty palate with a juicy toffee, dry finish.

FOOD PAIRING: Roast beef is an ideal companion as the caramel, toasty notes of the beer clamp onto the flavour of the meat and bring out its sweetness.

PURKMISTR
SVĚTLÝ LEŽÁK

PURKMISTR
PIVO WASABI

PURKMISTR
POLOTMAVÝ LEŽÁK

U MEDVÍDKŮ

Brewing made a welcome return to At The Little Bears restaurant in Prague in 2005. This resolutely "micro microbrewery" brews for the onsite restaurant and bar, which is a great favourite with both visitors and locals.

THE FACTS...

OWNER U Medvídků
FOUNDED 2005
ADDRESS Na Perštýně 7, 100 01 Praha 1
WEBSITE www.umedvidku.cz
PHILOSOPHY To show the manufacturing process at its best using traditional methods

U MEDVÍDKŮ MICROBREWERY was founded in 2005 in the At the Little Bears restaurant and bar, one of Prague's most popular outlets for Budvar. This was an overdue return to brewing in a historic building where beer had been made from the 15th century until the end of the 19th. It was later home to a cabaret before being left to deteriorate after the Socialist government confiscated it from its owners after World War II. Following the Velvet Revolution in 1989, the building was returned to the descendants of its rightful owners and was carefully and painstakingly restored into a characterful hotel and restaurant, which reopened in 2005. Part of the complex is in the old maltings, while some of the hotel rooms feature old brewing paraphernalia as a reminder of the past. The first beer was brewed in the restored brewery on 17th November 2005, exactly 15 years after the revolution in 1989. It's a small, almost Lilliputian, operation, seemingly invisible alongside the tables and chairs of the eating area in the maltings. But size is not what matters: the brewery says, "Our goal is not to manufacture the most beer, but to show the manufacturing process at its best, including procedures and equipment no longer in use today, such as stock cooling, open fermentation tanks, wooden lager barrels, and manual racking into bottles with patented caps".

The brewery can produce 250l (1.5 barrels) at a time and after the boil, the cooling occurs in an open vessel, reminiscent of a micro coolship, popular in the lambic breweries of Flanders. Open fermentation takes place in oak barrels, while maturation is in pitch-lined barrels. Maturation is usually carried out for a month, although the extra strong X-Beer 33 is left to mature for 200 days – the brewery claims that it is the strongest lager in the world when the level of alcohol content and the extract of the original wort content are taken into consideration. To complete its appeal to the beer lover, the brewery has a scheme whereby enthusiasts can pay to come and brew for a day and then collect their efforts when it is ready.

Time well spent
Maturation of at least a month helps bring out complex flavours

U MEDVÍDKŮ OLDGOTT

U MEDVÍDKŮ X-BEER 33

TASTING NOTES

OLDGOTT VIENNA/AMBER LAGER, 5.2% ABV
Caramel, roasted barley, and a hint of tantalizing spice aromas float upwards from a glass of this unfiltered, amber-coloured lager, which has been matured in oak barrels. The palate is sweetish, with more caramel, some dried fruit flavours, and a bittersweet finish.

FOOD PAIRING: Delicately flavoured meats such as pork schnitzel would be ideal with Oldgott, as the beer's roasted caramel notes would bring out the meat's sweetness.

X-BEER 33 STRONG LAGER, 12.6% ABV
A creamy collar of foam sits atop a dark chestnut-coloured beer; on the nose there's a pleasingly vinous, alcoholic sweetness with hints of musty cellar-like earthiness. The complex palate has a vinous, sweet, almost dessert wine mouthfeel with hints of cherry and honey, and all balanced by an earthy sternness.

FOOD PAIRING: A beer to drink on its own, offering up a contemplative sense of pleasure, or go dessert-crazy and match it with a bittersweet treat such as chocolate pudding.

BERNARD

www.bernard.cz

THE VELVET REVOLUTION OF 1989 brought with it both boom and bust for the Czech brewing industry. In the town of Humpolec, it initially looked like bust for the struggling local brewery, but ended up boom as the Bernard family stepped in and restored its fortunes under their own name. The brewery is now a thriving concern with its own maltings, while the beer is uniquely micro-filtered rather than pasteurized, giving beers such as the elegant pale lager Celebration and the luscious Dark a rich yet refreshing palate.

ČERNÁ HORA

www.pivovarcernahora.cz

MORAVIA IS BETTER KNOWN for its wine, but Černá Hora – named after the Black Mountain in the locality and the village it calls home – is one of the region's beer heroes and is based on a site where brewing has taken place since the late 19th century; written records indicate local brewing from the Middle Ages. Now part of the Lobkowicz brewing group, the brewery magics up a tempting range of beers including a crisp Světlý Ležák.

DĚTENICE

www.pivovardetenice.cz/en_pivovar.html

MEDIEVAL BANQUETS, buxom wenches, and jousting knights are a regular sight at the historic Dětenice château in north-eastern Bohemia. There was a brewery here once, but it closed during the Communist era. However, like many a medieval tale, there was a happy ending and brewing returned in 2003. Two beers are brewed: a pale aromatic lager and a dark brooding one, both fermented in wooden barrels.

JEŽEK

www.pivovar-jihlava.cz

JEŽEK HAS BEEN MAKING BEER in the Bohemia-Moravia border town of Jihlava since the 1860s. The name of the brewery means "hedgehog", but there's nothing remotely spiky about its range of beers, which cover the traditional and tempting spectrum of Czech classics including pale and dark lagers. The brewery is fairly unique in that it also produces a strong 8.1% ABV honey-gold lager – some would say Imperial Pils – and the rich and strong Jihlavský Grand 18°.

HEROLD

www.pivovar-herold.cz

IN THE AFTERMATH OF THE Velvet Revolution and the privatization of the brewing industry, Březnice-based Herold was one of the first to remind Czech beer lovers of their wheat beer heritage with its so-called Wheat Lager. Despite being discontinued in 2007, it was brought back two years later when the brewery came under Czech ownership. It remains a valuable part of their beer portfolio, which also includes a rich and creamy dark lager and a fresh, sprightly pale 12°.

KOZEL

www.beer-kozel.cz

THE TOWN OF VELKÉ POPOVICE has been home to Kozel since the 1870s, which is also when the brewery launched its famous goat emblem – "kozel" is Czech for goat – after a passing French artist painted it as thanks for the hospitality he had received. Now part of the SABMiller empire, Kozel produces a popular range of beers, including its award-winning 3.8% ABV dark lager. It also brews the dark and rich Master Tmavý 18° for Pilsner Urquell.

KRUŠOVICE

www.krusovice.cz

KRUŠOVICE IS A ROYAL BREWERY, no less. This long-established brewery in central Bohemia supplied beer to the Austro-Hungarian Emperor Rudolf II in 1583 and was royal-owned at one stage as well. A lot of beer has been brewed since then and nowadays, Krušovice is part of another empire, Heineken, which it joined in 2007. Its Imperial 12° is a superb expression of the spell that Moravian malt and Saaz hops can cast.

OSTRAVAR

www.pivovary-staropramen.cz/en/our-brands/ostravar

OSTRAVA IS THE CZECH REPUBLIC'S third largest city and the eponymous brewery has been here since the end of the 19th century. The city once had a strong industrial base, whose workers no doubt refreshed themselves with lashings of the local beer. The industry has gone, but the brewery still thrives with the likes of its bittersweet Premium 12° and the mixed-gas dark beer Velvet. Since 1997, it has been part of the Staropramen group, which itself is part of Molson-Coors.

PROTIVÍN MERLIN

PERNŠTEJN

www.pernstejn.cz

THIS VENERABLE BREWERY with its own maltings has been a rock-solid part of the eastern Bohemian city of Pardubice since 1872, although brewing in the locale goes back a few centuries earlier. A traditional and well-made selection of pale, amber, and dark lagers keeps locals happy, but what really makes Pernštejn stand out is its Pardubický Porter, an 8% ABV, richly malty, darkly sensuous beast of a Baltic porter that was first brewed in 1891 and is a rare survivor of this particular style.

PIVOVAR EGGENBERG

www.eggenberg.cz

EGGENBERG IS IN THE GORGEOUS old town of Český Krumlov and is the only brewery in the world to be actually located in a UNESCO site. Beer has been made here since the Middle Ages, although the brewery was previously called the Schwarzenberg Brewery. Traditional pale lager beers are very much Eggenberg's main focus, but it also produces an appetizing smoke beer, hinting at German brewing practices; Český Krumlov had a German majority population until 1945.

PROTIVÍN

www.pivovar-protivin.cz

EVEN THOUGH THE BREWERY is named after Protivín, a small south Bohemian town where it has been making beer for several centuries, Platan is the branding by which most drinkers know these highly accomplished beers. The name refers to the beautiful avenue of plane, or platan, trees leading to the brewery. One of its highly regarded beers is the rich and bittersweet Prácheňská Perla 14°. In 2008, the Lobkowicz group bought the brewery and alongside its own beer, it also brews a dark and a low-alcohol beer.

SVIJANY

www.pivovarsvijany.cz

AS FOR MANY LONG-ESTABLISHED breweries, life has been a bit of a rollercoaster for Svijany. Thought to have first started brewing in the northern Bohemian village of the same name in the 1560s, it was owned by various families until nationalization after World War II. Post-Velvet Revolution, various companies

SVIJANY KVASNIČÁK 13°

and corporations became involved, but in 2010, a Czech investment group became the owner. As for the beer, there is a tantalizing range of various well-made varieties on a Czech theme – Kvasničák 13° is rated as a stand-out unfiltered light beer.

U FLEKŮ

www.ufleku.cz

IF THERE'S ONE BEERY ATTRACTION that even the most discerning beer tourists should visit in Prague, it's this brewery's beer hall. Only one beer is brewed here, and while the waiters can be somewhat imperious, this is a small price to pay for sampling this wonderfully luscious dark lager. The hall was built in 1499 and brewing has occurred on the site since then.

ŽATEC

www.zatec-brewery.com

THE TOWN OF ŽATEC has been at the centre of the major hop-growing area of the Czech Republic for centuries – Žatec is Czech for Saaz. The brewery was built at the start of the 19th century, although it was two weeks from closure in 2001 before two Czech businessmen stepped in and saved it. The brewery is atmospheric, with rambling corridors and beers, such as Blue Label, which make the best of the region's noble hop character.

ZLATOPRAMEN

www.zlatopramen.cz

EVEN THOUGH THE AROMA of brewing has been filling the air of Zlatopramen's hometown Ústí nad Labem since the 16th century, the name Zlatopramen (meaning "golden well") dates from 1967, when a local maltster won a naming competition. In 2008 the brewery joined Heineken, and now focuses on several beers, including its highly regarded 11° pale lager.

ZUBR

www.zubr.cz

IT'S WINE VERSUS BEER in the region of Moravia, and the brewery, whose name means "bison" is in the heart of it in the town of Přerov. It's one of the Czech Republic's biggest volume producers – a lot of beer goes for export. Standouts include its Classic Dark, with a rich roast aroma and a bittersweet taste, and its strong Maxxim (6.5% ABV), fermented in open tanks and matured for three months.

ŽATEC BLUE LABEL

IMPORTANT EUROPEAN NATIONS

From the north, almost up to the Arctic Circle, down to the sun-kissed islands of the Mediterranean, people are brewing beer, and brewing it well. In Denmark and Spain breweries with rich heritages of more than 100 years can be found alongside a new breed of brewers, who are inspired to develop beers made with locally foraged herbs and spices. In Finland there is a revival of one of the world's oldest surviving beer styles, Sahti, while in nearby Norway and Sweden, brewers are discovering their countries' ancient brewing traditions.

In recent years, Italy has become one of the hottest beer destinations in the world, and it is not uncommon to find groups of US brewers travelling the country in search of new beers. Nearby Austria is renowned for its Vienna lager, but it's also home to a new generation of brewers who are exploring the process of wood-ageing in former spirit barrels. In France brewers are showing that fine food and good beers make perfect partners. The Netherlands, meanwhile, sees a new wave of brewers who want to develop new beers of different styles and tastes. And Ireland is home to the black stuff, Guinness, one of the world's most iconic beer brands.

In Portugal, there are hopes that the land of the grape could become the land of the grain, and Switzerland contains a host of brewers who treat brewing as an art and are proud of their commitment to locally sourced ingredients. Cyprus' small brewpub brews beers for discerning travellers, while on Malta the beers are highly influenced by UK traditions. Poland sees the stirrings of a craft beer industry, and across the former Eastern bloc countries of Croatia, Estonia, Hungary, Romania, Russia, Serbia, Slovakia, Slovenia and Ukraine there are early signs of a new beer revolution.

BØGEDAL BRYGHUS

Hand-made beers of quality are the order of the day at the Bøgedal Bryghus, where no two brews are ever the same. Founded in 2004, it keeps its production levels relatively low, concentrating instead on quality and respect for the beer.

THE FACTS...

OWNER Bøgedal Bryghus

FOUNDED 2004

ADDRESS Høllundvej 9, 7100 Vejle

WEBSITE www.boegedal.com

PHILOSOPHY Respect for the character of each beer

BØGEDAL Hvede

Type: Lys hvedeøl med appelsin og korianderfrø
Alkohol: 7,0 %   Bryg No: 324
Brygget: 8/11 2012
Tappet: 21/11 2012

Indhold: 75 cl. Holdbarhed: 31.11.13 Indhold: Byg- og hvedemalt, gær, humle, appelsin, koriander
Opbevaring hos forbrugeren: mørkt, optimalt ved 8 gr. Bøgedal Dk-7100 Vejle www.boegedal.com

BØGEDAL BRYGHUS
HVEDE

BØGEDAL №288

Type: Lys øl
Malt: Nøgen 6-radet byg landsort 1849 Nordisk Genbank No. 13416 og gl. dansk 2-radet byg 1849 Nordisk Genbank No. 9441
Humle: Centennial og Perle
Alkohol: 6,8 %
Brygget: 25/1 2012
Tappet: 7/2 2012

Indhold: 75 cl. Holdbarhed: 31. december 2014 Brygget af Bygmalt, gær, humle, vand
Opbevaring hos forbrugeren: mørkt, optimalt ved 8 gr. Bøgedal Dk-7100 Vejle www.boegedal.com

BØGEDAL BRYGHUS
NO 288

Sweet disposition
These strong, very rich beers are brewed with many of the natural sugars still intact

BØGEDAL BRYGHUS NO 321

NO TWO DAYS AND NO TWO BEERS are the same at the Bøgedal Bryghus, a small craft brewery in Jylland, Denmark. Brewers Gitte Holmboe and Casper Vorting are passionate about their beers. Every batch is nurtured and allowed to develop its own character. So even though recipes are followed, the results vary slightly. Each of the brewery's numbered brews is unique and is limited to a production run of 700 bottles. These are labelled with the name of the beer, the hops used, and the brewing and bottling dates. A visit to the brewery is like visiting a vineyard as the respect for the beer produced is tangible.

Holmboe and Vorting want their beers to taste of the land in their part of the world. They don't set out to mimic beer styles and tastes from elsewhere but try to ensure that the character of the ingredients, shaped by the terroir of the land, comes to the fore.

Wherever possible, everything in the brewery is done by hand, without the use of technology. Gravity and a series of pulleys are used to transfer ingredients around the brewery, and the wort is heated by a direct flame. From filling and emptying the mash tun to putting the caps on bottles, it is a manual process and the brewer says the beers are better for that. The unfiltered and unpasteurized beer produced here is among the best in Scandinavia.

TASTING NOTES

HVEDE WHEAT BEER, 7% ABV
Hvede is sweeter than a classic Belgian-style wheat beer, but still has the refreshing zest delivered by the use of coriander and orange. Its nose is a robust bouquet of citrus aromas, which give way to the fragrant flavours of citrus peel and sage.
FOOD PAIRING: Pair with a plate of sashimi and sliced pickles.

NO 288 PALE ALE, 6.8% ABV
A lacing of delicate, carbonated white, the bubbles are seemingly embroidered onto the inside of the glass. The beer is sweet, with hints of almond and citrus – any bitterness is understated.
FOOD PAIRING: It's a beer for a long, languorous lunch accompanied by some sweet ham and pickles.

NO 321 STOUT, 6.1% ABV
Liquid chocolate in a glass. This stout's dark chocolate, vanilla, and coffee flavours give way to a sweet citrus bitterness from the Cascade, Centennial, and Perle hops, and the unrefined aromatics of muscovado sugar.
FOOD PAIRING: Pair it with a dark bittersweet chocolate mousse torte. Or be bold and try it with a rich Belgian pâté.

HORNBEER

Being a great brewer is no accident, instead it's a journey of discovery. Like a great artist, Jørgen Rasmussen is always striving to perfect his wide range of beers in order to create the perfect drink.

NOTHING SEEMS TO DAUNT Jørgen Rasmussen, who set up the Hornbeer Brewery in eastern Denmark in 2008. Not even the fire that burnt the brewery down 12 months later. His attitude is that you just have to pick yourself up and get on with it. Well, phoenix-like, Rasmussen did just that, and has since gone on to win countless accolades at Danish beer festivals for his impressive "let's just have a go at it and see if it works" beers. But don't be fooled – this seemingly cavalier approach is underpinned by a superb understanding of the chorus of notes that comes from malts and hops. It has been said that if Jørgen's beers were music they would star at the Copenhagen Jazz Festival.

Rasmussen's beers are sheer style, both in the bottle and in the glass. His perceptive, textural artistry is supported by his wife Gundhild. Not only does she make a contribution to what ingredients are put into the beer, but it is her swirling, stylish designs that adorn the bottle labels. The beers themselves are sometimes smooth, even elegant, and will often deliver a hoppy surprise. The wide range produced includes a Russian imperial stout, a sour raspberry fruit beer, a Caribbean "rumstout", an oak-aged cranberry-flavoured sour beer, as well as a blonde, a brown ale, and an IPA.

According to Rasmussen, beer should have no boundaries: it is not a product that should be aimed at either the young or old exclusively. Such fripperies are the nightmares of marketing people. Instead, Rasmussen believes that beer is simply for discerning people. But, like a restless artist, his work is never done. Such is his search for the perfect beer. Wherever he goes he is always looking for inspiration for his next creation.

TASTING NOTES

DRYHOP ALE, 5% ABV
Amarillo hops are the star of this dry-as-a-sucked-lemon beer. They are a good choice for a single-hopped beer, being both bitter and aromatic. Highly attenuated, all the sweetness of the wort has been converted by the yeast, leaving a beer of dry grapefruit intensity.

FOOD PAIRING: Pair it with local treats such as a plate of pork crackling, mustard, gherkins, and slices of rye bread.

FUNKY MONK ALE, 8.8% ABV
This beer is big, bold, and brassy. It is laced with lashings of home-made candy sugar – only a good Belgian yeast could cope with so much fermentable sugar. Never buy just one bottle of this beer, buy two: drink one and give the other several more months to evolve.

FOOD PAIRING: Take your time sipping a beer like this and pair it with complex flavours such as a good strong cheese, caramelized roast potatoes, or a sweet rice pudding.

ESKIL OLD ALE, 5.6% ABV
Brewed in collaboration with famed Danish beer writer Carsten Berthelsen, this is Hornbeer's take on a Belgian-style monastery beer. It is named after a bishop who founded several monasteries in the 11th century. It is dark, unfiltered, full of molasses and fruit flavours, and you will taste the hops.

FOOD PAIRING: After a good walk, this is a big lunch beer. Enjoy with a Scandinavian smörgåsbord.

HORNBEER DRYHOP

HORNBEER FUNKY MONK

HORNBEER ESKIL

MIKKELLER

Since setting up in 2006, brewer Mikkel Borg Bjergsø has quickly proved himself as a craftsman, producing compelling, challenging, and always interesting beers. And he doesn't even have his own brewery.

TEACHER-TURNED-MASTER BREWER, Mikkel Borg Bjergsø is a modern-day prince of Denmark. But his story is no Shakespearean tragedy. The only revenge that Mikkel exacted was on the beer brewing rule book – he simply ripped it up. A former school teacher, Mikkel turned a classroom experiment into one of the most innovative breweries in the world. But there are no bricks and mortar to his brewery. He is a nomad, a travelling troubadour. His unusual brewing career has seen him journey to craft brewers worldwide, and collaborate with people who share his passion for emotion, excitement, and creating agitation in the world of beer. His travels have taken him to the UK, the US, Belgium, Norway, and of course, around his home country of Denmark.

His first commercial beer, developed with his then business partner Kristian Klarup Keller, was an astonishing stout, Beer Geek Breakfast. The pair virtually threw the kitchen sink at the beer – seven different malts and barley were poured into the mash tun, and hours were spent brewing the coffee needed to add extra flavouring. But even extreme beers need some balance, and the juggernaut of dark malts and coffee flavours is kept on the road by the addition of Centennial and Cascade hops. A bouquet of citrus blossom shines through the roasted blackness of the beer. Mikkel's other projects have included a series of single-hop IPAs, created to educate people about the attributes of different hops. Beers from the roaming brewer can be found in the Mikkeller Bar, located in Copenhagen's hip Vesterbro district, which offers a rotating selection of 20 draught beers.

THE FACTS...

OWNER Mikkeller
FOUNDED 2005
ADDRESS Viktoriagade 8, KLD, 1655 Copenhagen V
WEBSITE www.mikkeller.dk
PHILOSOPHY Rules are for breaking

TASTING NOTES

BEER GEEK BREAKFAST OATMEAL STOUT, 7.5% ABV
An intense beer, which is held together by a taut harmony of roasted barley, dark malts, and coffee flavours, with a refreshing wave of citrus flavours from the US hops. Variants of the beer have included chilli and chocolate versions.

FOOD PAIRING: Pair it with the comforting taste of some fresh warm croissants spread with extra salted butter.

BLACK IMPERIAL STOUT, 17.5%
Blacker than midnight on a moonless night, Black swirls with dark chocolate, coffee, and prune flavours that intertwine with vinous port and dark sherry flavours. It's hoppy, a little smoked, and dry as a desiccated bone.

FOOD PAIRING: Try pairing it with a plate of amaretto biscuits.

MIKKELLER BEER GEEK BREAKFAST

MIKKELLER BLACK

AMAGER BRYGHUS

www.amagerbryghus.dk

THERE CANNOT BE MANY BREWERIES THAT are housed in a former air-raid shelter. Amager Bryghus was founded in 2007 by friends Jacob Storm and Morten Lundsback, who turned a hobby and a dream into a commercial reality. Their beers are made using only natural ingredients with no artificial additives. Their motto is "what we don't know we can learn", and they draw on US brewing style rather than the British for their inspiration for their powerful IPA. Powered by Amarillo, Cascade, and Simcoe hops, the beer has a pleasant lingering finish.

BEER HERE

www.beerhere.dk

CHRISTIAN SKOVDAL ANDERSEN is something of a brewing legend and the creative force behind Beer Here, which he started in 2008. A brewing "cuckoo" or "gypsy", he perfects recipes using his home-brewing kit in Copenhagen before producing them in commercial quantities, in collaboration with other brewers such as BrewDog in the UK and Denmark's Herslev Bryghus. Andersen has won world renown among beer fans for his uncompromising, innovative brews and says his motto is "don't waste your thirst".

BREWPUB KØBENHAVN

www.brewpub.dk

BREWPUB KØBENHAVN IS AN INNOVATIVE microbrewery, bar, and restaurant in the centre of Copenhagen. Located in an attractive 17th-century building, many of the 11 beers on sale are brewed in its own cellar brewery, overseen by brewer Hans-Ole Kragelund. Producing brews modelled on those from around the world, its mission is to stay creative and to experiment. One of its most popular beers is Stevie Ray, a Danish interpretation of a US-style craft lager. With moderate bitterness, it has a distinctive floral aroma. The lightly roasted malt delivers fresh biscuit flavours.

CARLSBERG

www.carlsberg.com

ONE OF THE GRANDDADDIES in the world of Danish breweries, Carlsberg is the most influential of established breweries. It was founded in Copenhagen in 1847 by the legendary Jacob Jacobsen and was named after his son Carl. Jacobsen's legacy is his application of scientific techniques to the art of brewing. He popularized steam brewing and refrigeration. But his greatest contribution was the identification and propagation of a single yeast strain, making it easier to brew the same beer with a consistent taste, time after time.

CARLSBERG ELEPHANT

JACOBSEN WEISSBIER

DET LILLE BRYGGERI

www.detlillebryggeri.dk

SMALL IT MAY BE, but Det Lille Bryggeri's heart and imagination are big. Chillis, juniper, liquorice, and honey have all been used in its beers, which are equally influenced by US, British, Belgian, or German brewing styles – or a mixture of up to all four. One of its most strident beers is a powerful barley wine, which weighs in at 10% ABV. Aged in oak casks that once contained cognac, it should be laid down to drink in future years.

EVIL TWIN

www.eviltwin.dk

WHY, IN MYTHOLOGY, IS ONE TWIN GOOD and the other bad? The Romans have Romulus and Remus; the Danes have Mikkel and Jeppe Jarnit-Bjergsø. However, in this case, both identical brothers are a powerful, positive force for the good of beer. Mikkel is the creative force behind Mikkeller (see p.109) and Jeppe, under the name Evil Twin, is one of a growing band of "gypsy brewers" who is spinning fabulous fantasies with his IPAs, stouts, and pale ales.

GOURMETBRYGGERIET

www.gourmetbryggeriet.dk

"BEER IS MEANT TO BE DRUNK WITH FOOD" is the motto of the Gourmet Brewery, which was founded in 2005 by chef Lars Dietrichsen and brewer Michael Knoth. The upmarket brewpub is now owned by the Harboe brewery and, even though the founders are no longer involved, their ethos lives on. Four regular beers and a seasonal beer are produced, including a strong porter full of chocolate and coffee notes, which is as dark as any starless winter's night in Denmark.

HERSLEV BRYGHUS

www.herslevbryghus.dk

THE MANTRA OF Tore Jørgensen, the founder of the Herslev brewery, is that "Beers are inspired by the seasons". He is passionate about his farm and how the terroir of the land influences the beer he makes. "We make beer we can enjoy, and are inspired by the seasons – each brew has its own flavour and history", he says. He claims the soil on his farm and the climate around Roskilde have a profound effect on his organic and unpasteurized beers.

INDSLEV BRYGGERI

www.indslevbryggeri.dk

SPELT IS AN ANCIENT VARIETY OF WHEAT that provides the malt for Indslev's beers. Brewer Anders Busse Rasmussen is turning brewing theory on its head, by saying all beers can be made by using wheat and is very proud that the stout, made in the brewery founded in 1897 by his antecedent Frederik Christian Rasmussen, has won several awards. He says, "We are determined to show the world that wheat-based beer is so much more then hefeweizens and witbiers".

JACOBSEN

www.jacobsenbeer.com

HISTORY SEEMS TO OOZE out of every brick, rivet, and shining vessel housed in this brewery, which is much more than a working museum. Here, from 1847, Carlsberg founder Jacob Jacobsen turned his brewing theories on yeast into a reality. Today, the brewery produces a range of speciality beers. Modern in outlook, the brewers seek out ancient ingredients such as woodruff, a herb said to cleanse and renew, which is used in its spring beers.

MIDTFYN BRYGHUS

www.midtfyns-bryghus.dk

FOUNDED IN 2004, Midtfyn Brewery's fortunes were enhanced when American-born Eddie Szweda bought the company. He redesigned the range of beers produced in order to create a "wow experience" – sample the palate-tingling Chili Tripel, for example.

Located in Brobyværk on the island of Fyn, beers are brewed here for just about every season and occasion. One beer even celebrates England's Arsenal Football Club. Gunners Ale was developed for the club's many Danish supporters and, according to Eddie, should be drunk in the company of other "gooners".

NØRREBRO BRYGHUS

www.norrebrobryghus.dk

IT WAS ANDERS KISSMEYER'S DREAM to have his own brewery. Today he has made this dream a reality in the Nørrebro brewpub in Copenhagen. The brewery usually sells up to ten hand-brewed, traditional-style beers made on site. Kissmeyer's ambition is to renew Danish beer culture and he is not afraid to challenge ideas of what beer is and what it should taste like. In his fight against dogma, he believes quality is more important than tradition. Sour and wood-aged beers all have a starring role to play in his impressive portfolio.

ØERBAEK BRYGGERI

www.oerbaek-bryggeri.nu

THE FUTURE LOOKED PRETTY BLEAK for Øerbaek Brewery until Niels and Nicolai Rømer took it on in 1996. Founded in 1906, it had gone through a number of owners and the business had filed for bankruptcy in the 1990s. However, undeterred, the new owners decided they would restore

MIDTFYN CHILI TRIPEL

SVANEKE MORK GULD

brewing to the old, neglected buildings and produce a range of organic beers once again. These beers are today regarded as some of Denmark's best. Ingredients used include spelt and elderflower.

REFSVINDINGE

www.bryggerietrefsvindinge.dk

SINCE 1885 FOUR GENERATIONS of the same family, the Rasmussens, have brewed in the Refsvindinge farmhouse brewery. But it was the work done by the family during the 1990s that helped forge the brewery's reputation as an innovative brewer. Its Ale No 16, first brewed in 1995, drew a new generation of drinkers to the excitement of craft beer – it's a strongish, sweet, dark ale, brewed with English yeast. The popularity of some of its beers means that some are also brewed under supervision at the Vestfyen brewery.

SVANEKE BRYGHUS

www.svanekebryghus.dk

SINCE 2000, THE SVANEKE BREWERY in the small town of Svaneke, on Bornholm Island, has been producing unfiltered beers. In addition to its three core beers – a pilsner, a golden ale, and a sweet stout – it produces an interesting range of specials to caress its customers' palates. One such is the award-winning Mork Guld, 5.7% ABV, which is copper-hued and full of mildly bitter walnut and caramel flavours. Another is Red Hot Chili Ale – a top-fermented beer that is a striking red in colour and flavoured with fresh, spicy chillies.

THISTED

www.thisted-bryghus.dk

ONE OF DENMARK'S OLDEST BREWERIES, Thisted is owned by current and former residents of the town of Thisted. Annually, more than 1,000 of the shareholders gather for a tasting of the beers and for the company's annual general meeting. The company brewed Denmark's first organic beer in 1995 and produces a much sought-after, bottom-fermented Baltic Porter, which is laced with smoked malt and liquorice flavours.

UGLY DUCK

www.uglyduckbrewing.dk

ONCE FETED AS DENMARK'S youngest craft brewer when he founded the Rassted brewery in 2005, Martin Jensen is now responsible for Ugly Duck Beers, set up in 2006. Jensen has matured into one of the hottest brewers on the Danish craft scene and is constantly searching for new hop varieties to add texture to his raucous stouts and IPAs. He has also experimented with inoculating some barrels of beer with wild Brettanomyces yeast, just to see what happens.

THE FACTS...

OWNER Jämtlands
FOUNDED 1996
ADDRESS Jämtlands Brewery, Box 224, 831 23 Östersund
WEBSITE www.jamtlandsbryggeri.se
PHILOSOPHY Quality not quantity

JÄMTLANDS

Pilgrims travelling to the tomb of St Olaf in Trondheim are said to have revered the clear, sparkling, healing waters of Östersund. Today, it is beer fans who praise the heavenly qualities they bring to Jämtlands' beers.

FOR MOST OF THE 20TH CENTURY, Sweden had some of the most restrictive anti-alcohol laws in Europe. The production and sale of alcohol was largely controlled by the state and the temperance movement, resulting in the concentration of beer production in the hands of a few big brewers. Few believed that Sweden would ever have its own craft beer movement.

But all was not lost. In the 1990s, a few home-brewers, no doubt inspired by developments in the US, tried to turn a hobby into commercial activity. It was Sweden's accession to the European Union in 1995 that started to loosen the influence that the country's temperance movement had on the production of alcohol. One of the restrictions that was removed as a result of these changes was the ban on beer above 5.6% ABV being brewed.

Among the first companies to take advantage of the new rules was Jämtlands, which is based in a remote part of north-west Sweden. Each year head brewer David Jones produces a 6% ABV anniversary ale to celebrate his first brews. The brewery also has a large range of year-round and seasonal beers. English malt provides the power for the company's beers, while their renowned bitterness comes from hops sourced from England, Germany, Slovenia, and the US. The beer styles draw widely on the traditions of the UK, Germany, and Belgium, and like many brewers in the craft beer movement, a close eye is kept on developments in the US. All the beers are filtered but none are pasteurized. Clearly it's a formula that works, as the brewery has an oversized trophy cabinet and even that isn't big enough – it's bursting with awards from the Stockholm Beer Festival.

TASTING NOTES

HELL LAGER, 5.1% ABV
A golden beer that almost seems to fizz in the glass as the bubbles rise to form a nice, white head. A good lemon hop nose gives way to some soft fruit, honey, and orange peel flavours. Its finish is long, satisfying, and very moreish.
FOOD PAIRING: The clean flavours are not overpowered by Asian spices or Swedish smoked fish.

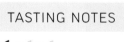

JULÖL ALE, 6.5% ABV
This is a seasonal, winter favourite. Big dark fruit and prune flavours rise from this dark red-brown beer. Alcohol warmth and orange fruit sweetness vie for attention and there are some spicy cinnamon notes. It is robust enough to warm the darkest and coldest winter's night.
FOOD PAIRING: The sweetness of the beer pairs well with pudding or cake made with dark fruit, or cinnamon rolls.

POSTILJON ALE, 5.8% ABV
A Swedish interpretation of a strong English ale. Amber in colour, it swaggers with bold flavours. There is a notable caramel taste over which can be detected Seville orange peel and even some fresh bready notes, all of which are balanced with a pronounced bitter English hoppiness.
FOOD PAIRING: This beer pairs particularly well with roasted and braised meats such as pork and beef.

Brotherhood of brewers
Craft brewers draw inspiration from other similar minded brewers across the world

JÄMTLANDS POSTILJON

NILS OSCAR

Nils Oscar must have been quite a man – his grandson Karl-David Sundberg named his brewing business after him. A childhood hero, Oscar possessed all the qualities that Sundberg wanted to promote through his business.

THE FACTS...

OWNER Nils Oscar

FOUNDED 1996

ADDRESS Fruängsgatan 2, 611 31 Nyköping

WEBSITE www.nilsoscar.se

PHILOSOPHY Honest at all times. Never afraid to do its duty

IF ONLY THEY COULD grow hops successfully on Karl-David Sundberg's land, Tärnö Manor, south-west of Stockholm, then all the raw materials for his beers would come from his farm to the glass. He already grows the barley, oats, rye, and wheat that his brewer, Patrick Holmqvist, needs to make his beers. However, the best latitudes for growing hops are between 35° and 55°, in both the northern and southern hemispheres. For a successful hop harvest, the plants require long hours of daylight and even in the land of the midnight sun, on a latitude of 58°, there are not enough daylight hours in the rest of the year for hops to prosper.

Nils Oscar is one of the new wave of Swedish brewers who were able to establish themselves following a relaxation of alcohol laws in Sweden. Founded in Stockholm as the Kungsholmens Kvartersbryggeri, it soon became the Tärnö Bryggeri and moved out of the city. In 1999, the name was changed to Nils Oscar. The Swedish brewing revolution has yet to match the exponential growth experienced by other countries in Europe, but this could be due to Sweden's *Systembolaget* – the state-owned organization that controls the shops where alcohol can be sold.

Sundberg gave the company its current name in memory of his grandfather, Nils Oscar, who was a big influence on him in early life. Born in 1865, Oscar emigrated to America at the young age of 17 and managed to establish himself successfully as a businessman and farmer both there and on his return to Sweden. Documents describe him as earnest, hard-working, and never afraid to do his duty. These are the qualities that Sundberg felt were important in setting up his brewery. Of the 15 or so beers made by the company, the best-selling lager is God Lager. This divine beer is no doubt heaven-sent but, in fact, it is named after the Swedish word for "good".

TASTING NOTES

IMPERIAL STOUT 7% ABV

This aged beer is well-rounded and full of dark chocolate and seared caramel flavours from the roasted malts, and softened by the use of oats, grown on the brewery's own farm. The hops bring a distinctive long bitterness.

FOOD PAIRING: It would pair well with a rich chocolate dessert or dark rum-flavoured chocolate truffles.

COFFEE STOUT 6.4% ABV

Coffee beans from the Fazenda Ambiental Fortaleza, Brazil, work in rich sweet harmony with the chocolate notes of the beer. It has a strong, vibrant, but not overbearing sweetness that duets with the citrussy lemon bitterness of the hops.

FOOD PAIRING: Pair it with a sweet chocolate cake or even one flavoured with coffee to match up its flavours.

GOD LAGER 5.3% ABV

A grainy, almost nutty-flavoured lager, which has some hints of unsalted butter. The hops add lemon blossom notes that lead to an enjoyable, long, almost warming finish. It is a clean and distinguished, easy-drinking beer.

FOOD PAIRING: The roasted roundness of the beer pairs well with barbecued, grilled, or fried meats.

NILS OSCAR IMPERIAL STOUT

NILS OSCAR COFFEE STOUT

NILS OSCAR GOD LAGER

ÅBRO BRYGGERI

www.abro.se

THE BREWMASTER at Åbro Brewery, Lennarth Anemyr, says beer is much more than what you get in a glass – it is a philosophy and a way to look at life. Åbro is Sweden's oldest family-run brewery, founded in 1856 in Småland Vimmerby. It sits at the foot of a ridge with access to its own fresh water source, which is used in the brewing process.

Today, Anemyr produces some of his best unpasteurized and unfiltered creations for the Stockholm Beer and Whisky Festival, and with his brewmaster specials he explores the full gamut of European beer styles, including his own subtle take on a smoked beer from Bamberg in Germany.

DUGGES ALE & PORTER

www.dugges.se

HOPS, MALT, AND PASSION are the essential ingredients for beer made by Mikael Dugge Engström. He thrives on visitors breathing in the atmosphere when visiting this "genuine craft brewery". He wants them to feel the taste of the ingredients and be infected by his enthusiasm. Located in Landvetter near Gothenburg, Engström draws inspiration from the US and the UK for his ale-style beers, and says that good malt and spicy hops brighten people's journey of discovery through the world of beer.

GOTLANDS

www.gotlandsbryggeri.se

GOTLANDS IS OWNED by Sweden's largest brewing company, the family-owned Spendrups, who use it for commercial and trial brews. Some say there are hops in the blood of Johan Spendrup, who oversees the brewery's output. A fourth-generation brewer, he learnt his craft in Bamberg, Germany. A smidgen of smoked malt is added to Wisby Stout, which Spendrup says lifts it to new heights: "It's so good that after two you would like a third".

HANTVERKS

www.hantverksbryggeriet.se

HANTVERKS WAS FOUNDED in 2003. The brewers say their vision is to increase the knowledge of brewing and beer culture

by producing beers that stand out from the crowd. The extensive range includes Alchemist, which draws on the Belgian tradition of adding fruit to lambic beers. With an intriguing blue hue, it contains Swedish blueberries and is left to mature for a year, creating an exquisite duet of acid and sour flavours. Chimney Sweep is a tasty black stout containing oats combined with caramel and chocolate malt, giving a bitter chocolate drinking experience.

MONKS CAFÉ

www.monkscafe.se

AFTER AN ABSENCE of many years, Monks Café brought brewing back to the city of Stockholm in 2008. It's a formula that seems to have been a great success, as the company has since expanded and opened a second brewpub, Monks Porterhouse. In the past there were probably many brewpubs like this in the city. Monks Café always has a range of interesting beers available. In addition to the regular beers, including an IPA and a porter, collaboration brews from visiting brewers and others from brewing students can be sampled. The brewpub also offers courses for those who wish to brew at home or start up their own brewery.

NÄRKE KULTURBRYGGERI

www.kulturbryggeri.se

"BEER IS ART", say Berith Karlsson and Rolf Larsson, the founders of Närke Kulture brewery, which opened in Grenadjärstaden in 2003 and produced its first beer in 2004. They are on a mission to stop the spread of mediocre industrial beer. Drawing on their experience as beer fans and home brewers they specialize in an extravagant range of unfiltered and unpasteurized hoppy light ales through to uncompromising porters. They recommend laying down and storing their stronger bottle brews.

NYA CARNEGIE

www.nyacarnegiebryggeriet.se

IN 2011, BROOKLYN BREWERY'S famed brewmaster Garrett Oliver (see p.152) collaborated with Carlsberg Sweden to produce a bourbon barrel-aged version of its famed Carnegie Stark-Porter, a historic beer first produced in 1836. The result of this coming

NYNÄSHAMNS INDIAN VIKEN PALE ALE

together has seen a new cross-Atlantic venture between the two companies, and the opening of a new brewery and restaurant in central Stockholm. With the brewing overseen by Brooklyn, the brewery is expected to become a focus for Sweden's craft beer fans.

NYNÄSHAMNS

www.nyab.se

WHEN A GROUP OF FRIENDS came together in 1988 to lament the poor choice of beer available to them, they probably didn't expect the discussion would lead to them eventually setting up one of Sweden's most influential craft breweries. Together they travelled Europe and discovered the exquisite joys of beers from both Britain and Belgium, but it was nearly another ten years before they took the plunge and opened their own commercial brewery, Nynäshamns. Its first beer, Bedarö Bitter, was inspired by English ales and went on to win a Gold at the Stockholm Beer Festival. Also worth trying is the award-winning, aromatic Indian Viken Pale Ale.

OCEAN

www.oceanbryggeriet.se

BREWER THOMAS BINGEBO'S passion for beer was nurtured on visits to London, where he developed a taste for malty brews. He set up Ocean Brewery in Gothenburg in 2007 with a group of friends, believing that malt should have the starring role in a beer, with hops providing some spice in the chorus line. Since then the brewery has grown substantially and its products are now sold throughout Sweden.

However, time must have mellowed Bingebo, as he now uses citrussy US hops in many of his well-balanced beers. Ocean's basic range includes the fruit-scented Glenn No 5, malty 12 Plato Lager, fruity-fresh West Coast, and Gothenburg Sports, which is packed with flavours of chocolate, blackcurrant, and liquorice. They also offer a wide range of seasonal and speciality beers.

OPPIGÅRDS

www.oppigards.com

IN 2004, BJÖRN FALKESTRÖM turned a converted barn on the farm that had been in his family for more than 250 years, into a brewery. The beers produced by Oppigårds, which include a core range of four ales – popular, malty Golden Ale, English-inspired Single Hop Ale, fruity Amarillo Ale, and

hoppy Indian Tribute Ale – are a well-crafted combination of good quality natural ingredients. It's a formula that has won the brewery much support.

SIGTUNA

www.sigtunabrygghus.se

AMBITION IS NO BAD THING and Sigtuna's founder Peter Forss says he wants to make his craft brewery the best in Sweden. The brewery opened in 2006 and since then production has grown quickly. Brewer Mattias Hammenlind attributes this to the fact that he plays loud rock and roll music – in particular AC/DC – to the fermenting brews. His rock and roll beers are a fusion of styles – lemongrass is added to a Belgian wit and the all-American IPA is augmented by luscious hops from New Zealand.

SLOTTSKÄLLANS

www.slottskallan.se

ORIGINALLY INSPIRED BY A TRIP to San Francisco in the 1990s, where its founder saw first-hand the emerging craft beer scene in the US, the Slottskällans Brewery now produces a range of easy-drinking ales and lagers. One of the goals of the brewery, based in Uppsala, is to make people think of beer in the same way that they think of wine. Each beer comes with accompanying food recommendations. For example, the strong and bitter Slottskällans Slottslager should be enjoyed with salads and fish dishes or with salty or fatty flavours, seafood, and meat. Taste and balance are the watchwords of the beers, which have gone on to win several awards at the Stockholm Beer Festival. Slottskällans has also gained many plaudits for its bottle-conditioned Imperial Stout.

SPENDRUPS

www.spendrups.se

SPENDRUPS, a family-owned company, has been making beer since 1897. Many of its beers draw inspiration from Germany's brewing heritage, and it brews a wide range of pilsner and Dortmund-style beers. With three large breweries, its beers are widely available. The most popular is Norrlands Guld. However, many choose to drink the Old Gold, a German-style pilsner, or Pistonhead Hot Roddin' Lager, a medium bitter lager with attitude; Pistonhead Plastic Fantastic is a full-bodied beer packaged in recyclable plastic.

SPENDRUPS PISTONHEAD HOT RODDIN' LAGER

ANNOEULLIN

One family has managed to keep the tradition of brewing fine beers at Annoeullin going for six generations and even survived moving its more-than-100-year-old coppers to a new site.

THE FACTS...

OWNER Lepers family
FOUNDED 1905
ADDRESS 199 Bis, Rue Marle 59930 La Chapelle d'Armentières
WEBSITE www.langelus.fr
PHILOSOPHY Believe in diversity

THE BREWERS OF FRENCH FLANDERS in the north-eastern corner of France are rightfully proud of their rustic traditions, and many of them make spicy, aromatic *bière de garde* – a delicious and interesting alternative to commonly available industrial lagers. Traditionally, *bières de garde* were made during the winter or cooler months of the spring. They were then stored for drinking on hot summer days, when many farm workers were thirsty after a day working in the fields and the temperatures were too warm for brewing. These days, the beer is brewed all year round.

Over time, most of these artisanal breweries have disappeared, but one family is still going strong. Recently, Charles Lepers took over the running of the Annoeullin brewery, which had been run by his parents, Bertrand and Yolande, since the 1970s. One of Charles' first tasks was to move the brewery to a new site in La Chapelle d'Armentières, at the defunct Motte-Cordonnier brewery where Stella Artois was once brewed. To ensure the aromatic malt and spice of his beer stayed the same, he moved the two old, fragile coppers, which were installed in 1905 by his great-, great-, great-grandfather. In the new location, there is space for brewery tours, a tasting room, and a shop, where the beers, many in champagne-style bottles, are sold.

TASTING NOTES

L'ANGELUS WHEAT BEER, 7% ABV
Barley malt, unmalted wheat, hops, and spices produce an aromatic chorus of citrus lemon and lime flavours, under which can be detected some green fruit and banana flavours. Unfiltered, it is a hazy, golden-yellow colour.

FOOD PAIRING: Try it with a meaty ale casserole.

LEPERS 8 BIÈRE DE GARDE, 8% ABV
Orange-coloured with streaks of blond in the glass, it is topped by a white, hazy head. It has strong notes of spice, a crisp, biscuit malt character, and a fragrant aroma of lychees and lemons.

FOOD PAIRING: Partner with a meaty dish such as a Flanders *pot'je vleesch* – a peerless stew of chicken, rabbit, and veal.

LEPERS 6 BIÈRE DE GARDE, 6% ABV
Light red-brown in colour, the beer brims with orange and lemon zest. It is sweet with hints of soft, buttery caramel, over which can be detected cloves and a pleasant medicinal flavour.

FOOD PAIRING: Try with pâtés, cheeses, and hunks of bread.

ANNOEULLIN L'ANGELUS

DUYCK

For four generations the Duyck family, makers of Jenlain beer, have kept the flag flying for French craft brewing, and they are making plans for the next generation to continue with the tradition.

THE FACTS...

OWNER Duyck

FOUNDED 1922

ADDRESS 113 Route Nationale, BP 6, 59144 Jenlain

WEBSITE www.duyck.com

PHILOSOPHY Evolving, while time does its work

DUYCK OR BIÈRE BLONDE

DUYCK AMBRÉE

THE DUYCK FAMILY have been brewing beer in the village of Jenlain, close to the border with Belgium in the north of France, since 1922. The brewery's founder was Félix Duyck, who got the brewing bug from his father Léon, a farmer and brewer who lived in Belgium. Brewing was a farmhouse tradition that prospered across Flanders for hundreds of years. It became home to some of the world's most remarkable beer styles – Belgian red, bruin, saison, and *bière de garde* – and although it's not known which beers Léon brewed, his rich Belgian heritage strongly influenced Félix when he set up his own brewery.

It was Félix who created the recipe for the brewery's traditional beers, and in 1950 introduced the use of recycled champagne bottles, to allow customers to drink Duyck beers at home. Over time, nuances between Belgian and French brewers developed. Belgian brewers tended to produce lighter-bodied, heartily hopped saisons or sour reds, while in France, brewers like Duyck developed maltier, stronger, and sweeter beers.

Today, Duyck's modern craft brewery is run by Raymond Duyck, who as well as making plans for his son to take over, hopes part of his own legacy will be that France will be known not just for its wine, champagne, and gastronomy, but also as a country of world class, exciting beer.

TASTING NOTES

OR BIÈRE BLONDE BIÈRE DE GARDE, 7.5% ABV
This is golden-blond in the glass and full of youthful vigour. A complex beer in which bold malt combines with earthy, citrus hops, aromatic spices, and a hint of cloves and vanilla.
FOOD PAIRING: Pair it with some sharp cheeses or perhaps a bowl of mussels, cooked in a splash of the beer.

AMBRÉE BIÈRE DE GARDE, 7.5% ABV
This unpasteurized beer glows with an amber hue. It is laden with flavours of stone fruit, plums, damsons, and some lightly toasted malt. This is no pallid brew – it is bold and big in taste.
FOOD PAIRING: An ideal partner with rich, sweet food. Try it with slow-roasted goose stuffed with prunes.

ÉCLATS D'AMBRE BIÈRE DE GARDE, 6.8% ABV
This is Christmas pudding in a bottle. Rich flavours of cinnamon and cloves combine with satsuma and candied peel. It is full of chewy malt flavours with layers of toffee and burnt caramel.
FOOD PAIRING: Enjoy with a rich steamed pudding or fruit cake.

Amber elegance
We should revere great beers in the same way others celebrate champagne

DUYCK ÉCLATS D'AMBRE

AU BARON

www.brasserieaubaron.com

IN THE VILLAGE OF GUSSIGNIES, in a part of France where French cuisine and Belgian beer culture entwine, father and son Alain and Xavier Bailleux brew beer for sale in the family's riverside restaurant. They have been brewing here since 1989. The spring seasonal is Cuvée des Jonquilles, a rich, golden ale. It is as vibrant in colour as the daffodils that crowd the river bank. An amber and a Christmas beer are also brewed.

BOURGANEL

www.bieres-bourganel.com

LIKE MANY FRENCH PEOPLE, Christian Bourganel is fiercely proud of the flavours of the region in which he lives. His Bourganel Brewery is located in the spa town of Vals les Bains in the shadow of the Ardèche mountains. It is an area famed for chestnuts, nougat, and bilberries, so it is no surprise that it was these he sought when he opened a brewery in 1997, and developed a range of blond and amber beers.

CASTELAIN

www.chti.com

IN NORTHERN FRANCE, there is a rich tradition of brewing a *bière de garde*, a strong ale or lager that is intended for keeping. Traditionally, these were brewed by farmers during the winter and spring months. The Castelain family have been brewing since 1926 and produce a range of beers, all of which have undergone a long period of cold conditioning. This adds great depth and complexity to the flavours. Their best-known brew is Ch'ti Blonde, a full-bodied beer.

LA CHOULETTE

www.lachoulette.com

LA CHOULETTE IS A RARE SURVIVOR from the hundreds of breweries that must have existed in the region of Nord-Pas-de-Calais in northern France in the late 19th century. The brewery was founded in 1885 and the current brewer, Alain Dhaussy, is proud of brewing beers the traditional way. His beers are bottled with the yeast, which allows for the development of complex flavour. His flagship beer is the richly robust Choulette Amber. Seasonal beers include one flavoured with fresh raspberries, Choulette Framboise.

GAYANT LA GOUDALE

DEUX RIVIÈRES

www.coreff.com

THIS REVOLUTIONARY French beer has its roots in an English brewery in Hampshire. Christian Blanchard and Jean-François Malgorn were part of a new wave of beer producers in Brittany, when they opened Deux Rivières in 1985. In the early 1980s, the pair had spent two years working in the Ringwood brewery (see p.49) in Hampshire under the tutelage of pioneering microbrewer Peter Austin. The full-bodied beers they produce are an unashamed mix of French and English malts.

LA FERME BECK

www.fermebeck.com

THE BECK FAMILY, who started brewing at La Ferme Beck in 1994, make good use of the hops they grow on their farm, which is right on the Belgian border in the Nord-Pas-de-Calais area. Quality not quantity is their guiding principle and each year they produce a batch of Hommelpap, made with freshly picked hops, which is produced in time to be drunk at their annual hop festival in September. Assertive in character, it is dominated by lemon and orange flavours.

GAYANT

www.brasseurs-gayant.com

THE GAYANT FAMILY has been running this brewery under the family name in Douai, in French Flanders, since 1919. One of their best known beers is Bière du Demon: at 12% ABV it claims to be the strongest brewed in France. They also produce Amadeus, a cloudy wheat beer, with hints of coriander and orange, and La Goudale, which uses a recipe taken from the Middle Ages. The brewers are proud of their craft tradition, preferring quality to quantity, and favouring traditional methods over industrial production. They say all their beers are brewed with the same care and attention usually given to fine wines.

LORRAINE

www.brasseurs-lorraine.com

IN 2003, RÉGIS BOUILLON and Jean-François Drouin decided to revive the tradition of brewing in Lorraine, and they set up Brasseurs Lorraine – historically it was a craft that had prospered in the region. The brewery produces top-fermented beers using both barley and wheat malts, and shuns the use of additives. Its Duchesse de Lorraine is based on an 18th-century recipe and includes red and smoked malts and the herb sassafras, which brings a spicy zing to the palate of the unpasteurized beer.

MÉTÉOR

www.brasserie-meteor.fr

BREWING FIRST STARTED on this site in Hochfelden in 1644, making Météor the longest-established family brewery in France. Its best-known beer is Météor Pils, which was developed in 1927 by Louis Haag and his son Frederick, to mimic beers from the town of Pilsen in the Czech Republic. It is made with Czech Saaz hops and locally grown Strisselspalt malt. Sold in local bars, the unpasteurized beer is refreshing, with a hint of biscuit malt and a generous floral bitterness from the hops.

MICHARD

www.bieres-michard.com

JEAN MICHARD was something of a revolutionary when he set up his first brewpub, Bières Michard, but he was confident in his belief that there would be a market for fresh unpasteurized beers. Working with his daughter, Julie, he developed a range of beers that drew inspiration from Bavarian brewing. Although Michard brews in a state-of-the-art brewing hall, craft and tradition are still at the heart of the beers. Ambrée is a crisp, refreshing beer with a satisfying hint of bitterness.

PIETRA

www.brasseriepietra.com

WHEN ARMELLE AND Dominique Sialelli decided to return to their native Corsica, they took with them the madcap idea of opening their own brewery. They wanted to be able to drink locally produced Corsican beer in Corsica. They opened Pietra in 1992 and were determined that their beers would capture the fragrant freshness of wild flowers on the island. So chestnut, juniper, myrtle, and arbutus are among the flavours used.

Their flagship beer, Pietra, is an amber beer brewed with Corsican chestnut flour, while Colomba, a white beer brewed from barley and wheat, is flavoured with local wild herbs. Serena is a light, purely malt beer, and Pietra de Nöel is a festive drink developed using the chestnut flour of the island.

ST SYLVESTRE 3 MONTS

THIRIEZ ETOILE DU NORD

ROUGET DE LISLE

www.brasserie-rouget-lisle.fr

LOCATED AT THE FOOT of the Jura mountains, Rouget de Lisle brewery was named after the composer who wrote *La Marseillaise* in 1792. It opened in 1994 and produces a wide range of beers, using local ingredients foraged from the surrounding hills to add spice and piquancy. These include wormwood, dandelion, blackcurrant, and gentian. The brewery's golden Absinthe Lager has a distinct bitterness from the wormwood.

SAINT GERMAIN

www.page24.fr

THE TWO BREWERS WHO set up Saint Germain Brasserie in 2003 remain adamant that their beers will retain their artisanal character and close links with French farmers. In 2008, they decided to only use hops produced by a French Flanders cooperative and so maintain production in the area. All the beers are top-fermented and one is named in honour of Saint Hildegard, a German abbess who is often wrongly credited with using hops for the first time to make beer.

ST SYLVESTRE

www.brasserie-st-sylvestre.com

ANYONE STANDING ON top of one of the three hills after which Brasserie St Sylvestre's most famous beer is named can see the hop fields and malthouses where the brewery's raw material comes from. One of Flanders' classic artisanal breweries, it is run by brothers François and Serge Ricour, who are inspired by the passion of their father who took over the brewery in 1954. The brewery's 3 Monts is a bold, vibrant example of a robust, golden, unpasteurized *bière de garde*.

THIRIEZ

www.brasseriethiriez.co

WHEN DANIEL THIRIEZ moved to rural Esquelbecq in the heart of Flanders in 1996, no brewing had taken place in the village since World War II. In 1997, he set up a new brewery, Thiriez, in an old barn, which had once been the home of the Poitevin brewery. His Etoile du Nord was developed in partnership with English brewer John Davidson of the Swale Brewery. Blond and light in alcohol, the generously used aromatic hops from Kent give it its unique character.

BROUWERIJ 'T IJ

A career on the road as a rock star gave brewer Kasper Peterson a taste for strong Belgian beers and a passion to brew them for himself. From humble beginnings his brewery has grown to be an Amsterdam institution.

BROUWERIJ 'T IJ OPENED IN 1985. It was founded by rock musician Kasper Peterson, who had spent a lot of time criss-crossing Europe to get to gigs, and of course, sampling the local beer. His particular favourites were strong Belgian beers, and he was determined to learn how to brew them and make them available in his homeland. In 1983 he set about the task with gusto, using a room in the squat he was living in on the banks of the 't IJ in Amsterdam.

Peterson's hobby gradually became a business, and within a few years Brouwerij 't IJ, with its bar and waterside seating, was opened; it is located in a former town bathhouse next to one of Holland's tallest wooden windmills. After 20 years, Kasper retired from the business and it was bought by Patrick Hendrikse and Bart Obertop, who are determined to keep the brewing tradition going.

Over the years, the business has grown, and a second brewery has opened just a short distance away from the original site. Here, beer is brewed for bottling, while the original brewery continues to produce draught beer for the bar. Very little of the raw material used by the brewery goes to waste.

Once used, the malted barley, which gives the beer its taste, colour, and alcohol content, is ideal as an animal feed. 'T IJ's spent grains, which are still rich in protein, go to a local sheep farmer. They must be very happy sheep as they produce a beautiful soft cheese called Skeapsrond, which of course is on sale in the bar.

There aren't many breweries that can boast that they are housed next to a windmill, but Batemans (see p.42), one of England's oldest family brewers is another. How appropriate that they should show their craft-brewing pedigree by collaborating on brewing a bock with 't IJ for a beer festival in England.

THE FACTS...

OWNER Brouwerij 't IJ
FOUNDED 1985
ADDRESS Funenkade 7 1018 AL Amsterdam
WEBSITE www.brouwerijhetij.nl
PHILOSOPHY Brewing characterful beers

BROUWERIJ 'T IJ ZATTE

TASTING NOTES

ZATTE TRIPEL, 8% ABV
This golden beer draws its inspiration from the Belgian tradition of strong, blond beers. Aromas of soft red fruit vie with layers of chewy malted bread and caramel. Its finish is warm and full of spice.
FOOD PAIRING: It works particularly well with lightly spiced lamb or chicken recipes.

IJWIT WHEAT BEER, 7% ABV
The beer pours like a swirling, golden cloud – the opaqueness comes from the use of wheat when making the beer. The tart freshness is augmented by banana, lemon, and medicinal clove flavours. It's a thirst-quencher.
FOOD PAIRING: In 't IJ's bar they recommend enjoying this beer with fresh peanuts, hard-boiled eggs, cheese, salami, and a Dutch speciality beef sausage.

SPECIALE VLO ALE, 7% ABV
A big brother to the brewery's Vlo, and created to celebrate the 25th anniversary of Amsterdam's De Bierkoning beer shop, it's something of a heavyweight. Full of rich coriander and caramel flavours, the aroma is citrussy from the use of Cascade hops.
FOOD PAIRING: The sugars in the beer work well with anything with lots of basil and with asparagus dishes.

BROUWERIJ 'T IJ
IJWIT

BROUWERIJ 'T IJ
SPECIALE VLO

DE MOLEN

In just a few years, De Molen, named after its hometown in the western part of the Netherlands, has taken the craft beer world by storm with its use of unusual ingredients, collaborations with other brewers, and its quirky sense of humour.

THE FACTS...

OWNER De Molen

FOUNDED 2004

ADDRESS Overtocht 43 2411 BT Bodegraven

WEBSITE www.brouwerijdemolen.nl

PHILOSOPHY Searching for the ultimate beer

THE BREWERS AT DE MOLEN are not afraid to explore new flavours in their quest to develop the ultimate beer, and are confident in taking on almost any style – in particular they have a penchant for emboldened porters and stouts. They do not shy away from a good argument either, although they do have their tongues firmly planted in their cheeks. In one infamous example, the brewery had started to export Rasputin, one of its range of imperial Russian stouts, to the US and ended up in a bit of a bar room spat. The US brewer of the similarly named Old Rasputin got hot under the collar about the Dutch invaders' use of the name. But instead of paying good money to already well-heeled lawyers, De Molen simply changed its beer's name in the US to Disputin and printed this message on the label: "This stout used to be called Rasputin, but the people who make Old Rasputin in California thought you were too dumb to tell the two products apart, and threatened to sue us for trademark infringement".

The brewery was founded in 2004 by Menno Olivier. A true craft brewer, he believes in collaboration with brewers from around the world in order to develop new beers or rediscover old styles. His super-charged collaborations, especially with US brewer Flying Dog (see p.158), are legendary. The inspiration came from De Molen's award-winning stout Hell and Damnation and Flying Dog's multi-faceted and enigmatic Gonzo Imperial Porter. Thus the hop-laden, black-as-night imperial stout Bat out of Hell was born. The brewery has had a lot of success – in 2010 it was the only European brewery to make the Top 10 in RateBeer's Best Brewers in the World awards. The brewery is also home to a restaurant and a shop, which sells some of the best craft beers from around the world. The annual Borefts Beer Festival is also held at the brewery in early autumn.

DE MOLEN KOPI LOEWAK

DE MOLEN TSARINA ESRA

DE MOLEN HEMEL & AARDE

TASTING NOTES

KOPI LOEWAK IMPERIAL STOUT, 9.5% ABV

This beer is made with Kopi Luwak, the most expensive coffee bean in the world. The beans have been eaten by the Asian palm civet, a small squirrel-like animal. The beans are indigestible, and once excreted are collected, washed, and roasted. The beer has an intense, coffee bitterness.

FOOD PAIRING: It pairs well with handmade, bittersweet milk or dark Belgian chocolates.

TSARINA ESRA IMPERIAL PORTER, 11% ABV

As dark as a starless night, this beer is ebony in colour with a small creamy, pale brown head. It tastes of honey, vanilla, black malts, espresso coffee, dark chocolate, ginger, port, and prunes. It's full-bodied with soaring alcohol notes.

FOOD PAIRING: Try with strong flavours such as a rich blue cheese, tiramisu, or even a bowl of chocolate ice cream.

HEMEL & AARDE IMPERIAL STOUT, 9.5% ABV

Heaven and earth in a bottle. The earth comes from the heavily peated malt used to make Bruichladdich whisky, while heaven is the soaring angelic chorus of roasted chocolate, burnt liquorice, and smouldered pinewood.

FOOD PAIRING: Search out dark chocolate flavours, ripe blue cheeses, or woodchip-smoked chicken or salmon.

GROLSCH PREMIUM LAGER

ALFA

www.alfabier.nl

THERE ARE NOT MANY BREWERIES left in the Netherlands that can trace their roots back to the 19th century. Joseph Meens founded the Alfa brewery in 1870 and to this day, it brews using water from its own well. It is one of the few Dutch brewers still to adhere to German purity laws and its best- known beer is Edel Pils, an easy-drinking beer that has a subtle aroma of citrus hops.

BUDELS

www.budels.nl

AN ANCHOR, A SYMBOL OF HOPE, has been linked to the Budels brewery since it was founded in 1870 in the Brabant city of Budel by Gerardus Arts. It still appears on the beer labels today. The brewery is now managed by the fourth generation of the Arts family and produces a range of top- and bottom-fermented beers. Many of its beers are inspired by German brewing traditions.

DE 3 HORNE

www.de3horne.nl

PUSHING THE BOUNDARIES OF BEER is a passion for Sjef Groothuis, who founded the 3 Horne brewery in 1991. He was one of a new wave of brewers in the Netherlands, fighting back against the predominance of mass-produced pilsner-style beers in his country. At first Groothuis drew inspiration from Belgian beers, but he has also experimented with many fruits including apricots and blackcurrants. He is best known for his banana beer, Bananatana, a 7% ABV top-fermented ale.

DE BEKEERDE SUSTER

www.beiaardgroep.eu

THURSDAY OR FRIDAY are always good days to have a beer in the "Converted Sister", if you want to enjoy the sweet smell of brewing. Standing at the back of this small and often crowded bar is a tangle of pipes and shining copper vessels, with more behind some glass doors, where the brewers work. The brewmaster is the experienced Harrie Vermeer, who produces a range of blonds, dubbels, and tripels, including a 4.9% ABV wheat beer flavoured with citrus and coriander.

DE PRAEL

www.deprael.nl

"TOGETHER WE CAN MAKE BEER" is the motto of the De Prael brewery, which can be found down a rather unprepossessing alley, a short walk from Central Station in Amsterdam. It was set up in 2002 by two home-brewers, Arno Kooy and Fer Kok, who worked in a nearby psychiatric hospital. They employed several rehabilitating patients as members of staff, and the brewery has now started using volunteers from the hospital. The brewery has since grown, but is still run with a strong social conscience. All the beers in the excellent range of Dutch- and Belgian-style beers are named after singers who are known for singing sentimental Dutch folk songs.

DE SCHANS

www.schansbier.nl

THE SMALL DE SCHANS BREWERY and distillery is located in the village of Uithoorn, on the river Amstel, just beyond the suburbs of Amsterdam. Former home-brewer Guus Roijen designed the original brewery, and installed it in 1998 in a former barber's shop on a street called Schans. The brewery's small output contains some interesting gems including an American Stout of some complexity, a saison, and a strong Belgian abbey-style ale.

EMELISSE

www.emelisse.nl

EMELISSE IS ONE OF A GROWING BAND of Dutch breweries who are turning their back on producing only pils-style beer. Its range, produced onsite in view of the attached restaurant, includes a heavily hopped IPA, a smoked beer, and even a robust imperial stout. Brewmaster Kees Bubberman is a keen fan of flavoured hops and often uses varieties from the US and New Zealand. The flavours in his Espresso Stout beer are boosted by coffee beans from Italy. The brewery's annual production is growing steadily and much of its beer is now exported to countries including the US, Brazil, and Europe.

GROLSCH

www.grolsch.nl

THE GROLSCH BREWERY can trace its roots back to 1615, but today it is owned by international brewer SAB-Miller. Its beers

are often sold in distinctive swing-top cap bottles, doing away with the need for an opener. Grolsch's best-known beer is its Premium Pilsner, also known as Premium Lager, which is a bold, spicy beer with a touch of sweetness. Its wide range of brews also includes a traditional hefeweizen.

GULPENER

www.gulpener.nl

A COMMITMENT to the local environment sees the Gulpener brewery sourcing all its malted barley, wheat, rye and spelt, and hops from a cooperative of farmers in the Limburg region. Brewer Jan Willem den Hartog says he is proud to work closely with farmers and has recently introduced a range of three organic beers. One of his most interesting beers is Korenwolf, a flavourful Belgian-style white beer that tastes of elderflower; the brewery also produces Korenwolf Rosé – a sweet, balanced beer flavoured with raspberries.

HANZE-STADS

www.hanze-stadsbrouwerij.nl

IN THE MIDDLE AGES, there were more than 40 breweries in the ancient Hanseatic city of Zutphen. Sadly, they are now all gone. However, a small brewpub in the city's centre is now open and is attempting to bring brewing back to the city. At Hanze-Stads, a range of top-fermented and unfiltered and unpasteurized beers are produced. Always on the bar is a blonde, a dubbel, and a tripel. Seasonal beers include a 12% ABV barleywine, described as a "dark digestive beer for the winter months".

HEMEL

www.brouwerijdehemel.nl

HEAVEN ("HEMEL") is indeed a special place. The brewery was set up by Dutch beer veteran Herm Hegger in 1983. Operating as the Raven, it produced the first Dutch white beer style, White Raven. It enjoyed such commercial success that the brand was sold to Oranjeboom and the brewery closed down.

Now the town of Nijmegen has had a second coming and the revived brewery, launched in 1996, has made a conscious decision not to grow too large. Located within a 12th-century cloister, it describes itself as a living brewery museum. The brewery produces several traditional Dutch-style beers and a cask-matured beer brandy.

HERTOG JAN

www.hertogjan.nl

NOW A VERY SMALL COG in the international wheels of the Anheuser-Busch InBev empire, the Hertog Jan ("Duke John") brewery is still viewed with affection by many Dutch beer fans. They remember it from 1981, when it was saved from closure by a management buyout. In the years that followed, it contributed to a revival of beer culture in the country with its range of bottom-fermented beers. Its Dubbel, a dark ale made with roasted malt, wheat, and brewing sugar, is brewed in the style of a strong Belgian beer.

JOPEN

www.jopen.nl

JOPEN BREWERY WAS FOUNDED in 1994 by a group of beer enthusiasts who wanted to revive the lost beer styles of the Dutch city of Haarlem, which was once famed for brewing – the last brewery had closed in 1916. The first beer produced was Hoppenbier, which is made to a recipe from 1501 and is named after the *Jopen*, an ancient type of brewing vessel. Strong in alcohol, at 6.8% ABV, it is made with barley, wheat, and oats. Top-fermented, it has a high hop content that brings a floral aroma and then a long bitter finish. Jopen's Bokbier is the highest-selling beer produced by an independent brewery in the Netherlands.

KLEIN DUIMPJE

www.kleinduimpje.nl

FORMER HOME-BREWER Erik Bouman has turned a hobby and a passion into a business – the Klein Duimpje, which translates as "Tom Thumb" brewery. The brewery might be small, but the range of beers it produces is large. Erik looks to the US, England, and Belgium for his top-fermented creations. Bouman's best-known beer is an espresso coffee and chocolate porter. It is the beer that launched his career, winning a major Dutch home-brewing competition in 1997.

LA TRAPPE

www.latrappe.nl

LA TRAPPE IS A TRAPPIST BREWERY within the walls of the Onze Lieve Vrouw van Koningshoeven Abbey. Beers can be called Trappist if they are brewed within a monastery, with the monks showing some involvement in the management of the brewery. A portion of the profits goes towards the abbey's charitable works. La Trappe is probably the most commercial of all Trappist breweries and produces a wide range of beers including a tongue-tingling 10% ABV brew called Quadrupel, which is matured in oak casks. Visitors are invited to sample the whole range in the monastery's tasting shop.

LINDEBOOM

www.lindeboom.nl

LINDEBOOM IS A SMALL FAMILY BREWER from Limburg, a province in the southernmost part of the Netherlands. The brewery was founded in 1870 by Willem Geenen and is still owned by members of his family; it was named after a lime tree growing next to the brewery. It produces a range of bottom- and top-fermented beers. The brewery's pilsner has some sweetcorn notes and a floral herbal hoppy note with, of course, a hint of lime.

MOMMERIETE

www.mommeriete.nl

TWO FORMER HOME-BREWERS, Gert and Carina Kelder, have been conjuring up great beers commercially for nearly a decade. The pair were inspired by strong Belgian beers and they spent 15 years experimenting with recipes, ingredients, and yeasts before summoning up the courage to turn a hobby into a business. Among their core range of beers is Scheerse Triple, at 9.9% ABV, which has won them many fans. It is laden with handfuls of spicy hops, while flavours of honey, tobacco, and pepper dance across the tongue. Other regulars include Blond, Meibock, Klokhenne's Weizen, Gramsbarger Najaars Bock, and Bisschops Bier.

ST CHRISTOFFEL

www.christoffelbier.nl

FOUNDED IN 1986, the St Christoffel brewery is named after the patron saint of the former mining town of Roermond in Limburg. It is one of the oldest of the new wave of Dutch breweries and all of its beers are bottom-fermented in open vessels. It best-known beer is Christoffel Blond, at 6% ABV, which is full of crisp, spicy flavours. An unfiltered and unpasteurized beer, it has been named the best beer in Holland on several occasions. A dark, wintery doppelbock, brewed for at least four months, is another regular.

BALADIN

BALADIN XYAUYÙ

More than just a brewer, Teo Musso at Baladin is in the vanguard of a movement to transform people's discernment of beer. He is on a mission to spread the culture of beer into the world of gastronomy.

THE EVER-CONFIDENT Teo Musso's brewery and bar is in Piozzo, a small village high up in the Piemontese hills above Asti and Barolo wine country. "Baladin" is a French word meaning "storyteller" and Teo seeks to express himself through his beers, which he sees as an extension of himself. Musso opened his brewpub in 1996 and designed his beer bottles in a style similar to that of wine bottles, so that the beers would also be consumed in restaurants alongside food. Some consider him to be the Frank Zappa of the beer world and like the late US musician, he is tall, languid, and studiously unkempt. His adventurous dedication, desire to be different, and search for perfection, make him, like Zappa, stand out from

the crowd. His beers are eclectic and experimental and a challenge to many people's preconceptions. For a start, they are not heavily advertised, bland, yellow, or always served chilled.

Teo is on a mission to get wine to leave centre stage and for beer to take its place. His creations are as much fine art as craft and science. As a man with a firm idea of his place in the pantheon of brewers, his Xyauyù has the "drink-by" advice on the label, "to be consumed by the end of the world". He even plays music to his beers using headphones, just like some expectant parents do with their unborn children. After all, his fermentation vessels are the wombs of his creations. One composer has even written a piece of music to be played at different stages of the fermentation.

So what notes does he use to compose his beer symphonies? The rhythm section is of course barley and hops. There could be a chorus of fruity flavours and spices. Often beer yeast will have to play second fiddle to wine or whisky yeasts. But, in front of it all, is the conductor, Teo Musso, armed only with his imagination and creativity.

A work of art
Brewer Teo Musso wants his beers to stand out from the crowd

BALADIN ISAAC

BALADIN NORA

TASTING NOTES

XYAUYÙ BARLEY WINE, 14% ABV
This complex brown beer is aged in a barrel for at least 18 months, which brings out exceptional swirling sherry flavours. It sits very still and brooding in the glass, with no head or carbonation. The result is a complex, rich, nutty beer with aromas of raisins, prunes, and well-polished old furniture. A vintage beer, it evolves with age.

FOOD PAIRING: A perfect nightcap, it pairs well with rich chocolate biscuits.

ISAAC WHITE ALE, 5% ABV
There is something precocious about the citrus and spice of this beer, which almost scrambles out of the glass. But the energy of the curaçao and coriander is softened by the fruit flavours of figs and poached pears. Chilled, it's a real refresher.

FOOD PAIRING: Serve on its own to guests before dinner or pair it with a light salad or fish.

NORA SPICED ALE, 6.8% ABV
Made with unmalted kamut, an ancient wheat variety, it is laden with ginger and orange zest. Amber in colour, on the nose there are wafts of vanilla and red roses. It has a long, almost vinous finish. Myrrh provides a balsamic bitterness.

FOOD PAIRING: Pair with sweet desserts such as a sticky ginger and pear pudding, or an Arabian rose water pudding.

BIRRIFICIO ITALIANO

Agostino Arioli, founder of Birrificio Italiano, is a master brewer and an artist with superb technical ability and meticulous attention to detail, who eloquently expounds the complexity and poetry of brewing.

ARIOLI IS REGARDED as one of the pioneers of the Italian brewing scene. He regards his beers as works of art and the ingredients he uses are the colours he uses to construct his pictures. He started to brew while he was still at school, but it was a trip to the Granville Island Brewery in Vancouver, Canada that opened up his mind to the seemingly inexhaustible potential of the brewing process.

He set up Birrificio Italiano brewpub in Lurago Marinone near Lake Como, with his brother Stefano and some friends. At first he concentrated on German-style beers and his ambition was to brew the very best. His attention to detail demanded that he visit Bavarian farms to choose the hops he needed. His production processes are complex and time-consuming, but always intended to draw the flavours he seeks from the ingredients. His ambition was to emancipate a style such as pilsner from the thrall of international brewers and show that it can have flavour and hop aroma. As Arioli's own beer palate widened, so did the beers he produced. Flowers, cinnamon, sour cherries, ginger, blackcurrant, and wild yeast have all been used in his creations. His desire to create easy-drinking, challenging beers full of flavour is as undiminished as ever.

THE FACTS...

OWNER Birrificio Italiano
FOUNDED 1994
ADDRESS Nuovo Birrificio Italiano srl, Via Monviso, 1, 22070 – Limido Comasco, Como
WEBSITE www.birrificio.it
PHILOSOPHY Transforming emotions and ideas into wonderful beers

BIRRIFICIO ITALIANO
FLEURETTE

BIRRIFICIO ITALIANO
TIPOPILS

TASTING NOTES

FLEURETTE ALE, 3.8% ABV
Light, sparkling, and pink in colour, it has flavours of roses, violets, and elderflowers, and even hints of honey. There is a natural sourness to the beer, which is satisfying and piquant.

FOOD PAIRING: The perfect way to start a dinner party, Fleurette also drinks well while watching the sun set over the mountains of northern Italy.

TIPOPILS PILSNER, 5.2% ABV
Dry to taste, the golden beer swirls, with floral, grassy hop flavours and a hint of honey. Its finish is refreshing with a pleasing, lingering bitterness. It is easy to appreciate why it is regarded as one of the best craft pilsners in the world.

FOOD PAIRING: The beer's clean crisp flavours pair with pizza, spicy dishes, fatty foods, and good Italian cheeses.

SCIRES CHERRY ALE, 7.5% ABV
This beer has a feral personality, from the use of lactic bacteria, wild yeast, and black Vignola cherries. The beer is long-matured in a wooden barrel before being transferred to a bottle, where its swirling, sour, vinous flavours continue to evolve.

FOOD PAIRING: The tartness of the beer works surprisingly well with oysters or a creamy dessert such as a cheesecake.

BIRRIFICIO ITALIANO SCIRES

32 VIA DEI BIRRAI

www.32viadeibirrai.com

CRAFT BREWING AS A JOURNEY to exploring unknown paths is the philosophy of the three partners who founded 32. They have a passion for brewing and are proud to be recognized for only using 100 per cent Italian ingredients. Italians are renowned for the finesse and functionality of their designs – think Ferrari, for example – and it is these skills that they bring to their beers and the bottles they are put into. Golden-hued Audace, a strong Belgian-style ale that swirls with spice and citrus notes, is drinkable art.

ALMOND 22

www.birraalmond.com

THE GREAT ITALIAN composer Claudio Monteverdi once said "the end of all good music is to affect the soul". Jurij Ferri, the founder of Almond 22, believes good beer should similarly affect the soul. Many of the ingredients for his unpasteurized and unfiltered beers come from the rolling green hills and mountains of Abruzzo, where his brewery is. Ferri's "expressions" draw inspiration from English and Belgian styles, but he delights in a search for new tastes.

BARLEY

www.barley.it

"BEER AND WINE should share the same table", says brewer Nicola Perra, who founded the Sardinian brewery in 2006 with Isidoro Mascia. Like many Italian brewers, he uses local ingredients in his beers. Deep red Cannonau grapes grown in his vineyard add vinous character to Perra's BB10 barleywine; the grapes' must is boiled down to form a rich syrup. The strong sipping beer soars with rich, dark fruit flavours and is wonderful enjoyed with a fresh Sardinian sheep's cheese.

BEBA

www.birrabeba.it

WHEN THE BEBA BREWERY was founded in 1996, the number of craft brewers in Italy could probably be counted on the fingers of two hands. Now there are more than 400 of them. BEBA's pioneering founders, brothers Alessandro and Enrico Borio, like bold, fresh flavours. Rye is used in the seasonal Talco to produce a tart, refreshing summer beer.

One of BEBA's strongest beers is Motor Oil. Dark, full-bodied, and bursting with liquorice and burnt roast malt flavours, its finish is long and memorable.

BI-DU

www.lebirredelbidu.altervista.org

HIGH UP IN THE ALPINE MOUNTAINS, up a seemingly tortuous road, where Italy and Switzerland meet, is the Bi-Du brewpub. The beers produced there are as big and bold as the owner and brewer, the rugged, bearded man of the mountains, Beppe Vento. Beppe likes hops – lots of them – and they partner well with the dishes he sells, which are hearty portions of sausages and sauerkraut or risotto flavoured with ginger. But Beppe also has a softer side and his Rodersch is a subtle interpretation of a German kölsch. Other beers include Artigian ("Artisan") Ale, a copper-red brew with 6.2% ABV and Confine, a dark English-style porter.

BIRRA DEL BORGO

www.birradelborgo.it

THE FIRST COMMERCIAL BEER that former home-brewer Leonardo Di Vincenzo made when he opened Del Borgo in 2005 was ReAle APA, a British-inspired American Pale Ale that he peppered with US hops. Di Vincenzo's exploration of the flavours that hops bring has produced My Antonia, an imperial pilsner made in collaboration with US brewer Sam Calagione of Dogfish Head Brewery (see pp.154–155). It includes fistfuls of Saaz, Simcoe, and Warrior hops. He has also used tobacco, tea leaves, and gentian roots in his beers. In collaboration with Teo Musso of Baladin Brewery (see p.124), Leo has also been involved with Open Baladin, a brewpub in the heart of Rome and Birreria in New York.

BRÙTON

www.bruton.it

THE MINOANS of ancient Crete are reputed to have drunk a beer called Brùton. No records of this Bronze Age beer exist, so the brewers at this smart brewpub in Tuscany have looked to the US and Belgium for inspiration for many of their creations. One of their most interesting beers is Bianca, which is made with Italian-grown spelt and unmalted wheat. The waspish, opaque beer has a sharp acidity with layered flavours of coriander and the zest of orange peel.

CITABIUNDA

www.birrificiocitabiunda.it

THE ROLLING HILLS OF PIEDMONT are seemingly filled with endless rows of grape vines. The region is famed for the quality of its wines, but it is also home to a little piece of beer-heaven, the brewpub Birrificio CitaBiunda. In the local dialect, the brewery's name means "blonde girl", and perhaps brewer Marco Marengo was thinking of her when he created his take on a Belgian witbier, Biancaneive. This curvaceous brew bursts with flowery notes from the use of champagne yeast.

DUCATO

www.birrificiodelducato.net

THE BEER CREATIONS of brewer Giovanni Campari of the Ducato microbrewery are as soaring and exhilarating as a chorus singing opera written by local legend Giuseppe Verdi. Campari founded the brewery in 2007 and is renowned as one of the country's most creative and passionate brewers. He weaves together art, science, and time to create some great beers. One is the award-winning Sally Brown, which Giovanni first brewed as a home-brewer. Featuring ten different malts, it is as dark and smooth as blackened silk.

GRADO PLATO

www.gradoplato.it

SERGIO AND GABRIELE ORMEA'S dream came true when they were able to open their own brewpub in Chieri near Turin in 2003. People liked the beers, and such was their success that they had to move to new premises in 2008 to accommodate demand for their brews. Regional favourites feature in their restaurant – especially snails – which are cooked in 20 different ways. Snails have not been used in their beers yet, although other native treats such as locally grown chestnuts have.

LAMBRATE

www.birrificiolambrate.com

COPIED BUT NEVER BETTERED, Lambrate was the first brewpub to open in the high-fashion city of Milan in 1996. The owners were inspired by visiting the famed Brouwerij 't IJ (see p.120) brewery in Amsterdam, Holland. Together, they created a mecca for the Italian craft beer movement, which continues to gather pace. It's a busy, bustling, dark brown bar and the perfect place to drink their range of brews.

MALTUS FABER IMPERIAL

L'OLMAIA

www.birrificioolmaia.com

BREWER MORENO ERCOLANI of L'Olmaia is fanatical about one thing – high-quality craft beer. After two years learning to brew at home, he installed a small commercial brewery in a farmhouse. It was 2005, the farmhouse was known as L'Olmaia, after the three elm trees ("olmi") that cast their shadow across the building, and another brewery was born. Now on a larger site in Montepulciano, Siena, Moreno is still dedicated to producing the perfect beer. His Christmas brew uses honey made by bees that have feasted upon the local elm blossom.

MALTUS FABER

www.maltusfaber.com

A LOVE OF BELGIAN BEERS led two home-brewing friends, Fausto Marenco and Massimo Versaci, to set up the Maltus Faber brewery in 2007. It is located in a derelict building in Genoa, which was once a large brewery owned by Dreher and then Heineken. Massimo is a well-known collector of brewery artefacts, so it is hardly surprising that the brewery has many objects on display from Genoa's brewing history. One of its best beers is an imperial stout, which is full of chewy liquorice flavours with an aroma as intense as freshly brewed Italian espresso.

MONTEGIOCO

www.birrificiomontegioco.com

PEACHES, GRAPES, SAGE, AND CORIANDER all grown on the Tortona Hills have been used as ingredients in the beers made by former home-brewer Riccardo Franzosi at the Montegioco Brewery. He set up the brewery in 2005, and delights in ageing his ales in oak barrels to produce astringent vinous lemon and tannin flavours, which make them marvellous partners to fish dishes. The sourness in his Quarta Runa, a sour peach ale, comes from wild yeasts on the fruit's skin.

PANIL (TORRECHIARA)

www.panilbeer.com

IS IT REALLY TRUE THAT one of the world's best sour red beers – a historic style derived from Belgian Flanders and the Netherlands – is made in Italy, in a brewery founded in 2000?

Brewer Renzo Losi's love of ageing beer in barrels is perhaps inherited from his wine-making father. Panil's Barriqueè Sour is vinous, uncompromising, and spends three months brooding in a cognac barrel. The lacto and wild brett yeasts work in mysterious ways that are never predictable, but are always guaranteed to be interesting.

PICCOLO

www.piccolobirrificio.com

THERE IS NOTHING HALF-SIZED about the beers from Piccolo Brewery – brewer Lorenzo Bottoni hits the high notes with his brews, which easily charm the tastebuds. He set up the brewery in 2005 in the beautiful old town of Apricale, close to the Italian border with France. Probably his best-known beer is Chiostro. Belgian in style, it's a spiced blonde ale with strong yeast notes, spiced with wormwood, which adds some woody, bitter, and anise flavours.

SCARAMPOLA

www.birrificioscarampola.it

HOME FOR THE SCARAMPOLA BREWERY is the former Abbey of St Stephen in Millesimo, and it is here that brewer Maurizio Ghidetti devotes his time to creating his heavenly brews. Having spent five years in England studying local beers, he returned to Italy and worked at the Baladin Brewery (see p.124) alongside Teo Musso before setting up his own brewery in a former barn. He likes to use local ingredients, which is how chestnuts and the rare orange variety chinotto find their way into his beer. His Italian take on an IPA is flavoured with grapefruit, which adds a bitter piquancy and some intense citrus notes to those already present in the Cascade hops.

ZAHRE

www.zahrebeer.com

HIGH UP IN THE MOUNTAINS in the small village of Sauris, close to the Austrian and Slovenian borders, a local delicacy is smoked ham. When Sandro Petris set up his brewery there in 1999, it seemed only right to produce a beer to complement it. Petris's Affumicata, which has a light but unmistakable aroma of smoked barley malt, is one of an interesting range of lagered beers produced. The Canapa is flavoured with Campagnola hemp flowers, which add a gentle floral sweetness.

GUINNESS

Often known simply as "the black stuff", Guinness is the perfect pint of blacker-than-night stout with a bold white collar on top. Thanks in part to its iconic advertising, it is one of the most recognizable brands in the world.

THE FACTS...

OWNER Diageo

FOUNDED 1759

ADDRESS St James' Gate, Dublin 8

WEBSITE www.guinness.com

PHILOSOPHY It's good for you

THE FOUNDER OF THE BREWERY, Arthur Guinness, probably began to brew porter in the 1770s. At the time, the brewing industry was moving from the farm cottage into the factory. Ambitious brewers were not only transporting their beers to England's fastest-growing industrial cities, but they were following soldiers and civil servants to the far flung corners of the world as the British Empire grew.

By 1880, the brewery's fame and its beer, a full-bodied stout, had travelled far and wide; Guinness was the biggest brewer in the world, producing more than 1.6 million hl (one million barrels) a year. Although many brewers would have brewed their own stout, Guinness gained a near-monopoly of the style during World War I, when fuel restrictions made it difficult for British maltsters to roast their own grains – there were no such restrictions in Ireland.

By the late 1920s, however, the beer's fortunes were waning in the UK: consumers were turning away from dark stouts towards lighter beers. But never afraid to make a bold move, the company took a decision that would ultimately seal its success. In 1927, it trialled an advertising campaign in Scotland. The success of the slogan "Guinness is good for you" led to a dynamic campaign in the UK in 1929. The health properties of Extra Stout were proclaimed far and wide – advertisements stated that Guinness was good for the nerves, digestion, insomnia, and tiredness. At one stage, pregnant women and new mothers were advised to drink Guinness to help prevent anaemia – doctors even prescribed it. These days, brewers can no longer make health claims for their beer in advertisements, but the legacy of them lives on. A display of Guinness' iconic advertising is on show at the brewery's visitor centre in Dublin. Its well-known advertisements, created by John Gilroy from 1930 to 1960, use slogans such as "Good things come to those who wait", "My Goodness My Guinness", and "Lovely day for a Guinness" (see left).

Today, Guinness is brewed in more than 50 countries worldwide and there are a number of variants, including the three draught variations – Red, Extra Smooth, and Extra Cold – described on the facing page. In many of these countries, it's fermented from an extract made in Ireland to which local grains are added; the Nigerian variant uses some sorghum, which adds a banana flavour. Drinkers in the UK and Ireland usually see it sold on draught, but in many other parts of the world it is sold in bottles in a variety of strengths ranging from 4.1% ABV to 8% ABV.

Guinness is distinguished from other stouts by its intense dryness and the smoky, roasted flavours that come from unmalted barley that has almost been burnt to a cinder. Inside the the St James' Gate Brewery, which was the first steel-framed multi-storey building in the British Isles, there is a giant drum, where the barley is roasted, filling the air with luscious, burnt coffee aromas.

A feature of the Guinness served in Irish pubs is the length of time taken to pour it. Often a pub will start to pour several pints before opening time, and then let them stand before customers come in. In the UK, publicans are advised to take 119.5 seconds to pour the perfect pint of the black stuff.

Lovely day for a GUINNESS

JOHN GILROY POSTER
"LOVELY DAY FOR A GUINNESS"

GUINNESS DRAUGHT

Black beauty
A distinct dryness and smoky flavours mark Guinness out from other stouts

GUINNESS FOREIGN EXTRA

GUINNESS ORIGINAL

TASTING NOTES

DRAUGHT STOUT, 4.1% ABV

Fruit, cream, and dark toffee flavours mingle with tones of liquorice. There is a notable but not overpowering hop flavour. Its finish is intensely dry.

FOOD PAIRING: Dry stouts are traditionally paired with fresh oysters and champagne.

FOREIGN EXTRA STOUT, 7.5% ABV

Deep, dark ruby-brown in colour with a rich and powerful taste of burnt liquorice and a hint of wild yeast. When made in Dublin, some beer is stored in vats for 100 days, which produces an intense lactic flavour. This is then blended with a freshly matured stout.

FOOD PAIRING: Pair it with a dark, not too sweet, chocolate cake or a spicy sausage like chorizo.

ORIGINAL 4.3% ABV

The colour is dark and topped by a wispy brown head. The nose is dominated by hops but this gives way to notes of burnt toast and rich malty flavours, including coffee and liquorice.

FOOD PAIRING: Partner it with a well-matured cheddar cheese or a hearty beef stew. Alternatively, use the Guinness as a float for vanilla ice cream.

RED STOUT, 4.1% ABV

Slightly sweeter than Guinness Draught, this beer's blackness is tinged with wisps of red. The trademark toasted barley is still in evidence but it lacks the coffee and liquorice intensity of its older sister beer. Light to drink, there is a good bitter finish.

FOOD PAIRING: Sausages and a sweet onion gravy with potato mash were invented for this beer.

EXTRA COLD STOUT, 4.1% ABV

The same beer as Guinness Draught, it's a ruby-black-bodied beer that is topped by the trademark Guinness head, which is created by the injection of nitrogen into the beer as it is served. Served at 3.5°C (38.3°F) to give a chilled crispness to the taste.

FOOD PAIRING: Pair it with a plate of battered fish and a bowl of piping hot chips with a sprinkling of crunchy sea salt.

EXTRA SMOOTH STOUT, 5% ABV

A Ugandan version of the beer, this is brewed in Kampala. Local ingredients are underpinned by an unfermented but hopped extract that is shipped from Dublin. It has the distinctive Guinness tang, but the extra alcohol gives it a warmer finish.

FOOD PAIRING: Pair with a hearty, slow-cooked red meat stew with a stock made of Guinness.

FINLANDIA

There is something elementally primal about a glass of Sahti, one of the world's oldest beer styles. Sahti was probably first made by Nordic farmers in medieval times, but its origins could go back even further than that.

THE FACTS...

OWNER Finlandia Sahti Ky
FOUNDED 1992
ADDRESS Palomäentie 342, Sastamala 38510
WEBSITE www.finlandiasahti.fi
PHILOSOPHY Keeping an ancient tradition alive

SAHTI IS PRIMITIVE BEER THAT CAN BE MADE from a variety of grains – malted and unmalted, including barley, rye, wheat, and oats; sometimes bread made from these grains is fermented instead of the malt itself, often using a baker's yeast. Whatever grain is used, the mash is always strained through juniper twigs, which are traditionally placed in a wooden trough-shaped tun, called a *kuurna* in Finnish. The *kuurna* is said to add mystery and complexity to the beer, as it contains many wild yeasts.

Finland historically had some of the most restrictive alcohol laws in Europe and for many years there was a tradition of making alcohol at home illegally. However, a change in the laws allowed Antti Vesala to set up a small brewery in 1992 and sell Sahti beer on his farm at Matku, north of the town of Forssa. He was one of the few people trying to keep this ancient beer style alive.

Finlandia's wort is predominately rye and some oats, which, following tradition, are boiled and strained through a bed of tart juniper branches. A true ale, there are no hops used in its production. Instead juniper brings gin-like and botanical flavours to the beer.

Petteri Lähdeniemi and Auli Mattila took over the production of the beer from Antti Vesala in 2011 and started selling in 2012. While the production of Sahti is likely to remain small and available to buy only in Finland, they are determined to ensure this beer, with its ancient heritage, lives on. Home-brew kits of Finlandia can be bought outside Finland for those curious to taste this ancient brew. Finlandia Sahti was recognized at the Helsinki Beer Festival in 1999 and 2003.

TASTING NOTES

SAHTI STRONG 10% ABV
This amber, protein-hazy beer is topped by a rough white head. The aroma is earthy with rising notes of juniper and cloves. It tastes of bubblegum, bananas, and rye. Slightly oily, it is sweet and full-bodied.
FOOD PAIRING: Try this brew with Scandinavian classics such as pickled herring and slices of rye bread.

TAVALLINEN SAHTI, 8% ABV
Orange in colour, it has a slightly medicinal nose with lots of banana notes. Although it lacks the body of Sahti Strong, it offers an equally interesting beer experience.
FOOD PAIRING: Pair with a a sharp Wensleydale cheese, slices of rye bread, and sour cranberry relish.

FINLANDIA SAHTI STRONG

KARJALA

Karjala beer has been brewed in Finland since 1932. In the early days it was made by a cooperative. Now owned by the mighty Heineken group, the brand is recognized as a national icon.

THE FACTS...

OWNER Heineken
FOUNDED 1932
ADDRESS Atomitie 2a, FI-00371 Helsinki
WEBSITE www.hartwall.fi
PHILOSOPHY Proud to be Finnish

Finland is not an easy place to be a brewer. The country has always had a difficult relationship with alcohol. Most is sold through a national chain of state-owned and carefully controlled Alco stores, which prefer imported beers to locally made types. Other shops are banned from selling beers that are stronger than 4.7% ABV. It is hardly surprising that many Finns take the ferry to Estonia and bring beer back by the vanload to drink at home, and are regular visitors to Sweden to drink there.

The environment is hardly one that encourages small brewers to prosper. In Finland, beer is differentiated according to five different tax bands: I, II, III, IVA, and IVB, which are based on the strength of the beer, from a low alcohol content to a maximum of 8% ABV. These bands came to be used as a way of distinguishing between different beers, including those in Karjala's range.

Karjala beers were first brewed by the East-Karelian cooperative company in 1932. This was taken over by Finnish soft drinks company Hartwall group in 1966, who went on to buy other breweries in Finland, including Lapin Kulta. In 2002, the group was bought by Scottish & Newcastle, which, in turn, was taken over in 2008 by a consortium comprising Carlsberg and Heineken, with the Dutch brewer Heineken assuming full control.

Finland often had a strained relationship with its giant neighbour the Soviet Union. This wasn't helped when in the 1960s, a Soviet diplomat criticized the image on Karjala's logo and beer labels, which he claimed represented a western sword brushing aside a Russian sabre. While the spat was bad for diplomatic relations, it was good for the brewer, as many Finns started to buy the beers to show their patriotism.

Prized ales
Some Finns regard it as their patriotic duty to drink Karjala beers

KARJALA IVA   **KARJALA IVB**   **KARJALA III**

TASTING NOTES

IVA LAGER, 5.2% ABV
Barley sugar flavours can be detected in this deep golden beer, which has a rich, malty taste and a large, foaming head. IVA has a warming, satisfying alcohol finish.
FOOD PAIRING: The sweetness of the beer will partner with hearty meat stews.

IVB LAGER, 8% ABV
A Swedish take on a doppelbock style. This strong lager has a deep golden colour and a large foaming head. Sweet to taste, the alcohol finish is long.
FOOD PAIRING: Pair with sweet, crunchy popcorn.

III LAGER, 4.6% ABV
An easy-drinking, pale golden-yellow beer, with a large white foaming head. Sweet to taste, there are tantalizing layers of toffee and caramel in this brew.
FOOD PAIRING: Pair with hot dogs, mustard, and some freshly baked bread rolls.

1516 BREWING CO

A small brewpub in Vienna, 1516 Brewing is determined to show that it is not just US brewers who can use aromatic hops to great effect – its beers offer a window into the exciting world of Austrian craft brewing.

THE FACTS...

OWNER 1516 Brewing Co
FOUNDED 1998
ADDRESS Schwarzenbergstraße 2, 1010 Vienna
WEBSITE www.1516brewingcompany.com
PHILOSOPHY To use hops and lots of them

VIENNA PLAYED AN IMPORTANT ROLE in the development of beer. It was here in 1841 that the great brewer Anton Dreher established a new style of beer – Vienna lager. He introduced a rich malted barley, with a glowing amber nuance and a subtle sweet texture to its flavour. He went on to use it in the first bottom-fermented lager, using large cold maturation tanks to condition and clear the beer.

Then, as now, brewers were inspired by other countries and breweries. Dreher, who came from a family of brewers, was a great student of the brewing process. He visited England and Scotland in 1833, where he admired the techniques used to produce beers of consistent strengths and colour.

Dreher's malty, amber, clear beer quickly became popular and was taken to the US by German-speaking immigrants, who no doubt brewed it there. But the style fell out of favour as US brewers started to brew large volumes of pale, light lagers. Thankfully, it was revived by the new wave of US craft brewers. A good thing too, as it had all but died out in Europe. 1516 Brewing has brought Vienna lager back to its hometown and sells it in its cosy, unashamedly American-style brewpub. Considered one of Vienna's most adventurous and

exciting pubs, it draws inspiration for many of its beers from across the Atlantic and it is not uncommon for visiting brewers to roll up their sleeves and do a spot of brewing there. 1516's founder Horst Asanger is on a mission to show that there is more to brewing in Austria than just the triad of helles, pils, and hefeweizens – and that they know how to use hops, too.

TASTING NOTES

WEISSE BAVARIAN WHEAT BEER, 5.2% ABV
Brewed with a yeast strain from a brewery near Frankfurt, it is a cross-continent collaboration. Turbid and overflowing with banana and clove flavours, it swirls with lemon flavours from the US Cascade hops.

FOOD PAIRING: Pair it with sweet-savoury dishes such as grilled chicken with rice and satay peanut sauce.

SAVINJSKI IMPERIAL IPA 10.3% ABV
This beer is aged in wooden casks formerly used by Château Mouton Rothschild and the Glenmorangie distillery. Belgian pale and crystal malts and aromatic hops from Slovenia – Magnum and Savinjski – create a soaring fruit bowl of red fruits, lemon, and whisky flavours. The finish is long and bitter.

FOOD PAIRING: Try it with a sticky and rich Black Forest gâteau or similarly rich dessert.

AMERIKANSKY IPA, 5.8% ABV
This American-style pale ale is brewed by a Ukrainian brewer. Hints of brown sugar and burnt orange vie with the citrus aromas from the Slovenian hops, Magnum and Dana, and whole-leaf Cascade hops from Washington State.

FOOD PAIRING: Pair it with a good steak and potato wedges.

1516 BREWING CO WEISSE

SCHLOSS EGGENBERG

Every year, on the same day in December, the brewers at Eggenberg start the long process of brewing one of the world's most famous beers, which was for many years renowned as the strongest ever made.

LIKE MANY BREWERIES whose history seems impossibly long, brewing on the site at Eggenberg, an area north of the Alps, first began in the 10th century. The current brewery was established in 1640 and today it is run by the seventh generation of the Stöhr family, who have owned it for over 200 years. It is perhaps now best known for a beer it began to brew in 2000 – the world-famous doppelbock called Samichlaus Bier, once regarded as the strongest beer in the world.

The beer was first brewed on 6 December 1979 (St Nicholas' Day or Samichlaus, in Austria) for sale over the Christmas season in 1980 by the Swiss brewery, Hürlimann. Its long, cold maturation of nearly ten months eats all the sugar in the malt, converting most of it into alcohol, creating a beer of some force and singular fruity intensity.

For many years, drinkers eagerly looked forward to the new Samichlaus beer coming on sale. They would compare it with vintages from previous years, while those with serious collections would seek out dusty, ageing bottles of the beer from their beer cellars, to reacquaint themselves with an old friend and see how it had changed.

However, the world of Samichlaus fans was shattered in 1997 when the brewery closed and was converted into offices for international companies, a shopping mall, and expensive apartments. But St

Nicholas must really exist, as the beer's fans got the present they'd been waiting for in 2000, when some ex-Hürlimann brewers, armed with a copy of the beer's original recipe, started to brew it again at the brewery in Eggenberg.

The family remain committed to ensuring that every year, while others celebrate St Nicholas' Day, their brewers will be starting the long, slow process of making this iconic brew ready for the following year. Other notable Eggenberg beers include Mac Queen's Nessie, a whisky malt red beer, and the award-winning Doppelbock Dunkel.

THE FACTS...

OWNER Eggenberg
FOUNDED 1640
ADDRESS Eggenberg 1, A-4655, Vorchdorf
WEBSITE www.schloss-eggenberg.at
PHILOSOPHY Custodian of a beer icon

TASTING NOTES

SAMICHLAUS BIER DOPPELBOCK, 14% ABV
Intense plum and prune flavours are exuded by this dark ruby prince of a beer. It's a biscuit tin of sweet malt flavours, which gives way to a long and warming alcohol finish.

FOOD PAIRING: Try with a slice of a fruit-rich cake, such as a German stollen seasonal cake, or with chocolates.

HOPFENKÖNIG PILSNER, 5.1% ABV
As its name suggests, Hopfenkönig has a hoppy, spicy citrus aroma and is the colour of pale hay. Light in body, its initial sweetness is followed by a short dry bitterness.

FOOD PAIRING: Pair with a plate of ham or a mild cheese.

URBOCK 23° DOPPELBOCK, 9.6% ABV
Dark and intense, Urbock 23° broodingly lagers for nine long months. A penetrating sugar sweetness is balanced by a bold hop bitterness.

FOOD PAIRING: Pair with a sugar-coated and roasted ham or a similar sweet cut of meat.

SCHLOSS EGGENBERG SAMICHLAUS BIER

SCHLOSS EGGENBERG HOPFENKÖNIG

SCHLOSS EGGENBERG URBOCK 23°

HAAND BRYGGERIET

In 2005, a fantastic foursome of beer enthusiasts, Arne Eide, Rune Eriksen, Egil Hilde, and Jens Maudal, decided to live their dream and set up their own brewery to explore the sublime and infinite variety of beer.

THE FACTS...

OWNER Haand Bryggeriet
FOUNDED 2005
ADDRESS Skogliveien 4, Bygg H, Sundland, 3047 Drammen
WEBSITE www.haandbryggeriet.net
PHILOSOPHY Making brewing fun

HAAND BRYGGERIET
HAANDBAKK

HAAND BRYGGERIET
FYR & FLAMME

For the love of beer
At Haand, the brewers try and encapsulate the adventure of brewing in all their beers

HAAND BRYGGERIET DARK FORCE

BREWING ISN'T WORK for the team at Haand Bryggeriet; it's an adventure – they volunteer at the brewery in their spare time. Their ambition was to learn how to recreate some of the craft beers they had sampled while travelling through Europe, while at the same time keeping Norway's ancient brewing traditions alive. They have a love of farmhouse brewing and take pleasure in the mysterious, transcendental qualities that wild yeast and lactic acid bacteria can bring to beer.

Some of their beers are aged in oak barrels – the first time this process has been used in Norway for more than 100 years. Brewer Jens Maudal says the barrels have been used for maturing red burgundy wine in France, and so they contribute some yeast and bacteria of their own. The first beer out of the barrels was sour and acetic, and they continue to experiment with this technique.

A battered wooden stick full of holes hangs from the ceiling in the brewery. It is the brewery's yeast stick. In the days of farmhouse brewing, a brewer would roll a wooden stick in the residue left over from a brew, which contained the yeast, and then place it in a new brew to start the process of turning sweet wort into beer. Such sticks are home to a complexity of wild flavours. They have yet to use the stick, but you can be assured that when they do, it will be a great adventure into the world of beer.

TASTING NOTES

HAANDBAKK OAK-AGED ALE, 8.5% ABV
This rustic vintage brew is fermented with a wild yeast and then stored in a wine barrel. Its ever-changing taste is tart and cheesy. Hints of leather, strawberry, and cherries can be detected.
FOOD PAIRING: Pair it with a good conversation – beers like this merit discussion and not distraction.

FYR & FLAMME AMERICAN STYLE IPA, 6.5% ABV
The citrus hops confirm the US heritage of this beer. There are swathes of herbal notes and some pine on the nose. It is not too sweet and there is a dry, satisfying citrus-hop finish.
FOOD PAIRING: American IPAs always go well with grilled, fatty foods, spicy foods, or pizza.

DARK FORCE WHEAT STOUT, 9% ABV
Liquid silk with dark fruits of the forest flavours; the wheat malt imparts a light touch. For beer of its strength, it drinks easily.
FOOD PAIRING: Pair with dark chocolate or a sweet dessert.

 # NØGNE Ø

The unflinching desire to produce the perfect bottle-conditioned ale has seen Nøgne Ø put Norway firmly on the map as a place where craft beers of real quality are produced.

Micro-might
Small might be beautiful but that doesn't stop Nøgne Ø being Norway's largest producer of bottle-conditioned beers

THE BEERS FROM NØGNE Ø are as uncompromising as the weather and sea-hewn rocks of the many craggy islands around Grimstad, the brewery's home. The company's name is taken from a phrase meaning "naked island", which was used by playwright Henrik Ibsen to describe the area. The 19th-century writer is renowned for bringing a new vitality to the theatre and for putting Norway on the map. The brewing team at Nøgne Ø hope their legacy will be that they've done the same for beer.

Co-founded by brewer Kjetil Jikiun, who had learnt to home-brew in the US, the early days were hard and work was often done for free. In a country where 98 per cent of beer consumption is of mainstream, industrial lagers, a brewery producing bottle-conditioned ales took time to become established. However, Nøgne Ø's refusal to cut corners, stint on raw materials, or compromise on their stubborn belief that better was preferable to bigger has seen the company become Norway's largest supplier of bottle-conditioned ales.

The best English Maris Otter barley goes into the beer, and the hops are usually chosen from the golden US quartet of Cascade, Centennial, Chinook, and Columbus. In addition to its range of more than 20 different beers, the brewery is the only European maker of sake, a traditional Japanese drink made from the fermentation of rice grains. Nøgne Ø's sake is made using a long and meticulous fermentation, unlike most commercial sakes.

TASTING NOTES

IMPERIAL STOUT 9% ABV
The beer's depth of flavour and ebony colour come from roasted and dark chocolate malt. It's a duet of rich, sweet malt flavours and bitterness from the aromatic and bittering hops.
FOOD PAIRING: Pair with chunks of dark bitter chocolate or freshly made vanilla ice cream.

SAISON 6.5% ABV
Like all good saisons, it's summer in a glass. A golden haze, with aromas of hay and citrus zest, it is a real refresher.
FOOD PAIRING: Pair with seafood such as fresh oysters.

BITTER ALE, 4.5% ABV
A great interpretation of an easy-drinking, hoppy English ale. A good malt body is topped by a soaring aroma from the hops.
FOOD PAIRING: Pairs well with many foods – particularly cheese.

NØGNE Ø IMPERIAL STOUT   **NØGNE Ø** SAISON   **NØGNE Ø** BITTER

AMBER

The end of Communist rule in Poland created a business environment that allowed new breweries to open. Amber Brewery is an independent family-run business producing unique regional beers in the tradition of the Gdańsk area.

THE FACTS...

OWNER Amber
FOUNDED 1992
ADDRESS Bielkówko ul, Gregorkiewicza 1, 83-050 Kolbudy
WEBSITE www.browar-amber.pl
PHILOSOPHY To continue the brewing tradition of Pomerania, famous since the Middle Ages

IN POLITICAL TERMS, Poland has played a pivotal role in the recent history of central and eastern Europe, sparking a movement that contributed to the end of Communism in 1989. But the political revolution didn't lead to a craft beer revolution. Many small breweries opened in Poland in the early 1990s, but multi-national companies, quick to see the size of the Polish beer market, moved in and bought up many of the country's breweries.

However, the Amber brewery, set up by farmer Andrew Przybyło soon after the end of the Communist era, has managed to survive. Mindful of the region's close links with the UK and the sea trade that brought in imperial stout, it brews its own Grand Imperial Porter. It also produces a number of other beers including a hefeweizen. Historically, a lot of brewing took place in the Gdańsk area – including the production of lower strength beers for drinking at breakfast time and stronger beers for sea travel. In 2008, the brewery produced, together with the Gdańsk History Museum, a well-lagered, amber-coloured beer, Johannes, in honour of one of the city's greatest brewers, Johannes Hevelius. However, the brewery has yet to take up the challenge of brewing a Grodziskie, a top-fermented, smoked wheat beer, once widely drunk in the region and now all but died out.

Native namesake
Koźlak is named after a rare goat that lives in the Tatra mountains

AMBER
GRAND IMPERIAL PORTER

AMBER
PIWO ZYWE

AMBER KOŹLAK

TASTING NOTES

GRAND IMPERIAL PORTER 8% ABV
A dark ebony colour with a ruby edge. There is a rich liquorice and roasted malt taste with hints of sweet chocolate and fresh black fruits. Quite sweet, it contains little hoppiness.

FOOD PAIRING: Pair with a chocolate mousse or a slice of sweet chocolate gâteau topped with strawberries.

PIWO ZYWE PILSNER, 6.2% ABV
Strong for a true pilsner, this unpasteurized beer is warm in alcohol and has some almost grass-like notes from the aromatic Polish-grown Lublin hops.

FOOD PAIRING: Pair with spicy Mexican or Asian dishes that contain chillies.

KOŹLAK DUNKEL BOCK, 6.5% ABV
A red-coloured beer, it is full of toffee and soft caramel flavours. There are hints of soft fruits, some freshly made bread, and a little hop bitterness.

FOOD PAIRING: Pair with sweeter-flavoured barbecued meats, roasts, and sausages. This beer can cope with some spice.

BROWARMIA KRÓLEWSKA

A small restaurant and microbrewery in the centre of Warsaw is flying the flag for craft brewing in Poland. Browarmia Królewska uses traditional European recipes to produce beers that cater to every taste.

THE FACTS...

OWNER Browarmia Królewska

FOUNDED 2005

ADDRESS Królewska 1 Str, Warsaw, Entrance from Krakowskie Przedmieście Str

WEBSITE www.browarmia.pl

PHILOSOPHY Proud to be Warsaw's first brewpub and restaurant

FEWER PEOPLE GO TO WARSAW to drink beer than travel to Munich in Germany or Brussels in Belgium. But if they do go, many seek out one of the city's few brewpubs, Browarmia Królewska, located in a vibrant part of the city centre.

The restaurant and microbrewery is a lively place, with a good selection of local food, although you can drink at the bar if you want to. Browarmia, which opened in 2005, was Warsaw's first restaurant and brewery and today produces 12 of its own beers. Customers who want to try a range of the beers produced can try a selection on a tray of four. Unusually for a Polish brewery, Browarmia produces not only bottom-fermented beers but also some made with top-fermented yeast.

Part of the joy of drinking in a brewpub is drinking close to where the beers are produced, and Browarmia is no exception. In the bar are two glistening copper vessels where the ingredients are heated and boiled. Behind glass windows are the open fermenters where the sweet wort, usually made with sweet Bavarian and Czech barley malts, ferment with aromatic Polish hops, Lubelski and Marynka. The brewers here have a healthy sense of humour and an understanding of the brewing process – they shun the hyperbolic and extravagant claims made by many others about their water, saying, "We use neither crystal waters of mountain streams or springs, nor water from artesian wells, rather our own high-quality municipal water". Also worth seeking out if you are an inquisitive beer hunter are the city's two other brewpubs, which operate under the name Bierhalle.

Beer beginnings
The joy of drinking in a brewpub is being close to where the beers are made

BROWARMIA KRÓLEWSKA PILS

TASTING NOTES

PILS 5% ABV

A hazy yellow, this unfiltered lager pours with a small white head. It has a pleasant bread malt taste mingled with grassy flavours, and a strong scent of aromatic hops.

FOOD PAIRING: Try it with sausages and potato wedges.

WHEAT 4.8% ABV

Just to be confusing, the bar does a light and dark version of this beer; the blonde is rugged but not too medicinal while the bruin has some nice sweet toffee notes.

FOOD PAIRING: Try it with delicate flavours such as salmon marinated in lemon, or even a knuckle of pork.

STOUT 5.2% ABV

This stout is both sharp and soft, as coffee and sweet chocolate flavours vie for attention. The Marynka hops add a potent, tongue-caressing bitterness.

FOOD PAIRING: Pair it with super-sweet desserts such as a sweet cheesecake topped with a hot cherry sauce.

ALHAMBRA

Time for a beer? After a hard day's work, many Andalucians will pop into their local bar for a small glass or two of one of Alhambra's delicious, clean-tasting beers and some spicy tapas.

THE FACTS...

OWNER Alhambra
FOUNDED 1925
ADDRESS Avenida de Murcia 1, 18012 Granada
WEBSITE www.cervezasalhambra.es
PHILOSOPHY Good beer takes time

SPANISH BEER might bring to mind pints of yellow, fizzy lager drunk by holidaymakers from the UK and Germany. But don't be fooled. Spain has its own established breweries that make some interesting beers, and there are signs that the country could soon experience a growth in craft breweries similar to the one experienced in Italy. After all, Spaniards drink a lot of beer – especially during the hot summer months when many like to sip cold, refreshing beer in preference to other alcoholic drinks. And the demand for creative, challenging beers is growing.

Alhambra Brewery opened in 1925 and is named after Granada's celebrated Moorish Alhambra palace. Indeed, the brewery's logo features two lions from the Patio de los Leones in the palace. By 1979 the company had grown to employ more than 400 people. During the 1990s, the brewery came under new management, who revitalized and expanded the product line and invested in new machinery and technology. In 1998 the award-winning Alhambra Reserve 1925 was introduced. Its simple bottle design, which has no label, is based on the original bottles produced by the company. The beer has been widely admired for its artisanal qualities. Other beers produced include the malty, copper-coloured Mezquita, the smooth, crisp Especial, dark, liquorice-flavoured Negra, and blonde, citrussy Premium Lager, all of which are widely available in Granada and the rest of Andalucía.

A great deal of care and attention is lavished on Alhambra's beers. The water used for brewing comes from the nearby Sierra Nevada mountains, reputed to be the purest water in Spain. The time taken when making a beer is often a way of distinguishing the interesting from the industrial, and the brewers at Alhambra always like to ensure that their beers have a slow fermentation and are conditioned for 39 days. This helps to release deep flavours in the beer as the flavour compounds settle, slow down, and mellow.

ALHAMBRA MEZQUITA **ALHAMBRA** PREMIUM LAGER **ALHAMBRA** NEGRA

TASTING NOTES

MEZQUITA LAGER, 7.2% ABV
Dark copper in colour, its style is similar to a Belgian abbey beer, with lashings of dark sugar on the tongue. The finish is dry coupled with the warmth of the alcohol. It is a beer with considerable complexity.

FOOD PAIRING: Accompany it with plates of Spanish tapas.

PREMIUM LAGER 4.6% ABV
A Spanish take on a classic beer style. Crisp and golden, it's an ideal thirst-quencher. Sweet and with a hint of citrus, it's best served well chilled. It also has some vanilla and honey notes.

FOOD PAIRING: A good all-round partner with food, it pairs well with simple fish dishes and salads.

NEGRA DARK LAGER, 5.4% ABV
As dark as a stick of liquorice, the use of dark barley malt exudes roasted coffee flavours on the nose. There is a spicy pepperiness and a sweet, sugary finish.

FOOD PAIRING: Pairs well with sweeter dishes and would be a good companion to rice dishes such as a paella.

DAMM

One of Spain's best-known breweries, Damm is taking beer-and-food matching to a whole new level with the creation of a beer for one of the world's best restaurants and the holder of three Michelin stars.

THE FACTS...

OWNER Damm
FOUNDED 1876
ADDRESS Carrer del Roselló 515, 08025 Barcelona
WEBSITE www.damm.es
PHILOSOPHY To maintain links with Spanish society and culture

DAMM
VOLL

DAMM
ESTRELLA

IT WAS THE FOG OF WAR and events 900km (560 miles) north of Barcelona that led to the opening of one of the grand old dames of European brewing, Damm. In 1871 the Franco-Prussian war was in full swing in the seemingly endless *pas de deux* between the two countries fighting over Alsace Lorraine. The region has a deserved reputation for its gastronomy as well as a long tradition of brewing. One Strasbourg resident, August Kuentzmann Damm, joined a stream of refugees making the journey south in search of peace in the sunnier climes of the Mediterranean. A brewer by trade, it was a natural step for Damm to set up a brewery in 1876, which today has risen to be a star of Catalonia.

As in the beginning, the beers are inspired by those of the Strasbourg region. They are light and easy-drinking, and tend to err on the side of sweetness rather than citrus hoppiness. Beer and food in Spain have always had a close link, but Damm has gone further than most in its attempt to ease wine off the dinner table of upmarket restaurants. Working with Ferran Adrià, chef of the famed restaurant El Bulli, the brewery created Inedit, a sparkling bottle-conditioned beer that swirls with notes of coriander and orange zest. At the restaurant it is served well-chilled in an ice bucket and carefully poured into white wine glasses.

TASTING NOTES

VOLL DOPPELBOCK, 7.2% ABV
A beer of some character, Voll is dark and golden. It exudes alcohol on the palate and there is a lingering sweetness that duets with roasted barley notes.

FOOD PAIRING: The beer has the strength of character to work with fatty foods like a cheese-laden pizza.

ESTRELLA PILSNER, 5.4% ABV
Don't be fooled by the colour – pale yellow to the eye – this is a beer of some strength. Dryness and bitterness from the malt and hops make it a refreshing thirst-quencher.

FOOD PAIRING: Pair it with a local surf and turf. In Catalonia, locals tuck into plates of chicken with prawns.

AK DAMM LAGER, 4.8% ABV
This Spanish beer has a strong German heritage. AK Damm is light golden in colour. It's an easy-drinking, refreshing beer with a light malt flavour.

FOOD PAIRING: Serve with mild cheese or unsalted ham.

DAMM AK DAMM

CROATIA

LIČANKA

www.pivovara-licanka.hr

LIKE MUCH OF THIS part of Europe, the beer scene in Croatia is dominated by a small number of international beer producers. However, Ličanka, founded in 1997 by Karlo Starčević, is regarded by many as one of the best brewers in the country. Based near Gospić in the Velebit mountains, the company produces beers under the Velebitsko name and says the brewing water, taken from the mountainous Lika region, is very good for lagers. It produces a light ale, Velebitsko Svijetlo, and a dark ale, Velebitsko Tamno.

CYPRUS

DRAUGHT

www.carobmill-restaurants.com

IT MIGHT BE A WHILE before a brewpub can be found on every Mediterranean island, but a start is being made. Carob Mill operates the brewery, along with a number of bars and restaurants in Cyprus – Draught can be found at the Lanitis Carob Mill complex in Limassol, near to the medieval castle. A small, modern microbrewery, it primarily brews German- and Czech-style beers for pairing with the restaurants' Tex Mex-, German-, and US-style food.

ESTONIA

A LE COQ

www.alecoq.ee

A LE COQ has played a proud role in the history of brewing. Originally founded in Prussia in 1807 by a French Huguenot family escaping persecution in their homeland, they later settled in London. In 1912 the brewery set up in the Russian empire where it could brew its Imperial Stout without paying export duties. However, the Russian revolution stopped the production of a beer with such royal connections. Imperial Stout is now brewed by Harveys (see p.34) in England. After further turmoil during World War II, the brewery operates under the same name today and is now the market leader for beer in Estonia, producing a wide range of brews.

HUNGARY

GYERTYÁNOS

www.gyertyanos.hu

BANANA, CHERRY, PUMPKIN, and chocolate are all used in beers produced by Gyertyános, founded in 1996 and based in the city of Miskolc. The brewery is widely regarded as one of the best of the new wave of craft brewers in Hungary. Their beers are a Hungarian rhapsody of local ingredients, which swirl up and down the taste scales. Beer lovers wanting to seek out these beers should go to Budapest in September and try them at the remarkable Főzdefeszt – Hungary's first national craft beer festival.

SERFORRÁS

www.serforras.hu

THERE IS A NEW HUNGARIAN revolution – craft beer. It's a revolution that is taking place in bars across the country and in animated conversations between beer fans who want to have the choice of their own local beers and not only those from the major international beer producers. One of the new brewers in the vanguard of this beer insurrection is Serforrás from Felsőzsolca, a small town in the north of Hungary close to the border with Ukraine. One of its most interesting beers is Corvinus Rex, which is flavoured with Tokaji wine from the Hernád Valley.

MALTA

SIMONDS FARSONS CISK

www.farsons.com/brewery.htm

WHEN YOU TAKE INTO ACCOUNT the history of Malta for the last one hundred or so years, it is hardly surprising that Simonds Farsons Cisk Brewery is strongly influenced by UK brewing styles. Among its brews are an easy drinking, lemon-flavoured lager that is ideal for hot Mediterranean days and an idiosyncratic range of well-hopped UK-style ales, including the Hopleaf range, which dates back to 1928. But seasoned beer travellers will probably seek out the Farsons Lacto. It is a classic milk stout and its black softness caresses the tongue before giving a cheeky lactose kiss.

PORTUGAL

PRAXIS

www.praxis.pt

FROM SMALL BEGINNINGS a beer revolution could be happening in Portugal. The Praxis microbrewery and restaurant is located in the former capital of Portugal and the renowned university city of Coimbra. Currently it makes a pale pilsner, a cloudy weiss, an almost Vienna red amber, and an enjoyable and nicely sweet roasted dunkel. The easy-drinking beers are a sign that even in the land of wine, a beer revolution is starting.

ROMANIA

S.C. MARTENS

www.martens.ro

THE BELGIAN-OWNED BREWERY S C Martens draws on its Low Country heritage with a range of beers that includes a number of wheat-style beers. The brewery was established by Josef Ploll in 1888 before becoming state-operated until it was privatized in 1998. Its SuperBrew 15, a weighty imperial-style lager at 15% ABV, has a cult following among US beer fans.

RUSSIA

MOSCOW BREWING

www.mosbrew.ru

ONE OF THE NEW BOYS on the Russian brewing block, Moscow Brewing opened its state-of-the-art brewery in 2008. A keen supporter of festivals for local and imported beers, it has ambitious plans to develop a Russian beer brand. It makes an interesting Vienna-style lager, Khamovniki Venskoe, which has the distinctive aroma from the Tettnanger hops.

TVER

www.afanasy.ru

THE ROOTS OF THE TVER BREWERY go back to 1887. Its best-known beer is named after a famed Russian explorer, Afanasy Nikitin, who was reputed to be one of the first Europeans to travel to India in the 15th century. Afanasy Tver is a well-balanced Bavarian-style beer with hints of soft fruit on the nose.

SERBIA

BLACK TURTLE

www.theblackturtle.com/srb

ONE OF THE STANDARD BEARERS for craft beer in Serbia, Black Turtle sells its beer through a small chain of pubs of the same name in the Belgrade area. The brewers draw heavily on German traditions for their beers and the range includes a smoked beer and a wheat beer. However, they also look to Belgian traditions for the Amber Abbey and Stout. They recently started to brew a number of fruit-flavoured beers using blueberries, strawberries, and lemons.

SLOVAKIA

KALTENECKER

www.kaltenecker.sk

THE KALTENECKER MICROBREWERY opened in 1997 within a long-established restaurant near the historical city of Košice. Despite Slovakia's wine culture, it has proved that it has demand for and interest in craft brewing. It produces a well-received range of unpasteurized beers, many of which are seasonal. One of its most interesting beers, Brokát 27, is wood-aged in former wine barrels and flavoured with spruce needles, juniper, and coriander.

PILSBERG

www.pilsberg.sk

LOCATED IN THE CITY of Poprad, up in the High Tatra mountains, the Pilsberg Brewery can trace its heritage back over more than 200 years. Over that time the brewery has had many owners and periods of being state-run, but took on its current structure in 2005. It produces a range of light and dark lager beers. Its pilsner-style beers have a pronounced hop bitterness and a sweet malt flavour.

SLOVENIA

KRATOCHWILL

www.kratochwill.si

SLOVENIA IS UNDERGOING something of a brewpub revolution, with many now open and others planned. One of the best is Kratochwill, opposite the main station in

LOCHER VOLLMOND BIER

Ljubljana. Its range includes a Bohemian-style lager, a hazy wheat beer, and a dark beer that is full of chocolate malt flavours.

Also worth seeking out is the Adam Ravbar, which is located in the suburbs of Ljubljana near the Rodica station. Its bar is dominated by the shiny copper brewing equipment.

SWITZERLAND

BRASSERIE TROIS DAMES

www.brasserietroisdames.ch

"BREWING IS A PASSION that must be shared in the same way a painter or musician creates a work of art", says the head brewer at Brasserie Trois Dames, Raphaël Mettler. He started to home-brew in 2002, but a sabbatical in the US and Canada persuaded him to open his own commercial brewery in 2008. He named it the Bière Trois Dames after his wife Sylvie and daughters Julie and Elise. His range includes US-style IPAs and wood-aged beers.

LOCHER

www.appenzellerbier.ch/

A LOCAL BEER with a national reputation, the Locher Brewery is proud to use only organic, Swiss-grown ingredients from the Appenzeller region. All the beers that ferment on a Sunday are said to be "godly blessed". At Locher they say their best beer, Vollmond, is always brewed when there is a full moon. This is said to trigger the yeast into a more vigorous action, as it converts the malt's sweet sugars into alcohol.

UKRAINE

PIVARIUM

pivarium.com.ua/en

THERE ARE SIGNS that beer culture is stirring in Ukraine and it is becoming easier to find locally brewed beer and brewpubs. Most draw on German and Czech beer styles for their inspiration. The Pivarium Brewery is in full sight of its customers at this smart, modern brewpub in Kiev. It produces a good range of easy-drinking beers including one made of honey, a light, a premium, and a coffee and wheat variety.

THE AMERICAS

UNITED STATES OF AMERICA

There is an amazing new world of beer in the US. From a country once known for the sameness and blandness of its beers, there now come some of the most intensely flavoured beers made in a seemingly endless variety of styles. From black-as-night oatmeal stouts to ales and wheat beers brewed with fruit, vegetables, spices, and herbs, this is a country that is ready and eager to barrel-age, bottle-condition, and dry-hop its way to new, exciting flavours.

The taste revolution began in the 1970s – at the time there were only 44 companies brewing beer in the US; most were large conglomerates and the beer was known for being rather bland and uninspiring. But changes in the law that made it legal for people to brew at home saw many people take up home-brewing as a hobby. Many of these home-brewers came to realize that there was a market for exciting, flavourful beers and that they could turn their passion into a business. Starting on the West Coast, a revolution rolled out across the US. These enthusiastic beer pioneers drew on the traditions of the Old World, saving several styles from extinction in the process. They also developed new distinctive US beer styles, which were full of big, bold aromas and tastes. The success of this revolution is evidenced by the number of companies now brewing. The number of craft brewers has gone from eight in 1980 to more than 2,000, and most Americans now live within ten miles of a brewery. The revolution shows no signs of slackening – it's estimated that more than one million Americans are now creating their own brews at home.

ALASKAN

Few beers are more obviously a product of the place where they are brewed than those from Alaskan Brewing. They reflect the brewery's regional roots and the environmental stewardship needed to brew on "The Last Frontier".

THE FACTS...

OWNER Alaskan Brewing Co

FOUNDED 1986

ADDRESS 5429 Shaune Drive, Juneau, Alaska 99801-9540

WEBSITE www.alaskanbeer.com

PHILOSOPHY Putting a little bit of Alaska in a bottle

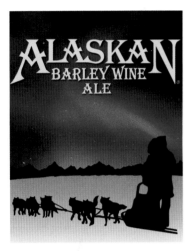

ALASKAN
BARLEY WINE ALE

ALASKAN
SMOKED PORTER

GEOFF AND MARCY LARSON founded Alaskan Brewing in 1986 and their priority is to keep things local. They based their Amber Ale on a recipe a brewery on the other side of Gastineau Channel had used 100 years before, and their most famous beer, Smoked Porter, is made with malt smoked over alder wood, used for centuries by the native Tlingit to smoke fish. They can tell a similar story about many other beers.

The Larsons aren't native Alaskans but clearly they belong there. "There are different elements that affect us, obstacles and challenges we'll encounter that others don't", Marcy Larson has said. One of those elements was disposing of spent grain. There are no roads in or out of Juneau, and sending the grain off to cattle farmers as other brewers do is not an option as there are not enough cattle in the whole of Alaska to consume it. Instead, Alaskan became the first brewery in the world to use its spent grain as the fuel source to power the steam boiler it uses in making beer. Implementing the process was only one of many environmental firsts by the brewery. As Geoff Larson says, "the uniqueness of our location means we don't always do things like others".

TASTING NOTES

BARLEY WINE ALE 10.7% ABV
This brew looks rich, deep red, and inviting. Complex aromas of burnt sugar, dark fruits, and hot caramel rise from the foam. Similar flavours linger through the finish.

FOOD PAIRING: Its strong flavour will overpower most dishes, although some find this a good match for fatty foods. Generally it works best with a dessert or alongside a strong cheese.

SMOKED PORTER 6.5% ABV
Pungent and smoky from the beginning, smoked porter smells like a walk on a south-east Alaskan beach when fires are glowing. Oily on the tongue, the texture melds with chocolate and dark burned fruits in aged bottles.

FOOD PAIRING: A delightful complement to smoked seafood, but also excellent with dessert, perhaps vanilla ice cream and raspberries.

AMBER ALE, 5.3% ABV
This beer pours bright copper, its nose primarily bready malt with a hint of fruit. Caramel emerges on the palate, with a satisfying, dry finish. Amber goes down alarmingly quickly.

FOOD PAIRING: Rich but crisp, it is a fine match for Alaskan king salmon, flavourful meats, and hearty Italian dishes.

ALASKAN AMBER

ALLAGASH

Rob Tod started Allagash Brewing as a one-man operation, determined to sell Belgian-inspired beers in the US. He learnt at the outset the importance of experimentation and of establishing that his beers belong on the dining table.

THE FACTS...

OWNER Allagash Brewing Co
FOUNDED 1995
ADDRESS 50 Industrial Way, Portland, Maine 04103
WEBSITE www.allagash.com
PHILOSOPHY Hand-crafting the best Belgian-inspired beers in the world

"FOR THE FIRST EIGHT YEARS people weren't interested in Belgian beers", he said. "People would ask us, 'Why don't you make the White more accessible? Get rid of that classic wheat character, take out some spices'". Allagash White was the first beer Tod brewed and it is now his flagship brew. Accounting for about three-quarters of sales, it tastes almost exactly the same as when he put the first keg on tap at the Great Lost Bear pub in the brewery's hometown of Portland in Maine.

"I didn't know if we'd do one beer or ten beers, but I knew we'd focus on Belgian beer", he said. The brewery now makes more than ten every year, some regularly, some annually, and some that are brewed only once. "One of the things about brewing Belgian beers is the whole style encourages experimentation", Tod has said. Those experiments include many not even attempted in Belgium – at least at the time – such as ageing beers in barrels that have first been used for other alcoholic beverages. However, the boldest experiment was probably building a small shed beside the brewery and installing a "koelschip" – a shallow pan that exposes wort (the liquid produced during the brewing process) to local microflora – so that they could make spontaneously fermented beers. At the time, this process had not been seen outside the Senne Valley near Brussels.

Almost as revolutionary was Tod's decision to team with the Institute for Culinary Education in New York City for a "Cookin' with Allagash" contest, in order to demonstrate how well his beers work with food. In the competition, up-and-coming chefs were invited to concoct original recipes using Allagash beers as an ingredient. New England's original Belgian-style brewery is now a successful and well respected brand.

ALLAGASH WHITE

ALLAGASH CURIEUX

ALLAGASH INTERLUDE

TASTING NOTES

WHITE BELGIAN WHITE ALE, 5% ABV
Cloudy in the glass, Belgian White Ale shimmers white in the right light. Spicy on the nose, it has herbal, fruity, citrus notes. Light on the tongue, there are crisp wheat notes accenting a hint of tartness that follows ongoing fruity, citrus flavours.

FOOD PAIRING: Its fruity flavours but cleansing acidity make it a fine match for many dishes. It is light enough to accompany a salad, but hefty enough to enhance even spicy seafood.

CURIEUX BOURBON BARREL TRIPEL, 11% ABV
A portion of the brewery's honey-ish tripel is aged in bourbon barrels, then blended with young tripel to produce Curieux. Bright golden, it has bourbon and vanilla flavours apparent at the outset. These merge with fruity aromas and flavours, including banana, leading to a smooth finish.

FOOD PAIRING: A dessert in itself, it pairs well with many sweet dishes, ranging from cheesecake to crème brûlée.

INTERLUDE FARMHOUSE ALE, 9.5% ABV
A beer of astonishing complexity, Interlude is fermented with two yeast strains, and a portion is aged in used wine barrels. It pours reddish-orange, smelling of tropical and stone fruits, becoming more vinous on the tongue. Its texture recalls bread crust. Moderately tart, it slides into a mildly tannic finish.

FOOD PAIRING: Its "farmhouse funk" matches pungent cheeses or smoked meats, its tart finish wiping away any fattiness.

ANCHOR BREWING

Before words like "microbrews" and "craft beer" became part of the American beer vocabulary, there was Anchor Brewing. Fritz Maytag not only saved the brewery in 1965, but he also became the godfather of the US beer revival.

ANCHOR FIRST BREWED BEER in 1896 and owns the trademark for "steam" beer. Stories differ about the origin of the name, but the most persuasive version is that it resulted from the practice of fermenting beers on San Francisco rooftops because ice was not available to chill the wort. Instead, brewers let the cool, often foggy, air control the temperature, with steam rising off shallow warm pans. Any West Coast beer brewed by this process, which would have tasted different because it had not been lagered as cold as elsewhere, became known as "steam". Anchor still cools its Steam Beer in much the same way in shallow pans, although it is now done inside the brewery after filtering the air.

In 1965, Fritz Maytag, a member of the family famous for making washing machines, was able to buy a controlling share of Anchor for a few thousand dollars as it was on the verge of bankruptcy. He not only improved the quality of Steam, but in so doing, he also kicked off a revolution. He proved that, given a choice, American drinkers would support beers beyond mainstream lagers, which by the early 1970s were growing blander and more

alike. Maytag introduced, or reintroduced, his countrymen to many styles of beer, such as porter, barley wine, and wheat ale. When he brewed Liberty Ale in 1975, initially as his Christmas ale, he was the first to showcase the Cascade hop, which added aromas unique to American-bred hops. Cascade became a cornerstone for American small-batch brewers, as did other hops of similar character that until then had been considered by brewers to smell and taste "rank". Maytag sold the brewery to Keith Greggor and Tony Foglio in 2010. Faced with capacity restraints, the new owners announced in 2013 that Anchor would build a second, larger brewery that would begin operations on San Francisco's waterfront in 2016.

The original
First brewed in 1972, this was the first US porter and has become the keystone for the style

TASTING NOTES

LIBERTY ALE PALE ALE, 5.9% ABV
A shocker in 1975. Darker than golden, it has a hugely floral, citrussy nose. Sweet on the tongue, but light, it is balanced by resiny hop flavours that give way to a distinct, still smooth, bitterness.
FOOD PAIRING: Very versatile. For instance, its sweet malt brings out caramelized flavours in grilled meat.

PORTER 5.6% ABV
Almost black, Porter smells of roasted grains, chocolate, and burnt toffee. Rich in both flavour and texture, with a caramel sweetness at the outset, it has an abundant hop flavour, with plenty of bitterness from both the hops and roasted grains.
FOOD PAIRING: Go ahead, try it with a porterhouse steak. Also an excellent match for spicy Mexican food or Cajun jambalaya.

STEAM BEER HYBRID, 4.9% ABV
Bright copper in the glass, Steam Beer begins with woody, herbal, mint aromas, followed by hints of caramel. The herbal hops give caramel sweetness on the tongue a quick hook, leading to a long, dry, bittersweet finish.
FOOD PAIRING: Bold and cleansing enough to take on Thai and Caribbean dishes or battered fried fish.

ANCHOR BREWING LIBERTY ALE

ANCHOR BREWING PORTER   **ANCHOR BREWING** STEAM BEER

AVERY BREWING

When a worldwide shortage of hops sent prices skyrocketing in 2008, many brewers cut back on how much they used. Not Adam Avery at Avery Brewing – he announced he would be putting more hops in some of his beers.

THE FACTS...

OWNER Avery Brewing Co

FOUNDED 1993

ADDRESS 5763 Arapahoe Avenue, Boulder, Colorado 80303

WEBSITE www.averybrewing.com

PHILOSOPHY Committed to producing eccentric ales and lagers that defy styles and categories. We brew what we like to drink

FOR MANY YEARS, Ellie's Brown Ale, a classically balanced ale, was Avery's best-selling beer, and it remains an important part of its portfolio, along with several other beers of conventional strength. However, starting with Hog Heaven in 1997 – 9.2% ABV and spectacularly hoppy – and accelerating with the release of The Reverend – a 10% ABV Belgian dark ale – in 2000, the brewery has earned a reputation for its intensely flavoured beers.

Adam Avery says of The Reverend brew, "we found out we could make a beer that wasn't super hoppy, that would get people's attention, and that they'd drink". Uniting Hog Heaven and The Reverend with a strong golden Belgian ale called Salvation, Avery created a "Holy Trinity of Ales".

Another group of beers is known as the "Dictator Series". This includes three imperial-size suitably titled beers, each weighing in at around 10% ABV. The Maharaja is "regal, intense, and mighty", The Kaiser, a copper-coloured, malty-spicy brew, while The Czar is inky black with toffee and sweet molasses flavours.

The "Demons of Ale" series went a step further again, with each beer between 15–17% ABV. Samaels is a strong, English-style ale, The Beast is dark with spicy, rum-like flavours, and Mephistopheles' Stout is coal black with hints of chocolate and cherries. The "Barrel-aged" series is more experimental and could include any category of beer and some that defy definition, including some fermented with wild yeast. These innovations have been a success, with sales, which declined in the three years before 2000, climbing every year since, necessitating construction of a new brewery. The brewery hosts several festivals every year, with tickets for the Boulder Strong Ale Fest and the Boulder SourFest selling out almost instantly.

TASTING NOTES

ELLIE'S BROWN ALE 5.5% ABV

The dark brown body and tan head signal rich aromas, and sweet chocolate and toffee-caramel flavours that are just as apparent on the tongue. Roasty, toasty, richly textured flavours are augmented by earthy hops.

FOOD PAIRING: Ellie's maltiness makes it an excellent match for smoky, roasted meats or beef tacos with spicy sauce.

HOG HEAVEN BARLEY WINE, 9.2% ABV

Dark red to copper, Avery calls Hog Heaven a barley wine, while others call it an imperial red ale. You can smell the citrus hops at 20 paces, mingling with the sweet aroma of cotton candy. There are complex and layered flavours of stone fruits and citrus on the tongue, yielding to a long bitter finish.

FOOD PAIRING: Because this beer finishes hop-rich and dry it pairs well with slighty fatty meat and game, as well as pulled pork or beef brisket from the smoker.

INDIA PALE ALE 6.5% ABV

Pours a bright orange colour with a billowing head. Citrus aromas leap from the glass, particularly grapefruit, and perhaps a bit of pine. Fresh on the nose and in the mouth, it is lean of body, bitter, and satisfyingly dry.

FOOD PAIRING: Classically, the acidity and hoppiness of IPA cut through creamy flavours, making it perfect for pasta dishes like fettucine alfredo or carbonara.

AVERY BREWING ELLIE'S BROWN ALE   **AVERY BREWING** HOG HEAVEN   **AVERY BREWING** INDIA PALE ALE

BELL'S

Inspired Brewing®

Larry Bell, the founder and president of Bell's Brewery, has always known how to throw a party. Eccentric Day each December has kept fans connected even as the brewery has expanded over the years.

PATRONS DRESS UP FOR ECCENTRIC DAY at the Bell's Eccentric Café in Kalamazoo, home to the original brewery for Kalamazoo Brewing. This site remains in use even though the company has now expanded and changed its name to Bell's Brewery. On this one day of the year, the massive draught menu includes an exclusive Eccentric Day beer, and the café serves a variety of eccentric foods, such as squid stuffed with bison cornbread. In the spring, Michigan bars hold parties to celebrate the return of Oberon Beer, some even tapping the beer at midnight.

Bell opened his brewery in 1985, making his first beers in a large soup pot, and quickly earned a reputation for big, bold beers, particularly stouts. In fact, around the beginning of the new millennium he turned all of November into a stout party. "Craft brewing had been declared dead in the *New York Times*", Bell said. "I saw a lot of my competitors make a run for lighter beers. I said, 'That's not why I got into this.' So to reinforce our commitment to full-flavoured beer, we decided to do the 10 Stouts of November."

The brewery outgrew itself in Kalamazoo and Bell built a new one nearby in Comstock. That expanded, then expanded again. After workers finish their shifts, they often head back to the Eccentric Café for a beer. "You find guys in the brewhouse down here drinking porter and stout", said production manager John Mallett. "We have an immense amount of pride in these beers."

TASTING NOTES

OBERON WHEAT ALE 5.8% ABV
This ale pours golden and hazy, and for Michigan residents signals the arrival of baseball season. Spicy, citrus, and other fruity aromas combine in the mouth, while the wheat adds a tart note. Finishes slightly sweet, but refreshing.

FOOD PAIRING: Light on the tongue but with enough acidity that it pairs well with delicate fish, salads, or sushi.

TWO HEARTED ALE INDIA PALE ALE, 7% ABV
Named Two Hearted after a Michigan river of that name, this ale could equally be called grapefruit perfume. Citrus is prominent in both the aroma and flavour, joined by stone fruits. Bready malt flavour and a touch of sweetness is quickly swept away by hop bitterness riding a final citrus wave.

FOOD PAIRING: Two Hearted Ale is a classic pairing for curry and Asian cuisine, or dishes flavoured with citrus or coriander, such as ground beef tacos.

EXPEDITION STOUT IMPERIAL STOUT, 10.5% ABV
Expedition may not be the blackest of Bell's stouts, but it is forbidding. An intoxicating nose reveals dark fruits, chocolate, roasted coffee beans – all flavours that open up in the mouth – mingling with earthy hops. The viscous body of this stout is never cloying.

FOOD PAIRING: Best thought of as port wine when pairing. It has the weight to match smoked, oily goose, and is also excellent for dessert with chocolate truffles or raspberry tart.

BELL'S OBERON

BELL'S TWO HEARTED ALE

BELL'S EXPEDITION STOUT

BOULEVARD BREWING

THE FACTS...

OWNER Boulevard Brewing Co

FOUNDED 1989

ADDRESS 2501 Southwest Boulevard, Kansas City, Missouri 64108

WEBSITE www.boulevard.com

PHILOSOPHY Fine beers since 1989

It seems fitting that, located in America's "breadbasket", Boulevard Brewing would sell more wheat beer than most. However, booming sales of its specialities illustrate just how far its richly flavoured beers have spread.

UNFILTERED WHEAT BEER still accounts for most of the sales at Boulevard. "The grain is a part of many Midwesterners' lives, especially Kansans, and there is a feeling of local support when you purchase it", longtime, but now former, Boulevard employee John Bryan said in 2009. "Around here we sell Unfiltered Wheat in rural taverns, Veterans of Foreign Wars halls, places where you would not expect to see craft beer as part of the line-up."

However, when Boulevard bought a new brewery in 2007, the brewery finally had capacity to produce a Smokestack Series of speciality beers. In 2012, those brands grew by 70 per cent. "I think that Midwestern beer aficionados are on a par with Belgian beer drinkers", said brewmaster Steven Pauwels, who grew up and trained in Belgium before going to work at Boulevard in 1996. "There is a lot of tradition in Belgium while there is a lot more experimentation going on here."

One of the first beers in the Smokestack line was Saison Brett, so named because it is dosed with the wild yeast Brettanomyces. "The inspiration came from some of the great Belgian saisons and also from my childhood when I grew up on a farm in Belgium", Pauwels said. "We would help out farmers during hay harvest. The dusty smell of hay when we were loading it on the field and the barn smell when we were unloading it are completely different but very unique. The beer doesn't smell like these memories but I tried to get the fresh hay smell through dry hopping and the barn smell with the Brett." Other beers in the series include the intense Tank 7 Farmhouse Ale, liberally hopped and "twister-proof" Double Wide IPA, and Dark Truth Stout, which the brewery claims holds the "secret to transforming the elemental into the extraordinary".

Belgium's best
A childhood spent on a Belgian farm was the inspiration for a range of saison beers

BOULEVARD BREWING
PALE ALE

BOULEVARD BREWING
UNFILTERED WHEAT BEER

BOULEVARD BREWING
TANK 7

TASTING NOTES

PALE ALE 5.4% ABV
Appears a touch orange, with a persistent white head. It has a complex but understated nose that is fruity, pleasantly floral, and with aromas of pine. There is malt sweetness in the mouth balanced by spicy hop flavour and solid bitterness.

FOOD PAIRING: The solid malt backbone and persistent hops make it a great equal to wild game, but it's also a perfect match for casual dishes like chicken wings and other fried food.

UNFILTERED WHEAT BEER 4.4% ABV
Follow the pouring instructions on the six-pack holder and it will land cloudy and pale in the glass. Grainy and spicy at the outset, there are hints of citrussy aromas. The flavour has a hint of gently toasted bread and more citrus. Light on the tongue.

FOOD PAIRING: Unfiltered Wheat Beer is light, but crisp on the palate, and works well with delicate and not so delicate sushi, manchego cheese, and pizza.

TANK 7 SAISON, 8.5% ABV
The straw colour is perhaps deceiving. Its oversized floral aroma is citrussy, spicy, and with a hint of cloves and even stone fruit. Double that intensity in the mouth, when it is spicier still, then pleasantly, but make no mistake, bitter.

FOOD PAIRING: This particularly assertive beer may overwhelm delicate dishes, but its citrus character and acidity nicely complement herb-roasted chicken and pork.

BREWERY OMMEGANG

The brewery is nestled on 135 acres outside Cooperstown, New York, home of the Baseball Hall of Fame. Although it opened in 1997, you don't have to squint too hard to see a Belgian farmhouse circa 1880.

THE FACTS...

OWNER Duvel Moortgat
FOUNDED 1997
ADDRESS 656 County Highway 33, Cooperstown, New York 13326
WEBSITE www.ommegang.com
PHILOSOPHY Where brewing is an art and partaking is a passion

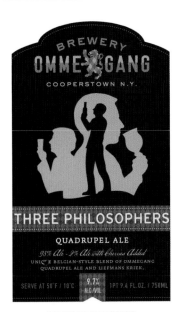

BREWERY OMMEGANG
THREE PHILOSOPHERS

BREWERY OMMEGANG began as a partnership between an American importing company and Belgian breweries, and emphasized its links to Belgian brewing and gastronomic cultures from the outset. They built the white-washed brick brewery on farmland that was once in the centre of the largest US hop-growing region, and their true-to-tradition beers quickly earned them an avid following. Duvel Moortgat bought total control in 2003, and has, at times, brewed Brewery Ommegang beers in its Belgian brewery, when the New York brewery could not keep up with demand.

This link to tradition and Europe was one reason cable television giant HBO approached Brewery Ommegang about creating a series of beers inspired by its *Game of Thrones* TV series – the first of them released in 2013. "Even though the show takes place in a mythical land and mythical time, we recognize that it gives off a European feel, a medieval and feudal feel", Brewery Ommegang spokesman Larry Bennett said when the announcement was made.

"So, that connection allowed this to make sense, for them and for us. If we made a beer for, say, Sea World, I don't think that would make much sense. We'd have to put in some serious work to figure that one out."

Appropriately, Brewery Ommegang hosts a festival each summer called "Belgium Comes to Cooperstown", which is best experienced by camping on the property. Fifty breweries from around the world pour beer on a Saturday, and those lucky enough to snag a VIP ticket – they sell out quickly – enjoy a four-hour dinner on Friday.

TASTING NOTES

THREE PHILOSOPHERS STRONG BELGIAN ALE, 9.8% ABV
A blend of a strong dark beer often found in monasteries with a kriek. Beautiful red highlights at the edges, and a complex nose and flavour: rich dark fruits mingle with tart red ones, one darting to the fore, then the other.
FOOD PAIRING: The rich combination of flavours can overwhelm many dishes, but this makes an excellent dessert along with pungent cheeses. Can be sublime as a marinade or used in sauce.

ABBEY ALE STRONG BELGIAN ALE, 8.2% ABV
Burgundian out of the glass, with tan-coloured, tight bubbles. Spices are apparent on the nose, notably liquorice. There are abundant flavours of chocolate, dried plums, raisins, more spices, and a hint of earthy hops. It has a magically dry finish.
FOOD PAIRING: Wine drinkers might think of this beer like Zinfandel, best paired with rich, gamey meats or matched with linguine with cheese.

HENNEPIN SAISON, 7.7% ABV
Effervescent when poured, this beer has a large head – the bubbles toss floral and spicy notes straight to the nose, along with hints of ginger and orange peel. There's a suggestion of sweetness on the tongue, and more spices, all met with a solid bitterness.
FOOD PAIRING: Light enough but packing enough punch that it works well with Asian cuisine or sushi.

BREWERY OMMEGANG
ABBEY ALE

BREWERY OMMEGANG
HENNEPIN

BROOKLYN BREWERY

Brooklyn was once a US brewing hub, home to 48 breweries – many operated by famous brewing families. None remained when Brooklyn Brewery opened in 1987. It has played a crucial role in reviving its surrounding neighbourhood.

THE FACTS...

OWNER Brooklyn Brewery

FOUNDED 1987

ADDRESS 79 N 11th Street, Brooklyn, New York 11249

WEBSITE www.brooklynbrewery.com

PHILOSOPHY Modern craft brewing is the perfect intersection of art and science... passion focused through technical skill

Citrus blast
Sorachi, a Japanese developed hop, sourced from a farm in Washington, gives a citrussy kick to this saison

FOUNDERS OF BROOKLYN BREWERY, Steve Hindy and Tom Potter, contracted at the outset to have their beer made at Matt Brewing in Utica, where much of it is still produced, but built their own brewery in 1996. It has expanded several times since, and has been joined in Brooklyn by several smaller breweries. "Brooklyn Brewery has played a big role in Brooklyn's resurgence", Williamsburg Small Business Services commissioner Robert Walsh said after a major expansion was completed in 2011. "By investing in his business, in the manufacturing sector, and in this great borough, Steve Hindy has made a real difference in New York City."

Brooklyn sells beer in 25 states and 20 countries, exporting more beer than any other US craft brewery. In 2013, it became the first to join an overseas venture, entering a partnership with Brooklyn, D Carnegie & Co, and Carlsberg Sweden to build a waterfront brewery in Stockholm. Brewmaster Garrett Oliver and his team take turns visiting Sweden to brew special beers.

Oliver is the face of the brewery and is particularly prominent. The author of *The Brewmaster's Table* and editor-in-chief of *The Oxford Companion to Beer*, he has travelled the world promoting US beer as well as his own, and is highly regarded – the *New York Times* called him "the greatest ambassador for craft beer in this country for the past 10 years".

TASTING NOTES

LAGER 5.2% ABV
Bright amber in the glass, suggesting a touch of rich caramel that persists from beginning to end. With a floral nose, this beer is spicy with citrus notes. Solidly bitter without being harsh.

FOOD PAIRING: Pair with a range of casual dishes, including pizza, burgers, Mexican food, barbecue, and Chinese food.

BLACK CHOCOLATE STOUT 10% ABV
This stout is the colour of dark chocolate, with chocolate on the nose and in the mouth, although it is far from one dimensional.

FOOD PAIRING: Best served as dessert or with a rich, chocolate dessert, fruit tarts, or strong cheese such as Stilton.

SORACHI ACE SAISON, 7.6% ABV
Like pouring liquid lemon – citrussy-lemon aromas rise as the golden-yellow beer splashes into the glass. Has a spicy, complex, and fruity aroma with a bready malt flavour and hop bitterness.

FOOD PAIRING: The lemon zesty aroma enhances the flavours of dishes such as fish tacos, sushi, curries, and grilled meats.

BROOKLYN BREWERY
LAGER

BROOKLYN BREWERY
BLACK CHOCOLATE STOUT

BROOKLYN BREWERY SORACHI ACE

DESCHUTES

When Deschutes Brewery & Public House opened in 1988, Bend in Oregon had a population of 20,000. As the brewery celebrated its 25th anniversary, the town had grown almost four-fold and had a dozen breweries.

THE FACTS...

OWNER Deschutes Brewery
FOUNDED 1988
ADDRESS 901 SW Simpson Avenue, Bend, Oregon 97702
WEBSITE www.deschutesbrewery.com
PHILOSOPHY Bravely done

"PEOPLE LOOK AT US NOW and don't realize we weren't always successful", said Deschutes owner Gary Fish; the brewery had been around for ten years through boom and bust. "I certainly do, and I hope I never forget. We had a time we couldn't make a batch of good beer (because of infections). We dumped ten straight batches."

Fish had no plans to sell beer beyond the restaurant he owned. However, tavern owners from Portland, who had stayed in Bend, told a distributor they wanted to put Deschutes beers on tap. It was simply a matter of finding the kegs, as soon the brewery was bursting out of the back of the building. "There was equipment in the middle of the street. We had to do something." That was the beginning of the first Deschutes brewery, and it has continued to expand ever since.

Deschutes makes its share of intense beers, but sensible balance has been the brewery's hallmark. This is particularly true of brews like Mirror Pond and Black Butte Porter, which is the best-selling porter in the US despite the fact that it is only available in limited markets. Deschutes beers have also been successful in international competitions, such as the International Brewing Awards, European Beer Star, and World Beer Awards.

The brewery makes several "fresh hop" beers in autumn, rushing hops to the brewing kettle right after they are picked, bypassing traditional kilning. Former brewmaster Larry Sidor even commissioned a nearby hop farmer to grow special "heirloom" Cascade hops for a beer called Chasin' Freshies.

TASTING NOTES

THE ABYSS IMPERIAL STOUT, 11% ABV
Deschutes puts a "best after" date on The Abyss one year after it is bottled. A cornucopia of aromas and flavours – liquorice, molasses, dark fruit, vanilla, bourbon, and oak tannins – are held together by the texture of the beer itself.

FOOD PAIRING: A contemplative beer, happy on its own. However, Deschutes does suggest serving it with caramelized onions and cream cheese on pepper crackers.

MIRROR POND PALE ALE 5% ABV
Bright orange in the glass, with a billowing white head. The aroma is a breath of fresh flowers and grapefruit. Light, clean, and biscuity on the palate, the flavours are much like the aroma. It has a restrained bitterness and is long and relatively dry.

FOOD PAIRING: Pair it with a goat's cheese pizza. It is also excellent with steamed clams.

INVERSION IPA 6.8% ABV
Pours amber with a large white head, leaving lacing that lasts through the whole beer. The hop aroma, most notably orange zest, is almost dizzying. A solid bready body, every bit is needed to support bracing bitterness.

FOOD PAIRING: The balance in the beer makes a good match for rich, sometimes gamey or fatty foods. Its malt character complements a burger loaded with bacon and blue cheese, while the hops cut through those flavours.

Experimental stouts
Deschutes have taken imperial stouts to heart, and beers such as The Abyss demonstrate a willingness to develop them in new, exciting ways

DESCHUTES THE ABYSS

DESCHUTES MIRROR POND PALE ALE

DESCHUTES INVERSION IPA

DOGFISH HEAD

To celebrate exporting his first Dogfish Head beer from Delaware in 1997, Sam Calagione built a boat and rowed it 18 nautical miles to deliver it to New Jersey. "It was a long, strange trip", he said later. It hasn't ended.

THE FACTS...

OWNER Dogfish Head Craft Brewery
FOUNDED 1995
ADDRESS 6 Cannery Village Center, Milton, Delaware 19968
WEBSITE www.dogfish.com
PHILOSOPHY Off-centred ales for off-centred people

CALAGIONE IS ONE OF THE MOST FAMOUS brewers in the US, although he now leaves most of the brewing to others in his fast-growing company. He and his wife Mariah opened Dogfish Head Brewings and Eats in 1995. Calagione originally brewed beer 12 gallons at a time – not nearly enough to keep up with demand at the Rehoboth Beach brewpub. But this start gave Calagione the creative edge, he claims, "we quickly got bored brewing the same things over and over – that's when we started adding all sorts of weird ingredients and getting kind of crazy with the beers!"

Dogfish Head is notorious for brewing with unusual ingredients, creating a series of "ancient ales", and for brewing what are generally known as "extreme beers". Calagione defines these as beers made with extreme amounts of traditional ingredients or beers made extremely well with non-traditional ingredients. For example, to brew Palo Santo Marron, the brewery imported Paraguayan Palo Santo wood and had a tank made specially to produce the beer. To continuously hop his 60 Minute IPA for the first time, Calagione rigged up a plastic bucket and vibrating electronic football game, dosing the beer throughout the boil. The brewery has since built a mechanical hopper to make 60 Minute, as well as a 90 Minute and a 120 Minute. To add more hop character in the glass, Calagione invented "Randall the Enamel Animal", a device packed with hops that beer is pumped through just before serving.

In 2009, Calagione was featured prominently in the movie *Beer Wars*, a documentary about the challenges small breweries face in the American marketplace, as well as a 2011 Discovery Channel television series called *Brew Masters* that focused on Dogfish Head. He has also written three books, started a Manhattan restaurant with Mario Batali, and generally attracts attention to his brewery on a regular basis. The trip continues.

TASTING NOTES

RAISON D'ÊTRE BELGIAN ALE, 8% ABV
A lovely red-brown, this beer is complex the moment it hits the nose – almost rummy, and rich with fruit and sweet, dark toffee. More of the same in the mouth; a bit smoky with a hint of spice.
FOOD PAIRING: A versatile beer, it can be ordered alongside steak or matched with mussels.

WORLD WIDE STOUT 18% ABV
Black, with a thick tan head. Dark fruits and ripe berries mingle with chocolate and roasted malt, which add texture that keeps it from being cloying. Overall it is complex and boozy.
FOOD PAIRING: The malt sweetness and overall heft make it a good match for steak or chorizo sausage. It also makes a good dessert along with mature farmhouse cheddar.

60 MINUTE IPA 6% ABV
It pours orange, which is appropriate as citrussy orange is prominent on the nose, along with floral and piney aromas. It has biscuit and sweet malty notes on the palate, along with more citrus and hop flavour. The bitterness is kept in balance.
FOOD PAIRING: This IPA is restrained enough that it will match, but not overwhelm, spicy foods, grilled salmon, or pizza.

DOGFISH HEAD RAISON D'ÊTRE   **DOGFISH HEAD** WORLD WIDE STOUT   **DOGFISH HEAD** 60 MINUTE IPA

PALO SANTO MARRON STRONG ALE, 12% ABV

Not quite black in the glass, but close. Aromatic and intense, with woody, nutty aromas and scents of dark fruit, roasted malt, and molasses. Flavours are much the same, with vanilla, chalky, and charred notes. This beer is complex and satisfying.

FOOD PAIRING: This beer is robust enough to match big flavoured cheeses such as blue cheese or goats' cheese.

FESTINA PÊCHE WHEAT ALE, 4.5% ABV

Labelled a "Neo-Berliner Weisse" and fermented with peaches, it pours a hazy gold and peaches are apparent from the start. The fruit sweetness, including stone fruits beyond peaches, is nicely balanced by tart wheat and slightly sour elements.

FOOD PAIRING: Light fruitiness and tartness at the finish nicely complement a salad as well as grilled chicken or fish.

MIDAS TOUCH HONEY ALE, 9% ABV

The ingredients – white Muscat grapes, honey, and saffron – create layers of flavour, tied together with subtle acidity.

FOOD PAIRING: The honey sweetness goes well with Pan-Asian dishes, risotto, curries, or roast chicken.

Ageing well
Palo Santo Marron is aged in the largest wooden brewing vessel built in the US since before Prohibition

Wooden wonder
The Palo Santo wood used to produce the beer is used in South American wine making and imparts a sweet vanilla flavour

DOGFISH HEAD PALO SANTO MARRON   **DOGFISH HEAD** FESTINA PÊCHE   **DOGFISH HEAD** MIDAS TOUCH

FIRESTONE WALKER

The first attempt at Firestone Walker failed miserably, but laid the foundation for the brewery to draw on English brewing tradition, incorporate New World tastes, and become one of the world's most decorated breweries.

THE FACTS...

OWNER Firestone Walker Brewing Company

FOUNDED 1996

ADDRESS 1400 Ramada Drive, Paso Robles, California 93446

WEBSITE www.firestonebeer.com

PHILOSOPHY Passionately in pursuit of the perfect beer... and never satisfied. We are living beer

FIRESTONE WALKER
ANNIVERSARY ALE

FIRESTONE WALKER
UNION JACK

CO-FOUNDERS OF FIRESTONE WALKER, David Walker and Adam Firestone, initially tried to age beer in Chardonnay barrels stored in a corner of the Firestone family vineyards, but the barrels were infected and yielded beer "not even as good as shampoo". Today, brewmaster Matt Brynildson oversees the patented Firestone Union, which takes inspiration from the Burton Union system once common in Burton upon Trent and still used by Marston's (see p.36) today. The Burton system, developed in the 1840s, linked wooden casks in order to manage yeast during fermentation but it was not designed to take flavours from the wood. Firestone uses new US oak barrels, and rotates fresh ones in regularly, so they add oak character.

A batch of Firestone ferments for one day in stainless steel, then a portion is transferred into the series of oak barrels. After fermenting for a week in wood, the beer is blended back with steel-fermented beer – wood-fermented beer accounts for about 15 per cent of DBA. Firestone brewers also blend about 15 per cent of DBA with steel-fermented beer to make Pale Ale 31. "Blended beers have a different level of depth we can't seem to get with a single-fermented beer", Brynildson said. "We take the beer apart and put it back together again."

Not all Firestone beers touch wood. When Brynildson began working on the recipe for an IPA in 2006, he envisaged it would be brewed with English malts and fermented in the Union. "It (oak) just didn't work with hops", he said. Instead, Union Jack is a prototypical American IPA, lean of body and dry-hopped to deliver a of blast of fruity, piney Northwest US hops from the outset.

To celebrate the brewery's 10th anniversary in 2006, Firestone created several strong, special beers and aged them in a variety of barrels, many previously used to make spirits. Brynildson then invited wine-makers from the Paso Robles area to help make the blend for its anniversary beer. That tradition has continued annually, and the brewery's inventory of ageing barrels has grown into the thousands. Firestone opened a separate facility, Barrelworks, with its own tasting room to showcase them. As a company, Firestone Walker is not one to rest on its laurels: Brynildson also works as a consultant for the Hop Growers of America, conducting classes for brewers around the world.

The dark side
Wookey Jack is Firestone's first black IPA and is left unfiltered so that what's in the bottle is as flavourful as possible

Best before
All Firestone Walker beers have the date that they were bottled shown on their neck or label and are best drunk within 120 days

FIRESTONE WALKER
DBA

FIRESTONE WALKER
WOOKEY JACK

Oatmeal renaissance
Oatmeal stouts had all but died out in Europe... and then the Americans discovered and revived them

Burton blend
Some of the blended Pale 31 is fermented in Firestone's version of the famous Burton System

FIRESTONE WALKER
VELVET MERLIN

FIRESTONE WALKER
PALE 31

TASTING NOTES

ANNIVERSARY ALE STRONG ALE, ABV VARIABLE
Every vintage varies, of course, starting with the appearance. Every batch has grown more complex as it ages, an ebb and flow of dark fruits, sweet notes of molasses and toffee, flavours of the spirits the barrels held before, and others associated with wood.

FOOD PAIRING: When Firestone Walker debuts the beer in its pub, it lays out a selection of aged cheese, such as Stilton or Bleu d'Auvergne.

UNION JACK INDIA PALE ALE, 7.5% ABV
Bright golden in the glass, Union Jack is topped by an off-white head, followed by generous lacing. With pine and citrus perfume on the nose, it has a touch of cotton candy underneath. The lean malt backbone stands up to persistent hop flavour and bitterness.

FOOD PAIRING: Not every IPA works with a spicy curry, but in this case the big and balanced combination of malt sweetness and hop character is perfect.

DBA PALE ALE, 5% ABV
Attractive, bright copper in the glass, topped by an off-white head. Oak and vanilla are apparent on the nose, but don't detract from underlying fruit aromas and flavours. Rich, but clean on the palate, with citrussy hops, lingering spiciness, and woody tannins.

FOOD PAIRING: The hop character and light fruitiness nicely match sweet, sour, and spicy Thai and Vietnamese dishes.

WOOKEY JACK BLACK INDIA PALE ALE, 8.3% ABV
This beer brings everything to the glass the name promises, pouring a double dark brown, with a swirl of spicy pine and citrus hop aromas, along with roasted notes. Much the same in the mouth, it is rich but balanced by crisp rye character and hop bitterness.

FOOD PAIRING: The bold flavours and hoppy notes have the heft to match smoked cheeses such as gouda, but, perhaps surprisingly, this beer is light enough for salads with a touch of citrus dressing.

VELVET MERLIN OATMEAL STOUT, 5.5% ABV
Pours black and smells of coffee, perhaps espresso, and cream. Tastes much the same, but also delivers on the velvet promise – it is rich, textured, and a touch oily. Sweet chocolate notes balance roasted coffee flavour. It has a subtle earthy bitterness.

FOOD PAIRING: A beer to order alongside filet mignon – its sweetness will meld with the tender meat and its roast flavours will play off charred character.

PALE 31 PALE ALE, 4.9% ABV
Pours a rich amber colour, topped by a thick head. Has a floral, citrus note with layers of fruit and malt on the tongue, bright hop flavour, and persistent bitterness.

FOOD PAIRING: The hops cut through foods like blue cheese or work well with spicy, heat-charred flavours.

FLYING DOG

Although they are now brewed far from their original home in Colorado, the beers made at the Flying Dog Brewery in Maryland remain true to their origins, reflected in the cutting-edge labels created by UK artist Ralph Steadman.

GEORGE STRANAHAN founded the Flying Dog Brewpub in Aspen in 1990, not far from Woody Creek, home to "gonzo" journalist Hunter S Thompson and other celebrities who gathered and drank at the Woody Creek Tavern. After Thompson committed suicide in 2005, the brewery – which moved from Aspen to Denver and larger quarters in 1994 – brewed Gonzo Imperial Porter as a tribute.

Ralph Steadman, who had illustrated Thompson's work, drew his first label for Flying Dog in 1995. The Colorado Liquor Enforcement Division rejected it because it felt that the language it used was inappropriate. Six years of legal tussles followed before the brewery and free speech triumphed.

Flying Dog closed its Denver brewery in 2008 and moved to Maryland. Some newer releases reflect its new surroundings. Pearl Necklace Oyster Stout is brewed with Rappahannock river oysters and proceeds from the beer benefit the Oyster Recovery Partnership, which coordinates and conducts oyster bed restoration in the Chesapeake Bay. Beyond its wide range of year-round and seasonal beers, Flying Dog's Brewhouse Rarities are available only in the mid-Atlantic states. These have included beers such as Pumpernickel IPA and Pineapple Saison.

FLYING DOG
GONZO IMPERIAL PORTER

FLYING DOG
PEARL NECKLACE OYSTER STOUT

TASTING NOTES

GONZO IMPERIAL PORTER 9.2% ABV
It pours dark brown but its thick head and lacing are both tan-coloured. It has aromas of coffee, fruits, and piney hops. It has flavours of chocolate and caramel then bittersweet roasted notes.
FOOD PAIRING: Its bold flavours match smoked meats, so pair with a variety of barbecue dishes. It's also excellent as dessert itself or with chocolate- or coffee-flavoured dishes.

PEARL NECKLACE OYSTER STOUT 5.5% ABV
Looks and smells a bit like coffee, with plenty of roasted grain on the nose and hints of chocolate. Light on the tongue, it has rich toffee-like flavours and a solid bitterness. It can taste slightly salty, especially when accompanying oysters.
FOOD PAIRING: The obvious choice is oysters.

SNAKE DOG IPA 7.1% ABV
Bright amber in the glass, the white head lingers. Citrus fruits, notably grapefruit, dominate the nose. There is malt sweetness in the mouth, although the balance is towards hops.
FOOD PAIRING: A hoppy beer like this stands up well to wasabi mayonnaise, while the malt sweetness contrasts with the spices, making Snake Dog an excellent match for a deep-filled sandwich, anything from tuna to a beefburger.

Revolutionary style
Radical images by Ralph Steadman adorn the brewery's labels

FLYING DOG SNAKE DOG IPA

FOUNDERS

THE FACTS...

OWNER Founders Brewing Company

FOUNDED 1997

ADDRESS 235 Grandville Ave SW, Grand Rapids, Michigan 49503

WEBSITE www.foundersbrewing.com

PHILOSOPHY Brewed for us

Co-founder Dave Engbers keeps a pair of bolt cutters on his desk, a reminder of the week in 2001 when he and partner Mike Stevens thought the bank was about to padlock the doors on the fledgling Founders Brewing Company.

MIKE STEVENS AND DAVE ENGBERS quit their jobs to start Founders and started off making fine, if unremarkable, beers. "It really took us until we were on the brink of bankruptcy to realize that we were the ones who should set the trends and do it our own way", Engbers told a local newspaper in 2012 just before the brewery celebrated its 15th anniversary. "We started talking about making the beers we liked to drink." After a benefactor stepped in to guarantee their loan, they stopped brewing beers for a wide audience and started producing bold, complex ones that made Founders one of the fastest growing not-so-small brewers in the US.

These include beers like Breakfast Stout, coffee-infused and 8.3% ABV; Devil Dancer, a "triple" IPA, 12% ABV and immensely bitter; Dirty Bastard Scotch Ale, 8.5% ABV; Backwoods Bastard, aged in bourbon barrels and 10.2% ABV; and an entire Backstage Series of limited releases, most 10% ABV and above. The fifth in the series, a 15% ABV blend of barley wines, some aged in bourbon barrels, was released for the brewery's 15th anniversary and called, appropriately enough, Bolt Cutter.

The most notorious Founders beer is KBS, an 11.2% ABV imperial stout brewed with coffee and chocolate, cave-aged in oak bourbon barrels for a year, and released once a year. The appetite for KBS causes long queues wherever it is sold. In 2013, fans crashed the website of an online service selling tickets intended to bring order to the process.

Not every beer is quite as strong as KBS. Rübæus, a popular raspberry wheat ale, is 5.7% ABV. Likewise, All Day IPA nicely balances 4.7% ABV malt character with bright hops, providing a lower alcohol alternative to Centennial IPA. Founders is now recognized as one of the most well-known breweries in the US and the winner of four medals at the 2010 World Beer Cup, two medals at the 2010 Great American Beer Festival, and one medal at the 2012 World Beer Cup.

TASTING NOTES

PORTER 6.5% ABV
Dark brown on the pour, but black in the glass. There are bold aromas at the outset: roasted malts, chocolate, and earthy hops. It has an almost chewy texture, with burnt caramel and chocolate sweetness offset by solid bitterness.

FOOD PAIRING: An excellent mate for grilled steak or prime rib. It also makes espresso-based desserts even more decadent.

CENTENNIAL IPA 7.2% ABV
The amber colour hints at a solid malt backbone, but the first and last impressions are hops. It smells like a basket of citrus fruits, notably grapefruit and tangerines. Fruity fermentation character blends with hops in the mouth before giving way to a long, bitter finish.

FOOD PAIRING: A versatile beer, Centennial IPA is strong enough to stand up to fatty cheeses or deep-filled sandwiches, but is likely to overwhelm more delicate dishes.

BREAKFAST STOUT 8.3% ABV
It pours the colour of coffee but appears thicker. A wake-me-up nose, with rich, roasted coffee at the outset, is complemented by dark chocolate notes. The balance flips to chocolate in the mouth and the finish is long and bittersweet.

FOOD PAIRING: Fans do drink it for breakfast. Its rich flavours, thick mouthfeel, and bitter finish nicely match US favourite syrup-covered waffles with bacon on the side.

FOUNDERS
PORTER

FOUNDERS
CENTENNIAL IPA

FOUNDERS
BREAKFAST STOUT

THE GLEAMING, SENSUOUS CURVES OF THE COPPERS, LIKE THESE AT ANCHOR BREWING (SEE P.147) IN SAN FRANCISCO, CALIFORNIA, ARE USUALLY THE CENTRE OF ATTENTION IN A BREWING HALL

AFTER A TOUR OF THE DOGFISH HEAD BREWERY (SEE PP.154–155) IN MILTON, DELAWARE, THERE IS NOTHING BETTER THAN TO SAMPLE THE WIDE RANGE OF BEERS IN ITS TASTING ROOM

GOOSE ISLAND

THE FACTS...

OWNER Anheuser-Busch InBev

FOUNDED 1988

ADDRESS 1800 W Fulton St, Chicago, Illinois 60612

WEBSITE www.gooseisland.com

PHILOSOPHY Creating a diverse selection of unique beers

GOOSE ISLAND
312 URBAN WHEAT ALE

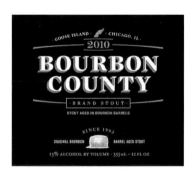

GOOSE ISLAND
BOURBON COUNTY STOUT

Goose Island took its beers national in 2013, two years after acquisition by Anheuser-Busch InBev. The production of its more esoteric brews remains in Chicago, the city where the brewery originated.

FORMER BREWMASTER AT GOOSE ISLAND, Greg Hall, lays claim to being the first brewer to age a commercial beer in barrels that had previously held spirits. He used bourbon barrels in 1992 when brewing an imperial stout for the 1,000th batch at Goose Island. Bourbon County Stout (BCS) was a once-a-year speciality until 2002. Now the brewery stacks thousands of used barrels full of beer in its warehouses, many of them BCS and variations on it. Its Vintage Ales include a variety of Belgian-inspired ales, some aged in barrels, often under the influence of wild yeast.

When Greg Hall's father, John, opened the Goose Island brewpub in 1988 it focused on lagers because that's what locals expected then. "But we always tried to educate people on ales", John Hall said when the brewery reached its 10th anniversary. By then he'd built a separate production brewery. "One thing that set us apart in Chicago – we didn't care that a lot of people didn't like our beer, we cared about the people who did like our beer. We spent a lot of time educating people. That's the secret."

John Hall retired in 2012, after selling the brewery to A-B InBev. To distribute the beers nationwide, A-B began producing the core beers – 312 Urban Wheat Ale, IPA, and Honker's Ale – as well as some seasonals at its own breweries. That leaves more space at the Chicago brewery for barrel-ageing.

TASTING NOTES

312 URBAN WHEAT ALE 4.2% ABV
This unfiltered ale is hazy in the glass. Floral, spicy hops announce themselves at the outset and there is a smooth and tart one-two combination on the tongue. It's a thirst-quencher.

FOOD PAIRING: Its light, spry character makes 312 Urban Wheat Ale an excellent choice to serve with a salad or fish.

BOURBON COUNTY STOUT 13% ABV
Pitch black, complex, and a bit boozy from start to finish, the bourbon is apparent in the beer, alongside chocolate, toffee, dark fruits, vanilla, and anise. Rich, but roasted bitterness and hops balance the abundant sweetness.

FOOD PAIRING: The perfect match for this beer is a warm fire and a snifter. Otherwise try with a flourless chocolate cake.

INDIA PALE ALE 5.9% ABV
This IPA is light amber with a thick, tight head. Quite floral with a combination of fruits, it's spicy on the nose with earthy spices on the palate. A hop bitterness balances rich malts.

FOOD PAIRING: Try this UK-style beer with a rich curry.

GOOSE ISLAND INDIA PALE ALE

GREAT LAKES

When Patrick and Daniel Conway founded their brewpub they called it Great Lakes because they wanted it to grow into something bigger. Now it takes more than 20 trucks full of honey just to make their Christmas Ale.

THE FACTS...

OWNER Great Lakes Brewing Company

FOUNDED 1988

ADDRESS 2516 Market Avenue, Cleveland, Ohio 44113

WEBSITE www.greatlakesbrewing.com

PHILOSOPHY Committed to crafting fresh, flavourful, high-quality beer and food

GREAT LAKES BREWPUB was founded in 1988 in Cleveland. Although it has now grown to become a major regional brewery, it continues to emphasize its Cleveland roots. It occupies six historic buildings near the West Side Market, one of the last US indoor-outdoor city markets of its kind. Its brewhouse – across the street from the brewpub – is housed in what were the stables of a former 19th-century brewery. The Conway brothers, who founded Great Lakes, have given their beers names like Eliot Ness Lager, because the lawman – portrayed in the film *The Untouchables* by Kevin Costner – moved to Cleveland after earning fame in Chicago. Burning River Pale Ale is so named because the Cuyahoga River nearby was once so polluted that it caught fire eight times. One name that didn't stick was The Heisman, given to their first beer. It was named after John Heisman of football fame, who was born near the brewery's site. Although the beer won a Gold medal at the 1990 Great American Beer Festival, the organization that takes charge of choosing a winner of the coveted Heisman Trophy football award objected to them using the name. The brothers renamed their beer Dortmunder Gold for its colour and because it had won them a Gold medal.

Great Lakes' beers, both ales and lagers, earned praise from the outset for their quality and reverence for tradition. The company has garnered equal respect for its environmental practices. Its logo has three waves rippling under its name, representing what Patrick Conway calls "our Triple Bottom Line: we felt it was important to emphasize, beyond the financial, the social and environmental".

GREAT LAKES
EDMUND FITZGERALD

GREAT LAKES
DORTMUNDER GOLD

GREAT LAKES
CHRISTMAS ALE

TASTING NOTES

EDMUND FITZGERALD PORTER, 5.8% ABV

With an imposing black body and thick brown head, this porter has a complex nose that is nutty with a solid roasted coffee punch, and chocolate and earthy hop notes. Lighter on the tongue that its appearance would suggest, it has rich chocolate and lighter caramel flavours; the flavours and bitterness linger.

FOOD PAIRING: The porter is bold enough to take on a well-charred steak or equally bold, spicy Cajun food, particularly rich gumbo.

DORTMUNDER GOLD LAGER, 5.8% ABV

Bright golden with a snow-white head, there is a hint of sweetness at the outset, mixed with understated hoppy notes. The firm body is bready; the malt sweetness builds but is balanced by hop bitterness and a hint of citrus.

FOOD PAIRING: The malt sweetness in this beer nicely complements a variety of grilled meats, and likewise pairs well with a pizza topped with meat.

CHRISTMAS ALE SPICED ALE, 7.5% ABV

Christmas cookies in a glass, appearing amber but smelling like your grandmother's kitchen when Christmas cake or cookies are in the oven. There are cinnamon, nutmeg, and cloves layered on top of sweet, fresh-out-of-the-oven baked flavours.

FOOD PAIRING: This seems like a perfect beer to have while decorating cookies, enjoyed fresh out of the oven, before covering them with anything sweet.

GREEN FLASH

At the start of 2013, Green Flash introduced "Hop Odyssey": six diverse hop-centric beers released throughout the year. But the brewery's own hop odyssey began in 2004, when innovative brewmaster Chuck Silva came aboard.

CONSIDERING SAN DIEGO'S REPUTATION for hop-forward beers, the fact that Green Flash decided to name one West Coast IPA was nothing if not bold. "When we decided to roll out our IPA we wanted it to be not just one of many IPAs, we wanted it to be almost a benchmark, a standout", Green Flash's brewmaster, Chuck Silva, said at the time. Even by local standards, he's inclined to go to extraordinary lengths to add hop character to Green Flash beers. For example, a beer called Palate Wrecker, an imperial IPA, is mashed and sprinkled with hopped wort rather than the traditional hot water. Another big difference between this brew and more traditional IPAs is that it is made with 2.7kg (6lb) of hops per barrel – generally, brewers making pale lagers use about 57g (2oz) of hops per barrel. Green Flash distributes its wide range of beers to much of the nation. Rayon Vert (French for Green Flash) is a Belgian-inspired pale ale, moderately hopped, and, under the influence of the wild yeast Brettanomyces, beguiling and effervescent. Another beer, Le Freak, has earned praise since it was introduced in 2008. "It's a creative style and I'm pretty proud of it", Silva said, not long after first brewing the beer. "I call it 'Belgian-style tripel meets San Diego Imperial Pale Ale.' I guess I was inspired by Belgian brewers. If they can do a hoppy Belgian, I can do a Belgian beer my way."

The brewery's indoor/outdoor tasting room is enormous, with 30 beers regularly on offer, and on a busy Friday night there is little that can be compared with attending a beer festival… or indeed, heading off on a hop odyssey.

GREEN FLASH
IMPERIAL

GREEN FLASH
WEST COAST IPA

GREEN FLASH
LE FREAK

TASTING NOTES

IMPERIAL INDIA PALE ALE, 9.4% ABV

This IPA is intense and floral from the start, with zingy grapefruit flavour and thick foam. It is oily, resiny, and spicy on the palate as those aromas turn into flavours. Bitterness lingers through a long, dry finish.

FOOD PAIRING: This beer can easily overwhelm at the table, but pairs well with grilled meats, charred and caramelized on the outside, rare on the inside, and slathered in barbecue sauce.

WEST COAST IPA 7.3% ABV

Perhaps the zesty, piney, citrus-packed nose creates a hop-induced fog, but this beer appears to have a green cast in the glass. It has gigantic hop flavours, hanging on a solid malt backbone and is delightfully bitter.

FOOD PAIRING: This beer is more intense than many IPAs, so plan accordingly. Dishes flavoured with citrus or coriander, such as slightly greasy ground beef tacos, work nicely against the fruitiness of the beer.

LE FREAK AMERICAN BELGO, 9.2% ABV

A slightly cloudy orange in the glass, this beer brims with fruity aromas, citrus, and a bit of spice. It has sweet malt, complex fruit flavours, and an unapologetic bitterness in the mouth. It's a brilliant merger of fermentation and hop-induced flavours.

FOOD PAIRING: A bold beer perfectly suited for bold, creamy, and/or pungent cheeses. It can be interesting with everything from a Danish blue cheese to smoked gouda, or even a limburger cheese sandwich.

LAGUNITAS

Lagunitas was founded in California in 1993 by Tony Magee. What sets it apart is its individual and exciting interpretations of traditional beers, sold with irreverent wording on the labels.

LAGUNITAS OPERATES LARGE brewing facilities in northern California, where Tony Magee founded the company that reflects his irreverent personality; Magee still writes the entertaining copy for the beers' labels and other promotional material. Many of the recipes are his originals, although today he acts more as "art director" when new beers are designed. "They're an expression of my own personal aesthetic. I don't really even know what my aesthetic is, but I work very hard to get those things on the labels so people see the personality", he says. So although Lagunitas's flagship IPA is not actually made with "43 different hops and 65 various malts", as the label states, it certainly represents the brewery's penchant for bold and bolder beers. Like most of the beers Lagunitas sells, it is generously dry-hopped and brimming with aromas and flavours rather than pure bitterness. Its label says "Thanks for choosing to spend the next few minutes with this special, homicidally hoppy ale. Savour the moment as

the raging hop character engages the Imperial Qualities of the Malt Foundation in mortal combat on the battlefield of your palate!"

A series of beers from 2006 likewise reflected the personalities of Magee and his brewers. Starting with Freak Out! ale, Lagunitas had hoped to brew a unique beer for each of Frank Zappa's albums, using the LP art for each label. However, the Zappa trust pulled the plug after five beers. Despite this, the brewery's success is growing. After struggling to keep up with booming demand for its beers in 2011, the brewery did not make Brown Shugga, a very popular seasonal. Instead they brought out Lagunitas Sucks holiday ale. It was a hit, and proved that fans love the brewery even when it "sucks".

"I'd like to think none of our beers are today's interpretation of yesterday's anything", Magee says, and the brewery continues to expand its eclectic range. It's no surprise that both Brown Shugga and Lagunitas Sucks, a barley wine, returned in 2012 for the winter season.

THE FACTS...

OWNER Lagunitas Brewing Co
FOUNDED 1993
ADDRESS 1280 N McDowell Blvd, Petaluma, California 94954
WEBSITE www.lagunitas.com
PHILOSOPHY Beer speaks, people mumble. Obey the buds, word

TASTING NOTES

PILS 6% ABV
Pale gold in the glass and topped by a thick white head, the aromas are floral, spicy and a bit grassy. It is cracker-clean in the mouth, with more spicy hop flavour and a bracing bitterness that remains long after the beer itself is gone.
FOOD PAIRING: A bit heftier than your average pilsner, this beer still nicely matches lighter fare, such as a summer salad, grilled chicken, or sushi.

IPA 6.2% ABV
It pours bright amber and the foam leaves circles of lace after each sip. Fruity, piney, and citrussy on the nose, there is more of the same on the palate; herbal hop flavours emerge and a touch of bready malt sweetness is balanced by hop bitterness.
FOOD PAIRING: The classic balance of sweetness and hop punch blend perfectly with south-east Asian dishes, such as spicy pork, poultry, or fish.

HOP STOOPID IMPERIAL IPA, 8% ABV
This IPA includes hop extracts, and no apologies, in the recipe, which boosts the massive hop presence without adding lingering vegetative notes. Hop aroma – citrus, pine, and all you'd expect – virtually jumps from the glass, followed by a solid bitter punch, the blow softened by malt sweetness.
FOOD PAIRING: The complex sweet malt-alcohol-hop bitterness combination perfectly accompanies a simple bowl of home-made vanilla ice cream.

LAGUNITAS
PILS

LAGUNITAS
IPA

LAGUNITAS
HOP STOOPID

NEW BELGIUM

Jeff Lebesch, founder of the New Belgium brewery, was inspired to start his own craft brewery in Colorado after a cycling trip around Belgium. The company is now the third-largest craft brewery in the United States.

THE FACTS...

OWNER New Belgium Brewing Co

FOUNDED 1991

ADDRESS 500 Linden St, Fort Collins, Colorado 80524

WEBSITE www.newbelgium.com

PHILOSOPHY Alternatively empowered, 100% employee-owned

NEW BELGIUM
FAT TIRE

KIM JORDAN AND JEFF LEBESCH, wife and husband, started the New Belgium brewery in their Fort Collins basement in 1991. They soon moved to larger quarters in a railway station, then built a state-of-the-art facility, which has since expanded many times over. After several years of searching, the company settled on Asheville, North Carolina, as the site for a second brewery, scheduled to begin operations in 2015. Beyond its obviously popular beers, New Belgium annually wins accolades as one of the best places to work in the US, having long ago established itself as committed to environmental issues, as well as being 100 per cent employee-owned. When employees have worked at New Belgium Brewing for one year they receive a Fat Tire bicycle. After five years they are taken on a guided tour of Belgium, and they all have an opportunity to become part-owners.

Fat Tire Amber Ale is at the heart of its success, once accounting for three-quarters of sales, although today many fans are as likely to drink

Ranger IPA as one that takes its inspiration from Belgium. A bicycle resembling the one employees receive is on the company logo and Tour de Fat – a travelling festival that visits more than a dozen cities each year and includes a costumed bicycle parade, New Belgium beer, bizarre bicycle contests, and more – has raised millions of dollars for charity.

The addition of brewmaster Peter Bouckaert in 1996, a native Belgian who had worked at Rodenbach (see p.88), boosted the brewery's "Belgian cred". He bought used wine barrels, filled them with beer and inoculated them with "wild" yeast. The first beer to result was La Folie. Now the brewery has a room full of large oak fermentation tanks.

TASTING NOTES

FAT TIRE AMBER ALE, 5.2% ABV

It pours a rich amber – caramel notes blend with earthy hops on the nose and are joined by a hint of citrus. Caramel malt seems more toast-like in the mouth, its sweetness not quite offset by subtle hops. The finish is on the sweet side of dry.

FOOD PAIRING: A very versatile beer, but best with foods that aren't sweet, because they detract from the maltiness. Excellent for lunch with a grilled chicken sandwich and a Mid-western US speciality – beer cheese soup.

LA FOLIE SOUR BROWN ALE, 6% ABV

Each vintage appears and tastes a bit different, with some batches a deeper red in the glass, some more mouth-puckering than others. Complex fruity aromas and flavours, from citrus to cherries, combine with a varying wood character. The magic in this beer is the balanced acidity.

FOOD PAIRING: Playing up that acidity, New Belgium suggests matching La Folie with a bitter green salad and ahi tuna.

RANGER INDIA PALE ALE, 6.5% ABV

Bright gold in the glass with a rocky head, this beer is pungent with citrussy, piney hops jumping from the glass. There is lean malt flavour on the palate, dominated by resiny hops, more pine and citrus, and a crisp bitterness. It has a long spicy-dry finish.

FOOD PAIRING: New Belgium's "Beer Rangers" are their representatives in the field. It's easy to imagine grilling beefburgers outdoors, loading them with every topping imaginable, and opening an IPA.

NEW BELGIUM
LA FOLIE

NEW BELGIUM
RANGER

NEW GLARUS

On a hilltop overlooking the town it shares a name with, New Glarus Brewery looks almost Bavarian. However, brewmaster Dan Carey makes clear: "It's a Wisconsin brewery, a Wisconsin sensibility, a Wisconsin way of thinking".

THE FACTS...

OWNER New Glarus Brewing Co
FOUNDED 1993
ADDRESS 2400 State Hwy 69, New Glarus, Wisconsin 53574
WEBSITE www.newglarusbrewing.com
PHILOSOPHY From barley to bottle, true to style without compromise... ever

NEW GLARUS
SPOTTED COW

NEW GLARUS
MOON MAN

DEBORAH AND DAN CAREY founded New Glarus in 1993. Deborah is the company president and was chosen as Wisconsin's Small Business Person of the Year in 2011. The brewery logo features her thumb-print in the shape of the state of Wisconsin and the words "Drink Indigenous" around the bottom. Theirs is the only brewery in the US to sell more than 120,000hl (73,000 barrels) a year without shipping beyond state borders, although there is plenty of demand.

By the time they started New Glarus, Dan Carey had worked at a microbrewery in Montana; interned at Ayinger Brewery in Bavaria; been valedictorian of a Siebel Institute Course in Brewing Science and Technology; installed breweries; and been brewing supervisor at Anheuser-Busch's Fort Collins plant (see p.189). He also passed the Diploma Master Brewer exam at the Institute of Brewing in London, becoming the first American in 19 years to do so.

The Wisconsin farmhouse ale, Spotted Cow, perfectly represents the brewery. Dan created the beer after wondering what Wisconsin farmhouse beers would have tasted like in the 19th century. It is made using indigenous ingredients such as corn, some unmalted barley grown on land the brewery owns, and is left unfiltered.

TASTING NOTES

SPOTTED COW WISCONSIN FARMHOUSE ALE, 5.1% ABV
Pale yellow and a bit hazy in the glass, with hints of stone fruit and a bit of hay on the nose. Fruity in the mouth, it has honey-like sweetness, a touch of spicy hop flavour, but little bitterness.
FOOD PAIRING: The perfect beer for a Friday night fish fry or other Wisconsin favourites: grilled fresh bratwurst, cheese curds, or a cheese sandwich.

MOON MAN NO COAST PALE ALE, 5% ABV
Bright and golden, the head is effervescent. Citrus hop aromas dominate the nose, with a swirl of grapefruit, lemon zest, orange, and tangerine rind. Bready malt and stone fruit flavours are nicely balanced against citrus hop notes and bitterness.
FOOD PAIRING: Hops character gives Moon Man the heft to stand up to diverse, richly flavoured fare such as Thai food, spicy curries, or jambalaya.

TWO WOMEN PALE LAGER, 5% ABV
Pours a rich gold with a white head and thick lacing. The aroma is floral and spicy, tinged with citrus and a hint of graininess. It is bready in the mouth with fruity, spicy notes and bitterness.
FOOD PAIRING: An excellent match for rich pork dishes like schweinebraten – pork goulash wiener schnitzel.

Hometown heroes
New Glarus is fiercely proud of its Wisconsin heritage

NEW GLARUS TWO WOMEN

NINKASI

Naming an IPA Total Domination before selling a drop was either optimistic, arrogant, or both. "Total domination" might have been an over-statement, but Ninkasi's quick success was unprecedented.

Divine offering
A rich, dark, complex beer, truly dedicated to the admirers of Ninkasi

NINKASI
BELIEVER

TOTAL DOMINATON BECAME the best-selling 1 pint (470ml) bottle of beer in Oregon, and one of the best-selling in the United States, despite limited distribution. Ninkasi grew into a regional brewery within three years and the rocket ride has barely slowed since. Partners Nikos Ridge, who previously worked in the financial industry, and Jamie Floyd, a charismatic figure within the brewing community, sold their beers in grocery stores, warehouse stores, and other chain operations.

"Nikos and I are not making beer just for beer geeks. We don't want just one one-hundredth of one per cent of beer… We're here for everybody", Floyd states. He puts a premium on balance, which is not to say he aims for the bland flavours in the middle. His hop-forward beers attract the most attention, starting with Total Domination and including wildly popular beers made with fresh unkilned hops during harvest season. To make Total Crystalation, the brewers pack the mash tun with Crystal hops hours off the plant, then circulate already generously hopped wort through the freshly picked cones.

The brewery was named for the Sumerian goddess of beer and Floyd talks about the role of beer in civilization. "Being connected with my community is the important thing for me, and being the village brewer is the perfect way to do that", he says.

THE FACTS...

OWNER Ninkasi Brewing
FOUNDED 2006
ADDRESS 272 Van Buren Street, Eugene, Oregon 97402
WEBSITE www.ninkasibrewing.com
PHILOSOPHY To perpetuate better living. The ancient Sumerians worshipped the beer they made and praised the goddess Ninkasi for the miracle of fermentation. Beer is a staple of civilization and a valuable part of a happy life

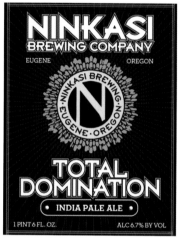

NINKASI
TOTAL DOMINATION

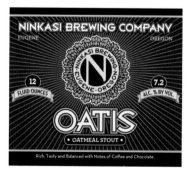

NINKASI
OATIS

TASTING NOTES

BELIEVER DOUBLE RED ALE, 6.9% ABV
Deep red with rich malty aromas and flavours, including caramel and toffee. It has prominent citrus hop character, both on the nose and in the mouth. The sweetness lingers, but isn't cloying.

FOOD PAIRING: Its bold malt character and crisp bitterness make Believer a good choice to go with a four-cheese pizza, layered with big-flavoured varieties.

TOTAL DOMINATION INDIA PALE ALE, 6.7% ABV
Pours cloudy and deep orange. Its citrus-laden nose is floral with prominent grapefruit zest. It has a solid malt middle, a bit of caramel sweetness, and is balanced by bitterness.

FOOD PAIRING: Try with poultry, seafood, and spicy Mexican dishes. Makes an excellent dessert alongside sharp cheeses.

OATIS OATMEAL STOUT, 7.2% ABV
Almost black with a firm tan head, it has a complex nose with flavours of sweet chocolate, malts, molasses, and dark fruits. It is full and creamy, with roasted malts and hop bitterness.

FOOD PAIRING: A potent stout; try with meaty dishes and thick stews. May also be served with fruit salad after dinner.

ODELL

Odell began brewing in 1989 when craft brewing was hardly known in the US. Like many of its beer-making neighbours, Odell pays close attention to its footprints – environmental, historic, and those still fresh.

ODELL'S REGIONAL FOOTPRINT SUMS UP the ethos of the brewery. It includes ingredients from each of the ten states where the company sells beer. The brewers took several small batches and blended them into Footprint, using hops and barley from Colorado and Idaho, wheat from Kansas and Wyoming, Arizona prickly pear, Minnesota wild rice, Nebraska corn, New Mexico green chillies, South Dakota honey, and oak barrels from Missouri. It is not a regular offering, yet reflects the concern for sustainability and commitment to community shared with nearby New Belgium brewery (see p.166).

Doug, Wynne, and Corkie Odell located their first brewery in a grain elevator built in 1915. Due to Doug's respect for UK brewing tradition, they used all four of its floors to install a traditional gravity-fed system and employed open fermentation. "I would say that my brewing style is all about flavour balance", he said. His Scottish-inspired 90 Shilling ale, available the day the brewery opened, remains the best-selling beer, but others, like the progressively hoppy trio of 5 Barrel Pale Ale, IPA, and Myrcenary Double IPA, flaunt US hop character. A Woodcut Series features barrel-aged beers, while the Cellar Series tends to push boundaries. Research into growing organic hops in its home state is one of the local initiatives Odell has funded.

THE FACTS...

OWNER Odell Brewing Co
FOUNDED 1989
ADDRESS 800 E Lincoln Avenue, Fort Collins, Colorado 80524
WEBSITE www.odellbrewing.com
PHILOSOPHY Keeping the craft in craft brewing

Tangy Twist
The addition of aromatic US hops gives the traditional IPA a bold flavour and distinctive bitterness

TASTING NOTES

IPA 7% ABV
Bright on the nose and in the glass, IPA is golden with an orange note that also appears in the aroma, joined by mango and tangerine. Citrus hop flavours meet biscuity malt on the tongue, balanced by firm, dry hop bitterness.
FOOD PAIRING: Drinking this beer along with Thai curry is one of Doug Odell's favourite beer-food pairings.

THE MEDDLER WILD ALE, 8.9% ABV
Appears muddy brown with a blanket of beige foam. It has a complex nose, mostly dark fruits like raisins and plums, but also berry and cherry notes. Its pleasant acidity, tart rather than sour, cuts through chocolate and toffee flavours with a malt richness.
FOOD PAIRING: Try in a sauce for venison or pork, or a beef stew.

90 SHILLING SCOTTISH ALE, 5.3% ABV
Pours a rich copper topped with a tan-coloured head and a rich caramel aroma and flavours. There is chocolate and fruitiness on the palate, with earthy hops. It finishes dry, but not bitter.
FOOD PAIRING: A comfortable beer, it nicely suits comfort food, like meatloaf or roasted chicken and steamed vegetables.

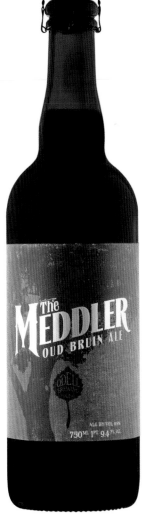

ODELL
IPA

ODELL
THE MEDDLER

ODELL
90 SHILLING

OSKAR BLUES

The year Oskar Blues became the first small US brewery to package its beer in cans, it sold 800hl (475 barrels). Ten years later it produced 102,300hl (62,500 barrels) and now more than 200 other breweries also put their beer in cans.

THE FACTS...

OWNER Oskar Blues Brewery
FOUNDED 1999
ADDRESS 1800 Pike Road, Longmont, Colorado 80501
WEBSITE www.oskarblues.com
PHILOSOPHY Ride bikes. Drink beer. Repeat

AN ALABAMA NATIVE, DALE KATECHIS opened Oskar Blues Grill in 1997, using southern-inspired recipes from his mother. He installed a tiny brewery in the basement in 1998, and began selling beer the following year. When he decided to invest $10,000 on a hands-on canning line in 2002, craft beer fans and breweries alike considered cans taboo, suitable only for tasteless mainstream beers. The first beer he packaged, Dale's Pale Ale, helped change that perception. In 2005 it finished atop a blind tasting of US pale ales conducted by the *New York Times*.

Katechis calls it the "Canned Beer Apocalypse" and it took his business well beyond the village of Lyons, Colorado. Oskar Blues Grill & Brew remains in Lyons but the company operates a large brewery, with a popular tasting room, and a spacious restaurant in nearby Longmont; it raises cattle for beef served in its restaurants and grows hops to put in its beer at Hops & Heifers Farm; it runs Lyon Soul Distilling; and it opened a brewery in North Carolina to meet demand on the East Coast. In 2012, Katechis was named the Ernst & Young Entrepreneur of the Year for his Mountain Desert Region. An avid cyclist, he also started his own fixed wheel bicycle company. One of the brewery's first promotions was to give away a performance bicycle to the first three customers to recycle 3,501 cans – the number that fit on a shipping pallet.

TASTING NOTES

TEN FIDY IMPERIAL STOUT, 10.5% ABV
Pouring it from a can adds to an initial impression of pitch-black motor oil. There are moderately roasty, sweet, and dark chocolate aromas mingling from the start. It is thick and chewy, redolent of rich chocolate and dark fruits, with chocolate and roasted bitterness emerging at the end.
FOOD PAIRING: A dessert in itself, but the menu in Lyons suggests tempting partners, like a warm fudge brownie sundae or chocolate bourbon balls.

DALE'S PALE ALE 6.5% ABV
Pours copper with a fluffy white head and a piney, citrus, biscuity nose. The palate is rich, and abundant bready malt and juicy-fruity hop flavours are offset by a long, bitter finish.
FOOD PAIRING: A solid match for tuna tacos at the original restaurant – a dish that includes jalapeños, coriander dressing, fresh mango salsa, and rocket.

MAMA'S LITTLE YELLA PILS 5.3% ABV
This beer is yellow with a floral aroma and subdued, slightly grainy notes of citrus and spice. There is crispness on the tongue – a combination of malt and hops – and it is full of hop flavour with a firm but not harsh bitterness.
FOOD PAIRING: Pairs wonderfully with any sandwich.

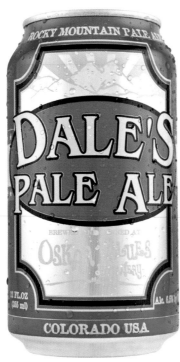

"Can do" attitude
Oskar blues led the trend for small brewers to can beer

OSKAR BLUES TEN FIDY

OSKAR BLUES DALE'S PALE ALE

OSKAR BLUES MAMA'S LITTLE YELLA PILS

PORT BREWING

San Diego-based brewery Port Brewing has two brands – Port and Lost Abbey – both catering to different markets. US West Coast-style beers are sold under the Port brand, while Belgian-inspired brews have the Lost Abbey label.

THE FACTS...

OWNER Port Brewing Co
FOUNDED 2006
ADDRESS 155 Mata Way #104, San Marcos, California 92069
WEBSITE www.portbrewing.com, www.lostabbey.com
PHILOSOPHY We brew the beers others can't

PORT BREWING WAS STARTED IN 2006 by the people behind the Pizza Port brewpub chain. They had been producing beer for their restaurants but demand had exceeded supply, so they opened a separate brewery in a larger facility. Brewmaster Tomme Arthur's beers often take inspiration from Belgium, based on understanding rather than imitation. "For a while there people were trying to replicate the world styles, but I don't know that I ever set out to copy another beer", Arthur said.

Instead of discussing style, he prefers to talk about "flavour-driven beers" and how creations like Cuvee de Tomme changed the conversation in the US. He first brewed Cuvee at the Pizza Port pub in

Solana Beach in 1999, ageing a strong, dark beer fermented with Belgian yeast, in used bourbon barrels, dosed with 50lb (23kg) of cherries and three different strains of the wild yeast Brettanomyces. Now he uses a variety of brandy and French oak barrels as well.

Lost Abbey has beer ageing in more than 1,000 barrels, and blending their flavours is a hallmark of the brewery. Although the resulting beers often feature bold, intense characteristics, they also include complex, nuanced notes that only emerge over time. In 2012, Arthur and crew blended 13 special beers during the year. Their "Ultimate Box Set" was inspired by rock music with each monthly "track" showcasing a different anthem, different types of barrels, and different base beers from the Lost Abbey portfolio. At the end of the year, the dozen single releases and a 13th bonus beer were packaged in a "roadie"-worthy trunk along with liner notes.

PORT BREWING
RED POPPY ALE

PORT BREWING
10 COMMANDMENTS

PORT BREWING
HOT ROCKS LAGER

TASTING NOTES

RED POPPY ALE WILD FRUIT BEER, 5% ABV
Almost brown with ruby highlights, this beer is aromatic, particularly with dark fruits and cherries. Sweet caramel and red fruit flavours are quickly met in the mouth with tart sour cherries and a pleasant note of balsamic vinegar. There is a lingering impression of wine – this beer is wonderfully complex.

FOOD PAIRING: The fruitiness and acidity in Red Poppy match, balance, and cut through the richness of duck, particularly one glazed or in sauce.

10 COMMANDMENTS STRONG BELGIAN ALE, 10% ABV
Pours a very dark brown, looking substantial and smelling the same. There are plenty of dark fruits, chocolate, and caramel in both the aroma and flavour, but nicely melded. There are tart, earthy, spicy notes on the tongue, finishing dry.

FOOD PAIRING: The dark fruit flavours and caramelized notes make an excellent match for flavourful meat, such as braised short ribs.

HOT ROCKS LAGER STEIN BEER, 6.2% ABV
Part of the Port Brewing family, this beer is brewed in the German tradition by adding hot granite to the boiling kettle. There is abundant caramel aroma, along with toffee, even chocolate. This full-flavoured lager with rich caramel flavours is offset by earthy and spicy hops, and a smooth bitterness.

FOOD PAIRING: A very food-friendly beer that is excellent with casual but relatively flavourful foods like burgers, pizza, barbecue, and Mexican dishes.

R🟊GUE **ROGUE**

Although not the largest of the new wave of US breweries, Rogue sells its beer in every state and more than 20 other countries. It has further built on its outsize reputation by recruiting its fans to join its "Rogue Nation".

THE FACTS...

OWNER Rogue Ales
FOUNDED 1998
ADDRESS 2320 OSU Drive, Newport, Oregon 97366
WEBSITE www.rogue.com
PHILOSOPHY Dedicated to the Rogue in each of us

ROGUE
DEAD GUY ALE

ROGUE
MOCHA PORTER

Naughty but nice
Rogue might be irreverent but it exudes class in a glass

ROGUE SHAKESPEARE OATMEAL STOUT

PACKAGING BEERS in glow-in-the-dark bottles or pink ceramic ones (a Bacon Maple Ale, no less), Rogue constantly brandishes an irreverent attitude, but still makes its beer, and brewmaster John Maier, the star. When the national Brewers Association initiated its annual award for innovation in craft brewing in 1997, Maier was the first recipient. Although he uses bold amounts of less than traditional ingredients, he established a reputation for using hops, and brewed one of the first commercial Double IPAs.

That's one reason why Rogue acquired its Micro Hopyard in Oregon's Willamette Valley, about 120km (75 miles) east of its Newport brewery. Rogue leases land on an established hop farm, complete with picking machine and kilning facilities. It also grows a portion of its own barley on the Tygh Ranch, to the north-east of the hop yard. The farm is off the beaten track, but is packed at weekends. The tasting room keeps regular hours and during the summer and harvest there are tours every day. "This is about the Rogue experience", co-founder Jack Joyce has said. It's also about education. "We believe origin matters." Special events include musical concerts and presentations on subjects such as bee-keeping. The facility is available for weddings, and there's accommodation at the Hop 'N' Bed, a farmhouse that overlooks acres of hops as well as the processing facilities.

TASTING NOTES

DEAD GUY ALE MAIBOCK, 6.6% ABV
Its copper appearance announces rich, toasty, caramel aromas and flavours; the hops are herbal-spicy on the nose and bitter in the mouth. The caramel sweetness is balanced by the hops.
FOOD PAIRING: Well suited for bold game, pork, or sausages, with potatoes on the side. The one-two sweet and hoppy punch is powerful enough to match Cajun food as well.

MOCHA PORTER 5.1% ABV
Pours coffee-black, leaving tan lacing. The roasted notes give way to chocolate, while rich caramel is more apparent in the mouth. Well balanced, the hops supplement a bittersweet finish.
FOOD PAIRING: The chocolate, hint of smokiness, and spicy hop character intermingle with barbecued beef.

SHAKESPEARE OATMEAL STOUT 6% ABV
Dark roasted coffee and chocolate aromas mingle with dark fruit. There is a husky malt presence, plenty of hop flavour and bitterness, with an almost creamy, smooth mouthfeel.
FOOD PAIRING: A dessert unto itself, Shakespeare Oatmeal Stout might also be served with chocolate or vanilla ice cream.

RUSSIAN RIVER

A sign taken from the New Albion Brewery, which opened nearby in 1977, hangs behind the bar at Russian River Brewing, connecting the beginning of microbrewing in the US with its present and probably its future.

FIRST AT BLIND PIG BREWING in southern California, then at Russian River in northern California's wine country, brewmaster Vinnie Cilurzo found an enthusiastic audience for, and inspired other brewers with, his hop-forward ales. Cilurzo called the first beer he made at Blind Pig in 1994 a Double IPA, probably the first commercial version of what since has become recognized as a distinct style. He went to work at Russian River, a subsidiary of Korbel Champagne Cellars, in 1997, and when the owners of the company decided to leave the brewing business he and his wife, Natalie, bought the brand and opened their brewpub in 2004. They have since built a separate production brewery nearby.

Cilurzo also began to experiment with ageing beers in used wine barrels at Russian River, starting with some that once held Chardonnay. "It started with the idea that I wanted to make a blond barrel-aged beer. I love lambics, so I decided to take one component of lambic and do that in this beer. The idea of extracting some of the wine flavour (from the barrels) happened on its own", he said. He had settled on the idea of making an entire series of "-tion" beers, and called the first barrel-aged one Temptation. The first beer in the line, the strong golden Damnation, is another of his most popular.

The Double IPA Cilurzo brews now, Pliny the Elder, is very different from his first one, reflecting in part how many new bold hop varieties have become available during the last 20 years, and certainly since Jack McAuliffe started New Albion. Cilurzo also makes a Triple IPA, Pliny the Younger, once a year, releasing it each February.

TASTING NOTES

PLINY THE ELDER DOUBLE IPA, 8% ABV
Pours bright golden with a thick white head. The aroma is that of hop cones rubbed together, with pine and citrus, and particularly grapefruit. It is lean of body, but with a firm malt backbone, abundant hop flavours, peppery notes, and pure bitterness. It has a long, lingering, bitter finish.

FOOD PAIRING: Pizzas are outstanding at the brewpub, and Pliny stands up to the boldest of them. Try one made with mozzarella, pesto, sausage, spinach, and caramelized onions.

TEMPTATION BARREL-AGED ALE, 7.5% ABV
Golden in the glass, but hazy if you empty the whole bottle. There are white grapes and citrus (particularly pineapple) on the nose, followed by earthy, musty, wild notes. Stone fruits blend with grapes, oak, and vanilla on the palate. Temptation is complex and ultimately acidic.

FOOD PAIRING: Vinnie Cilurzo has called Temptation and Humboldt Fog goat cheese from Cypress Grove his favourite pairing for his beers. If you can't get to California, try it with your favourite goat's cheese.

SUPPLICATION BARREL-AGED ALE 7% ABV
The colour of a not-quite-ripe cherry, both Pinot Noir (from the barrels) and cherries (from the fruit) are apparent from the start. The aroma and flavour quickly merge – sour cherries, ripe grapes, raspberry, and strawberry notes, smokiness – and the fruity flavours are balanced by tart acidity and oak tannins.

FOOD PAIRING: A perfect match for a simple green salad with a vinegar-based dressing – the acidity of the dressing will complement the beer.

RUSSIAN RIVER
PLINY THE ELDER

RUSSIAN RIVER
TEMPTATION

RUSSIAN RIVER
SUPPLICATION

SAMUEL ADAMS

At the forefront of the microbrewing boom in the US, the Boston Beer Company has been brewing Samuel Adams, named after the American founding father traditionally believed to have been a brewer, since 1985.

JIM KOCH, A SIXTH-GENERATION BREWER who originally embarked on a career in management consulting, began brewing and selling beer in 1985. Within four years, Boston Beer Company's sales of Samuel Adams beer exceeded those of Anchor Brewing. It has remained the largest US craft brewery ever since. At the outset, most of the beers were brewed under contract at heritage breweries – older breweries with excess capacity reopened after Prohibition. Today, Boston Beer owns its own breweries, the largest of which is in Pennsylvania's Lehigh Valley. Their small pilot brewery in Boston is open to visitors.

Koch's first beer, Samuel Adams Boston Lager, has been the top seller from the first day. He based it on the recipe his great-great grandfather, Louis Koch, had used in St Louis in the 1870s. Boston Beer has gone to extraordinary lengths to assure the quality of that beer, supporting the Hallertau Mittelfrüh hop in Germany when others didn't, while also demanding hop growers deliver it fresher and with the specific qualities Boston Beer wanted.

In 1993, Koch introduced Samuel Adams Triple Bock, then the world's strongest beer at 17% ABV. "At the time, everyone was trying to make one new classic style. That's what was driving innovation", Koch said. "I wanted to step outside of that, to try to expand the boundaries of beer rather than expanding on traditional styles." An extreme brew, Triple Bock laid the groundwork for Utopias, an ultra-strong beer of almost 30% ABV, which was the strongest beer available at the time. Each Utopias blend includes beers from barrels used for Triple Bock.

Koch understands better than almost anyone how much American beer changed in a few decades, and why. In 2013, he collaborated with craft beer pioneer Jack McAuliffe to brew McAuliffe's original New Albion Ale. Boston Beer gave all the profits to McAuliffe, who was an essential player in launching the American "microbrewery movement". He opened New Albion Brewing in 1976. It closed in 1982, but inspired thousands of brewers who followed – including Koch.

Vintage variation
Each vintage of Utopias will have nuanced differences in flavour and aroma

SAMUEL ADAMS
UTOPIAS

SAMUEL ADAMS
NOBLE PILS

SAMUEL ADAMS
OCTOBERFEST

SAMUEL ADAMS
LATITUDE 48 IPA

SAMUEL ADAMS
BLACK LAGER

Leading lager
Samuel Adams proudly claim that Boston Lager "helped to lead the US beer revolution"

Golden delicious
Samuel Adams' first beer is renowned for its gloriously frothy head and gleaming golden colour

SAMUEL ADAMS BOSTON LAGER

TASTING NOTES

UTOPIAS STRONG ALE, 27% ABV OR MORE

Imagine top-flight port and sherry blended together, dark fruits, melted toffee, woody notes, and more than just a whiff of alcohol. Multiply it by ten and you have an idea of Utopias.

FOOD PAIRING: A dessert on its own, Utopias is doubly decadent when served with crème brûlée.

NOBLE PILS PILSNER, 5.2% ABV

Pours straw-coloured and golden, with perfume-like hop aromas. It is floral, spicy, and has a citrus scent unlike that given off by American hops. Bready in the mouth, it is spicy with a crisp bitterness leading to a clean finish.

FOOD PAIRING: A perfect choice to accompany bruschetta, its bready malt character matches the bread, while the hops cut through the acidity of tomatoes.

OCTOBERFEST 5.3% ABV

It would be a pity to hide the orange-red body of Octoberfest in an opaque glass. Rich malts on the nose and in the mouth, perhaps a hint of spicy hops, but bitterness for balance. A complex but never busy beer.

FOOD PAIRING: There's a reason that roast chicken is a dish *de rigueur* at Oktoberfest in Munich. The caramelized flavours in Octoberfest and the chicken blend perfectly.

LATITUDE 48 IPA 6% ABV

Latitude is darkish amber in the glass, topped by a large white head. A mash-up of hop aromas, citrus, melon, and pine, gives something different with each breath. There are the same flavours in the mouth, and a solid malt backbone balanced with obvious bitterness.

FOOD PAIRING: The richness of body nicely complements a dish such as smoked salmon or a hamburger loaded with salty extras like bacon.

BLACK LAGER SCHWARZBIER, 4.9% ABV

More like a dark brown lager when the light hits it right, Black Lager has roasted malts and notes of chocolate that make it smell darker. Rich and smooth, more hop spicy than bitter, although a hint of roasted coffee lingers through the finish.

FOOD PAIRING: The roasted malts in this beer nicely balance sweet caramelized onions and cheese in French onion soup.

BOSTON LAGER 4.8% ABV

Bright copper in the glass, Boston Lager promises sweet malts, which are more apparent in the flavour than on the nose. It starts with floral, spicy aromas, its hop bitterness and flavour perfectly balancing the rich malt. It has a long, but smooth finish.

FOOD PAIRING: Particularly versatile with food, able to take on blue cheese, doughy chicken, or highly seasoned sausage.

SIERRA NEVADA

Sierra Nevada offered a blueprint for more than a thousand small breweries that followed, one built on boldly flavoured and often hop-centric beers, sustainable environmental practices, and strong community involvement.

THE FACTS...

OWNER Sierra Nevada Brewing Company

FOUNDED 1980

ADDRESS 1075 E 20th Street, Chico, California 95928

WEBSITE www.sierranevada.com

PHILOSOPHY With a passion for innovation, pushing at the boundaries of beer, anything is possible

CO-FOUNDERS OF SIERRA NEVADA, Ken Grossman and Paul Camusi, took inspiration from Anchor and New Albion before assembling a business plan that called for a maximum production of 3580hl (2186 barrels) annually. "We figured we could make money at that, we wouldn't get rich but we'd get by", said Grossman, who later bought out Camusi. The brewery in Chico now produces nearly 1.2 million hl (750,000 barrels) a year, and a second one has been built near Asheville, North Carolina.

Grossman and Camusi dumped the first 10 full-size batches of Sierra Nevada Pale Ale they brewed before they decided they had one of high-enough quality to sell. It became the standard for what was long the most popular craft beer style, notable for the quantity of hops and the floral, fruity aromas and flavours they provided. Pale Ale showcases the Cascade hop, which itself became a bold signature for many craft beers.

When national sales of the India pale ale style passed those of pale ale in 2011, one of the beers at the forefront was Sierra Nevada's Torpedo Extra IPA. It acquired that name because a vessel that looks like a torpedo is used to make the beer – it is packed with hop cones and beer is circulated through it to add resiny hop oils and bright aromas. In 2010, the US Environmental Protection Agency named Sierra Nevada its Green Business of the Year. It earned praise for its zero-waste policy and its investments in renewable power, which supplies 85 per cent of its electricity needs. The brewery has one of the largest privately owned solar installations in the country. Another scheme sees beers brewed to benefit the nearby abbey of New Clairvaux, a Trappist monastery. Proceeds help the monks in Vina, just north of Chico, rebuild a chapter house that once stood in Trillo, Guadalajara, Spain.

Professor emeritus Michael Lewis, who began teaching brewing classes at the University of California, Davis, in 1962, might be able to put Sierra Nevada in better historical perspective than anybody. "Sierra Nevada Brewing Company is the most perfect brewery on the planet", he has said. "Because the people at Sierra Nevada have committed themselves to quality and integrity."

Set the bar
An early example of an "American" IPA, Celebration is considered a benchmark of the style

SIERRA NEVADA
CELEBRATION

SIERRA NEVADA
RUTHLESS RYE

TASTING NOTES

CELEBRATION INDIA PALE ALE, 6.8% ABV
A seasonal, the brewery's first IPA is deep orange and brimming with resiny citrus and pine aromas. It has a rich caramel sweetness, met by solid bitterness and more hop flavour. There is a long, dry, back-of-the-throat finish.

FOOD PAIRING: Made with the freshest kilned hops from the current harvest, and perfect at a Thanksgiving table complete with roasted turkey and dressing.

RUTHLESS RYE INDIA PALE ALE, 6.6% ABV
This IPA is a deep copper colour with an off-white head and thick lacing. Citrus and pine aromas arrive first, followed by bready and spicy notes. Light on the tongue, the flavours are complex spices and peppers with a touch of malt sweetness and herbal hops. The bitterness does not linger.

FOOD PAIRING: The malt sweetness and spicy notes in this beer bring out the different flavours in a Jamaican-style jerk chicken.

TORPEDO INDIA PALE ALE, 7.2% ABV

Pours a deep orange with a thick white head. It is quite floral, with something of a fruit salad, but not overdone. The caramel malt sweetness on the tongue is met quickly by the firm bitterness of resiny hops and fruit hop flavours. It is unapologetically bitter.

FOOD PAIRING: The citrus character and caramel malt sweetness mingle nicely with a chicken oriental salad – hop bitterness providing the same sort of balance it does in the beer.

BIGFOOT ALE BARLEYWINE STYLE ALE, 9.6% ABV

Dark amber, even a bit vinous-looking, with resinous hops, husky malts, and almost woody aromas on the nose. Rich, dark, caramel flavours are accompanied by earthy hops and a robust bitterness. A contemplative beer, this is one to let warm and spend an evening with.

FOOD PAIRING: A popular beer to store in the cellar and serve multiple vintages of at one time. A platter of pungent, flavoursome blue cheeses turns such a "vertical tasting" into an event.

PALE ALE 5.6% ABV

Bright orange in the glass and on the nose, Pale Ale is floral and fruity. Toasted bready malt flavours are well balanced by assertive hop bitterness, with memories of citrus lingering beyond a crisp, dry finish.

FOOD PAIRING: This beer shows its versatility through an entire meal, for instance starting with a salad that includes citrus, followed by a grilled steak and roasted vegetables on the side.

ESTATE INDIA PALE ALE, 6.7% ABV

Made with organic unkilned hops and malted barley grown on brewery property. It has vibrant hop aromas, both grapefruit and lemon zest, and is a bit grassy. The bready malt sweetness and grainy notes are balanced by smooth hop bitterness.

FOOD PAIRING: The fresh citrus notes in this beer and spiciness of the hops complement similar flavours in chicken tamales garnished with sweet Thai chilli sauce.

Hop-centric
Bold hop flavours are the signature of Sierra Nevada's beers

SIERRA NEVADA
TORPEDO

SIERRA NEVADA
PALE ALE

SIERRA NEVADA
BIGFOOT ALE

SIERRA NEVADA
ESTATE

STONE

The Stone brewing empire includes not only one of the fastest growing breweries in the country since 1996, but also its World Bistro and Gardens, Stone Farms, other cosmopolitan endeavours, and a rather famous Arrogant Bastard.

THE FACTS...

OWNER Stone Brewing Co
FOUNDED 1996
ADDRESS 1999 Citracado Pkwy, Escondido, California 92029
WEBSITE www.stonebrew.com
PHILOSOPHY We brew the beers we want to drink

BREWMASTER AND CO-FOUNDER of Stone Brewing, Steve Wagner, says that Arrogant Bastard Ale, perhaps as well known for the words on the bottle as what's inside, resulted from an accident. He added too many hops to a test batch when he was working on the recipe for Stone Pale Ale. "Oh, man, I screwed up", he said to co-founder Greg Koch. Koch tasted the beer, then told Wagner it was the best beer he had ever drunk. They joked it would be too good for others to appreciate and when trying to choose a name "started off with the 'You're not good enough for it' stuff", Wagner said. The rest turned out to be history. All of those original thoughts and more are on the label, including the phrase, "It is quite doubtful that you have the taste or sophistication to appreciate an ale of this quality and depth". It doesn't seem to have put off its many admirers who have made the beer famous.

Stone has expanded in multiple directions since moving from its original warehouse brewery in 2006. Its spacious Bistro and Gardens showcases Stone and other beers from around the world with an eclectic menu featuring local, organic produce. The brewery has also started Stone Farms, which grows produce for its restaurant, and has plans to build another restaurant and hotel. At the same time, Koch and Wagner continue to scout possible locations for a Stone Brewery in Europe.

The brewery produces nine regular beers: Pale Ale, Smoked Porter, IPA, Ruination IPA, Levitation Ale, Cali-Belgique IPA, Sublimely Self-Righteous Ale, Arrogant Bastard Ale, and Oaked Arrogant Bastard Ale. A similar number of limited release beers, such as Old Guardian Barley Wine Ale, Imperial Russian Stout, Ruination Tenth Anniversary IPA, Smoked Porter with Vanilla Bean, and Smoked Porter with Chipotle Peppers are also available. Despite the wide range, the hop-centric beers such as the IPA and Arrogant Bastard are its trademark. Head brewer, Mitch Steele, is the author of *IPA: Brewing Techniques, Recipes and the Evolution of India Pale Ale*. In 2012 the brewery began an "Enjoy By" series of IPAs, intended to be drunk fresh when their aroma and flavours were at a peak, putting the date they should be consumed by in large numbers on the front of the bottle.

The popular tours of the brewery see over 50,000 people annually visiting the site in Escondido to find out more about the craft beer culture.

Extreme ales
Much admired for their depth and intensity, Stone beers are not for the faint of heart

STONE
ARROGANT BASTARD ALE

STONE
RUINATION IPA

STONE
SUBLIMELY SELF-RIGHTEOUS ALE

Head start
IPA has a thick, creamy, persistent head

Master glass
Good glassware adds to the pleasure of great beer

STONE IPA

TASTING NOTES

ARROGANT BASTARD ALE STRONG ALE, 7.2% ABV
Mahogany in the glass, there are rich dark fruits in the aroma intermingling with piney hops from the outset. There is more of the same in the mouth, fruit blending with caramel sweetness, always balanced by hop bitterness and flavour.

FOOD PAIRING: The Bistro menu suggests drinking this with its pan-seared salmon risotto, with baby rocket and grape tomatoes, seasonal fruit gastrique (a sweet and sour fruit sauce), and fried shaved parsnips.

RUINATION IPA 7.7% ABV
A light shade of orange, but the bright hop aroma quickly turns up the citrus volume. Layers of fruit on the palate come from both the hops and fermentation. It is pungent, piney, and spicy, but bitterness never overwhelms the solid malt backbone.

FOOD PAIRING: An excellent match for assertive cheese, such as aged cheddar, parmesan, roquefort, or mimolette.

SUBLIMELY SELF-RIGHTEOUS ALE BLACK IPA, 8.7% ABV
Pours as black as promised, but smelling very IPA-like; it is resiny and piney with waves of citrus. Chocolate and dark caramel flavours are joined by the same hop character as on the nose. Solidly bitter, but without the acrid notes common in, say, a stout this colour.

FOOD PAIRING: Enjoy with pretzels seasoned with sea salt and served warm with cheddar cheese sauce and mustard.

IPA 6.9% ABV
Pale golden, this IPA has thick, clinging lace that leaves a ring after each sip. Bold citrus and pine aromas jump from the glass, and are balanced by a measure of sweet malt on the palate. It has a long, bitter, finally dry finish.

FOOD PAIRING: If you're lucky enough to visit the Bistro, enjoy this with the tilapia ceviche on the lunch menu. Alternatively enjoy with Mexican-style food served with chilli-lime tortilla chips.

VICTORY

The three best-selling beers from Victory Brewery – a Belgian tripel, a hop-focused US IPA, and a German pilsner – represent different brewing cultures, the respect for the tradition behind them, and a bit of independent thought.

THE FACTS...

OWNER Victory Brewing Company
FOUNDED 1996
ADDRESS 420 Acorn Lane, Downingtown, Pennsylvania 19335
WEBSITE www.victorybeer.com
PHILOSOPHY With our German training we apply our boundless American creativity to the best brewing traditions of Europe to create memorable brews

"WE WORK A LOT ON THE FRINGE of traditional beer styles – all pilsners have hops, but ours is a little hoppier than most", said Ron Barchet, who co-founded Victory with Bill Covaleski. The two were in fifth grade in 1973 when they first met on a school bus. They have remained friends ever since, and in 1985 Covaleski gave Barchet a home-brewing kit as a Christmas present. What started as a hobby turned into more. Both worked at Baltimore Brewing, which was well known for its German beers until it closed, and both attended brewing school in Germany, although not at the same time. "When we compared SAT (college admission test)

scores in high school it was apparent that we had different strengths, and so it continues. We rely on one another to handle the tasks that that person was built for", Covaleski said of the partnership that emerged. They opened Victory Brewing in a former bakery products factory in 1996, operating a restaurant and production brewery that both expanded several times, constantly earning accolades for its broad portfolio. They opened a second brewery in 2013 in nearby Parkesburg, again within an existing factory complex, saying that "environmental impact and water quality were major considerations. Nearly eight months of water-quality research found that the mineral composition of the water is nearly identical".

On the brewery's 16th anniversary, Covaleski wrote about the business plan the two assembled in 1994. "Even back then we noted that our competitive advantages would come from the ingredients we use and the techniques we employ. That remains true today. The imported malt and whole-flower hops we use today are the same stellar ingredients we proposed as we were getting started", he wrote.

TASTING NOTES

HOPDEVIL INDIA PALE ALE, 6.7% ABV
It pours a rich copper colour, so it's no surprise there's a touch of Munich malt sweetness on the nose and in the flavour. But this is a hop-first beer, brimming with aromas of pine and citrus, tasting of citrus and providing bracing bitterness.
FOOD PAIRING: The extra bit of body in this IPA matches quite nicely with Thai food, as do the citrus notes, bringing out more citrus in the dish.

PRIMA PILS, 5.3% ABV
Straw-coloured with a bit of gold in the light, Prima Pils is boldly floral at the outset, with fresh pilsner malt up front. The cracker-crisp palate, spicy hop flavours, and bitterness balance any malt sweetness. It finishes dry.
FOOD PAIRING: This beer is seafood- and fish-friendly. Try it with baked or grilled salmon; the texture of the fish will match the beer, and the hops will cut through the flavour.

GOLDEN MONKEY TRIPEL, 9.5% ABV
Pale with orange highlights and topped with clinging white foam, this beer has a spicy nose, with aromas of banana and stone fruits underneath. There is a hint of candy floss on the palate, more fruit flavours, and some cloves, balanced by a hop bitterness that leads to a dry finish.
FOOD PAIRING: There is plenty of punch here to enjoy with  flavourful cheese and ham, such as prosciutto or serrano.

VICTORY
HOPDEVIL

VICTORY
PRIMA

VICTORY
GOLDEN MONKEY

WIDMER BROTHERS

Like many other fledgling brewers in the 1980s, Kurt and Rob Widmer used their father's truck to make their first deliveries. What resulted was unique: a new US beer style and the largest brewery in the most beer-centric city.

THE FACTS...

OWNER Widmer Brothers Brewing

FOUNDED 1984

ADDRESS 929 North Russell Street, Portland, Oregon 97227

WEBSITE www.widmerbrothers.com

PHILOSOPHY Fostering the brotherhood of craft beer since 1984

THE WIDMER BROTHERS OF PORTLAND created a new beer style in their Hefeweizen, served cloudy like a Bavarian weissbeer but made with an altbier yeast that does not create the banana and clove flavours typical in a weiss. The Widmers also include a solid dose of Cascade hops, adding citrus character and much more bitterness than would be typical. "In 1986 we weren't thinking style. We were just brewing beer", Rob has said. The beer proved widely popular and by the mid-1990s Widmer was the largest draught-only brewery in the western hemisphere, before it began bottling beer.

Widmer and the Redhook Ale Brewery merged in 2008 to form the Craft Brew Alliance, later acquiring Kona Brewing (see p.193). However, the brands continue to operate independently, and there's certainly more to Widmer than hefeweizen. A Rotator IPA series showcases new hop varieties and a Collaborator Series features winning recipes produced by local home-brewers. The Brothers' Reserve Series includes beers they never envisaged when they first opened. "I'm not sure this could have happened anywhere else in 1985. The people

in the North-west are the grandsons and granddaughters of pioneers. They are willing to try anything", Kurt stated.

In 2012, Widmer introduced a new brand, Omission, under the Craft Brew Alliance label. What is omitted is the gluten compounds found in barley and wheat, to which a portion of the population is allergic. Some brewers use alternative grains, such as sorghum, to make gluten-free beers, but have struggled to make them taste beer-like. By instead using barley, removing the gluten during the brewing process, Craft Brew Alliance creates gluten-free beer that tastes more like beer.

TASTING NOTES

OMISSION PALE LAGER, 4.6% ABV
Sunny yellow in the glass with refreshing lemony notes on the nose and a touch of malt sweetness. The flavours are clean, but muted, almost white bread-like. The hops provide more citrus notes that are slightly harsh. Otherwise, it is nicely balanced.
FOOD PAIRING: Widmer's Gasthaus Pub offers this beer with a gluten-free menu and recommends dishes such as salad with diced chicken breast and bacon.

HEFEWEIZEN WHEAT ALE, 4.9% ABV
Pours a hazy yellow with an abundant white head. Citrus, particularly lemon zest, aromas, and flavours, matched against clean bready-yet-tart wheat. Crisp, smooth bitterness at the end, leaving a final impression of grapefruit.
FOOD PAIRING: An excellent match for fresh North-west seafood, which could be anything from salmon to crab, including well spiced dishes.

DROP TOP AMBER ALE 5.3% ABV
Bright amber, this beer is topped with a thick white head, and is balanced from the start with gentle floral hops and caramel sweet notes. It has a creamy texture, with toasty caramel, malt, and honey flavours that blend with spicy hops on the palate.
FOOD PAIRING: Drop Top is a less filling choice than a "bigger" beer at the end of a meal. Its caramel malt blends nicely with a caramel cheesecake; its spicy hops cut through the sweetness.

WIDMER BROTHERS
OMISSION

WIDMER BROTHERS
HEFEWEIZEN

WIDMER BROTHERS
DROP TOP AMBER ALE

4 HANDS

www.4handsbrewery.com

TRULY A DOWNTOWN BREWERY, operating a short walk from Busch Stadium in St Louis, 4 Hands' tasting room is always open on baseball game days – its Prussia Berliner Weiss is a quenching antidote for Missouri's summer humidity. They sell a typically wide range for a newish brewery, with hop-forward beers and food-friendly choices. One example is Smoked Pigasus, a porter made with rye, maple syrup, and grain smoked at a local barbecue restaurant. Others are aged in barrels that held wine or spirits.

5 RABBIT

www.5rabbitbrewery.com

PARTNERS FROM MEXICO and Costa Rica started 5 Rabbit in 2011, the country's first Latin American-inspired brewery, based in Chicago. Their beers, designed by well-known beer author Randy Mosher, take inspiration from the flavours, textures, and aromas of Latin cuisine, rather than attempting to replicate modern Mexican beers or ancient Mayan ones. For instance, 5 Lizard Latin-Style Witbier is made with lime peel, passionfruit, and spices. Motueka hops from New Zealand further enhance the passionfruit-tropical character.

(512) BREWING

www.512brewing.com

KEVIN BRAND, founder of (512) Brewing, was a college student at the University of Texas in Austin when he visited the local Celis Brewery (now closed) and learned that beer "could be brewed here, not just in St Louis". Some years later, he returned to start his own locally focused brewery selling only draught beer, using both organic and local ingredients. Pecan Porter is made with roasted pecans, a staple in the Texas Hill Country.

10-BARREL

www.10barrel.com

PERHAPS ITS FOUNDERS should have stuck with the first name they gave the brewery, Wildfire, because 10-Barrel is one of the fastest-growing in Bend, the Oregon town full of breweries and the Bend Beer Trail. Brewers Jimmy Seifrit, Tonya Cornett (2008 World Beer Cup Small Brewmaster of the Year), and Shawn Kelso are the faces of the organization.

ABITA

www.abita.com

ABITA IS BREWED IN ABITA SPRINGS, which is across Lake Pontchartrain from New Orleans, and had been famous for its spring water for more than 100 years. Abita's beers are the ones drinkers across the country associate with "*Laissez les bons temps rouler*" ("let the good times roll"), stocking up on beers like Amber and the raspberry-infused Purple Haze during Mardi Gras season and for crawfish boils. Established in 1986, it was the first craft brewery in the South and remains the largest.

AC GOLDEN

www.acgolden.com

AC GOLDEN IS TUCKED INSIDE THE MillerCoors brewery in Golden, Colorado, which until recently was the largest single site brewery in the world. It is responsible for Colorado Native, which is brewed with all-Colorado ingredients, and also both classic continental lagers and beers from what is called the "Hidden Barrel Project". These include strong beers aged in barrels that held spirits, as well as decidedly sour, and delightfully complex, beers that take their inspiration from Belgium.

ALCHEMIST

www.alchemistbeer.com

TWO DAYS AFTER tropical storm Irene created a flood in 2011 that destroyed The Alchemist – a Vermont brewery's downtown Waterbury pub – the first cans of Heady Topper rolled off the line at its nearby production brewery. The immensely popular Double IPA, appropriately rich in tropical fruit and other bold flavours, funded growth that has since allowed Alchemist to resume brewing other beers. These are sold at the brewery door.

ALE ASYLUM

www.aleasylum.com

THE ALE ASYLUM BREWERY IS POISED TO become one of Wisconsin's three largest craft operations. It moved into a new Madison facility in 2012 due to demand for its hop-forward beers and Belgian-inspired ales. Brewmaster Dean Coffey adds Cascade hops at 11 different stages to brew Hopalicious, a pale ale. Not surprisingly, Ballistic IPA is even more forceful, and a beer called Bedlam! balances assertive American Citra hops and a Trappist monastery yeast.

5 RABBIT 5 LIZARD

ALESMITH

www.alesmith.com

THE CAPACITY OF ALESMITH has grown from its modest roots and has reached that of a regional brewery. However, this San Diego brewery's reputation remains much bigger than its physical size and output. Internet rating sites have, at times, ranked it the No 1 brewery in the world. Founded in 1995 by one home-brewer and sold in 2002 to another, Peter Zien, it is proud of its home-brewing credentials. AleSmith sells a dizzying array of big, bold beers, such as its popular IPA and the coffee-infused Speedway Stout.

ALPINE

www.alpinebeerco.com

EX-FIREMAN PATRICK MCILHENNEY founded Alpine in 1999. The beers were originally brewed under contract at AleSmith but are now brewed in the small town of Alpine, west of San Diego. McIlhenney makes his intentions clear by giving his beers names such as Pure Hoppiness and Exponential Hoppiness – exponential because the amount of hops doubles with each addition – both considered Double IPAs. Although they may sound innocent, the likes of Nelson and Duet are also aggressively hoppy.

ANDERSON VALLEY

www.avbc.com

SINCE OPENING IN 1987, Anderson Valley has emphasized its ties to the Mendocino County valley it was named after. That includes using Boontling, the local language spoken only in Boonville, to name beers such as Hop Ottin' IPA or its Bahl Hornin' ("good drinking") Series of innovative beers. The brewery has won awards for its environmental initiatives.

ANHEUSER-BUSCH

www.anheuser-busch.com

MUCH HAS CHANGED HERE, but the Budweiser brand and Anheuser Busch's Clydesdale horses remain international icons. The brewery's roots in its hometown of St Louis go back to 1852, although the mother company – Anheuser-Busch InBev – is headquartered in Belgium. A wholly owned subsidiary, A-B operates 12 breweries across the country that produce nearly half the beer sold in the US, including the world's second best-selling brand, Bud Light, and Shock Top beers.

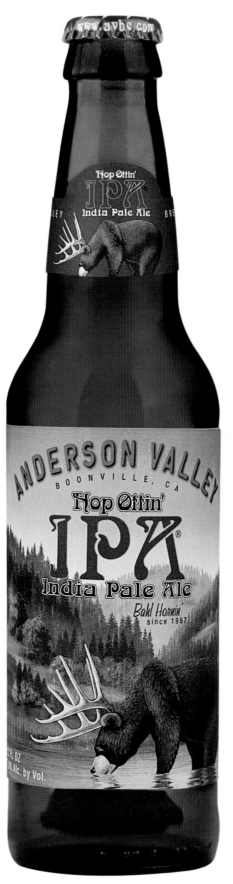

ANDERSON VALLEY HOP OTTIN' IPA

ARCADIA

www.arcadiaales.com

THE BATTLE CREEK BREWERY has drawn on English tradition since it opened in 1996, using one of the many Peter Austin brewing systems Alan Pugsley installed around the world. Arcadia still imports English malts, and uses the classic Ringwood yeast strain in open fermentation tanks. Beers such as London Porter and Scottish Ale reflect that tradition, but the brewery also offers American hop-centric and barrel-aged ales.

ATWATER

www.atwaterbeer.com

ATWATER BLOCK BREWERY opened with a flourish in 1997. Its lagers, which were made in a brewhouse imported from Germany, quickly began to win awards. However, it closed, resumed operations, then closed again before reopening in 2005. Now simply called Atwater Brewery and housed in a 1919 factory warehouse in Detroit's historic Rivertown district, traditional German lagers remain at the core of its business, but they are packaged in cans, and joined by popular ale styles.

AUGUST SCHELL

www.schellsbrewery.com

GERMAN-BORN AUGUST SCHELL established the country's second-oldest, surviving, family-run brewery in 1860, in New Ulm. Appropriately, given the popularity of the brewery's traditional German beers, it hosts Bock Fest each February, attracting thousands despite the freezing Minnesota weather. It produces a strong range of year-round beers as well as a good choice of seasonal specials.

AUSTIN BEERWORKS

www.austinbeerworks.com

IT SEEMED A DOZEN BREWERIES, including Austin Beerworks, opened in Austin in 2010, each with a different approach. "Hell-bent on excellence", a foursome of friends gambled on producing hop-forward beers packaged in cans – they quickly won design awards and sold almost 4770 hl (2900 barrels) in their first full calendar year. Fire Eagle American IPA packs the citrus, fruity punch of American hops, while Pearl Snap Pils is a Texas heat-quencher featuring continental hops.

BALLAST POINT

www.ballastpoint.com

HOME-BREWERS GET MUCH of the credit for turning San Diego from a beer wasteland into a mecca. Jack White and Yuseff Cherney started their brewery, Ballast Point, in 1996 in the back of a home-brew store that White had opened in 1992. By 2010, they had won three gold medals at the prestigious World Beer Cup and Small Brewery of the Year. Not surprisingly, the recipe for one of their most heralded beers, Sculpin IPA, was written in collaboration with local home-brewers.

BAXTER

www.baxterbrewing.com

LUKE LIVINGSTON BEGAN home-brewing in college, until his dormitory supervisor took his kit away. He wrote the business plan for this Maine brewery when he was 24, and by the time he was 27 years old in 2011, he was on *Forbes* magazine's "30 under 30 list" in the food and wine category. Baxter is yet another brewery that successfully parlayed hop-forward ales, such as its Stowaway IPA, and packaging in cans into double-digit growth.

BAYERN

www.bayernbrewery.com

OWNER AND BREWMASTER of Bayern Brewery, Jürgen Knöller, is a German diploma master brewer who began brewing in 1978 at the age of 16. He spent many years in Germany moving up from apprentice to journeyman to master brewer. Local legend is that when Knöller moved from his Bavarian home to Missoula, Montana, in 1987 to help start this brewery, he brought two suitcases, one with his clothes and the other with brewing books. He bought Bayern Brewing outright four years later, and it remains the only German brewery in the Rocky Mountains. The brewery focuses solely on German styles, although some beers have more whimsical names, like Face Plant (a weizen bock) and Dump Truck (a helles bock).

BEAR REPUBLIC

www.bearrepublic.com

ALTHOUGH FIREMAN-RACE CAR DRIVER-brewmaster at Bear Republic, Richard Norgrove, makes many sought-after beers, including Hop Rod Rye, this California brewery can barely keep up with the demand for Racer 5, a particularly fruity, resinous IPA. Norgrove invented his own unique way to "dry hop" this beer, circulating it through separate small vessels he calls "hop babies" to extract hop oils and create more aroma. The family-run operation also has a brewpub in Healdsburg, in Sonoma County wine country.

BERKSHIRE

www.berkshirebrewingcompany.com

FOUNDERS OF THE BERKSHIRE Brewing Company, Gary Bogoff and Chris Lalli, built much of this brewery themselves, in a former cigar factory in western Massachusetts. They sold mostly draught beer, but continued to bottle by hand until sales passed 12,000 hl (7300 barrels). "We're living our own destiny", Bogoff said after the brewery, founded in 1994, grew to regional status. They brew a wide range, but Drayman's Porter represents the brewery well.

BIG BOSS

www.bigbossbrewing.com

STARTING WITH TOMCAT BREWING in 1996, breweries with five different names operated in the same space in Raleigh, North Carolina. Then Geoff Lamb bought the brewery and along with brewmaster Brad Wynn renamed it Big Boss after one of its top-selling beers. The swagger in the name suits the beers well, whether they are traditional, like the brown ale Bad Penny, or more exotic like Big Operator, a Belgian chocolate raspberry stout.

BIG SKY

www.bigskybrew.com

BIG SKY BREWERY IN Missoula, Montana, makes a wide range of bold, interesting beers, but it is best known for its Moose Drool – a brown ale. The story behind the name is that the mother of one of the founders painted a picture for possible use on the new brewery's labels. On seeing the image, which showed a moose lifting its head from a pond, one of the brewers said, "Let's call it Moose Drool".

BISON

www.bisonbrew.com

CO-OWNER OF BISON BREWING, Daniel Del Grande, is particularly adamant about green practices. The brewery was founded in Berkeley, California, in 1989, but production has now moved to Mendocino Brewing. After production moved, Del Grande hired a firm to benchmark the brewery's carbon footprint. The online green consumer directory Greenopia now gives the brewery a three (out of four) green leaf rating. The company has sold certified organic beers since 2002. These include their top-selling Chocolate Stout and the intriguing Honey Basil Ale.

BJ'S CHICAGO PIZZA AND BREWERY

www.bjsbrewhouse.com

BJ'S OPERATES MORE THAN 130 restaurants in 15 states, a few of them brewery-restaurants, others serving beer made at BJ's own microbreweries or under contract elsewhere. Each location offers eight regular beers and several seasonals, and generally promotes small-batch beers at other brewpubs. For example, one of their beers, Camaraderie, was made in collaboration with the Bavik Brewery in Belgium, then served in dozens of its restaurants.

BLACK RAVEN

www.blackravenbrewing.com

A VINTAGE PHOTO OF A MAN surrounded by wood barrels and titled "brewer with tame raven" on the home page of the Black Raven Brewing website explains a mystical brewery-raven connection behind its name. Since the brewery opened in 2009, Robert "Beaux" Bowman has proven adept at hop-forward beers, such as Trickster IPA, and hefty beers, like Old Birdbrain, which won medals three years in a row at the prestigious Great Alaska Beer and Barley wine Festival.

BLUE MOON

www.bluemoonbrewingcompany.com

THE MIGHTY MILLERCOORS OWNS the Blue Moon brand and brews its beers at several of its breweries. However, when Coors first assigned a single brewer and one marketeer to start a brand on a shoestring in 1994, they had to find a small brewery to make Blue Moon Belgian White under contract. Today the brand outsells the most popular craft brands in the US including Sierra Nevada Pale Ale and Samuel Adams Boston Lager. The brewmaster Keith Villa, who was responsible for its success, continues to write recipes for other new Blue Moon beers.

BLUE POINT

www.bluepointbrewing.com

STARTING WITH EQUIPMENT acquired in auction from failed microbrewery start-ups, partners Pete Cotter and Mark Burford built Blue Point Brewing in a former Long Island ice factory and took their name from the local "Blue Point Oysters". Toasted Lager, a Vienna-style lager that gets some of its colour from direct-fire boiling, was the flagship from the beginning. It has been joined by more fashionable beers, such as RastafeRye Ale and Hoptical Illusion.

BOSCOS

www.boscosbeer.com

THE REGIONAL CHAIN OF Boscos Brewery restaurants opened in suburban Memphis in 1992. It appears briefly in the Tom Cruise movie *The Firm*, and broke new ground in the mid-South with, eventually, a choice of 50 or so different brands a year. The most famous, appropriately, is Famous Flaming Stone Beer – a traditional German stein beer. As well as running four brewpubs in Tennessee and Arkansas, the company operates a separate brewery, Ghost River, which distributes beer in the Memphis area.

BOULDER

www.boulderbeer.com

BOULDER BEER COMPANY MADE three beers in a goat shed outside the town of Boulder in Colorado when it began selling beer in 1980. These were Boulder Porter, Stout, and Extra Special Bitter. The brewers used American Cascade and German Hallertau hops because of the largesse of brewing giant Coors, which also sold the start-up brewery malt. The range is much broader today, including beers such at the heavily dry-hopped pale ale Hazed & Infused and Flashback India Brown Ale.

BOUNDARY BAY

www.bbaybrewery.com

ONE OF THE LARGEST BREWPUBS in the country, Boundary Bay distributes much of what it brews beyond its gate. However, the pub remains the hub. "If you take a snapshot of who's here, it's a good slice of the people in Bellingham", general manager Janet Lightner said when the brewery celebrated its 10th anniversary in 2005. A wide range is on offer, from the hop-centric Inside Passage Ale (IPA) to the consistently outstanding Dunkles Bock.

BRECKENRIDGE

www.breckbrew.com

BRECKENRIDGE OPENED IN 1990 as a brewpub in the town of the same name and expanded into Denver in 1992, later trying unsuccessfully to operate pubs beyond Colorado's borders. By focusing on five brewpubs and alehouses within the county of Denver, and its production brewery, the company grew to the point that in 2013 it announced plans to build a new brewery on farmland south of Denver.

BREWERY VIVANT

www.breweryvivant.com

BREWERY VIVANT IS LOCATED in a Historic Grand Rapids neighbourhood and occupies a 100-year-old environmentally reclaimed building that was once the livery for a funeral home. The brewery's pub is housed in the former chapel. The beers, on the other hand, taste of a Franco-Belgian farmhouse brewery, albeit one that packages in cans. They range from the traditional, like the saison Farmhand or the abbey-style Solitude, to the bold, such as Zaison at 9% ABV.

BRIDGEPORT

www.bridgeportbrew.com

FIRST CALLED THE Columbia River Brewery when it opened in 1984, BridgePort is the oldest surviving craft brewery in Oregon, which has since become known as Beervana. The brewpub and brewery fill a 100-year-old Portland rope factory, expanding more than once since San Antonio-based Gambrinus bought the brewery in 1995. BridgePort IPA, which many considered stunningly bitter when it was introduced in 1995, remains its flagship beer.

BRISTOL

www.bristolbrewing.com

BRISTOL BREWING has been a fixture in Colorado Springs since 1994, when Mike and Amanda Bristol settled in the area. They expanded in 2013, installing a German-designed brewhouse in a century-old elementary school, almost across the street from the previous brewery. Although it more than doubled its capacity, the brewery only sells its beer in Colorado. Its Laughing Lab Scottish Ale has won more medals at the Great American Beer Festival than any other Colorado beer.

BOULDER HAZED & INFUSED

THE BRUERY

www.thebruery.com

WHEN FOUNDER Patrick Rue wrote his business plan, he boldly envisaged barrel-aged beers would account for 20 per cent of sales. By 2013, five years after the brewery opened, it was at capacity – he owned 3,000 barrels, and 40 per cent of production went into barrels. It took time to assemble the "parts" – for instance, Oude Tart is a blend of Flemish-style red ales aged in wine barrels for up to 16 to 20 months. The brewery proudly states that all its bottled beers are 100 per cent bottle-conditioned, such as the award-winning Saison Rue.

CALDERA

www.calderabrewing.com

FOR THE FIRST eight years after it opened in 1997, Caldera sold only draught beer and remained rather small. However, business boomed when it became the first microbrewery in Oregon to install a small-run canning line in 2005, funding a major expansion completed in 2012, and allowing the company to also begin distilling. Its beers – notably its IPA and Pale Ale – have won medals in competitions all over the world.

CAMBRIDGE

www.cambrew.com

ONE OF THE FIRST BREWPUBS in New England, Cambridge Brewing still has the same comfortable refurbished factory feel, with exposed brick and high ceilings. Likewise, the core of traditional beers is as carefully cared for, without being stuck in 1989. Brewmaster Will Meyers offers a constantly changing line-up of innovative beers – be it a strong Belgian-inspired beer like Benevolence, or one called The Wind Cried Mari made with heather flowers, jasmine, and lavender.

CAPITAL

www.capital-brewery.com

USING A BREWHOUSE acquired from a failed German brewery, Capital has made beer true to German tradition – most of the time – since 1986. Autumnal Fire could best be described as a cross between an Oktoberfest – it is made for the same season – and a pale doppelbock – it is brewed to the same strength. Although the portfolio includes a few US-centric beers, the true German-style brews, such as Capital Pilsner and Capital Dark, represent its true soul.

THE BRUERY SAISON RUE

CAPTAIN LAWRENCE

www.captainlawrencebrewing.com

WHEN SCOTT VACCARO was 17 years old he decided he wanted to be a brewer. So he travelled across the country to study brewing science in California, interned at several breweries, then got on-the-job training at Sierra Nevada Brewing (see pp.176–177). He returned to his New York home to start Captain Lawrence in 2006 with the help of his family. The brewery is best known for its Belgian-influenced and barrel-aged beers, some of them sour, all of them complex.

CASCADE

www.cascadebrewingbarrelhouse.com

CASCADE OPERATES a brewpub in Raleigh Hills and its Barrel House in Portland. It is the latter, specializing in sour beers, that aficionados flock to. In 2005, owner Art Larrance and brewmaster Ron Gansberg decided to explore sour beers aged in barrels, seeking to offer an intense sensory experience beyond that found with hops. Gansberg's experiments have been endless, including beers made with all manner of fruit. The Barrel House regularly serves live beer – in which the yeast or bacteria are still active – from a barrel.

CENTRAL WATERS

www.centralwaters.com

THIS BREWERY TAKES some issues more seriously than others. It was the first to be invited into the state of Wisconsin's Green Tier programme for its environmental practices. Yet its brewhouse vessels have names like The Dude, Donnie, Walter, and The Big Lebowski – referring to the movie of the same name. Beers in Central Waters' reserve series include many aged in barrels and none more cleverly named than Kosmyk Charlie's Y2K Catastrophe Ale, a barley wine.

CHUCKANUT BREWERY

www.chuckanutbreweryandkitchen.com

THE CHUCKANUT BREWERY IS, among other things, a triumphant return to brewing for one of America's first craft brewers. Will Kemper and Andy Thomas founded a brewery, Thomas Kemper, in 1985, but it was soon swallowed up after a merger with a company that would become Pyramid Ales. Kemper travelled the world, helping other breweries start up, before setting up Chuckanut in 2008. The smallish Washington brewery simply makes some of the best German-inspired beers in the US. Kemper is particularly fond of the Chuckanut Pilsner.

CHURCH BREW WORKS

www.churchbrew.com

THE BREWHOUSE of the Church Brew Works sits on the altar of what was St John the Baptist Roman Catholic church in Pittsburgh's Lawrenceville neighbourhood, but it's not just an ornament in a beautiful setting. The brewery, which opened in 1996, won four medals at the 2012 Great American Beer Festival and Large Brewpub of the Year. It is best known for the quality of its German-inspired beers, including the always dependable Pious Monk Dunkel.

CIGAR CITY

www.cigarcitybrewing.com

AFTER OPENING IN 2009, Cigar City Brewing in Tampa quickly lifted the image of Florida brewing, with brewmaster Wayne Wambles' beers winning medals in each of its first four years at the Great American Beer Festival. The brewery leans heavily on Tampa's culture – its name a nod to a time when the city was America's "cigar capital". Jai Alai IPA points to the popular sport of the same name that used to be played in Tampa, and its Humidor Series beers are aged in Spanish cedar, the wood used in cigar boxes.

COLUMBUS

www.columbusbrewing.com

COLUMBUS BREWING is nestled in what is known as the Brewery District – an area of Columbus, Ohio, that was home to five breweries in the 19th century. The neighbourhood has undergone the same sort of revival as brewing in this city, and Columbus Brewing is the biggest of the newcomers. Although brewmaster and owner Eric Bean has an affection for lagers, and his unfiltered seasonal offering Summer Teeth is popular, the brewery's pale orange IPA with a hoppy edge has driven double-digit growth. The Pale Ale is another popular year-round offering.

CRAFTSMAN

www.craftsmanbrewing.com

MARK JILG BEGAN MAKING idiosyncratic beers in 1995, long before small-batch beer was hip in Los Angeles. "I like to do the things other people aren't doing", he said. That includes mainstay beers, like Craftsman 1903, a pre-Prohibition lager made with a generous dose of flavour. Cabernale is made with Cabernet Sauvignon grapes, leaving an impression between beer and wine, and Acorn Saison is just what the name implies.

CROOKED STAVE

www.crookedstave.com

FOUNDER OF CROOKED STAVE, Chad Yakobson, explains that the crooked stave is the one stave in the barrel that is different. "In the industry, we are the crooked stave", he said. He creates his beers in Denver using proprietary yeast strains cultured while he was working on his master's dissertation on Brettanomyces; most of the beers are blended after ageing in barrels. These include the saison Surette, a golden L'Brett d'Or, and HopSavant, a tropical, noticeably wild IPA.

DARK HORSE

www.darkhorsebrewery.com

EACH DECEMBER Dark Horse Brewery in central Michigan hosts its 4 Elf Winter Ale party, releasing a beer by that name, putting nearly 50 others on tap, and inviting customers to dress as elves. The brewery has retained its personality despite booming sales, largely driven by Crooked Tree IPA and an assortment of other generally bold beers. The taproom is jammed with mugs of club members, and space at the hand-made stone-top bar is precious.

DC BRAU

www.dcbrau.com

NO PRODUCTION BREWERY had operated in Washington, DC since 1955 until DC Brau opened in 2011. Founders Brandon Skall and Jeff Hancock are closely connected to the city's club scene, often spinning records themselves, and sometimes working music into the names of their beers, such as Your Favorite Foreign Movie (a Steely Dan lyric), and Ghoul's Night Out (a song by the Misfits). However, their best-selling beer, a pale ale, is simply called The Public and is packaged in cans.

DESTIHL

www.destihlbrewery.com

MICROBES FLOATING in central Illinois farm air provide the wild component for this brewery's popular sour beers. DESTIHL discovered this at its Normal brewery-restaurant (it also has one in Champaign), employing used barrels as "koelschips" during what brewmaster Matt Potts describes as a "spontaneous secondary/wild fermentation". He continued the practice after opening a production brewery, and also added fouders, large oak vessels imported from France, to keep up with demand.

DEVILS BACKBONE

www.dbbrewingcompany.com

THIS BREWPUB AND separate brewery in central Virginia quickly earned accolades for their beers, but particularly for those of German origin. Brewmaster Jason Oliver, who oversees production at both locations, was drawn to the styles in brewing school. "I like the precision of the process", he said. "I wanted to learn those old techniques." The four mostly widely available beers – Vienna Lager, Eight Point IPA, Dark Abby (a Belgian-inspired dubbel), and Danzig (a Baltic porter) – illustrate the breadth of his portfolio.

DIAMOND KNOT

www.diamondknot.com

TWO WORKERS AT BOEING, outside Seattle, started Diamond Knot Brewing in 1994, keeping their day jobs, milling grain at home and hauling it to their tiny brewery in the back of a bar in Mukilteo. Their IPA, dry-hopped in the keg with the then-newish Columbus hops, quickly became a cult beer in Seattle. They eventually bought the bar, and now own and operate three restaurants and two breweries.

DIXIE

www.paulanerhpusa.com/dixie

HURRICANE KATRINA, and the looters who followed, destroyed Dixie, a throwback New Orleans brewery in 2005. Its beers, including Dixie Lager and Blackened Voodoo (a schwarzbier), are now brewed under contract in Wisconsin, although there are those who hope a new brewery will be built in Louisiana. The original Dixie Brewing opened in 1907 and before the storm, still aged some of its beer in 1912-vintage cypress wood tanks.

DOUBLE MOUNTAIN

www.doublemountainbrewery.com

PARTNERS MATT SWIHART AND Charlie Devereux founded their Double Mountain brewery in Hood River, Oregon, in 2007. Its name is taken from the view to the north of Mount Adams and the one to the south – Mount Hood. Much they do is just a little different, such as using a yeast strain from Belgium to ferment most of their ales. They feel that using hop cones, rather than pellets, and a hopback adds to the undeniable hop character in their beers, which are packaged in 500ml (16 fl oz) returnable bottles.

DRAKE'S

www.drinkdrakes.com

WHEN ROGER LIND FOUNDED Lind Brewing in 1989 in San Leandro, he brewed, kegged, and delivered all the beer himself. Twice sold since and renamed Drake's, it remains a "hands on" brewery. But it is one that produces much more beer and has a taproom, the Barrel House, with two dozen of its beers on draught. Not surprisingly, most of the beers these days are made with larger doses of hops, starting with Drake's India Pale Ale.

DRY DOCK

www.drydockbrewing.com

THREE YEARS AFTER he bought the Brew Hut homebrew shop in 2002 in Aurora, Colorado, Kevin DeLange opened Dry Dock Brewing next door. Eight years later, the brewery moved into a six-acre complex large enough to accommodate further growth. His choice for the first four beers off a new canning line – Apricot Blonde, Hefeweizen, Amber, and the IPA Hop Abomination – illustrate a mission to brew "traditional styles really well".

DUCK-RABBIT

www.duckrabbitbrewery.com

FOUNDER OF DUCK-RABBIT, Paul Philippon, was a philosophy teacher. He knew that if he started a brewery he would use the distinctive Duck-Rabbit Brewing logo – a duck facing right, a rabbit left – based on the illustration made famous by Austrian philosopher Ludwig Wittgenstein that illustrates something can be seen in two ways. Philippon saw, unlike others, that he could specialize in selling dark beer in North Carolina. He was proven right after his beers – like Baltic Porter – earned a national following.

EEL RIVER

www.eelriverbrewing.com

EEL RIVER BREWING BECAME the first certified organic brewery in the country in 1999, and later came to be powered by biomass – leftovers from a saw mill. Its beers illustrate that organic beers, like its Porter, needn't forego flavour. The northern California brewpub occupies a former redwood mill in Fortuna; a separate production brewery was built in nearby Scotia in 2007.

ELYSIAN

www.elysianbrewing.com

LIKE MOST LARGER CITIES, Seattle is a collection of neighbourhoods, and Elysian Brewing serves many of them individually, with three brewpubs as well as its production brewery. Beers such as Dragonstooth Stout and Avatar Jasmine IPA have a national reputation, as does brewmaster Dick Cantwell's interest in beers made with various botanicals. Other regulars include Immortal IPA, Zephyrus Pilsner, and Perseus Porter. The brewery's annual Great Pumpkin Festival features more than 60 pumpkin beers from around the world, including its own Night Owl Pumpkin Ale.

EPIC

www.epicbrewing.com

UNLIKE OTHER UTAH BREWERIES, Epic Brewing chose from the outset not to make beers under 4% ABV to accommodate the state's curious laws related to beer, quickly earned a national reputation, and built a second brewery in Denver. Although "epic" refers to a perfect powder day in Utah or Colorado ski country, it aptly describes head brewer Kevin Crompton's bold approach, reflected in beers like Big Bad Baptist Imperial Stout, infused with coffee and aged in bourbon barrels.

FAT HEAD'S

www.fatheadsbeer.com

FAT HEAD'S SALOON was an early outpost for craft beer on Pittsburgh's South Side. Matt Cole was a well-travelled brewer who had established his reputation separately. They merged to become Fat Head's Saloon and Brewery, with both a brewpub in Middleburg Heights, Ohio, and a production brewery. It is best known for its Head Hunter IPA, but other beers, such as Battle Axe Baltic Porter and Güdenhoppy Pils, are equally interesting.

ELYSIAN NIGHT OWL

FIFTY FIFTY

www.fiftyfiftybrewing.com

BREWMASTER AT FIFTY FIFTY, Todd Ashman, was instrumental in the 1990s in establishing barrel-aged beers as a separate category when talking about American beer. Deemed "experimental" at the time, beers he made at an Illinois brewery won medals in back-to-back years at the Great American Beer Festival, which later gave barrel-aged beers their own category. He brews a wide range of beers in the tiny brewhouse in Truckee, California, but his barrel-aged beers are most in demand.

FISH

www.fishbrewing.com

LOCATED IN OLYMPIA, Washington, where former brewing giant Olympia made the slogan "It's the water" famous, Fish Brewing produces both organic ales under the Fish Tale brand name and German-inspired beers under the Leavenworth name. It acquired Leavenworth Biers in 2001. These had previously been brewed in a dying logging town that reinvented itself as a Bavarian village. The company operates Fish Tale Brew Pubs in both Olympia and Everett.

FLYING FISH

www.flyingfish.com

A SERIES OF BEERS named after the New Jersey Turnpike exits celebrates the relationship this suburban Philadelphia brewery has with its home state, New Jersey. It is also known as the brewery launched on the Internet, or as founder Gene Muller put it in 1995, "This Old House meets the World Wide Web". The range of Flying Fish's regular offerings, such as the Belgian-influenced Abbey Dubbel or the very American Hopfish, is as diverse as their Exit Series.

FOOTHILLS BREWING

www.foothillsbrewing.com

THE ANNUAL RELEASE OF Sexual Chocolate Stout at Foothills Brewing's Winston-Salem brewpub has turned into something of a festival, attracting fans across the south-east. First made as a homebrew for Valentine's Day, the beer – harder to find when aged in bourbon barrels – takes its name from a fictional band in the movie *Coming to America*. Foothills added a production brewery in 2011 to meet demand for beers such as Hoppyum IPA and People's Porter.

FORT COLLINS

www.fortcollinsbrewery.com

FORT COLLINS BREWERY is known both for its own brands and for producing gluten-free beers for New Planet Beer Company, based nearby in Boulder. Fort Collins built a new brewery complex in 2010 that also houses Gravity 1020, "a modern tavern", and installed a larger brewhouse in 2013, in part to meet growing demand for the New Planet beers sold nationally. Fort Collins' most popular brands include Kidd Black Lager and Chocolate Stout.

FOUR PEAKS

www.fourpeaks.com

PROBABLY MOST FAMOUS for its Kilt Lifter Scottish-Style Ale, Four Peaks Brewing added a second brewing facility in 2012 to keep up with soaring demand. The original brewery and restaurant in Tempe, Arizona, opened in 1997 in an inviting building that dates to 1892 and housed a creamery until 1965. Although well-balanced ales such as Kilt Lifter and 8th Street show brewer Andy Ingram's respect for balance, Hop Knot IPA played an equal role in driving ongoing growth.

FREE STATE

www.freestatebrewing.com

WHEN FREE STATE BREWING opened as a brewery restaurant in Lawrence in 1989, it was the first licensed brewery in Kansas to operate in more than 100 years. The state embraced Prohibition in 1881, long before the rest of the US, and did not legalize the sale of beer again until 1948. Free State built a production facility in 1989 and packages beers primarily for sale in Kansas, but also in neighbouring Missouri. These include both its flagship beers, like Ad Astra Ale, and specialities.

FULL SAIL

www.fullsailbrewing.com

BEER FANS OUTSIDE Oregon know Full Sail Brewing for a wide range of beers, from its throwback Session Lager to robust hop-forward and barrel-aged beers. All the beers are brewed by hand in the only manual brewhouse of comparable size in the US. Those who've been to the brewery itself speak mostly of the setting. The deck of the brewery's pub looks out over the Columbia River Gorge, which, weather permitting, is full of kiteboarders and windsurfers. Snow-topped volcanic peaks are visible all around. Opened in 1987, the brewery became employee-owned in 1999.

FULLSTEAM

www.fullsteam.ag

FULLSTEAM BREWERY, which opened in 2010, makes a statement about itself by choosing an .ag domain name for its website, and with a mission to "create a distinctly Southern beer style that celebrates the culinary and agricultural heritage of the South". That includes brewing beers with local ingredients: El Toro Classic Cream Ale is made with corn, Carver with sweet potatoes. A Forager series uses ingredients harvested by volunteers, and has included beers made with wild persimmon and paw paws.

FUNKWERKS

www.funkwerks.com

FUNKWERKS FOUNDERS Brad Lincoln and Gordon Schuck knew that if they were to specialize in making saisons, they needed to be surrounded by other choices, and in Fort Collins they certainly are. "We can't do what we're doing in a place that doesn't have a lot of breweries", said Lincoln. In 2010, within months of starting to brew, they bought a bigger brewing system. Two years later, Funkwerks Brewing won Small Brewing Company of the Year at the Great American Beer Festival.

GEARY'S

www.gearybrewing.com

IN 1986, DL GEARY BREWING was the 13th microbrewery to open in the US. Before starting the brewery, Dave Geary trained in England, working in a dozen small breweries from Scotland to the south of England. He hired English brewing consultant Alan Pugsley to set up his brewery, and his beers reflect a sense of balance and restraint. These include the flagship Pale Ale, which blends English malt and yeast with distinctive North-west-American hops. Hampshire Ale and London Porter also feature.

GENESEE

www.geneseebeer.com

ONE OF THE FEW pre-Prohibition breweries to still make beer, Genesee Brewing rebranded itself as High Falls at the beginning of this century, but has since returned to the name it used when it opened in Rochester, New York, in 1878. It produces its own line of adjunct lagers as well as the Dundee Ales and Lagers. The company opened the Genesee Brew House in 2012 and makes speciality beers on the premises.

GEORGETOWN

www.georgetownbeer.com

MANNY'S ALE, NAMED after Georgetown's co-founder, Manny Chao, accounts for more than 80 per cent of this Seattle brewery's sales – the brewery has grown into a regional-sized setup, despite selling only draught beer. Chao and partner Roger Bialous brewed in the old Rainier Brewery before building their own plant. Chao said he was looking for a "snappy hop finish" for the pale ale and kept adding hops to the back end. "Eventually, I added some to the front end, and it all came to life."

GIGANTIC

www.giganticbrewing.com

PARTNERS VAN HAVIG and Ben Love have outsized reputations in the Oregon brewing community, but chose the name Gigantic Brewing as their way of saying the brewery will remain small. They set only two goals when they opened in 2012: "Make the best damn IPA in Portland, Oregon, and produce seasonal, exciting flavourful beers, most of which will be brewed only once". One of their first releases beyond the promised IPA was The City Never Sleeps, a black saison.

GOLDEN ROAD

www.goldenroad.la

EVEN WITH NEW BREWERIES coming online in record numbers in 2011 and 2012, booming sales at Golden Road Brewing focused the spotlight on 27-year-old co-founder Meg Gill. "Meg Gill is a force – wrapped in a smart, surfer girl, no-messing-around style", New Belgium Brewing CEO Kim Jordan said. The Los Angeles brewery opened new accounts at a record pace for a start-up, primarily driven by "Anytime Beers" like Point the Way IPA, packaged in cans.

GORDON BIERSCH

www.gordonbiersch.com

SEPARATE COMPANIES now own the chain of Gordon Biersch brewery restaurants and a large brewery of the same name based in San Jose, California. They both brew German-inspired beers from recipes created by Dan Gordon, who trained for five years at Weihenstephan Technical University in Bavaria. As well as classic interpretations of beers such as its Märzen and Hefeweizen, Gordon's distribution brewery launched a series of limited edition, high-alcohol beers.

GRAND TETON

www.grandtetonbrewing.com

LOCATED IN IDAHO AT THE base of the Teton Mountains, Grand Teton Brewing ships its popular and strong speciality beers to many states west of the Mississippi. The brewery also claims a place in history. Not long after it opened as Otto Brothers Brewing in 1988, the brewpub reintroduced Americans to the "growler", at one time a metal pail, but reinvented as a glass 3-pint (1.7-litre) jug used to haul fresh beer home.

GRAY'S

www.graybrewing.com

THE GRAY FAMILY RESUMED beer-making in 1994 after a 72-year hiatus. The company was founded by JC Gray in 1856 but had discontinued brewing in southern Wisconsin in 1912, before the arrival of Prohibition. A 1992 fire destroyed the company's soda bottling plant and although it remains a small brewery, Gray's won two gold medals at the 1994 Great American Beer Festival, for its Honey Ale and Oatmeal Stout.

GREAT DIVIDE

www.greatdivide.com

LOCATED IN DENVER'S BALLPARK neighbourhood and surrounded by a growing number of brewery start-ups, Great Divide is an old timer. Surprisingly, the brewery did not add a taproom until 13 years after it opened in 1994, but that has become a top tourist destination. Massive, bold beers such as Hercules Double IPA and Yeti Imperial Stout are ranked among the best in the world by beer rating sites, but the portfolio includes numerous traditional choices – such as Colette – that are always sensibly balanced.

GREENPOINT

www.heartlandbrewery.com

GREENPOINT BEER WORKS in Brooklyn brews the beers for the Heartland Brewery chain in Manhattan and brewmaster Kelly Taylor's own Kelso brand. Heartland opened on Union Square in 1995 and now has six locations in New York City, most of them in Midtown. Kelly Taylor's previous brewing experience before he went to work for Heartland was at home, but he soon tweaked those recipes, for instance boosting the hops in its IPA, and in 2006 started his Kelso line.

GRITTY'S

www.grittys.com

THERE IS NO GRITTY – the founders made up the name – but the original Gritty McDuff's in Portland's Old Port has the sort of Old World feel the name implies. Maine's first brewpub, it opened in 1988 and has since been joined by two more Gritty's, the largest of which also packages beer for distribution on the East Coast. The equipment and yeast come from England and the Best Bitter, particularly when served cask-conditioned, shows it.

HAIR OF THE DOG

www.hairofthedog.com

ALTHOUGH IT HAS a national reputation and has been selling beer since 1994, Hair of the Dog Brewing produces less beer annually than the average brewpub. The beers are generally high in alcohol, sometimes barrel-aged, and always bottle-conditioned. They all have their own identity, "like the people who have inspired them". Chef-turned-brewer Alan Sprints takes his greatest inspiration from Belgian brewers, but his first beer, called Adam, was based on the extinct German "adambier".

HALE'S

www.halesbrewery.com

MIKE HALE OPENED HALE'S ALES in western Washington in 1983 after training at Gale's Brewery in England, and moved his brewery twice before settling between Seattle's Fremont and Ballard districts. Both the pub adjoining the brewery and the beer are true to Hale's vision to recreate what he discovered in England in the 1980s, but the range goes beyond English beer. For instance, both Mongoose IPA and Supergoose IPA are packed with North-west-American hops.

GREAT DIVIDE COLETTE

HALF ACRE

www.halfacrebeer.com

GOOSE ISLAND (SEE P.162) WAS the lone distributing brewery in Chicago until Half Acre Beer kicked off a new wave of start-ups, initially selling beer made under contract, then firing up its own brewhouse in 2009. The brewery was also the first in the city to package its beers in cans, opting for distinctively labelled 16 fl oz (500 ml) tall boys. Half Acre supplements its regular beers, including the assertive pale ale Daisy Cutter, with numerous seasonals, served at the taproom adjoining the brewery.

HANGAR 24

www.hangar24brewery.com

BEERS LIKE AMARILLO PALE ALE and Helles Lager have driven exponential growth at Hangar 24 Craft Brewery since it opened in 2008. However, owner-brewer Ben Cook – who previously worked in quality assurance at Anheuser-Busch – has also tapped into ingredients grown near the brewery's Redlands, California, home. His Local Fields Series includes Vinaceous, a beer brewed with red wine grapes, as well as others made with apricots, dates, and blood oranges.

HARPOON

www.harpoonbrewery.com

A SPACIOUS NEW BEER HALL at Harpoon's Boston visitor centre opened in 2013, using old and new construction materials from New England, symbolizing the link between traditional and modern practices here. Harpoon Brewery opened in 1986 and is one of the largest of the former microbreweries. The company operates breweries both in Boston and Vermont and serves a popular IPA, as well as many new beers with its 100 Barrel series of one-off brews.

HAYMARKET

www.haymarketbrewing.com

THE HAYMARKET RIOTS between Chicago police and labour organizers took place a few blocks away from Haymarket Brewery in 1886, and the building itself is more than 100 years old. However, while brewmaster Pete Crowley makes beer with a nod to many traditions, it's clearly 21st-century America at his pub and brewery. Crowley learned barrel-ageing skills at Rock Bottom Brewery in Chicago, and has a large barrel room here.

HEAVY SEAS

www.hsbeer.com

HUGH SISSON WAS the first brewmaster at Sisson's, a well known Baltimore beer destination that became a brewpub in 1989 after Maryland made them legal. Five years later he started Clipper City Brewing, since renamed Heavy Seas, after its most popular brand. Flagship Loose Cannon IPA, known as Hop3, has aided the brewery's exponential growth. The brewery has the largest cask-conditioned programme in the country, and has wooden casks for special occasions.

HIGHLAND

www.highlandbrewing.com

ASHEVILLE, North Carolina, attracted national attention in 2011 when both Sierra Nevada Brewing (see pp.176–177) and New Belgium Brewing (see p.166) announced they would build East Coast breweries there – but Highland Brewing laid the foundations 17 years before. The brewery started out in the basement of a pizzeria before moving to larger quarters, the first of several small breweries to open in what has become a beer-crazy city. Its flagship, Gaelic Ale, is an amber ale with a resiny hop bite.

HIGH POINT

www.ramsteinbeer.com

WHEN GREG ZACCARDI began selling the Ramstein brand beers in 1996, High Point Brewing was the first, and only, all-wheat brewery in the United States since before Prohibition. This was a time when weissbier breweries were tiny and made something that tasted more like sour wheat beers from Berlin. Zaccardi has since made other styles part of this New Jersey brewery's line-up, but its beers such at Ramstein Classic and Blonde taste of Germany.

HILL FARMSTEAD

www.hillfarmstead.com

LESS THAN THREE YEARS after Shaun Hill opened the Hill Farmstead Brewery on an isolated Vermont farm on land that's been in his family for eight generations, the reviewers at the Internet site www.ratebeer.com judged the brewery to be the best in the world. Many of Hill's beers are highly hopped, and at times he'll further accent citrussy New World hop character with the addition of citrus zest. "I've had a citrus obsession all my life", Hill said.

HINTERLAND

www.hinterlandbeer.com

BILL TRESSLER, A JOURNALIST who previously edited two beer magazines, and his wife, Michelle, founded Green Bay Brewing in 1995 in a small town outside Green Bay, Wisconsin. The brewery soon outgrew that space and the Tresslers moved their business into the city, later branding it Hinterland Brewery. They emphasize their beer's food-friendly attributes by operating a restaurant attached to the brewery and the Hinterland Erie Street Gastropub in Milwaukee.

HOFBRÄUHAUS

www.hofbrauhaus.us

HOFBRÄUHAUS, THE SPRAWLING Munich beer hall with roots that go back to the 16th century, opened its first American outpost in Newport, Kentucky, in 2003; by the beginning of 2013 it operated a dozen restaurants, beer halls, and beer gardens in the US. The full-size restaurants, such as in Las Vegas, are massive, some brewing beer on the premises and all serving the same traditional food and beer found in Munich.

HOPPIN' FROG

www.hoppinfrog.com

BREWMASTER AND OWNER of Hoppin' Frog, Fred Karm, says he's his own focus group. He clearly likes big, bold beers and has found an audience for them, shipping beer from Akron, Ohio, to 16 states and nine other countries. The "B.O.R.I.S." in his legendary B.O.R.I.S. The Crusher is short for Bodacious Oatmeal Russian Imperial Stout, and Karm also makes a version aged in used Heaven Hill Kentucky whiskey barrels. Even the seasonal pumpkin beer, Frog's Hollow Double Pumpkin Ale, is oversized, packing 8.4% ABV.

HOPWORKS URBAN

www.hopworksbeer.com

HOPWORKS URBAN BREWERY describes itself as the first eco-brewpub in Portland, Oregon. An Oregon Sustainability Grand Champion Award confirms its commitment to the environment. Founder and brewmaster Christian Ettinger made Portland's first organic beers when he was at Laurelwood Public House and Brewery, but didn't commit to organic hops until he was sure the quality would suit hop-forward award-winning beers like his Hopworks IPA.

INDEPENDENCE

www.independencebrewing.com

FOUNDED BY ROB AND Amy Cartwright, Independence Brewing has twice won a Good Food Award for its Convict Hill Oatmeal Stout, a national prize that recognizes excellent tasting and sustainably crafted food and drink. They've also created considerable goodwill with local Austin, Texas, drinkers by repackaging Independence Amber each autumn and calling it Oklahoma Suks before the University of Texas and Oklahoma University football teams play each other.

IRON HILL

www.ironhillbrewery.com

THE STILL-GROWING restaurant-brewery chain opened its first Iron Hill Brewery & Restaurant in Delaware in 1996 before spreading into Pennsylvania and New Jersey, with plans for more restaurants in the Mid-Atlantic. Each location keeps the same five beers on tap, but individual brewers then fill out the line-up and may have twice as many of their own beers available. Iron Hill's Media, Pennsylvania, brewery won Small Brewpub of the Year at the 2012 World Beer Cup.

ITHACA BEER

www.ithacabeer.com

AN EARLY BEER BEACHHEAD in New York's Finger Lakes region, otherwise known for its wineries, Ithaca moved into a larger brewery in the autumn of 2012, more than doubling its capacity. The brewery opened in 1998 and has been an early supporter of efforts to revive hop farming in New York, which was once the centre of hop-growing in the US. Its Flower Power IPA, so far brewed with hops from the North-west, is among its best-selling beers.

JESTER KING

www.jesterkingbrewery.com

BROTHERS JEFFREY AND Michael Stuffings made a commitment to mixed fermentations before they opened Jester King Craft Brewery in a farmhouse setting west of Austin, Texas, embracing the character "wild" yeasts might add. "Having our eyes opened to the world beyond Saccharomyces, there's no turning back", Stuffings said. They use organic ingredients when possible, age their beers in barrels, and brew low-alcohol (or "session") beers with colourful names and labels.

JOLLY PUMPKIN

www.jollypumpkin.com

WHEN FOUNDER RON JEFFRIES decided in 2004 that all the beers from Jolly Pumpkin Artisan Ales would be fermented in open vessels – often influenced by wild Michigan yeast – aged in oak, and bottle-conditioned, his plan seemed more outlandish than it would a few years later. "It's all about doing things the hard way", he said. Wonderfully rustic beers like La Roja and Bam Bière quickly earned followers, and Jolly Pumpkin now has café-breweries in Traverse City and Ann Arbor, as well as its production brewery.

KARBACH

www.karbachbrewing.com

BREWMASTER ERIC WARNER trained in Germany and wrote a book on German wheat beers, so his recipe for Weisse Versa Wheat made it clear from the start that Karbach Brewing, which opened in Houston in 2011, would not be bound by any rules. It is fermented with Bavarian yeast common to weissbeers, but spiced with coriander and citrus peel, which is very un-Germanic. Karbach's best beers include American-hop rich Hopadillo IPA and German-hopped Sympathy for the Lager.

KARL STRAUSS

www.karlstrauss.com

FOUNDERS OF KARL STRAUSS, Chris Cramer and Matt Rattner, opened their first brewpub in San Diego in 1989. They named it in honour of Karl Strauss, an icon in the brewing industry who provided them with key start-up advice. Today Karl Strauss Brewing operates both a production facility and seven brewery restaurants in southern California. Red Trolley Ale, the brewery's first holiday ale, is its best-seller.

THE KETTLEHOUSE

www.kettlehouse.com

IN 1995, THE SAME YEAR Big Sky started brewing across town in Missoula, Tim O'Leary and his wife opened a "brew on premises place", where customers could come in and make their own beer. That morphed into a small microbrewery and taproom. In 2009, they built a larger brewery on the north side of town and Kettlehouse became the first Montana brewery to package in cans.

JOLLY PUMPKIN LA ROJA

KONA BREWING FIRE ROCK PALE ALE

KONA BREWING

www.konabrewingco.com

THE BEERS HAWAII'S Kona Brewing sells in the continental US are brewed by Craft Brew Alliance partners in Portland, Oregon, and Portsmouth, New Hampshire. Drinkers can nonetheless taste Hawaii in beers such as Fire Rock Pale Ale and Pipeline Porter. On the Big Island where Kona started in 1995, its best-selling beer is the assertive Castaway IPA.

KUHNHENN

www.kbrewery.com

WHEN BIG STORES STARTED putting other small hardware stores out of business, brothers Bret and Eric Kuhnhenn talked their father into selling home-brewing supplies in the shop he'd run for 35 years and put together their own brewery, meadery, and winery north of Detroit. Beers include cult classics such as Raspberry Eisbock, and GRIPA, which has won Gold for the Best IPA at the World Beer Cup.

LA CUMBRE

www.lacumbrebrewing.com

JEFF ERWAY BEGAN home-brewing when he was teaching in western New Mexico. He quickly became obsessed and started talking about opening his own brewery. La Cumbre Brewing opened in Albuquerque in 2011. Before the brewery's first anniversary, Erway's Elevated IPA, which accounts for 70 per cent of sales, bested 175 others to win a Gold medal at the Great American Beer Festival.

LAKEFRONT

www.lakefrontbrewery.com

A MILWAUKEE ATTRACTION since it opened in 1987, Lakefront's popular tour showcases "Bernie Brewer's Chalet" from the old baseball stadium and historic lights from a 1916 beer hall. The brewery occupies a Cream City-brick building. A diverse line-up includes "all local" beers, like Wisconsinite Summer Weiss, made with only Wisconsin ingredients, including specially isolated yeast.

LANCASTER

www.lancasterbrewing.com

DESPITE A PROUD BREWING history – in 1868, The *Daily Intelligencer* newspaper had proclaimed, "Lancaster in America occupies the same position that Munich does in Germany in regards to the brewing industry" – Lancaster, Pennsylvania, was without a brewery for 40 years before Lancaster Brewing opened in 1995. Their Milk Stout has been particularly well received.

LAZY MAGNOLIA

www.lazymagnolia.com

BENEFITING FROM A CHANGE in Mississippi law, Lazy Magnolia Brewing – which in 2003 became the state's first production brewery since Prohibition – has grown to regional status. Southern Pecan Brown Ale, made with roasted pecans, remains the brewery's top seller, but the breadth of its line-up widened when Mississippi boosted the limit on alcohol in beer from six per cent to ten.

LEFT COAST

www.leftcoastbrewing.com

OGGI'S PIZZA & BREWING started Left Coast Brewing in 2004 to make beer for its southern California restaurants. The San Clemente brewery now sells beer in seven states and exports some internationally. It was one of the first breweries to regularly offer a Double IPA and its signature beer is called Hop Juice.

LEFT HAND

www.lefthandbrewing.com

WHEN ERIC WALLACE and Dick Doore learned that the first name they'd chosen in 1993 for their new brewery was already taken and went scrambling for another, they didn't envisage that the red left hand that now adorns bottles, six pack holders, silos outside the Longmont, Colorado, brewery, and even delivery trucks would become so ubiquitous. Left Hand Brewing's line-up includes many of its original beers, like Sawtooth Ale, but also popular newcomers such as Milk Stout Nitro.

LEGEND

www.legendbrewing.com

A FULLY FLEDGED microbrewery, Legend hides underneath a bustling restaurant in Richmond. The basement setting presents logistical challenges for the brewers, who brew more than 12,000 hl (7300 barrels) a year. Legend Brown Ale is the flagship, accounting for 60 per cent of sales, but Legend Lager and IPA reveal the diversity of the beer menu.

LEINENKUGEL'S

www.leinie.com

ALTHOUGH MILLER (now MillerCoors) bought the controlling interest in the Wisconsin brewery Leinenkugel's in 1988, family members are the faces of the brand, as they have been since Jacob Leinenkugel and John Miller started the Spring Brewery in Chippewa Falls in 1867. Leinenkugel bought out Miller in 1884. The range has broadened well beyond Leinenkugel's Original, a pale lager, with beers like Sunset Wheat, a witbier, and Summer Shandy, a wheat beer with lemonade flavour, getting the widest distribution.

LION

www.lionbrewery.com

ONE OF THE FEW BREWERIES established before Prohibition and still operating today, the Lion Brewery in north-east Pennsylvania has survived by contract-brewing and producing non-beer drinks along with two of its own lines – Lionshead and Stegmaier. The Lion Brewery bought Stegmaier in 1974, and in doing so acquired a portfolio that goes back to 1857. Although it has added fashionable styles like IPA, Lion shines with traditional offerings such as Stegmaier Porter and Stegmaier Brewhouse Bock.

LIVE OAK BREWING

www.liveoakbrewing.com

ALTHOUGH VISTORS TO THE TEXAS Hill Country around Austin have long appreciated how Czech and German immigrants created a distinctive barbecue style, it has taken longer for Live Oak Brewing to establish the same sort of respect for traditional beers. Selling draught beer only, the brewery uses Old World practices, like decoction mashing and open fermentation. Connoisseurs have sought out beers like Live Oak Pilz and Hefeweizen since the brewery opened in 1997, and today the beers are finding a wider audience.

LOGSDON FARMHOUSE

www.farmhousebeer.com

JUST SOUTH OF HOOD RIVER, OREGON, operating out of the same barn in which he started Wyeast Laboratories – the yeast supply company he ran for more than 20 years – Dave Logsdon operates Logsdon Farmhouse

LONERIDER SWEET JOSIE

Ales in partnership with Charles Porter. They use yeast that Logsdon collected in travels throughout Belgium, and include ingredients like local organic peaches, cherries grown on Logsdon's 20-acre family estate, and local hops. Beers like Seizoen Bretta were an instant hit with beer fans.

LONERIDER

www.loneriderbeer.com

THREE HOME-BREWING FRIENDS, who kept their day jobs while they got Lonerider Brewing up and running at the beginning of 2009, chose a gritty Western theme and made use of thoroughly modern social media tools to quickly establish themselves on the burgeoning North Carolina brewing scene. The "ales for outlaws" have names like Shotgun Betty, the labels are flashy, and the tap handles are designed with a spur motif. The robust Deadeye Jack porter and Sweet Josie, a brown ale, are both Great American Beer Festival medallists. Promotional items for outlaws are available at their online store.

LONG TRAIL

www.longtrail.com

ONE OF THE LARGER "SMALL" BREWERS in the US, Long Trail Brewing has earned a reputation for promoting "ECO (Environmentally Conscious Operations) Brewing" since opening in 1989. The Vermont brewery makes excellent German-style beers: its Long Trail Ale is brewed in the manner of an altbier, although not as bitter, and its popular Double Bag is a stronger variation on the theme. Not surprisingly, it was honoured by the Vermont "Governor's Award for Environmental Excellence" in 2009.

LOST COAST

www.lostcoast.com

FOUNDED IN 1990 AND KNOWN for beers like Downtown Brown, Alleycat, and Great White, the Lost Coast Brewery and Café long ago established itself as a vital member of the community in Eureka, California. Its city council made that clear in 2012, approving measures to help Lost Coast, already a good-size regional brewery, build a much larger facility. "A number of communities would like to have Barbara (Groom, co-founder and brewmaster) and her business. This agreement is part of accomplishing that," city manager David Tyson said at the time.

MAC & JACK'S

www.macandjacks.com

DRINKING AFRICAN AMBER from Mac & Jack's Brewery is an essential North-west beer experience. Malcolm Rankin and Jack Schropp started out brewing beer in a garage, making it at night and delivering it by day. The brewery in the Seattle suburb of Redmond has grown into a regional force, although it produces only draught beer. Its flagship African Amber is slightly cloudy because brewers dry-hop each keg with a bag of hop cones grown in the nearby Yakima Valley.

MAD FOX

www.madfoxbrewing.com

LOCATED IN THE UPMARKET Washington DC suburb of Falls Church, this brewpub has made brewmaster Bill Madden and his beers the stars even though Mad Fox's food – up-scale dining with an emphasis on local produce – also shines bright. Madden established a national reputation for his beers at Capitol City, mastering a full range of styles, from Hardly English-style Ordinary Bitter and Rock Star Red Irish Ale to an outstanding Kölsch.

MAD RIVER

www.madriverbrewing.com

THERE ARE MANY REASONS to visit Mad River, including an inviting beer garden, the beer itself, and the original Sierra Nevada Brewing equipment, which founder Bob Smith bought from Ken Grossman in 1989 to open his own brewery. The Humboldt County brewery has won multiple awards for its environmental practices as well as its beers, which include both Jamaica and Steelhead brands – the Extra Pale is particularly outstanding.

MADISON RIVER

www.madisonriverbrewing.com

BLACK GHOST, COPPER JOHN, HOPPER, Irresistible, Rubber Legged Razz, Salmon Fly, and Yellow Humpy are all names of fishing flies. At Madison River Brewing in south-western Montana they are also names of beers, which fill out a full range of styles. Black Ghost, for instance, is an award-winning oatmeal stout. It comes as no surprise that brewmaster Howard McMurry is an avid fisherman himself. Salmon Fly Honey Rye, the People's Choice award-winner at the 2012 Wyoming Brewers Festival, is the flagship.

MAGIC HAT

www.magichat.net

FOUNDED IN 1994, MAGIC HAT BREWING is now a subsidiary of North American Breweries, but offers those who visit its Burlington, Vermont, brewery a unique circus-like experience. "It doesn't have to be just about beer. It is about brand and lifestyle", co-founder Alan Newman observed before NAB bought Magic Hat. Beers like Pistil, made with dandelion petals, don't conform to style, and flagship #9 is a pale ale infused with apricot.

MAMMOTH BREWING CO

www.mammothbrewingco.com

HANDY FOR SKIING IN THE WINTER and on the eastern side of Yosemite National Park, Mammoth Brewing Co reflects its setting in many ways. Owner Sean Turner thinks the hop profile of the beers is softer because water boils at a lower temperature at 2,440m (8,000ft) above sea level. In addition, its popular and imperial-sized IPA 395, named for the highway corridor Mammoth Lakes sits on, is made with local sage and juniper.

MARBLE

www.marblebrewery.com

EACH LABEL AND TAP HANDLE for Marble Brewery's beers features a different colour marble. Appropriately, the founders chose the same green ball with an inlaid image of hop cones for the main logo as they use for their flagship India Pale Ale. Best known for its hop-forward ales, Marble offers an assertive, but nuanced, range of beers that have won numerous awards. Some are available only at its popular downtown Albuquerque taproom.

MARIN

www.marinbrewing.com

THE MARIN BREWPUB, located in Larkspur and easily reached from San Francisco by ferry, opened on April Fools' Day in 1989. Quickly proving that it was not a joke, it has won multiple awards for its beers. Although many of the original choices, such as Mt Tam Pale Ale and Point Reyes Porter, remain on tap, Arne Johnson, in charge of the brewery since 1995, is a master of cutting-edge beers. Co-founder Brendan Moylan also operates a second brewpub, Moylan's, nearby.

MARITIME PACIFIC

www.maritimebrewery.com

THE MARITIME PACIFIC BREWERY, founded in 1990, and its Jolly Roger Taproom, founded in 1997, are long-time fixtures in Seattle's Ballard district, which in recent years has turned into a hotbed for smaller breweries. The seafaring theme includes the beer names, vintage pirate flags draped in the taproom, and a treasure map painted on the floor. As per usual in the North-west US, there are plenty of hop-centric beers here as well as traditional lagers.

MATT BREWING

www.saranac.com

MATT BREWING, FOUNDED IN 1888 by FX Matt, is one of the largest and oldest breweries in the country, but not as well known as most its size. The upstate New York brewery put its familiar brands in the background in the 1990s, focusing on Saranac, which produces styles that are a hit with craft beer drinkers. Matt also makes popular craft beers under contract.

MCMENAMINS

www.mcmenamins.com

BROTHERS MIKE AND BRIAN MCMENAMIN run more than 65 drinking establishments in the North-west, primarily near Portland, Oregon. Many of them make beer on the premises, and Edgefield Manor outside Portland brews quite a lot. Not all locations trumpet the McMenamin name, some are large and historic, and others are neighbourhood gems that may serve other brands as well.

MCNEILL'S

www.mcneillsbrewery.com

OWNER AND FOUNDER OF MCNEILL'S, Ray McNeill, once told a reporter, "I have three passions. Cellos, bikes, and the beer thing." A classically trained cellist, McNeill settled on "the beer thing" in 1991, opening a brewpub in Vermont and then a packaging facility in 2008. He has also established a reputation for carefully researching the recipes for his beers, using traditional methods to make them, creating a pub atmosphere in Brattleboro, and serving excellent cask-conditioned beers.

MAUI BREWING CO

www.mauibrewingco.com

OBVIOUSLY, DRINKERS IN BOTH Hawaii and on the mainland like the beers from Maui. After opening a brewpub in 2005, founder Garrett Marrero added a production facility, then in 2013 announced construction of a second production brewery to open in 2014, followed by a new brewpub. In Hawaii, a blond ale and IPA are the bestsellers, but on the continent CoCoNut PorTeR rules. Liquid Breadfruit, a collaboration with Dogfish Head (see pp.154–155) containing ulu – local Maui breadfruit – and toasted papaya seeds, shows Marrero's interest in brewing distinctly Hawaiian beers.

MENDOCINO

www.mendobrew.com

MENDOCINO BREWING CLAIMS a direct link to the rebirth of US beer. The Hopland Brewery, using equipment and the yeast from the defunct New Albion Brewing – the brewery that showed other craft breweries the way – opened as California's first brewpub in 1983. In 1997, Mendocino Brewing built a new brewing plant nearby in Ukiah. It still makes some of the original beers, although no longer packaging them in 2.6-pint (1.5-litre) magnums, as well as others that reflect an expanding US palate.

MERCURY

www.ipswichalebrewery.com

MERCURY BREWING IN IPSWICH, on the Massachusetts North Shore, set up in 1991, has quietly grown into a regional-size brewery that produces its own brands. These include Ipswich Ales, Stone Cat Ales, and 5 Mile Ales, the latter using at least one ingredient grown locally – and numerous others under contract for companies mainly in Massachusetts. The brewery was called Ipswich Brewing when it first opened, and it is best known for the Ipswich brand, most prominently Ipswich Dark Ale and Ipswich Oatmeal Stout.

MIDDLE AGES

www.middleagesbrewing.com

SINCE MARC AND MARY RUBENSTEIN opened their Syracuse, New York, brewery in 1995 in a former Sealtest ice cream factory, they've focused on traditional English ales. They use English malts, the well-known Ringwood yeast strain, and make ales available to some accounts that want to sell cask-conditioned beers. The "Middle Ages" theme continues in the marketplace, where each of the distinctive labels recalls the days of King Arthur. Beers produced have suitably medieval names such as Impaled Ale, Wailing Wench, Swallow Wit, and Ape Hanger Ale.

MIDNIGHT SUN

www.midnightsunbrewing.com

ALTHOUGH MIDNIGHT SUN BREWING distributes beer to only a few of the Lower 48 states, the Alaskan brewery has developed a cult following with its esoteric ales, many of which come but once… ever. For instance, in 2007 the brewery offered a seven-beer "Deadly Sin Series": Lust was a strong dark Belgian ale aged in bourbon barrels and infused with sour cherries and Brettanomyces. Core beers like Sockeye Red IPA and Kodiak Brown Ale are readily available in Anchorage, including in cans.

MILLERCOORS

www.millercoors.com

INTERNATIONAL BREWING GIANTS SABMiller and Molson Coors created MillerCoors as a US joint venture in 2008. Its two best-selling beers during that year were Miller Lite and Coors Light. In 2010 it created Tenth and Blake Beer Co, which oversees several speciality craft brands. Its Batch 19 beer went into production in 2010 and is made using a recipe from the pre-Prohibition era. Other craft beers brewed at MillerCoors facilities include Blue Moon (see p.184), Leinenkugel's (see p.194), and AC Golden (see p.182). Tenth and Blake has also invested in smaller craft breweries, such as Terrapin (see p.203), based in Georgia.

MILWAUKEE

www.mkebrewing.com

NINE YEARS AFTER FOUNDING the Milwaukee Ale House in 1997, Jim McCabe built a production brewery, Milwaukee Brewing. Head brewer Robert "Bert" Morton earned a chef's diploma from the Culinary Institute of America and has drawn on that experience as one way to distinguish his beers from those of older, more established city breweries. The brewery's first two beers packaged in cans were flagship Louie's Demise, an amber lager, and Love Rock, a Vienna lager.

MINHAS

www.minhasbrewery.com

RAVINDER MINHAS TOOK OVER one of the US's oldest remaining breweries in 2006 when he bought the Joseph Huber Brewery, which had roots going directly back to 1843 in Monroe, Wisconsin. Now Minhas produces a variety of products sold in both Canada and the US. These include low-priced lagers made for Trader Joe's, brands such as Huber Bock that Wisconsin drinkers know well, and newcomers like Lazy Mutt "Farmhouse" Ale.

MOONLIGHT

www.moonlightbrewing.com

BRIAN HUNT HAS BEEN A one-man brewery since 1992, producing about 1,800hl (1,100 barrels) a year in Sonoma County, all of it draught beer, most of it sold in the San Francisco Bay Area. Hunt learned to brew at California-Davis in the 1970s, at a time when instructor Michael Lewis took his classes to visit New Albion Brewing. His beers, like the dark lager Death & Taxes or Reality Czeck Pils, are unfiltered and nuanced.

MOUNTAIN SUN

www.mountainsunpub.com

FROM THE MOMENT IT OPENED in 1993 on Boulder's popular Pearl Street, the Mountain Sun Pub & Brewery has been a favourite spot with the locals. It is laid back in the same comfortable way as the McMenamins pubs (see p.195), and serves a wide range of well-made beers. The company later added the Southern Sun on the south side of Boulder, then the Vine Street Pub in Denver. They don't take credit cards, but they do trust customers to send in payment later.

NAPA SMITH

www.napasmithbrewery.com

WINE-MAKERS READILY ADMIT "it takes a lot of beer to make good wine", so it is no surprise to find them at the Napa Smith Brewery, which also operates a brewpub and wine tasting room, in the centre of Napa Valley. Brewmaster Don Barkley was one of very few employees at the historic New Albion Brewery in the 1970s (the first new brewery since Prohibition), later moving along with the yeast and some of the equipment to Mendocino Brewing, where he worked for 25 years before joining Napa Smith.

NARRAGANSETT

www.narragansettbeer.com

THE NARRAGANSETT BREWING COMPANY has a history that goes back to 1888, although the brewery last made beer in 1983 and was for the most part demolished in 1998. Rhode Islander Mark Hellendrung and a group of investors bought the brand in 2005 and contract to have different beers made at various breweries. Some of the appeal of 'Gansett beer is nostalgia, but seasonals like a bock and porter have found fans.

NATTY GREENE'S

www.nattygreenes.com

WHEN CHRIS LESTER AND KAYNE FISHER, already successful operating beer-focused restaurants, opened their first brewpub in Greensboro in 2004 they named it Natty Greene's, after the revolutionary war hero who gave the North Carolina city its name. Their concept proved portable, and they built a packaging brewery in 2006, then a second brewpub in Raleigh in 2010. Both brewpubs offer a rotating selection beyond those available from the production brewery, and those in Raleigh get particularly high marks.

NEBRASKA

www.nebraskabrewingco.com

TO MAKE MELANGE À TROIS, Nebraska Brewing ages a strong (10% ABV) Belgian-style blonde ale in French oak Chardonnay wine barrels. The beer has won multiple awards and is one of the reasons the brewery, which was to be only a brewpub when it opened, now sells beer as far away as New York City. The brewery produces a full range of styles, but has built its reputation on bold beers like barrel-aged Apricot Au Poivre Saison.

NEW HOLLAND

www.newhollandbrew.com

NEW HOLLAND BREWING MANAGING partner Fred Bueltmann is known as a "beervangelist". Operating both a production brewery and a pub, New Holland puts a premium on beer education – encouraging its employees to become Cicerones, their beer knowledge certified through an independent programme – and its pub celebrates beer at the table. The pub has its own brewery and distils spirits as well. A family of IPAs and Dragon's Milk Bourbon Barrel Stout are particularly popular.

NO-LI BREWHOUSE

www.nolibrewhouse.com

MARK IRVIN FOUNDED Northern Lights Brewing Co outside Spokane, Washington, in 1993. He moved into the city in 2002, making his brewery a pub as well. The microbrewery produced a modest 1,900hl (1,165 barrels) in 2011 before John Bryant, who had previously worked with several breweries during periods of hyper-expansion, became a partner. After 2011, No-Li Brewhouse, renamed in order to avoid a conflict with a brewery selling a beer called Northern Lights, quickly expanded, and won numerous international awards by the end of 2012.

NODDING HEAD

www.noddinghead.com

A SECOND-STOREY brewery-restaurant located in Philadelphia's city centre, Nodding Head often serves unique beers seldom found elsewhere, such as George's Fault, a 9% ABV strong honey beer fermented with Belgian yeast. It took an entire summer for Nodding Head to sell 8hl (5 barrels) of Ich Bin Ein Berliner Weisse the first time it was brewed in 2001, but now the delightfully tart wheat beer is a popular summer regular.

NOLA

www.nolabrewing.com

NEW ORLEANS NATIVE Kirk Coco returned home in the aftermath of Hurricane Katrina and founded New Orleans Lager & Ale (NOLA) in 2009. "This market was still 95 per cent Bud-Miller-Coors two years ago", Coco said after the brewery opened. "The turnaround has been a lot of people who hadn't had craft beer getting out and trying it." They seem to like beers such as the assertive Hopitoulas IPA.

NORTH COAST

www.northcoastbrewing.com

ALTHOUGH FORT BRAGG, located on the picturesque northern California coast, is a popular tourist destination, it is not the handiest location for a brewery that ships its beer as far afield as North Coast does. However, it's where brewmaster Mark Ruedrich and his partners lived when they decided to open a brewpub in 1988. Popular beers include Le Merle, Red Seal Ale, Old Rasputin Imperial Stout, and Brother Thelonious Abbey Ale.

NORTH COAST LE MERLE

NOTCH BREWING

www.notchbrewing.com

CRAFT-BREWING VETERAN Chris Lohring started Notch Brewing in 2010, producing only "session beers" – those with 4.5% ABV or less. He doesn't own his own brewery, instead he produces his beer at Mercury Brewing in Ipswich (see p.196) and sells it only in Massachusetts. Notch Session Pils (4% ABV) and Session Ale (4.5% ABV, dosed with distinctive US hops) are the easiest to find. Beers like Černé Pivo, a black lager, have introduced drinkers to new styles.

OAKSHIRE

www.oakbrew.com

THE OAKSHIRE BREWERY HAS barrelled ahead full steam since its founders, schoolteacher Jeff Althouse and his brother Chris, convinced brewmaster Matt Van Wyk, himself a former science teacher, to move to Eugene, Oregon, from Illinois in 2009. Van Wyk established a reputation for his barrel-aged beers at Flossmoor Station in suburban Chicago. As well as Oakshire's Watershed IPA and Overcast Espresso Stout, both his bourbon-barrel and sour ales quickly grabbed attention.

O'FALLON

www.ofallonbrewery.com

O'FALLON BREWERY APPEARED to be on the verge of closing in 2011 before a former Anheuser-Busch marketing executive bought the brewery west of St Louis. Many of its "everyday" beers aren't so everyday, notably Hemp Hop Rye, Wheach, and Smoked Porter. Wheach is a peach-flavoured wheat beer, well suited for humid St Louis summers and available on tap at Busch Stadium. O'Fallon contracts with a Wisconsin brewery to produce the beers it sells in bottles.

OLD DOMINION

www.olddominion.com

FOUNDED IN ASHBURN, VIRGINIA, in 1989, Old Dominion grew to be one of the 50 largest brewing companies in the US before it was sold to Fordham Brewing in 2007. All operations eventually merged at Fordham's facility in Delaware, under the umbrella brewery Coastal Brewing. The Fordham and Old Dominion brands remain separate, and beers such as Dominion Ale, Octoberfest, and Millennium remain favourites.

OTTER CREEK

www.ottercreekbrewing.com, www.wolavers.com

ALTHOUGH VERMONT BREWING giant Long Trail became much larger in 2009 when it bought the Otter Creek Brewery and the Wolaver's Organic brands, it has maintained Otter Creek as a separate brewery, with its own visitor centre. Otter Creek has expanded beyond its well-regarded traditional beers to add trendy new offerings like Alpine Black IPA. Wolaver's was one of the first USDA certified organic breweries in the country and benefits from growing interest in organic products.

PABST

www.pabstblueribbon.com

PABST BREWING COMPANY, with roots that go back to 1844 in Milwaukee, long ago became a "virtual brewery" that contracts to have its beers made at plants with excess capacity. Sales had been in decline for 25 years before they sprang back to life in 2002, after urban hipsters adopted Pabst as an "anti-brand". Pabst Blue Ribbon, or just PBR, is often found as a cheaper alternative at bars that otherwise sell only craft beer.

PELICAN

www.yourlittlebeachtown.com/pelican

THE ONLY OCEAN FRONT BREWERY in Oregon, right beside the oft-photographed Cape Kiwanda landmark, Pelican Pub and Brewery's beers have won awards from Grand Champion Beer at the Australian International competition to the European Beer Star in Germany, but it was usually necessary to visit Pelican to find those beers, including Imperial Pelican Ale, Kiwanda Cream, and Doryman's Dark. A separate brewery in nearby Tillamook now produces beer for distribution, making it a little easier to find.

PENN

www.pennbrew.com

LOCATED IN THE FORMER EBERHARDT and Ober Brewery in Pittsburgh's Deutschtown, the Pennsylvania Brewing Company is a modern-day brewing pioneer. It first opened in 1986 and then reopened in 2009 after being closed briefly. The brewery produces first-rate German-style beers, such as Penn Pilsner and Penn Weizen. Its on-site restaurant sells "Euro-Pittsburgh" fare and has a welcoming beer hall and outdoor beer garden.

PIKE MONK'S UNCLE

PERENNIAL ARTISAN ALES

www.perennialbeer.com

ONE OF THE FIRST BEERS released by Phil Wymore after Perennial opened in St Louis in 2011 was made with fresh local strawberries and rhubarb and was designed to recall rhubarb pie. His goal was to layer beers with ingredients that create complexity. Other beers have included relatively straightforward offerings, like his dry Belgian-influenced Hommel Bier, to the very complex. Abraxas is an imperial stout aged on ancho chilli peppers, cacao nibs, and cinnamon sticks.

PIECE

www.piecechicago.com

PIECE BREWPUB in Chicago's Wicker Park neighbourhood has won so many awards since it opened in 2001 that it's become a destination for beer fans, particularly those who like thin-crust pizza – the full name is Piece Brewery and Pizzeria. Brewmaster Jonathan Cutler, who previously worked at Goose Island (see p.162) and Sierra Nevada (see pp.176–177), has proved to be adept at making everything from true-to-Bavaria weiss beers to US pale ales brimming with hops.

PIKE

www.pikebrewing.com

THE OWNERS OF PIKE, Charles and Rose Ann Finkel, have played a pivotal role in the US beer revival. They began by importing beers from classic European breweries in 1978, introducing drinkers to varieties they had never tasted. They founded Pike Brewing in 1989 in Seattle, sold it in 1997, and bought it back in 2006, to the benefit of both the brewery and restaurant. It houses much of Finkel's extensive breweriana collection, which is more impressive than in some museums. Its beers include Monk's Uncle Tripel Ale.

PIZZA PORT

www.pizzaport.com

BROTHER AND SISTER Vince and Gina Marsaglia bought a struggling pizza restaurant in Solana Beach in 1987 and in 1992 turned it into their first Pizza Port brewpub. There are now five of the pubs in southern California. In 2006, the Marsaglias and two other partners founded Port Brewing in a separate facility (see p.171).

PORT CITY

www.portcitybrewing.com

PORT CITY BREWING FOUNDER Bill Butcher stepped into the US limelight in 2012 when he spoke at the Democratic National Convention about how a government loan helped him get his suburban Washington DC brewery open in 2011. Until then the metro area had been without a packaging brewery. Brewmaster Jonathan Reeves' beers, such as Monumental IPA and Downright Pilsner, quickly won attention for their balance.

POUR DECISIONS

www.pourdecisionsbrewery.com

PART OF THE PHILOSOPHY WHEN Kristen England and BJ Haun opened Pour Decisions in suburban Minneapolis-St Paul in 2012 was, "The pint is not the destination, only part of the journey." Scientists by day and brewers on the side, they offer several low-alcohol beers – such as the 3.1% ABV Pubstitute, a dark Scottish session ale – suitable for conversation, and others drawn from brewing history and other beer cultures.

PRETTY THINGS BEER & ALE PROJECT

www.prettybeer.com

DANN PAQUETTE, WHO HAS WORKED in breweries on both sides of the Atlantic, operates Pretty Things with his wife, Martha. They are sometimes referred to as "gypsy brewers" as they don't own their own brewing plant. The Paquettes, who call themselves "tenant brewers", make their beer at a facility south of Boston that has extra capacity. Jack D'Or, a Belgian-style saison, is particularly worth seeking, as are their historical recreations.

PROST

www.prostbrewing.com

HISTORY RADIATES FROM the gorgeous copper brewhouse at Prost Brewing, resurrected from a defunct Franconian brewery and brought to Denver's Highland neighbourhood. Bill Eye and Ashleigh Carter brew the same full-flavoured, traditional beers Brauerei Hümmer in Breitengüßbach, Germany, made for 350 years. Their Altfränkisches Dunkel Bier and Pils, among others, can be found in a growing number of locations around northern Colorado.

PYRAMID

www.pyramidbrew.com

LIKE MAGIC HAT (see p.195), Pyramid Breweries operates under the North American Breweries umbrella, brewing most of what it packages in Seattle. It also operates other brewery restaurants on the West Coast. Pyramid opened in 1984 as Hart Brewing and was an early US pioneer in wheat brewing. Its line-up still includes several wheat beers, and a seasonal wheat series, but also many styles currently in fashion, such as its 8.5% ABV Imperial IPA.

RAHR & SONS

www.rahrbrewing.com

ALTHOUGH RAHR & SONS BREWING was not able to make beer for most of 2010 after record-breaking snow caused its roof to collapse early that year, the Fort Worth brewery emerged stronger. Its Saturday tours have become a block party. "People come into our brewery and feel at home. There's a sense of ownership over the local brewery", founder Fritz Rahr said. Its lagers, like the black Ugly Pug, are well-suited for the Texas heat.

REAL ALE

www.realalebrewing.com

DESPITE ITS NAME, Real Ale Brewing does not specialize in cask-conditioned ales, although they are available for interested pubs. The brewery opened in the basement of a Hill Country antique shop in 1996, and grew into the largest Texas-owned brewery north of Shiner after building a new brewery in 2006. Fireman's #4 Blonde Ale is easiest to find, although Full Moon Pale Rye and a growing number of special offerings such as Phoenixx Double ESB and Devil's Backbone Tripel are more complex.

RED BRICK

www.redbrickbrewing.com

FIRST KNOWN AS ATLANTA BREWING, Red Brick opened in 1993 in an old Midtown red-brick printing facility, brewing with equipment from Ireland. The brewery moved to its current location in 2007 and changed its name to Red Brick Brewing in 2010. "Having two names has confused people for a long time, and now that we've expanded into six other states, there's no reason to confuse those people, too", brewery president Bob Budd said.

RED LODGE

redlodgeales.com

THE MONTANA TOWN OF RED LODGE sits at the gateway to the stunning Beartooth Highway drive that leads into Yellowstone National Park. Red Lodge Ales, including Bent Nail IPA, are sold across much of Montana and Wyoming, including at the taproom/restaurant that adjoins the brewery on the east side of town. The building has one of the largest solar thermal arrays in the state on top, with hop bines growing in the outdoor beer garden.

RED OAK

www.redoakbrewery.com

GERMAN-BORN AND TRAINED, brewmaster at Red Oak, Chris Buckley, makes beers on a German-built system and adheres rather vocally to the Reinheitsgebot, the Bavarian "beer purity law" that stipulates beer be brewed only with hops, malt, water, and yeast. The business opened as a brewpub in Greensboro, called Spring Garden, but took the name Red Oak in 2002, and now occupies a larger state-of-the-art production facility in Whitsett. Buckley does not filter or pasteurize the beers, which the brewery distributes itself.

REDHOOK

www.redhook.com

NOW PART OF THE CRAFT BEER ALLIANCE with Widmer (see p.181) and Kona (see p.193), Redhook is the oldest craft brewery in the North-west, and also operates a plant in New Hampshire. Brewing first began in Seattle in 1982, but Redhook did not begin to find a market until it introduced Ballard Bitter in 1984 and flagship ESB in 1987. After opening a new brewery in Woodinville in 1994, Redhook was briefly the fourth-largest craft beer company in the US.

REVOLUTION

www.revbrew.com

FOUNDER JOSH DETH and brewmaster Jim Cibak, both Goose Island (see p.162) alumni, had high expectations to meet when Revolution opened in Chicago's Logan Park in 2010. Their brewpub, and a production facility built nearby in 2012, produces a wide range of beers, from the assertive Anti-Hero IPA to the sessionable Workingman Mild. They picked up two medals in the 2012 World Beer Cup.

REVOLVER

www.revolverbrewing.com

NATIVE TEXAN GRANT WOOD started his brewing career at Pearl in San Antonio in 1985, but became better known as a brewer of Samuel Adams beers (see pp.174–175). "I kept asking myself if I wanted to stay (in Boston) or take a chance, create my own beer", Wood said. The beers he began making in 2012 at Revolver in North Texas certainly are his own, ranging from a traditional bock to a US wheat beer finished with blood orange zest, local honey, and spices.

RIVER HORSE

www.riverhorse.com

FOUNDED IN 1996 AND FIRST LOCATED in a lovely brick building that once housed the Original Trenton Cracker plant, River Horse Brewing moved out of Lambertville, a popular tourist town, to a bigger facility in nearby Ewing in 2013. Additional space allows the New Jersey brewery to resume making lagers, but its best-selling beers are hop-oriented (like Hop-A-Lot-Amus Double IPA) or rather strong (Hipp-O-Lantern, an 8.5% ABV pumpkin beer, and Tripel Horse, a 10% ABV Belgian-style ale).

ROCK BOTTOM

www.rockbottom.com

THE ROCK BOTTOM CHAIN of restaurant breweries is a subsidiary of CraftWorks Restaurants & Breweries, which also owns other brewery restaurants, including the Gordon Biersch and Big River Grille brands, and about 60 beer-oriented Old Chicago restaurants. Each location offers a menu of core beers, and some unique to that brewery. The Chicago Rock Bottom won Large Brewpub of the Year at the 2008 Great American Beer Festival.

SAINT ARNOLD

www.saintarnold.com

THE OLDEST AND LARGEST craft brewery in Texas, Saint Arnold retains a solid connection with the Houston community, for instance inviting fans to recycle six-packs for beer gear. Ten years after the brewery opened in 1994, founder Brock Wagner noted, "I've come to realize I may own the stock, but it's not my brewery. It belongs to everybody who drinks Saint Arnold beer." Beyond its core beers, look for its Divine Reserve and Icon Series.

SAINT SOMEWHERE

www.saintsomewherebrewing.com

BOB SYLVESTER BREWS FLORIDA farmhouse ales in Tarpon Springs, located north of Tampa. "(Saison) is less a style, more a philosophy of brewing", he said. Although Saint Somewhere, taking its name from a Jimmy Buffett song, is tiny, he ships his beers, packaged in 1.3-pint (750-ml) bottles decorated with stylish artwork originally created to promote Florida tourism, to 20 states. "I'm a traditionalist", he said, employing open fermentation – in a tank previously used to make wine – and whole hop cones.

SANDLOT

www.bluemoonbrewingcompany.com

LOCATED WITHIN COORS FIELD baseball stadium in Denver, this is both the pilot facility where Coors' Blue Moon beers are developed and a brewpub serving the ballpark, offering an interesting range of traditional styles. Only open during Rockies games, but it sells its beers at other venues. Particularly adept at styles developed in Germany, such as Move Back, a Dortmunder, and several cracker-sharp pilsners – some with amusing names, like Most Beer Judges Are Boneheads.

SANTA FE

www.santafebrewing.com

FIRST HOUSED in a horse barn in Galisteo, then a former motorcycle restoration shop, it took Santa Fe Brewing, now located in a purpose-built facility, almost 25 years to grow into New Mexico's first regional brewery. Mike Levis opened the brewery in 1988, buying Boulder Brewing's historic square brewing kettle, and many of the original beers remain, brewed to new recipes by his son and current brewer, Ty.

SCHLAFLY

www.schlafly.com

CO-FOUNDER OF SCHLAFLY, Tom Schlafly, wrote a book called *A New Religion in Mecca* about "sharing" the St Louis market with international giant Anheuser-Busch. The Saint Louis Brewery (its proper name) has done this since 1991. Schlafly brews at its taproom near downtown and at a larger facility, called Bottleworks, in suburban Maplewood. The 50 varieties that are brewed each year are all served during a September Hop in the City festival.

SHIPYARD

www.shipyard.com

SHIPYARD BREWING CO-FOUNDER and brewmaster Alan Pugsley has been nicknamed the Johnny Appleseed of brewing because he has consulted on and built 120 breweries around the world. Almost all of them, like Shipyard, use Ringwood yeast from England (a strain at least 160 years old), one he says gives the Shipyard beers their soft, easy-drinking character. Established in 1984, Shipyard briefly went into partnership with Miller Brewing, but has since bought back full control of operations.

SHMALTZ

www.shmaltzbrewing.com

JEREMY COWAN STARTED selling a single brand, HE'BREW, in 1996. That has turned into two distinct lines of beer, Shmaltz Brewing and Coney Island Craft Lagers, making beers such as Genesis Ale and Messiah Nut Brown Ale. Although Coney Island owns the licence for the world's smallest brewery, making 7 pints (4l) at a time, both the Shmaltz and Coney Island brands are brewed under contract. Shmaltz sells a special holiday pack of eight strong beers with Hanukkah candles and instructions on how to make a beer Menorah.

SHORT'S

www.shortsbrewing.com

JOE SHORT'S UNIQUE BEERS have established a wide following among those seeking unique offerings such as Key Lime Pie, Peaches & Crème, and PB&J, a blend of Über Goober (peanut butter) Oatmeal Stout, and Soft Parade fruit beer. Short's Brewing keeps 20 of its beers on tap at its Bellaire, Michigan, brewpub, while producing beer for distribution at a nearby facility. Offerings include Huma Lupa Licious IPA and Local's Light – a lager.

SIERRA BLANCA

www.sierrablancabrewery.com

SIERRA BLANCA BREWS BRANDS including Alien Ale and Stout. Located east of Albuquerque, the brewery started operations in Carrizozo, not far from Roswell, where a UFO from outer space was said to have landed in 1947. Sierra Blanca also brews under its own name, owns the Rio Grande brand, and makes Monks' Ale and Monks' Wit under contract for Christ in the Desert monastery north of Santa Fe.

SHMALTZ MESSIAH

SIXPOINT

www.sixpoint.com

FOUNDED IN BROOKLYN IN 2004, Sixpoint Brewery draws on the tradition of the six-point brewer's star, which looks like the Star of David and has been linked to brewers since the late 1300s. The brewery also uses 21st-century methods to connect to its fans, for instance, conducting an Internet poll that allowed them to choose the hop that in 2012 would be transported freshly from Washington state to be used in Sixpoint's autumn harvest, or "wet hop", beer.

SKA

www.skabrewing.com

IN 1995, FOUNDERS OF SKA BREWING, Dave Thibodeau and Bill Graham, met at 5 o'clock after work each day to begin brewing, often working until 3am. "Thank God we were as young as we were", said Thibodeau. They labelled their amateur home-brew "Ska Brewing" because they listened to Jamaican ska music when they made the beer, so that became the name of their brewery. It has grown into a regional producer, its beer names and labels still true to its ska roots.

SLY FOX

www.slyfoxbeer.com

FOUNDED IN 1994, SLY FOX BREWING operates two Pennsylvania pubs and a production brewery. Although it offers a full range of beers, Sly Fox has a reputation for its lagers, beginning with Pikeland Pils. The first Sunday of May each year it hosts the Sly Fox Bock Fest & Goat Race. Several varieties of bock are available, and the brewery taps the new maibock immediately after the goat race, naming it in honour of the winner.

SMUTTYNOSE

www.smuttynose.com

IT TOOK YEARS LONGER than anticipated, but Smuttynose, which opened in Portsmouth, New Hampshire, in 1994, has finally moved into a much-needed larger facility on a former farm in nearby Hampton, keeping their old brewery for experimental batches. Although fans admire the balance of its beers across the board, starting with Shoals Pale Ale, the brewery was one of the first to embrace "extreme beers", with each release in its Big Beer and Short Batch Series highly anticipated.

SNAKE RIVER

www.snakeriverbrewing.com

TWICE CHAMPION SMALL BREWERY at the Great American Beer Festival, Snake River Brewing sells most of what it makes in the restaurant above its basement brewery, but ships cans as far away as New York. It is a popular stop for tourists headed to national parks in summer, and skiing in the winter. It is adept at a full range of traditional styles, including excellent lagers, as well as specialities only occasionally available, like barrel-aged Le Serpent Cerise.

SOLEMN OATH

www.solemnoathbrewery.com

JOHN BARLEY – HIS REAL NAME – got a taste for Belgian beers when visiting his parents, who moved to beer-friendly Belgium when he was in college. So it should be no surprise that the brewery he and his brother, Joe, opened in the sprawling Chicago suburb of Naperville includes Belgo-US beers, made with Belgian yeast strains and citrussy-tropical US hops. Brewmaster Tim Marshall, a highly regarded veteran of the Rock Bottom chain, brews a remarkably diverse line-up.

SOUTHAMPTON PUBLICK HOUSE

www.publick.com

THE STYLISH LONG ISLAND brewery-restaurant Southampton Publick House began making beer in 1996, with brewmaster Phil Markowski introducing locals to world styles, such as saison, seldom seen in the US; Markowski left the company in 2012. Southampton, in partnership with Pabst (see p.198), has several beers brewed under contract and distributed widely by the Pabst network. Those brands, as well as others made only at the pub, remain available in Southampton.

SOUTHERN TIER

www.stbcbeer.com

"WE MAKE A LOT OF (different) beers, and that's one thing that sets us apart," said brewmaster Paul Cain. Southern Tier Brewing has been in expansion mode since it opened in Lakewood, New York, in 2002, producing unique, often strong, offerings like Imperial Crème Brûlée Stout (9.6% ABV) and Imperial Pumking (8.6% ABV). The beers are available in much of the US and exported to several markets.

SPEAKEASY

www.goodbeer.com

THE SAN FRANCISCO Speakeasy Brewery takes its name from the illegal establishments that served alcohol during Prohibition. Its top-selling beer, Big Daddy IPA, is named for David Keene, who founded Toronado, one of the US's premier beer establishments, and is nicknamed "Big Daddy". A production brewery first, Speakeasy added a taproom in 2013, complete with secret passageways and a heavy duty door with a working peephole.

SPOETZL

www.shiner.com

DRIVEN BY SALES OF SHINER BOCK, the Spoetzl Brewery in the small Texas town of Shiner has gone from being a brewery in danger of closing in 1990 to one that produces more than 596,000hl (364,000 barrels) annually, selling its beer in almost every state. Although Bock accounts for about 80 per cent of sales, the brewery continues to release new brands, both true to Shiner's Czech-German heritage, like its Bohemian Black Lager, and experiments that include its first ales ever.

SPRECHER

www.sprecherbrewery.com

RANDY SPRECHER MOVED to Milwaukee in 1980 to work for Pabst Brewing (see p.198), and after he was laid off, stuck around to open the Sprecher Brewery in 1985. Although Sprecher started a second brand, Chameleon, in 2010, to brew styles beyond the traditional ones Sprecher produces, his first recipes, for Black Bavarian and Special Amber, are the top sellers. Better known nationwide for its root beer, Sprecher began selling Hard Root Beer, containing 5% ABV, in 2013.

SQUATTERS

www.squatters.com

THE FIRST SQUATTERS brewpub opened in downtown Salt Lake City in 1989. The company now has three pubs, one of them in the airport at Salt Lake City, and brews and packages beer at the Utah Brewers Co-op (see p.205). Although there is no limit on the alcohol level of beer that may be sold in bottles in Utah, draught beer cannot be stronger than 4% ABV, putting a cap on what brewpubs can serve. Squatters proves that this rule does not have to limit flavour.

SPRECHER BLACK BAVARIAN

STARR HILL JOMO LAGER

STARR HILL

www.starrhill.com

CHARLOTTESVILLE NATIVE Mark Thompson returned to his hometown to start the Starr Hill Brewery in 1999, initially brewing his own beer only for pub sales. He moved the brewery to nearby Crozet and expanded in 2005, shutting the brewpub, broadening distribution after Anheuser-Busch (now AB-InBev) took a minority stake and committed to act as "master distributor". Starr Hill is best known for "minimalist" and traditional beers, such as Jomo Lager and Dark Starr Stout.

STEVENS POINT

www.pointbeer.com

POINT SPECIAL LAGER is brewed, as it has been since 1857, at the nation's fifth-oldest continuously operating brewery, Stevens Point. Over time, the brewery's line-up has expanded along with consumer interest, to include beers like Point Nude Beach, a summer wheat ale, and the golden Point Three Kings Ale. Point Special earned a bit of fame in 1973 when *Chicago Daily News* columnist Mike Royko anointed it the best beer in the country.

STILLWATER

stillwaterales.blogspot.com

BRIAN STRUMKE is a so-called "gypsy brewer", making his beer at breweries both in the US (primarily Maryland) and Europe (mostly Belgium). "Eventually, I'd like to have something of my own, whether it's a full production facility or a brewpub", he has said. Most Stillwater ales are made in the spirit of Belgian farmhouse ales, such as the excellent Stateside Saison, and Strumke likes that his beers have been described as "one foot in tradition, the other in outer space".

STOUDTS

www.stoudtsbeer.com

CAROL AND ED STOUDT STARTED Pennsylvania's oldest microbrewery, Stoudts, in 1987 with memories of their German honeymoon still fresh. The first beers were German-influenced, served at their German-themed restaurant. Stoudts Gold, a helles, and Pils are among the flagship beers, joined by a diverse modern line-up. Stoudts Brewing remains micro, brewing less than 18,000hl (11,000 barrels), because that suits Ed Stoudt: "Why get big? Big didn't work so good for the dinosaurs."

STRAUB

www.straubbeer.com

A FAMILY-RUN BUSINESS since it opened in 1872, the Straub Brewery in St Marys, Pennsylvania, is most famous for its "Eternal Tap", at which visitors are allowed to pour their own beer any time during main office hours. Located about 50 miles (80km) from Punxsutawney of *Groundhog Day* fame, Straub produces Groundhog Brew each year, using a recipe that has varied. Its flagship Straub Lager, however, has remained the same, made with shaved corn as well as malted barley, since 1872.

SUMMIT

www.summitbrewing.com

FOUNDER MARK STUTRUD buys Moravian barley to be malted and used in Summit Brewing's beer from a cousin; their shared grandfather was born in Norway. Although the brewery produces its share of new wave beers (an Unchained Series), the importance of such tradition is apparent everywhere in St Paul – quite obviously in the copper brewhouse from Germany, but also in classic, if not flashy, beers like Extra Pale Ale and Great Northern Porter.

SUN KING BREWING

www.sunkingbrewing.com

PUB BREWERS IN INDIANAPOLIS for ten years before they started Sun King Brewery in 2009, Dave Colt and Clay Robinson made becoming Indianapolis' brewery their first priority. Among other activities, they throw a great party about once a month at their tasting room, inviting in a local rock band to help celebrate the release of a new beer. They also turned heads in 2011 when their beers won a record eight medals at the Great American Beer Festival.

SURLY

www.surlybrewing.com

FOUNDER OF SURLY BREWING, Omar Ansari, has been called the "rock star of Minnesota's craft beer movement", although it is Todd Haug, Surly's head brewer, who creates the recipes for the bold beers that united the "Surly Nation". Fans travel to the Twin Cities from around the country for events like Darkness Day, when an imperial stout with that name is released. "We brew for people who didn't know they wanted it until they drank it", Ansari has said.

SWEETWATER

www.sweetwaterbrew.com

ALTHOUGH SWEETWATER'S flagship 420 Ale's name has marijuana connotations, co-founder Freddy Bensch says it was chosen because the beer was brewed on April 20. Sweetwater Brewing has embraced a counterculture image though, at the same time growing into the south-east's largest craft brewery.

TALLGRASS

www.tallgrassbeer.com

THE BEST-SELLING BEER from Tallgrass Brewing in Manhattan, Kansas, is an oatmeal milk stout, Buffalo Sweat. "When we first started, we tried to guess what people wanted. But now we make the beers that excite us", said Tom Mahoney, a member of the sales staff. Packaging its beer in cans, including 8-Bit Pale Ale with its blast of the tropical Galaxy hop from Australia, has also excited fans.

TERMINAL GRAVITY

www.terminalgravitybrewing.com

A PUBLIC HOUSE IN FRONT and brewery at the back, Terminal Gravity is located in Enterprise, Oregon, well off the beaten track, but its beers can be found in much of the state. When Steve Carper and Dean Duquette first opened their brewpub they leased space to a baker and built a sausage kitchen. "We're the brewer, the baker, and the sausage maker", Duquette said.

TERRAPIN

www.terrapinbeer.com

PERHAPS NO BREWER has done more than Brian "Spike" Buckowski to evangelize using malted rye in beer. When John Cochran and Buckowski started Terrapin in 2002, their first beer was Rye Pale Ale. They built their own brewery in 2008, and Buckowski has travelled the world making collaboration beers, most of them including rye, of course.

THOMAS CREEK

www.thomascreekbeer.com

BREWMASTER TOM DAVIS and his father, Bill, started Thomas Creek in Greenville, South Carolina in 1998, making contract beer as well as their own. Recently, the focus has been on the growing Thomas Creek brand, available in 15 US states and exported to Europe.

THOMAS HOOKER

www.hookerbeer.com

THE DEVELOPMENT FROM the Trout Brook Brew Pub, founded in 1997, to the Thomas Hooker Brewery, is a little hard to follow, because a new brand was forged, ownership changed, and the brewery moved from Hartford to Bloomfield in the process. Despite this, Thomas Hooker has begun to assert itself, as its label suggests, as "Connecticut's Beer". More accurately, this should be "Connecticut's Beers", since the wide range runs from its popular Blonde Ale to the quite assertive Liberator Doppelbock.

THREE FLOYDS

www.3floyds.com

DARK LORD DAY, THE ONE DAY A YEAR when Three Floyds Brewing releases an imperial stout with that name, has turned into a celebration that attracts beer fans from across the country, representing the ethos that surrounds the Hammond, Indiana, brewery. Its first beer, Alpha King, established Nick Floyd's hop-centric agenda in 1996. Those that followed, like Zombie Dust and Gumballhead, continue to build on it.

TOMMYKNOCKER

www.tommyknocker.com

IDAHO SPRINGS IS A FORMER mining town that provided the nearby Denver mint with half its gold needs in the 19th century. Cornish miners believed Tommyknockers – mythical men said to dwell in the mines – would give them good luck. Located on the town's main street (Miner), Tommyknocker Brewery also has an expansive restaurant, with some tables separated from fermentation tanks by a low railing. Its Butt Head Bock has won many Great American Beer Festival medals.

TRÖEGS BREWING

www.troegs.com

TRÖEGS IS NAMED after a family nickname. The founders, brothers Chris and John Trogner, combined their surname with the Flemish word "Kroeg," meaning "pub". They built a new brewery in Hershey, Pennsylvania, in 2011, closing their first, which had opened in 1997. Seasonals like the hoppy Nugget Nectar ale and Mad Elf holiday ale (11% ABV and infused with cherries) are immensely popular, as is a Scratch series of experimental beers.

TRUMER

www.trumer-international.com

A PARTNERSHIP BETWEEN Gambrinus (which also owns the BridgePort and Shiner breweries) and the Trumer Brauerei in Austria, the Berkeley-based Trumer Brauerei makes but one beer, Trumer Pils. Both breweries use the same recipe, and except for the water, the same ingredients. "We focus on process", said Lars Larson, the Berkeley brewmaster. They also routinely ship beer from one to the other for taste testing.

TWISTED PINE

www.twistedpinebrewing.com

ALTHOUGH GHOST FACE KILLAH is not the best-selling beer at Twisted Pine Brewing, it is the most interesting. It is made with six different peppers, including Bhut Jolokia, the Ghost Pepper, which is 200 times hotter than jalapeños. Brewers wear masks and gloves to cut up the peppers. The result is a throat-burning beer. Most drinkers will be happier sticking to the assertive and outstanding Big Shot Espresso Stout.

TWO BROTHERS

www.twobrothersbrew.com

BROTHERS JIM AND JASON EBEL developed an appreciation for traditional beers as students abroad, began home-brewing together, later ran a home-brew supply shop and then started Two Brothers in 1996. "We'd get together for family dinners and that's all we'd talk about. Eventually, our mother said, 'You either need to do this, or shut up, because you're driving me crazy!'" Jason said. They take great pride that their brewery, located west of Chicago, is family owned. Beers include the French-style Domaine DuPage.

TWO ROADS

www.tworoadsbrewing.com

BUILT IN 2012 PRIMARILY to make beer under contract for smaller Connecticut breweries, Two Roads is located in a historic Stratford industrial building dating from the 1920s. The brewery created a buzz for its own beer by hiring Phil Markowski as brewmaster. Markowski brewed at Southampton Publick House (see p.202) from 1996 until 2012, turning it into a beer destination. He is a recipient of the Brewers Association award for innovation in brewing and wrote the book *Farmhouse Ales*.

TWO BROTHERS DOMAINE DUPAGE

UINTA

www.uintabrewing.com

STARTED IN A SALT LAKE CITY garage in 1993, Uinta Brewing grew into Utah's first regional-size brewery. It has since pushed its distribution area wider, shipping cans to new markets. Some of its beers are low-alcohol products, common in Utah, and include excellent choices like Organic Baba Black Lager and Cutthroat Pale Ale. Uinta also created a Crooked Line of high-gravity beers, many aged in barrels. Wind-powered since 2001, the brewery has won multiple awards for its environmental practices.

UPLAND

www.uplandbeer.com

WHEN SOUR RESERVE from Upland won a Gold medal in the Belgian-style Lambic or Sour category at the Great American Beer Festival, fans of Caleb Staton's sour and wild beers simply nodded knowingly – they'd been chasing the small quantities available for years. Expansion at the brewery in 2012 now gives Staton space to produce such specialities as well as high-demand beers like Dragonfly India Pale Ale and Wheat Ale.

UPRIGHT

www.uprightbrewing.com

LOCATED IN THE BASEMENT of the Leftbank building in North Portland since 2009, Upright brews farmhouse-inspired ales, using open fermentation and often local ingredients. Founder Alex Ganum explains the brewery's name is a reference to Charles Mingus, the jazz double bassist whose work defied categorization. Ganum aims to do the same – his core beers simply carry numbers that give a sense of strength. Others like Flora Rustica, made with calendula and yarrow flowers, add a twist to saison.

URBAN CHESTNUT

www.urbanchestnut.com

OPENED IN 2011 in urban Midtown St Louis, Urban Chestnut produces a Reverence and Revolution series of beers that represent diversity. The former includes beers like those Bavarian native Florian Kuplent, the brewmaster, grew up with. Less traditionally, Winged Nut is a roasty weiss beer made with chestnuts, and STLIPA showcases fruity and piney hops from the north-west US.

UTAH BREWERS

www.utahbeers.com

SCHIRF BREWING, WHICH BEGAN at Wasatch Brewpub in 1986, and Squatters Pub (also known as Salt Lake City Brewing and founded in 1989) created the Utah Brewers Co-operative in 2000, a separate facility where they both make beer for distribution well beyond the pubs they still operate. Greg Schirf has a reputation for needling the powers that be in Utah, the result being beers with names like Polygamy Porter and Evolution Amber Ale. Utah also produce a range of high-alcohol beers including the Devastator (8% ABV).

VERMONT

www.vermontbrewery.com

CRAFT-BREWING PIONEER Greg Noonan, who died in 2009, opened Vermont Pub & Brewery in 1988, and his vision remains intact. It is a conversation-friendly pub with local beer, some traditional, some that pushes beer in a new direction, like Blackwatch IPA. Nearby American Flatbread houses Zero Gravity Brewery, which also makes excellent beer.

WACHUSETT

www.wachusettbrew.com

WACHUSETT WAS STARTED in 1994 by buddies who attended Worcester Polytechnic Institute. "There's just something fundamental about beer and what it represents to us", brewery president Ned LaFortune said. Wachusett Brewing grew into one of the largest in Massachusetts with accessible beers like its modestly hopped Country Pale Ale and by making beer under contract for other breweries. In 2012, LaFortune added a canning line, to package not only Wachusett brands, but also for contractees to use.

WEYERBACHER

www.weyerbacher.com

ONLY WHEN DAN WEIRBACK started making the more esoteric beers he enjoying brewing and drinking did Weyerbacher Brewing turn into a viable business. They weren't part of the plan when he opened his Easton, Pennsylvania, brewery in 1995, producing traditional English ales. But pretty soon a Belgian-inspired tripel, a barley wine called "Blithering Idiot" and a 9% ABV Double IPA made with pungent Simcoe hops became his top-selling beers, funding major expansion.

WYNKOOP

www.wynkoop.com

COLORADO'S FIRST BREWPUB, Wynkoop Brewing, was founded by John Hickenlooper, who went on to become the state's governor, and the late Russell Schehrer, a brewer memorialized for his innovation. The Denver brewpub packages some of its beers, and current brewmaster Andy Brown continues to create beers in Scheherer's spirit, such as a stout made with bull testicles. Wynkoop has hosted a national Beerdrinker of the Year competition since 1997.

YARDS

www.yardsbrewing.com

BREWMASTER TOM KEHOE, who co-founded Yards Brewing in 1994, has shepherded the company through four different locations, each with a larger brewhouse, the fourth in the Northern Liberties neighbourhood, historically a hotbed for brewing in Philadelphia. "I think we're keeping it alive… I think Philadelphians are always looking for something to be proud of", Kehoe said. He makes British-inspired beers like Philadelphia Pale Ale and Extra Special Ale.

YAZOO

www.yazoobrew.com

MISSISSIPPI NATIVE Linus Hall opened Yazoo Brewing in 2003 in Nashville and by 2010 had to find a bigger facility. Now a regional brewery, its beers can be found in most of Tennessee, Mississippi, and Northern Alabama. When hop shortages in 2008 made it difficult to get particular varieties, Hall launched Hop Project Series, changing the hop varieties used in his IPA with each batch.

YUENGLING

www.yuengling.com

THE OLDEST BREWERY in the US and also the largest US-owned one was built by DG Yuengling in 1829, rebuilt after a fire in 1831, and passed down from one generation to the next. The brewery produced 164,000hl (100,000 barrels) in 1985 when Dick Yuengling Jr bought it from his father, compared to about 3.6 million hl (2.2 million barrels) in 2012, although it can be found in only 14 states. As in Prague, where drinkers get Pilsner Urquell when they order "pilsner", in Pennsylvania "lager" means Yuengling Traditional Lager.

CANADA

Once upon a time, anyone seeking a beer in Canada could have been forgiven for thinking that its beer culture was starting to mimic the near mono beer culture that had existed in the US. For more than 50 years, two beer brands, Molson and Coors, had dominated the country's bars and refrigerators. But all that has changed and Canada is now experiencing its own craft beer revolution; drinkers are able to discover and enjoy outstanding beers produced by the nation's growing band of craft brewers. Most care passionately about the environment and pride themselves on making local beers for local people. They produce beers of great integrity that sparkle with passion and innovation. As with many beer revolutions, it was fuelled and sustained by a change in legislation. In 2006 the government cut the tax that small brewers were paying on their beer. Suddenly, breweries that had at best been able to break even, had money to invest in new equipment and marketing and were able to develop new ideas for beers.

One of the first of Canada's craft brewers was Vancouver Island, founded in 1984 by a group of people who felt that Vancouver Island ought to have a brewery of its own. Another early entrant was Amsterdam Brewing, which has been bringing passion and revelry to Toronto since 1986. They were shortly followed by Great Lakes Brewery, founded in 1987, which has gone on to establish itself as a brewer of some distinction. Unibroue was founded in 1992 and was another early Canadian pioneer, especially for its unfiltered, bottle-conditioned beers. These early trailblazers led where others have now followed and have fired a belief that beer can be interesting, fun, and unlike anything else that has been brewed before.

AMSTERDAM BREWERY

Toronto's beer scene leapt into life in 1986 when Dutch-born Roel Bramer founded the city's first brewpub. Today the brewery continues to grow and thrive with a blend of pub-friendly classics and adventurous one-offs.

THE FACTS...

OWNER Jeff Carefoote

FOUNDED 1986

ADDRESS 45 Esandar Drive Toronto, Ontario M4G 4C5

WEBSITE www.amsterdambeer.com

PHILOSOPHY We speak craft beer!

AMSTERDAM BREWERY
ALL NATURAL BLONDE

AMSTERDAM BREWERY
NUT BROWN ALE

NOWADAYS, TORONTO HAS SEVERAL BREWPUBS, but Amsterdam Brewery was the first. It started life in 1986 in a factory space that was originally home to a tyre re-treading business. Its novelty value probably attracted the crowds, but they swiftly came to recognize it for the quality of its beers. As for its name, founder Roel Bramer comes from the Netherlands, and it was only natural that he look homewards when thinking of what to call his new venture. The first beer he brewed was Natural Blonde, a crisp, refreshing, pale golden lager beer; this was followed by a range of British-style ales, wheat beers, and midnight-dark stouts and porters.

The brewery continues to mix and match its everyday beers with a selection of one-offs, such as the wine barrel-aged Belgian golden ale Goedenavond, and a powerful barley wine that is matured in a fresh whisky barrel. This mining of the rich vein of brewing lore has obviously served the brewery well as it has enjoyed constant growth. A second brewpub was opened in 1988 and then in 1993 the first brewpub – The Amsterdam Brasserie and Brewpub – became the Amsterdam Brewing Company, a business venture with a much greater focus on brewing. In 2002, Bramer sold the business to its current owner, Jeff Carefoote, who also bought Kawartha Lakes Brewing a year later. Further growth and success look likely to continue for Amsterdam Brewery.

TASTING NOTES

ALL NATURAL BLONDE PILSNER, 5% ABV

This pilsner is a refreshing pale gold in the glass with wisps of citrus lemon drifting across the nose. It has a clean, crisp character that strides across the palate.

FOOD PAIRING: Try with roast chicken or oysters on the shell.

KLB NUT BROWN ALE 5% ABV

This sleek chestnut-brown ale has soothing aromas of toffee, mocha coffee, and milk chocolate with orange citrus. A creamy mouthfeel and chocolate notes lead to a subtly sweet finish.

FOOD PAIRING: Enjoy with meatballs in tomato sauce as the sweetness matches the sauce's acidity.

(416) URBAN WHEAT WHEAT BEER, 4.16% ABV

Named after Toronto's area code, this golden-amber-coloured beer has citrus notes with subtle fruity flavours and a thirst-quenching quality; the finish is quick but with some dryness.

FOOD PAIRING: Grilled lemon sole or plaice is an ideal choice.

AMSTERDAM BREWERY (416) URBAN WHEAT

GREAT LAKES BREWERY

Toronto was a desert for craft beer back in the mid-1980s, but matters changed for the better when Great Lakes Brewery was founded in 1987. Since then both the brewery and the city's beer scene have grown up together.

TORONTO BEER WEEK is one of Canada's major beer events as the city and its outlying suburbs are home to a fair selection of breweries. Today, craft beer is king, but back in 1987, choice was not on the agenda and pale lager from big multi-national corporations ruled. The founding of Great Lakes in 1987 was the start of the change – it was the first brewery of its kind in Toronto. At first, just two beers were brewed, a lager and an ale, but by 1990 the money had run out and the brewery was closed. In 1991, Peter Bulut bought the business and Great Lakes beers started to flow once more. Throughout the 1990s and beyond the millennium, the brewery's beers were a fairly traditional selection of well-made lagers and ales, with Golden Horseshoe Premium Lager the best-seller. However, the release of Devil's Pale Ale in 2006 was a game-changer as it broke away from the brewery's regular portfolio. Marketing manager John Bowden said: "The success of Devil's Pale Ale encouraged us to brew a line of seasonal beers, including our Orange Peel Ale, Pumpkin Ale, and Winter Ale". The brewery celebrated its 25th anniversary in 2012 with a selection of special beers, including an imperial black IPA, a porter aged in wood, and a Belgian saison.

THE FACTS...

OWNER Peter Bulut
FOUNDED 1987
ADDRESS 30 Queen Elizabeth Boulevard, Etobicoke, Toronto, Ontario M8Z 1L8
WEBSITE www.greatlakesbeer.com
PHILOSOPHY Toronto's original craft brewery

GREAT LAKES BREWERY
DEVIL'S PALE ALE

GREAT LAKES BREWERY
CRAZY CANUCK

Pumpkin pioneers
Early American colonists used pumpkin mixed with malt to brew beer, a practice which has been revived by many craft brewers

GREAT LAKES BREWERY PUMPKIN ALE

TASTING NOTES

DEVIL'S PALE ALE AMERICAN PALE ALE, 6.6% ABV
Amber in colour, Great Lakes' game-changing beer has a giddy swirl of aromatic citrus fruit notes on the nose, while in the mouth the big, juicy, appetising citrussy character is kept in line by a crisp graininess. The big finish is bitter and dry.
FOOD PAIRING: A luscious burger with a generous helping of home-made coleslaw would cause fireworks on the palate.

CRAZY CANUCK AMERICAN PALE ALE, 5.2% ABV
The US West Coast provides the inspiration for this boisterously hopped pale ale, with grapefruit and orange notes on the nose, followed by juicy citrus fruits and a biscuity, bready sweetness, with a lasting bitterness in the finish.
FOOD PAIRING: Grilled fish with a creamy sauce would be a perfect foil – the bitterness would cut through the sauce, which in turn would accentuate the citrussy notes.

PUMPKIN ALE SPECIALITY BEER, 5.4% ABV
An amber-coloured ale, this autumn release is brewed with pumpkin, cinnamon, clove, nutmeg, and allspice, resulting in a warming, spicy, bittersweet flavour with a lasting dry finish.
FOOD PAIRING: Serve with roast chicken or turkey and the spicy notes will lift the sweetness and flavour of the bird.

UNIBROUE

Since it started brewing in 1992, Unibroue has grown to be one of the most notable breweries of the Quebec province, becoming famous for its Belgian brewing influences and a distinct and unique sense of branding.

THE FACTS...

OWNER Sapporo
FOUNDED 1992
ADDRESS 80 Des Carrières Street, Chambly, Quebec J3L 2H6
WEBSITE www.unibroue.com
PHILOSOPHY Belgian-style beers brewed with Quebecois style

UNIBROUE MAUDITE

UNIBROUE GRANDE RÉSERVE 17

GIVEN THE FRENCH INFLUENCE in Quebec, it is no surprise that Belgium and northern France usually influence the brewing traditions more than other beer countries. One of the biggest breweries in the province is Unibroue, which was started by André Dion and Serge Racine in 1992, whose aim was to tap into the growing craft brewery market and produce their own unique products. Bottle-conditioned beers – a rarity in this part of the world – were brewed to titanic Belgian-style strengths, and packaged with startling and colourful labels. A general sense of Gallic style and flair made the brewery stand out further. For instance, La Fin du Monde is a tripel, while Blanche de Chambly is often claimed to be North America's first abbey beer. There have been fruit beers – the Éphémère series – strong ales and lagers, and even a self-declared honey pilsner. As well as winning plenty of awards, the beers have been exported throughout the world and caught the attention of drinkers in the UK and France. Canadian brewery Sleeman invested in the company in 2004 and renamed it Sleeman Unibroue Inc. Two years later, Japanese giant Sapporo bought the whole company. Despite the fears of beer lovers, Unibroue has remained true to its roots and has continued to bewitch drinkers and win awards around the world.

TASTING NOTES

MAUDITE BELGIAN-STYLE STRONG ALE, 8% ABV
This powerful beer is red-amber in the glass with flavours of spice, caramel sweetness, and hints of orange, finishing with a warming alcoholic glow.

FOOD PAIRING: Try with a pasta dish with a tomato sauce, such as tagliatelle with bolognese ragù.

GRANDE RÉSERVE 17 BELGIAN STRONG ALE, 10% ABV
This Trappist-style beer is a chestnut colour, with aromas of vanilla, dark toasted malt, and oak. The palate has flavours of orange, spice, toasted grain, vanilla, and oak.

FOOD PAIRING: Pair with a stilton cheese. The creamy character and salty notes would be lifted and accentuated by the beer.

BLANCHE DE CHAMBLY BELGIAN-STYLE WITBIER, 5% ABV
As pale and golden as a watery sunset, this bottle-conditioned witbier has a mixed nose of spice, coriander seed, cloves, and orange peel. Soft on the palate with a subtle dusting of orange and spice notes, the finish is refreshing and clean.

FOOD PAIRING: Go Belgian with moules marinière.

French finesse
Gallic flair and panache help Unibroue's beer stand out from the crowd

UNIBROUE BLANCHE DE CHAMBLY

VANCOUVER ISLAND BREWERY

Frustrated by the lack of good beer on Vancouver Island, four beer lovers started making their own. Vancouver Island Brewery is now responsible for some of the most popular craft beers in British Columbia.

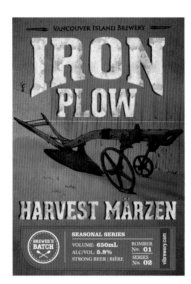

VANCOUVER ISLAND BREWERY
IRON PLOW HARVEST MÄRZEN

VANCOUVER ISLAND BREWERY began life in 1984. It was created by four local beer lovers who wanted an alternative to the big brands that ruled the bars and pubs on the island. A couple of years earlier, Molson had stopped brewing the island's favourite tipple, the locally brewed Lucky Lager, and knocked down the brewing site where it was made – this apparent act of vandalism probably helped motivate the start-up. The four founders – John Hellemond, John Young, Ray Moore, and Jim Clarke – set up their kit in the city of Victoria, on the southern tip of the eponymous island, and initially called their business Island Pacific Brewery. They started brewing one beer, Goldstream Lager, and the Garrick's Head pub in Victoria is recorded as their first customer. Along with several other microbreweries who started at this time, Island Pacific was part of an emerging movement in Canada, partly influenced by what was happening south of the border in nearby Seattle and Portland.

In 1986, local dairy farmer Barry Fisher bought a majority of shares and ten years later the brewery moved to a bigger plant. By this time it had already changed its name to Vancouver Island. The move, which increased capacity, and its re-branding were part of a plan both to give drinkers a sense of where the brewery was coming from, but also to start selling further afield in its home state of British Columbia. Vancouver Island Brewery has always had a strong emphasis on lager beers, which are all brewed according to the 1516 Bavarian Purity Law, but it also produced Piper's Ale quite early on – this pale ale was made to commemorate a local hero from World War I, James C Richardson, who was awarded the Victoria Cross. In the last few years, Vancouver Island has brewed a range of seasonal beers and also won plenty of awards. Hermann's Dark Lager leads the pack, having won over a dozen awards in both Canadian and American beer festivals. These days, the brewery tours are a popular item on the Victoria tourist trail, and the sad demise of Lucky Lager is a nothing but a distant memory.

VANCOUVER ISLAND BREWERY
HERMANNATOR ICE BOCK

TASTING NOTES

IRON PLOW HARVEST MÄRZEN OKTOBERFEST, 5.8% ABV
This German-style seasonal beer is polished copper in colour and has a shy nose of grain and caramel. In the mouth the beer is dry and bittersweet, with a bitter finish.
FOOD PAIRING: Enjoy with roast chicken that has been smothered in salt, lemon juice, and dry herbs.

HERMANNATOR ICE BOCK DOPPELBOCK, 9.5% ABV
This is a smooth charmer of a strong beer that was originally developed by brewmaster Hermann. It spends three months in maturation to emerge as a powerful strong bock with chocolate and caramel notes and a long, dry, and fiery finish.
FOOD PAIRING: Pair with grilled meat or try it at the end of the meal with a dessert such as tiramisu.

HERMANN'S DARK LAGER DUNKEL, 5.5% ABV

This creation was named after a favourite former brewmaster. Chestnut-amber in colour with a generously creamy yet spiky, toasty character to the brew, the mouthfeel is smooth and elegant, and the chocolatey notes lift the beer to noble heights.

FOOD PAIRING: The toastiness and creamy chocolate elegance of this beer would make it a natural companion to a big meaty steak pie. You could even put some of the beer in the pie as well.

STORM WATCHER LAGER, 5.3% ABV

This is a seasonal beer that provides warm and rich malty flavours that help to ward off winter weather. It pours amber into the glass from where subtle notes of honey and caramel drift upwards. There is more caramel and honey, plus toffee, and a hint of bitter lemon on the palate, and a refreshing wave of carbonation.

FOOD PAIRING: Slow-cooked beef brisket, home-made barbecue sauce, and a fresh crispy roll are the ideal accompaniment to this beer.

SPYHOPPER HONEY BROWN 5% ABV

Golden-amber in colour, this luscious beer has a dusting of honey and the suggestion of lemon on the nose, while the mouthfeel on the palate is smooth and slightly honeyed. There is also a hint of bitter lemon and the finish is pleasingly rather than overly sweet.

FOOD PAIRING: Duck breast with blackcurrant sauce seems a completely mad pairing, but the sweetness of the beer wraps itself around the berry sauce, while the beer's carbonation cuts through the rich meat.

PIPER'S PALE ALE 5% ABV

This aromatic ale is orange-amber in colour, and has a welcoming aroma of caramel with a light flurry of lemon and orange citrus in the background. In the mouth it's crisp and fruity before it finishes dry with echoes of the hop-driven fruitiness.

FOOD PAIRING: Fish and chips are the ideal pairing for Piper's Pale Ale: the beer's crispness will cut through the oiliness of the dish and bring out the sweetness of the fish.

VANCOUVER ISLAND BREWERY
HERMANN'S DARK LAGER

VANCOUVER ISLAND BREWERY
STORM WATCHER WINTER LAGER

VANCOUVER ISLAND BREWERY
SPYHOPPER HONEY BROWN

VANCOUVER ISLAND BREWERY
PIPER'S PALE ALE

DIEU DU CIEL! APHRODISIAQUE

BIG ROCK

www.bigrockbeer.com

BACK IN 1985, lawyer turned barley farmer Ed McNally so despaired of ever finding a decent beer to drink in his local area that he started up Big Rock in the western Canadian city of Calgary. He set out to produce beer using local ingredients as far as possible to create fresh, natural beer. The enterprise prospered, helped in no small measure by beer drinkers looking for something other than the pale lagers that dominated the market. Ed McNally stood down in 2012 but Big Rock classics such as Grasshopper, Traditional Ale, and Barghest Barley Wyne continue his legacy.

BRICK

www2.brickbeer.com

WHEN JIM BRICKMAN opened Brick in the city of Waterloo in 1984, it was the first microbrewery in Ontario. His research was punctilious: he travelled through nearly 30 countries and visited dozens of breweries in his quest to learn about making the perfect beer. This odyssey obviously worked, as Brick is now the fourth-largest brewery in Canada and although Brickman left in 2009, it remains noted for its varied selection of lagers and ales, plus the Laker brand of light and ice beers.

CHURCH KEY BREWING

www.churchkeybrewing.com

THE SACRED CAME UP against the profane in 2000 when John Graham began brewing in an old Methodist church on the edge of the Ontario town of Campbellford. No divine thunderbolts intervened in Graham's plans though, and since then drinkers have been blessed with an intriguing, complex roster of beers that range from barrel-aged barley wine and weizenbock to the more traditional – for craft breweries that is – double IPA.

CREEMORE SPRINGS

www.creemoresprings.com

CREEMORE SPRINGS IS LOCATED in the village of Creemore in Ontario and has been brewing since 1987. It's noted for using a direct-fired copper kettle for its boil, while the German-style beers it produces are not pasteurized. Beers such as Premium Lager, Traditional Pilsner, and urBock have been joined by Hops & Bolts India Pale Lager, a "Czech twist on an English IPA". In 2005, it was bought by Molson but happily little seems to have changed since then.

DIEU DU CIEL!

www.dieuduciel.com

DIEU DU CIEL! OPENED as a brewpub in Montreal in 1998 and quickly developed a reputation for its challenging range of beers: one included cocoa in the mix – Aphrodisiaque – another smoked malt, while their popular wheat beer contains hibiscus flowers. This exhilarating selection of beers is now brewed at both the original brewpub, which maintains its reputation as an ideal drinking and eating place, and at a larger production brewery in the town of Saint-Jérôme, 40km (25 miles) north-west of Montreal.

FERME BRASSERIE SCHOUNE

www.schoune.com

BELGIAN FARMING FAMILY the Schounes left Belgium and moved to Quebec in 1980 and set themselves up as grain farmers. A few years on, sons Patrice and Pascal realized that they had a passion for brewing and in 1997 the brewery came into operation, with the aim of making their beer with local raw materials. They famously made a gueuze in 2002, which won an award at the World Beer Montreal event. Other beers produced include La Schoune à l'Erable, which includes maple syrup, and the traditional Belgian wheat beer La Blanche de Québec.

GAHAN HOUSE

www.gahan.ca

PRINCE EDWARD ISLAND'S sole brewery, Gahan House, has been making beer since 1997 when it was called Murphy's and based in the city of Charlottetown. It changed its name in 2000 after it had moved to larger premises in the old part of the city. As well as the brewery, the Gahan House pub is the place to drink the full range of beers, which includes the nutty, earthy Iron Horse Dark Ale and the robustly bitter 1772 IPA as well as Island Red Amber Ale, Sir John A's Honey Wheat Ale, and Coles Cream Ale.

GARRISON BREWING

www.garrisonbrewing.com

FORMER NAVAL OFFICER Brian Titus started Garrison in 1997; aptly, given his background, basing it in the former garrison town of Halifax, Nova Scotia. The first beer was an Irish Red Ale, which is still brewed today and won Gold at the World Beer Championships in 2010; other beers include Tall Ship Amber Ale and an unfiltered imperial IPA. Garrison is also noted for a diverse selection of intriguing beers such as Jalapeño Ale, Spruce Beer, and Grand Baltic Porter, one of the few of its style to be brewed in Canada.

GRANITE

www.granitebreweryhalifax.ca

GRANITE BREWS IN TWO PLACES. First of all it began life in Halifax, beginning as a brewpub in 1985 and majoring in English cask beers, although not exclusively. Several years later, in 1991, a similar operation was opened in Toronto with cask beers once more part of the portfolio. Now, the Halifax operation is just a brewery, although Toronto still has its brewpub. As well as cask beers, such as the dry-hopped Best Bitter Special, Granite also produces Weissebier, Barley Wine, and Black IPA.

GRANVILLE ISLAND

www.gib.ca

THE FOUNDATION of Granville Island in 1984 is generally seen as the start of the Canadian microbrewing movement. Its first beer was the barbeque-friendly Island Lager, which still remains one of the brewery's best-sellers. In 2005, original owner Mitch Taylor sold the brewery and production was divided between its original site – which is used for small batch speciality beers such as Chocolate Imperial Stout and Fresh Hop ESB – and one in the town of Kelowna, where the regular beers are made. The brewery was sold once more in 2009, this time to Molson Coors subsidiary Creemore Springs (see facing page).

HART & THISTLE

www.hartandthistle.com

THE HART & THISTLE is a self-proclaimed gastropub down on the waterfront in Halifax, but it also happens to have its own microbrewery, from which there are usually two beers available (alongside other craft beers). Greg Nash is the brewer there, and if the likes of his Commissar Russian Imperial Stout, 37 Hr Simcoe SMaSH, and Hopalyptic Doom Double IPA are any guide, then drinkers should prepare to have their tastebuds seriously tingled.

HOPFENSTARK

www.hopfenstark.com

FRED CORMIER IS THE BREWER and founder of Hopfenstark, a man who has no place for the word "ordinary" in his brewing vocabulary. If you want a Baltic porter aged in a bourbon barrel, a Berliner weisse, or several styles of saison, then he is your go-to man. He also produces cask-conditioned beer. Cormier founded Hopfenstark in 2006 and the beers are sent out to be sold in local establishments as well as being available at his own bar, where they are brewed.

LE CHEVAL BLANC

wordp.lechevalblanc.ca/wp

MONTREAL'S FIRST BREWPUB appeared in 1986, three years after Jérôme Catelli-Denys took over the Cheval Blanc tavern when it was left to him by his uncle Angelo. The business had been in his family since 1945. Alongside Belgian-style beers such as a wheat beer with cranberries and raspberries, Denys also oversees a well-hopped American pale ale plus a pilsner with New Zealand hops instead of the usual Saaz. Uniquely, especially for Quebec, it also serves cask ale in the traditional manner beloved of English pubs. Nine cask ales are now available at all times.

LES TROIS MOUSQUETAIRES

www.lestroismousquetaires.ca

BROSSARD IS A SUBURB of Montreal and it was here in 2004 that Les Trois Mousquetaires – the three musketeers, a trio of workers who were made redundant when their factory closed – decided to make their mark on the world of Quebec brewing. As well as looking to Belgian brewing traditions for inspiration, this small but dedicated outfit is also influenced by German beer styles, which is why such beers as Impériale Weizen Grande Cuvée and Doppelbock Grande Cuvée Printemps wow beer lovers.

GARRISON BREWING TALL SHIP AMBER ALE

LE TROU DU DIABLE

www.troududiable.com

THE NAME OF THIS forward-thinking brewpub comes from the Devil's Hole, an apparently endless drop to hell, on the river that flows through the Quebec city of Saint-Maurice – home to the brewery since 2005. Freedom of expression runs rife in the beers brewed. Some might be influenced by Germanic lagering with a twist, while others are Belgian-influenced free-styles such as the extra-strong abbey ale La Buteuse or a collaboration with Brussels-based De La Senne (see p.87), Schieve Tabarnak. US mash-ups also get a look-in: an IPA aged with Brettanomyces in wine barrels makes a bold statement.

MAGNOTTA

www.magnotta.com/Brewery

GABE MAGNOTTA SET UP A WINERY in 1990 in the Ontario city of Vaughan. Then, six years later, along came the brewery, with a focus on high-quality, adjunct-free beers that were sold under the name of True North. Blonde Lager was a best-seller, but other beers in the range include an alt, an IPA, and a boisterous strong ale. Sadly, Magnotta passed away in 2010 at the early age of 59 but the brewery – as well as the winery – remains independent.

MCAUSLAN

www.mcauslan.com

HOME-BREWING HAS a lot to answer for, fortunately a lot of it being good beer. Take home-brewer Peter McAuslan who, in 1989, started his own brewery in Montreal. The microbrewing boom was well under way and the brewery's debut beer St-Ambroise Pale Ale was a success. Further triumph came when beer writer Michael Jackson declared it to be the best beer in Quebec. Other beers of note include Oatmeal Stout and the seasonal Vintage Ale. In April 2013, Peter McAuslan retired and the brewery was sold to Les Brasseurs RJ.

MICROBRASSERIE CHARLEVOIX

www.microbrasserie.com

QUEBEC HAS A VIBRANT craft-brewing scene and Charlevoix is regarded as one of the most inventive and consistently expressive of this community. It brews an eclectic selection of Belgian-inspired beers including the Dominus

LE TROU DU DIABLE LA BUTEUSE

Vobiscum range, plus specialities such as Imperial Milk Stout, part of the Vache Folle line. Founded in 1998, it was originally based at Restaurant Le Saint-Pub MicroBrasserie, but in 2009 it opened a stand-alone brewery, keeping the pub's brewkit for producing one-offs to be sold to eager customers.

MOOSEHEAD

www.moosehead.ca

TIME IS AN IMPORTANT INGREDIENT in brewing, but for the oldest independent Canadian brewery, time is also about survival. The brewery's roots go back to 1867, two years after the Oland family moved to Nova Scotia from England. The matriarch of the family, Susannah, opened up a brewery and, despite two fires and the brewery's destruction in 1917's Halifax explosion, Olands are still in charge at the site in the New Brunswick city of St John. Moosehead's beers are on the pale lager side, and they also contract-brew for Samuel Adams (see pp.174–175), among others.

NIAGARA'S BEST

www.davebush.com/NiagarasBestBeer/index.htm

SOME PEOPLE ENJOY themselves by going over Niagara Falls in a barrel, but the majority of visitors to one of North America's greatest tourist sites would rather plump for a beer from Niagara's Best, founded in 2005. Beers made include the best-selling Blonde Premium Ale, Drummond Hill Dark Ale, and the witbier Cascada Premium White Ale, though beer geeks are more likely to go for the monthly brewer's special, which can include anything from an IPA to a raspberry wheat.

PUMP HOUSE

www.pumphousebrewery.ca

DURING THE 1980S, home-brewer Shaun Fraser's dream was to brew professionally. He briefly worked at a brewery in the 1980s, but it wasn't until the end of 1999 that he and wife Lilia opened up their brewpub the Pump House. Its name came from his job as a local fire chief in the New Brunswick town of Moncton. The business has thrived. Crowd-pleasers like Blueberry Ale, Cadian Cream Ale, and the fruity Fire Chief's Red Ale sit alongside monthly seasonals including an Oktoberfest, Baltic porter and English-style brown ale made with star anise.

SLEEMAN

www.sleeman.ca

PIRACY AND PROHIBITION feature highly in the history of this famous Ontario brewery. John H Sleeman, descended from a family of Cornish pirates, began brewing in 1834, then 99 years later the brewery was closed due to its links with bootlegging. In 1988, John W Sleeman brought the brewery back to life, and it was bought by Sapporo (see p.245) in 2006. Alongside its own brands, such as Honey Brown Lager and Silver Creek Lager, Sleeman contract-brews US beers for the Canadian market including Pabst Blue Ribbon.

SPINNAKERS

www.spinnakers.com

THE LONGEST-SURVIVING BREWPUB in Canada, Spinnakers was founded by Paul Hadfield in 1984 with the help of microbrewing pioneer John Mitchell, after whom one of the brewery's most popular beers, Mitchell's ESB, is named. The brewery produces a range of US- (Seattle is not that far to the south) and UK-influenced beers, several of which are cask-conditioned. Located in downtown Victoria on Vancouver Island, it is part of a highly regarded bar and restaurant, where beer-and-food pairing is common.

STEAMWORKS

www.steamworks.com

THE HISTORIC GASTOWN AREA of Vancouver has been home to Steamworks since 1995 when Eli Gershkovitch set it up as a brewpub, using a steam heating system to brew. The brewery's portfolio features a range of influences including a Czech pilsner, saison, pale ale, and a rich coffee stout that has 1,200 double shots from a La Marzocco espresso machine added to the beer as it is conditioning.

STORM

www.stormbrewing.ca

NEWFOUNDLAND BREWERY STORM started life in 1997 when Michael McBride bought the brewing kit of a defunct local brewery called Freshwater. He set it up in Mount Pearl and proceeded to brew a compact collection of beers that now includes Raspberry Wheat, Coffee Porter, and Island Gold. As well as being known for the quality of its beers, McBride has attracted a lot of plaudits for turning Storm into a zero emissions brewery.

WELLINGTON SPECIAL PALE ALE

WOLF BREWING RANNOCH

WELLINGTON

www.wellingtonbrewery.ca

AS THE NAME MIGHT SUGGEST, the Duke of Wellington was the influence behind the name of this Guelph-based microbrewery, which was opened by Philip Gosling in 1985. The brewery was a pioneer in producing cask-conditioned beers such as Arkell Best Bitter, which is still brewed. Gosling has gone and the brewery is now run by Doug Dawkins – who has been there from the beginning – and Brent Davies. As well as its ales, including Special Pale Ale, Wellington produces an Imperial Stout, a seasonal winter warmer and a Vienna-style lager.

WOLF BREWING

www.wolfbrewingcompany.com

WOLF BEGAN LIFE IN 2000 as Fat Cat in the town of Nanaimo on Vancouver Island and gathered a fan club for its idiosyncratic beers, which were accompanied by colourful labels. In 2010, the brewery was sold to its current owners and renamed Wolf. The brewery makes a series of beers that tries to reflect both US West Coast and English ale styles, with Rannoch Scotch Ale and Black Tail Porter among the best-sellers.

YELLOWBELLY

www.yellowbellybrewery.com

SITUATED IN A HISTORIC 19th-century building in St John's, Newfoundland, the brewpub Yellowbelly started making beer in 2008. The brewmaster is Liam McKenna, who once worked for the Dublin Brewing Company; the beer he made then was so highly thought of that a certain large Dublin brewery went around paying publicans not to stock it for fear of it hitting their sales. Now he makes four regular beers, including the rich and roasty St John's Stout and a complex Irish Red called Fighting Irish Red Ale.

YUKON

www.yukonbeer.com

YUKON WAS FOUNDED BY long-time friends Bob Baxter and Alan Hansen in 1997. Then it was known as Chilkoot, becoming Cheechako before settling for Yukon in 1999. Despite its isolation in the far north of Canada, the beer has won awards and is sold in several Canadian regions. How about the creamy and dark Lead Dog Ale or its roasty, hoppy black IPA, A.D.D. Series 005 Cascadian, for starters?

MEXICO, CENTRAL, & SOUTH AMERICA

Mexico, Central, and South America are like many of the world's emerging beer markets: a battleground for some of the world's biggest brewers. Many of the local beers are derived from Germanic traditions of pale light lagers, with some dark strong beer styles. However, there are signs that an artisanal brewing culture is picking up some pace. In Brazil, brewers like Juliano Mendes, founder of Eisenbahn (see p.218), are keen to show that there is an alternative to mass-market beers. In fact, in the brewery's home city of Blumenau there are a number of other microbrewers and the city holds its own annual Oktoberfest.

Mexico is in the front line of takeover battles of national beer brands by international companies. Moctezuma (see p.224) is now owned by Heineken, and produces a highly drinkable Vienna-style porter. Countries such as Chile and Argentina might be better known for their wine than their beer, but here too there are some up and coming craft beer producers to be found – several have now opened in Argentina, such as Antares and Barba Roja (see pp.228–229). In Chile, a native Californian is leading the charge for new beer tastes at the Szot brewery (see p.230). His award-winning beers draw on US brewing traditions rather than German. In neighbouring Uruguay, Colombia, Bolivia, Peru, and El Salvador – indeed across the region as a whole – there are signs of craft beer appreciation developing.

Many Caribbean countries have a strong beer-drinking culture, although many of the beers produced are sweetish pale brews, such as those found in Trinidad and Tobago, Cuba, and Costa Rica. However, Jamaica is home to a beer well worth seeking out: Desnoes and Geddes' Dragon Stout is a powerful beer packed full of malt and molasses flavours (see p.231).

BIERLAND
STRONG GOLDEN ALE

 BIERLAND

Blumenau is perhaps one of the most Germanic cities in Brazil and it's entirely appropriate that it celebrates beer and its traditions with lederhosen-slapping gusto – since its founding in 2003, Bierland has celebrated this tradition.

HOME FOR BIERLAND is the southern city of Blumenau in Brazil, which is resolutely Germanic in its origins, having been founded by German immigrants to the country in the 19th century. It has held on to its beery identity with some skill – the city's Oktoberfest is the second-largest in the world after Munich's. In other ways, the beeriness has been watered down – at one stage it was home to dozens of small traditional microbreweries, though they eventually wilted before the onslaught of the large corporate breweries. In 2003, Bierland took up arms against this sea of troubles and set up its brewery in a neighbourhood with a large population of German descent. Its first steps were careful and predictable with the production of a brace of beers, the Pilsner and the Amber. Two years later, the careful steps were becoming confident strides as the Bock and the Weizenbock appeared. To make things even better that year, Bierland's beers were also available to be swigged to the strains of "Ein Prosit" at the Oktoberfest. The years since then have been ones

of constant growth, more equipment – especially for lagering – a tasting bar and, of course, further beers.

However, one of these newcomers might not have been so familiar to the Germans who founded the city – it is the Imperial Stout, whose worth and value have been recognized by a slew of awards, including a Gold medal at the prestigious European Beer Star in 2012. Just to demonstrate that the brewery hadn't lost touch with its heritage, though, Bierland's Bock won a Silver medal in its category in the same competition. As the song might have said: beer's coming home.

German gem
With Weizen, Bierland offers beer lovers a taste of Bavaria

TASTING NOTES

STRONG GOLDEN ALE BELGIAN-STYLE ALE, 9% ABV
This strong beer comes in a beautiful broad-shouldered, flat-bottomed 1.3 pint (750ml) bottle. Golden in colour, it has a full, spritzy nose, while the palate has a moussec-like richness, plus malt sweetness, some pear and a long, spirituous finish. It's bottle-conditioned and will improve with age.

FOOD PAIRING: Cheese is the most pleasing partner with this beer as the spritzy bubbles can cope with a pungent, salty blue cheese such as gorgonzola.

IMPERIAL STOUT 8% ABV
The German founding fathers of the city probably never set eyes on this rich brooding treat: chocolate and bonfire on the nose, and a luscious, creamy, chocolatey, mocha character kept in line with a gentle bitterness in the finish.

FOOD PAIRING: This is definitely a dessert beer because of the chocolate and sweet notes, so how about a couple of scoops of vanilla ice cream?

WEIZEN BAVARIAN HEFEWEISS, 4.7% ABV
Bierland's take on the classic Bavarian weissbier is orange-yellow in the glass, sitting beneath a fluffy head of meringue-white foam. The beer has a sparkling, slightly fruity, lightly spicy character with a quicksilver yet refreshing finish.

FOOD PAIRING: Make believe it's Bavaria and it's mid-morning: the classic second breakfast of weisswurst sausage and pretzels will make a perfect match.

BIERLAND
IMPERIAL STOUT

BIERLAND
WEIZEN

EISENBAHN

The desire to drink beer better than what was then available in Brazil was Juliano Mendes' motivation for opening Eisenbahn. The brewery has won many awards with its eclectic take on both German-style and world beers.

THE FACTS...

OWNER Brasil Kirin

FOUNDED 2002

ADDRESS Rua Bahia 5181, Salto Weissbach, Blumenau (Santa Catarina) 89032-001

WEBSITE www.eisenbahn.com.br

PHILOSOPHY Exemplary brewing based on the German style

IN THE WORLD OF BREWING the word "passion" is bandied about so much that it is almost in danger of becoming meaningless. But there are times you can judge passion by someone's actions rather than what a brewery's PR department writes. Such is the case with Juliano Mendes, who became totally dissatisfied with the choice of beers in Brazil and decided to do something about it. Based in the German-Brazil heartland of Blumenau, which has a rich beery heritage, Mendes' passion for beer and flavour came to fruition with the founding of Eisenbahn in 2002 – it was apparently named after an old railway that used to be near the brewery. As if to further underline the seriousness of the project, a German brewmaster was employed and given the job of cooking up a series of *Reinheitsgebot*-friendly beers. These included Pilsen, light in bitterness as the Brazilian palate likes it, Dunkel – though the brewery's description suggests that it is more of a Thuringian schwarzebier – and, as if to test the waters for other beers, a Belgian-style pale ale. The passion has worked and Eisenbahn has gone on to become one of the best known of the Brazilian microbreweries. Even being bought by Grupo Schincariol, now Brasil Kirin (2012), in 2008 has not stopped it displaying its craft beer credentials – its beers have attracted plenty of awards, though it was its Dunkel that began the avalanche in 2007 when it won the Bronze in its category at the European Star Awards; Weizenbock won a Bronze in its category at the same event. The brewery's current portfolio is one of German specialities plus several Belgian creations including the champagne beer of Lust, a unique creation for South America.

EISENBAHN DUNKEL

EISENBAHN PALE ALE

EISENBAHN PILSEN

TASTING NOTES

DUNKEL DARK LAGER, 4.8% ABV

Coffee and chocolate run riot on the nose and palate of this ruddy-chestnut-coloured beer. There's a crisp dryness, a medium body feel, and hints of toasted grain before a mild bitterness leads the way to a dry and appetizing finish.

FOOD PAIRING: The national dish of Brazil is the strong tasting meat stew feijoada – the Dunkel's crispness cuts through the sauce, while the chocolate and coffee notes embrace the richness of the meat and sauce.

PALE ALE 4.8% ABV

This orangey-yellow beer pours with a bubbly white head and has a sprinkle of hop aromatics on the nose with some malt sweetness. The palate is bittersweet, citrussy, and dry and bitter in the finish.

FOOD PAIRING: Roast lamb is a match for this beer as the meat's sweet and juicy notes are lifted by the beer.

PILSEN LAGER, 4.8% ABV

The most popular of Eisenbahn's beers worldwide, Pilsen is light golden in colour, with a large, foaming white head. It has a sweet grassy aroma and a refreshing, light, hoppy flavour with a dry finish.

FOOD PAIRING: Its crisp, refreshing finish means that it cuts well through rich, greasy foods, such as barbecued ribs or sausages, but it also partners well with delicate flavours such as seafood – try with prawns or other shellfish.

WAY BEER

Since its launch in 2010, Way has been winning friends and tantalizing beer drinkers with its explosively flavoured US-inspired craft beers. Its Amazonian wood-aged lager has a definite Brazilian edge.

TRAVEL BROADENS THE MIND and brings the traveller into contact with new cultures, different peoples, and a whole new way of life. Sometimes travel can take place without leaving home, especially when it relates to beer. Take Way Beer, for instance. Alessandro Oliveira and Alejandro Winocur founded the brewery towards the end of 2010 with a launch at the Brazilian Beer Festival in Blumenau. Their labels' bright abrasive colours and their beers' outstanding flavours caused an immediate stir. Critical success followed soon after, when in April 2011, American Pale Ale was voted Best Pale Ale at Maxim Beer Awards, Brasileiras. This was beer travel in the sense that Oliveira and Winocur brought the craft beer culture of North America to this part of southern Brazil, with styles such as Irish Red Ale, Double American Pale Ale, and Cream Porter as part of their repertoire; Belgium is also represented with Roller Coaster Dark Belgian

IPA. Way is based in the Pinhais municipality of Curitiba in the southern Brazilian state of Paraná and is a busy, modern concern. They brew five different beers, placing their emphasis on innovation and the creation of exemplary flavour. The brewery has organized its own Oktoberfest, while beer- and food-matching occasions are also regularly organized. As if to demonstrate that there is no standing still, the brewery also launched one of their most ambitious beers with Amburana Lager. Mindful of the ageing of beer in wood projects going on in the US and in other parts of the craft-brewing world, they produced a strong Doppelbock and then placed it to mature in amburana wood, which is native to Brazil – this complex, smooth, creamy, and sweet beer has been a great success. Way Beer helps to show that although travel may be good for the soul, sometimes the best ideas can be found on your doorstep.

THE FACTS...

OWNERS Alessandro Oliveira, Alejandro Winocur

FOUNDED 2010

ADDRESS Rua Pérola 331, Pinhais, Curitiba, Paraná, 83325-200

WEBSITE www.waybeer.com.br

PHILOSOPHY To produce bold vibrant beers influenced by the US craft-brewing revolution

Local flavour
Who needs oak to wood age beers when the locally grown amburana can be used?

TASTING NOTES

AMERICAN PALE ALE 5.2% ABV

The American hops Cascade, Citra, and Amarillo lead the aromatic charge for this gold-orange pale ale with hints of sweet caramel malt in the background. Appetizingly bitter, it is citrussy, honeyed, and lightly caramelized on the palate with a bittersweet finish.

FOOD PAIRING: Grilled steak and caramelized onions slapped between two slices of sourdough bread would be the perfect match for this ale.

CREAM PORTER 5.6% ABV

A creamy, luscious porter, this beer has mocha coffee notes on the nose; the palate has milky coffee, rich chocolate, some roastiness, and malt sweetness before it finishes bittersweet and lingering.

FOOD PAIRING: The beer has a creamy, sweetish texture and enough alcohol to both complement and stand up to a rich bread and butter pudding.

AMBURANA LAGER DOPPELBOCK, 8.4% ABV

This strong lager has up to three months' maturation in amburana wood. Dark chestnut in colour, the nose offers up notes of woody spice, some honey, and a hint of vanilla. In the mouth there's a vanilla smoothness, more light woodiness, some toasty notes, malt-derived sweetness, and a creamy texture; the finish is light and sweet with woody hints.

FOOD PAIRING: Try with rich, meaty dishes such as roast duck with cherry sauce, as the complexity of the beer plus its malt-sweet notes will add extra flavour to the dish.

WAY BEER
AMERICAN PALE ALE

WAY BEER
CREAM PORTER

WAY BEER
AMBURANA LAGER

ALTHOUGH **BRAZILIAN CRAFT BREWERS** ARE HUGELY OUTNUMBERED BY MASS-MARKET BRANDS, A VARIETY OF STYLES IS BEING PRODUCED

A BRAZILIAN STREET CAFÉ – SUCH AS THIS ONE IN BOTAFOGO, RIO DE JANEIRO – IS THE PERFECT PLACE TO RELAX WITH DINNER AND A BEER AT THE END OF A LONG DAY

2CABEÇAS

www.facebook.com/2cabecas.cervejas

TWO HEADS ARE BETTER than one in the case of 2Cabeças – which translates as "Two Heads" – a Rio-based brewing concern that was set up by home-brewers Bernardo Couto and Salo Maldonado towards the end of 2011. The duo don't have their own brewery but instead make their beers at Cervejaria Allegra in Rio de Janeiro. Not for them the lagered beers of the south, but instead they have chosen to make Brazilian versions of US craft styles, including Hi-5 Black IPA, the American pale ale Sunset, and Maracujipa, an IPA that has passion fruit added instead of dry hops.

ABADESSA

www.abade.com.br

WHILE MANY CRAFT BREWERS have turned their backs on the German beer purity law *Reinheitsgebot* (see p.52), Abadessa's brewmaster and founder Herbert Schumacher positively revels in brewing his beers within its boundaries. Based in the southernmost state of Brazil, Schumacher began work in 2005 with a range of German-influenced beers including a pils, helles, dunkel, rauchbier, and festbier. In 2009, the brewery was accepted as a member of the prestigious Berlin-based Society for the History of Brewing.

ANNER

www.cervejaanner.com

ANNER WAS SET UP IN 2007 in a suburb of Porto Alegre, the capital city of the state of Rio Grande do Sul. It has four regular beers along with some occasional seasonal releases, all of which are influenced by US and European brewing practices. Libertadora is a self-styled Imperial Red Ale that has dried fruit and spices on the nose and palate alongside the hops, while Maria Degolada, which translates as "Mary Slain" after a local story about a young woman's fate at the hands of an unwelcome suitor, is a very strong take on a Belgian tripel with lots of rich flavours.

BADEN BADEN

www.badenbaden.com.br

WHEN BADEN BADEN WAS BOUGHT by what is now the Brazilian subsidiary of Kirin (see p.243) in 2007, the fact that concern was expressed about the microbrewery's future direction showed how well-regarded it had become since being founded in 2001. The concern was misplaced – Baden Baden remains in its hometown of Campos do Jordão in São Paulo state and beers such as the rich and smoky Stout, the robust and fruity Red Ale Especial, and eminently drinkable ESB-style 1999 still pack a powerful, flavoursome punch.

BALDHEAD CRAFT BEERS

www.cervejabaldhead.blogspot.co.uk

BALDHEAD CRAFT BEERS is yet another brewery start-up in the south of Brazil in the city of Porto Alegre. The enterprise began in 2010, several years after Filipo Severo and Giuliano Vacaro took an inspirational trip to London, where they discovered the complexities of English ale. They also visited Belgium and Munich's Oktoberfest, which encouraged them to adopt the *Reinheitsgebot* when they started brewing. It's entirely appropriate that their three beers span the beery culture of their European jaunt: an English bitter, a German kölsch, and a Belgian dark ale. The name of the brewery was inspired by the bald founder of the brewery, Giuliano Vacaro, and the logo, a bald monk, reflects the fact that many beers were originally made within a monastic setting.

BAMBERG

www.cervejariabamberg.com.br

WITHIN THE TIME FRAME of Brazilian craft beer, Bamberg is a comparative veteran, having started brewing in a São Paulo suburb in 2005. Bamberg Brewery was set up by brothers Alexander, James, and Luke Bazzo. As the name of the brewery suggests, German beer is a big influence, in particular the smoked beers of the Franconian city of Bamberg, which the brewery pays homage to with a smoky, dry rauchbier. Other styles include a pils, helles, bock, and weizenbock, though they have also tinkered with wood-ageing barley wines.

BAR INVICTA

www.cervejariainvicta.com.br

THE CITY OF RIBEIRÃO PRETO is fast becoming a city known for its beer, with Bar Invicta run by Rodrigo Silveira joining both Colorado and Lund in selling craft beers to the local citizens.

COLORADO DEMOISELLE

Set up in 2011, the brewery, as the name might suggest, is a brewpub, a popular beer bar that sells Invicta's beers alongside other Brazilian and imported brews. Beers brewed include the ubiquitous German-influenced Pilsener and Weiss, but more intriguingly an India black ale, an imperial India pale ale, a porter, and an imperial stout. Lovers of good beer are invited to visit the brewery and try the beers on site.

BARLEY

www.barley.com.br

BARLEY STARTED OFF as a home-brewing hobby in 1992, but ten years later the beer was being sold commercially around its home area of Capela de Santana in the Rio Grande do Sul region of Brazil. Appropriately enough for a region in which a lot of German immigrants settled, Barley's beers are resolutely *Reinheitsgebot*, including its regular pilsner, Vienna, and weiss beer, plus a seasonal bock only served on draft. In 2010, the brewery opened a cosy wooden cabin where its beers could be studied.

BODEBROWN

www.bodebrown.com.br

IT WAS 2009 when Samuel Cavalcanti founded his microbrewery in the city of Curitiba in the southern state of Paraná. In an area where the beer tradition is predominantly influenced by German traditions, he went totally against the grain and looked to the US craft beer sector for his motivation. Hence a selection of beers with bright and outlandish labels such as Dangerous Imperial IPA, an intensely hoppy, fruity ale, and Black Rye IPA, a strong (7% ABV) American black ale with roasted flavours and a crisp mouthfeel. The brewery's Classic Scotch Ale, Wee Heavy, won a gold medal at the Mondial de la Bière in 2011. The brewery also runs courses for home-brewers and has a small library of brewing titles.

COLORADO

www.cervejariacolorado.com.br

MARCELO CARNEIRO DA ROCHA must have been a lonely man when he opened his brewery, Colorado, in 1995, as the city of Ribeirão Preto was already home to one of the behemoths of Brazilian brewing, Antarctica (as it was known before it merged with Brahma to form AmBev). Nevertheless he has persevered, and Colorado is now one of the shining lights of

microbrewing in Brazil. Not content with mimicking US craft beer, Colorado has its own Brazilian-flavour take on beer with a pilsner featuring cassava, a weiss with local honey and Demoiselle, a rich porter using coffee beans from the Upper Mogiana region. His distinctive, colourful labels truly make his beers stand out from the crowd.

CORUJA

www.cervejacoruja.com.br

CORUJA, WHICH TRANSLATES AS "OWL", began its brewing career in 2004, and it is another brewery without a brewery. Until 2010, its beers were contract-brewed by Gol Beer Bebidas in the Rio Grande do Sul region. Since then the beers have been moved next door into the Santa Catarina region and brewed by Saintbier. European, especially German, influences are strong and the ranges includes a weizen, weizenbock and, rather uniquely, a self-styled landbier.

FALKE BIER

www.falkebier.com.br

IN 2004 MARCO FALCONE quit his job as an engineer and set up Falke Bier in his family home just outside the city of Belo Horizonte in the state of Minas Gerais. He had been a home-brewer in the 1980s but then lapsed until a trip to Germany revived his beery passion. Falcone has a real sense of dedication to the beers he makes, which include an IPA, pilsner, a weiss, and a tripel – he uses a coffee roaster to kiln his own malt for his schwarzbier while playing classical and jazz music for the benefit of the yeast as his beers mature.

KRUG BIER

www.krug.com.br

KRUG BIER IS A BREWERY with a strong history and connection with Austrian brewing. It was set up in Belo Horizonte in 1997 by Theo and Hervig Gangl, who can claim kinship with a family that has been brewing in Austria for several centuries (there is also talk of a link with Warsteiner). Naturally, with such ties, the *Reinheitsgebot* rules the roost when it comes to brewing beers such as the bottled Austria Pilsen and Austria Weiss, as well as the draft offerings, which are served in the bar and restaurant attached to the brewery. The brewery has been a huge success and had to relocate to a larger site in 2004.

LAGOM BREWERY & PUB

www.lagom.com.br

2010 SAW THE START of the lively Lagom brewpub in Porto Alegre, which was put together by a band of home-brewers who wanted to sell their own beers as well as those brewed by others in the Rio Grande do Sul region. The freedom that home-brewers revel in is very much evident in the beers that the brewery produces, and at any one time visitors to the brewpub might find eight taps of Lagom's beer, including a smoked porter, an IPA – sometimes with a single hop – a weizenbock, an oatmeal stout or even a very strong barley wine. These are served alongside appropriately named dishes including "Meatballs from Hell". The business has been a great success and opened a second pub in 2012.

NACIONAL

www.cervejarianacional.com.br

SÃO PAULO'S ONLY BREWPUB, Nacional, is a lively spot that opened up in 2011 in a former factory and produces over 5,000 litres (42 barrels) of quality beer every month. More than 25 beers are brewed on one floor and then drunk on the one above – there's also a restaurant where ice cream that is made with the brewery's pilsner is served. The brewing team makes great play of the fact that beers such as Mula IPA and Kurupira Ale are free of preservatives and not served ice cold, as is the tradition in the majority of Brazilian bars.

SEASONS CRAFT BREWERY

www.cervejariaseasons.com.br

ANOTHER REASON TO MOVE to Porto Alegre – the Seasons microbrewery started brewing in 2011 with the avowed aim of spreading the message of "good beer" throughout the region and beyond. A US-style IPA, a Belgian blond, and a luscious coffee stout are among some of the regulars, with seasonal offerings including a harvest beer made with fresh hops and a Russian imperial stout that is fermented for 22 days and then matured for 11 months. At 10% ABV this is a beer not to be taken lightly! The brewery also runs various initiatives to involve the community in the craft beer revolution in Brazil, partnering with other breweries to spread the word.

CUAUHTÉMOC MOCTEZUMA

Dos Equis and Sol are just two of the popular beer brands produced by Cuauhtémoc Moctezuma. One of the largest breweries in Mexico, its best known brands are recognized around the world.

THE FACTS...

OWNER Heineken

FOUNDED 1890

ADDRESS Boulevard Ferrocarriles 247, Industrial Vallejo, Azcapotzalco, 02300 Mexico City, Federal District

WEBSITE www.cuamoc.com

PHILOSOPHY Even though the brewery is one of the largest in Mexico, it has a passion for quality

THE BUSINESSMEN who formed the Cuauhtémoc Moctezuma Brewery in 1890 (when it was just called Cuauhtémoc) could not have predicted how large their business would eventually grow. The brewery was founded in the city of Monterrey. Its debut beer was Carta Blanca, which very soon won brewing awards in Paris and Chicago. In fact, its win in Chicago was the first time a Mexican brewery had ever won a brewing award.

The history of Cuauhtémoc Moctezuma has been one of constant expansion, with various companies set up along the way to supply some of the essential elements of beer-making, such as packaging, glass, and malting barley. Its beers are currently brewed at six plants and its range includes a selection of pale and dark lagers, while its Bohemia brand has seen a chocolate stout and weizen variant. History has not always been kind to the brewery. In 1914, during the Mexican revolution, supporters of the president, Venustiano Carranza, briefly took over the brewery because the owners at the time supported his rival. The owners fled to Texas but later were able to take back control of their business with help from US and Russian diplomats. In 2012 the brewery was taken over by international giant Heineken.

TASTING NOTES

DOS EQUIS XX AMBAR 4.7% ABV
A Mexican take on a Vienna-style beer, it is red to the eye, has a soft caress of hops, and a palpable malt presence. An export success, it is proving popular north of the border in the US.

FOOD PAIRING: Serve well chilled and pair with a fiery chilli or honey-glazed ribs hot off the barbecue.

BOHEMIA CLÁSICA PALE LAGER, 5.3% ABV
Bohemia pours yellow-gold in colour, while the nose has an understated note of malt-derived sweetness. In the mouth, it is medium-bodied, crisp in character, with an undercurrent of sweetness and a slight bitterness.

FOOD PAIRING: The beer's crispness and hints of sweetness make it a divine match with grilled chilli prawns.

NOCHE BUENA DARK LAGER, 5.9% ABV
Light chestnut brown in the glass with a slight caramel, nutty, chocolatey nose. There's more caramel sweetness on the crisp, full-bodied palate, with hints of toffee and earthy hop before its lasting dry finish.

FOOD PAIRING: Given the alcohol, the crispness, and the full-bodied mouthfeel, this is a beer that would be excellent when paired with a meaty dish such as chilli con carne.

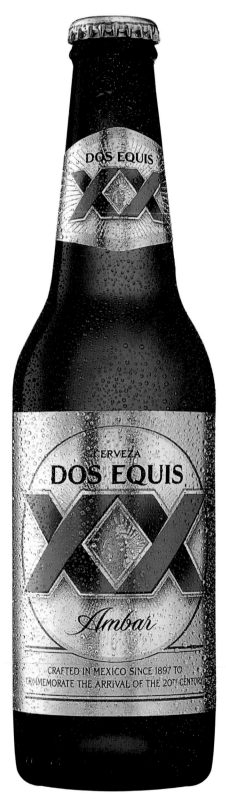

CUAUHTÉMOC MOCTEZUMA
DOS EQUIS XX AMBAR

GRUPO MODELO

Grupo Modelo started off as a modest-sized brewery in Mexico City, but has since become one of the largest breweries in the world; its light golden beer Corona Extra is famously served with a slice of lime.

WHILE THE US WAS IN THE THROES of Prohibition in 1925, Cerveceria Modelo, as it was then known, was founded in its southern neighbour, Mexico. One of the first beers to be produced by the company was Corona Extra, which has gone on to become the world's best-selling Mexican beer, though it is not recorded whether the habit of stuffing a wedge of lime into the bottle's neck took place when the beer was born or came later. Not long afterwards, the brewery started putting the beer into its trademark clear glass bottles. Two other beers that were produced at the beginning and remain favourites with Mexican drinkers were Modelo Especial and

Negra Modelo, which is Mexico's best-selling dark beer, though it was initially draught-only and not bottled until 1930. Whether the story that the popularity of dark beers in Mexico was due to Austrian immigrants who followed the self-proclaimed Emperor Maximilian in the 1860s is true or an easy legend is still disputed. Modelo was obviously getting things right with the thirsty Mexican population – and maybe a few border-crossing Americans – as within several years the brewery was selling eight million bottles of beer annually.

The history of Grupo Modelo (as it has become) then went on to become a familiar brewing tale of expansion and buyouts, including the purchase of Toluca in 1935 (brewer of the Victoria brand) and Pacifico in 1954, where Modelo's Pacifico had been brewed since 1900. Nowadays, it is the sixth-largest brewery in the world, produces 14 different brands, and has eight brewing sites throughout Mexico. It also imports big brands such as Budweiser and Tsingtao, and even makes its own bottled water.

THE FACTS...

OWNER Constellation Brands
FOUNDED 1925
ADDRESS Lago Alberto 156 Colonia Anáhuac, 11320 Mexico City, Federal District
WEBSITE www.gmodelo.mx
PHILOSOPHY Whether it's pale or dark in colour, or light or strong in flavour, Grupo Modelo has a beer for everyone

TASTING NOTES

CORONA EXTRA PALE LAGER, 4.8% ABV
Pale yellow in colour with a slight nose suggestive of lemon and sweetcorn. The mouthfeel is light to medium with crisp carbonation, a slim hint of citrus, and a dry finish. This is what is known as a "lawn-mower" beer.

FOOD PAIRING: This is a simple, uncomplicated beer that is best used for refreshment on a hot summer's day, though it would also work well with barbecued chicken.

PACIFICO CLARA PALE LAGER, 4.8% ABV
Clear gold in colour, Pacifico Clara has a sweetish, grainy nose with hints of citrus in the background. On the palate there is malt sweetness with a whisper of citrus, while the crisp carbonation helps refresh the mouth.

FOOD PAIRING: This is the ideal beer for a tortilla stuffed with shredded pork, freshly-made salsa, and a sprinkling of fiery jalapeño chillies.

MODELO ESPECIAL PALE LAGER, 4.4% ABV
Dark gold in the glass with undercurrents of sweet graininess on the nose. There's a crisp cutting carbonation on the palate with suggestions of caramel sweetness and citrus fruitiness before the quick finish, which has some bittersweet notes.

FOOD PAIRING: Another beer that works best as a thirst-quencher, though its crispness makes it a no-brainer with a spicy dish such as prawn fajitas.

GRUPO MODELO
CORONA EXTRA

GRUPO MODELO
PACIFICO CLARA

GRUPO MODELO
MODELO ESPECIAL

PRIMUS

THE FACTS...

OWNERS Rodolfo Andreu and Jaime Andreu

FOUNDED 2007

ADDRESS Av Revolución 344, Col Escandón, Del Miguel Hidalgo, 11800 Mexico City

WEBSITE www.primus.com.mx

PHILOSOPHY To make our own craft beers and work with other Mexican craft brewers

Primus founders Rodolfo and Jaime Andreu took three years to perfect their first beer before releasing it for sale. It was the first alt to be brewed in Mexico and they are now the leading lights of a growing craft-brewing movement.

THERE'S A LOT OF BEER IN MEXICO and a lot of different brands to choose from. A large amount of Mexican beer also travels abroad. All around the world Mexican beer has a certain style cachet – the drinker with a wedge of lime in the bottle of Mexican lager somehow feels that this gives them a certain amount of credibility. The flipside to this image of Mexico being awash with beer is that there are lots of brands but very few that deviate from pale and dark lager styles. That's where the likes of Primus come in – it is one of a small, select band of craft breweries, who, step by step, are showing the Mexican beer drinker that beer needn't always be served ice cold or slight in its flavour. It's a tough task though as the Mexican beer market is dominated by two giant brewers, which makes it hard to get small-batch beers to market. There's a similar issue with raw materials, which necessitates their importation, but Primus has initiated a scheme whereby the small band of craft brewers in the country work together to order large batches of malt. This sense of collaboration is just one aspect of the small but steadily growing thirst for craft beer in Mexico, a market perhaps influenced by the headline-grabbing growth of craft beer in its northern neighbour. However, a sense of realism has to be held onto – craft brewers only had 0.01 per cent of the market in 2011. Even though this was double the previous year's figures, there's still a long way to go.

The Primus Brewery is located in a suburb to the north of Mexico City, and in 2007 it laid down its brewing marker by producing the country's first-ever alt beer, Tempus. According to the brewery founders, Rodolfo and Jaime Andreu, it took three years of research and education before they were confident enough to release the beer. Their detailed sense of preparation shows how serious they were. To make things even more interesting, they then produced Tempus Doble Malta, a self-styled imperial alt, and the rich Scottish ale Tempus Reserva Especial. The brewery also hosts beer versus wine dinners. These guys are serious and their hard work is beginning to pay off in this difficult market. Hopefully in the future Mexican beer will be seen to have more variety around the world than it currently does.

Point to prove
Primus is out to show that Mexican beer is bigger than lager with lime

PRIMUS TEMPUS RESERVA ESPECIAL   **PRIMUS** TEMPUS DOBLE MALTA   **PRIMUS** TEMPUS DORADA

Practise makes perfect
*Good things take time
to produce – Primus spent
three years honing its
first beer*

Think outside the pint
*Beer does not have to be
served in big glasses. A
well-crafted glass enhances
the enjoyment of a beer*

PRIMUS TEMPUS ALT CLASSICA

TASTING NOTES

TEMPUS RESERVA ESPECIAL SCOTTISH ALE, 6.1% ABV
The beer shines amber beneath its fluffy white head of foam,
with a cascade of caramel and sweet honeyed notes on the nose.
It's a full-bodied beer on the palate with plenty of big biscuity
and toffee notes, some citrus and spice, and a spirituous
character, before it finishes with a distinctive bitterness.

FOOD PAIRING: A good beer to pair with a rich beef stew or
maybe wait until the end of the dinner and put it to good use
with a raspberry cheesecake.

TEMPUS DOBLE MALTA IMPERIAL ALT, 7% ABV
The brewery's signature beer gets an alcoholic makeover: more
malt, caramel, alcohol, and in the background the bracing
earthiness of hop. It's a big mouthful with plenty going on,
and a fabulous balance between big malty sweetness and spice
with earthy and herbal hop. The finish lingers.

FOOD PAIRING: The brewery suggests this as an apéritif,
though if being served at the table, it would make a good
companion to a ripe, stinky stilton.

TEMPUS DORADA BLONDE ALE, 4.3% ABV
Pale gold in colour, this beer has a drift of sweetish malt-
derived notes on the nose, suggestive of dried, slightly
sugary grain; there is also an undercurrent of spice and
citrus. The palate is spritzy, biscuity and features some citrus
before its dry fruity finish.

FOOD PAIRING: This is a light beer that would be best
enjoyed with a similarly light dish, such as grilled chicken
or even seafood sushi.

TEMPUS ALT CLASSICA 5.2% ABV
The brewery's debut beer is a sleek polished amber-copper
in colour. Caramel and toasted grain hover on the nose, while
there is sweet malt, spiciness, and toasted grain on the palate
followed by a bittersweet finish.

FOOD PAIRING: Serve with griddled scallops and pancetta and
enjoy how the beer lifts the seafood and matches the salty meat.

ANTARES

After a stint in the US, Leo Ferrari and Mariana Rodriguez were bowled over by the craft beers they discovered there and began to home-brew; the next step was opening Argentina's pioneering craft beer brewpub.

THE FACTS...

OWNERS Leo Ferrari and Mariana Rodriguez

FOUNDED 1998

ADDRESS 12 de Octubre 7749, Mar del Plata, Buenos Aires Province

WEBSITE www.cervezaantares.com

PHILOSOPHY Craft beer in a brewpub setting

BEER PASSION OFTEN HAS A HABIT of taking people by surprise – one day they're happy with their regular pint and just getting along nicely and then something totally unexpected happens. Take the founders of Antares, for instance. After finishing college, Argentinean graduates Leo Ferrari and Mariana Rodriguez travelled to the US to work, and in the process found themselves exposed to the vibrancy of the craft beer movement there. Beers such as pale ales, IPAs, and imperial stouts were light years away from the standard, freezing cold lagers that were commonplace at home. Their beer epiphany was on its way. After meeting and chatting with a US home-brewer, the couple followed suit and started making their own beer. Once back home, they hooked up with fellow student Pablo Rodriguez and beer passion completely enveloped them. Argentina was introduced to craft beer in 1998, when Antares was set up as a brewpub in the seaside resort of Mar del Plata. This was the first outlet for the beers, and has been followed by nine others in the years since, all of which are stand-alone, Antares-branded brewpubs producing and selling the beer. Naturally, given Ferrari and Rodriguez's experience in the US, the beers brewed are an eclectic bunch, including a dry-hopped Kölsch, a rich malt-driven Scotch, and a shellfish-friendly Cream Stout. When we think about Argentina and gastronomy we think wine, massive slabs of steak, and ice-cold beer, but thanks to Antares' efforts since 1998, craft beer is also now firmly on the menu.

TASTING NOTES

KÖLSCH 5% ABV
Antares' interpretation of the classic beer of Cologne is dark gold in colour with a light and easy-going flurry of sweetish, grassy notes on the nose. The medium mouthfeel has a dry, bittersweet, grassy character; the finish lingers with an appealing dryness.

FOOD PAIRING: The dryness and bittersweet nature of the beer work with cured cold meats such as salami and chorizo.

STOUT IMPERIAL 8.5% ABV
In the glass it's dark chestnut in colour sitting beneath an espresso-coloured foam. Chocolate and fruity notes swirl upwards on the nose, while the palate has a spike of roastiness and a soft luscious chocolate caress, all wrapped up with an earthy hoppiness. The long finish is appetizingly dry.

FOOD PAIRING: Grilled ribs, sticky with their smoky, sweet-sour marinade, would make an ideal partner for this beer.

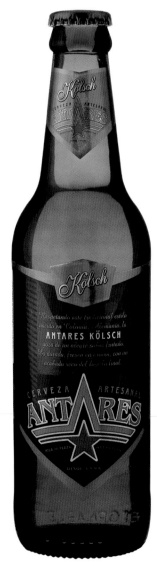

ANTARES KÖLSCH

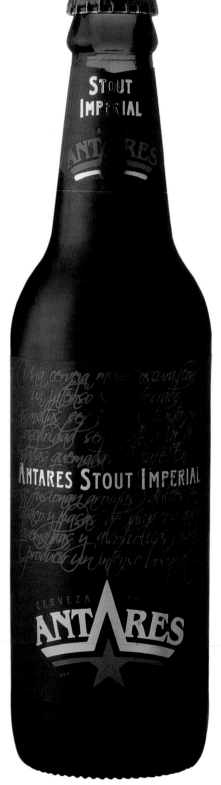

ANTARES STOUT IMPERIAL

BARBA ROJA

Antonio and Vivian Mastroianni set up Barba Roja in a leisure park in 2001, offering their beers in a pirate-styled bar. They began with a standard range of lagers, but have since gone on to make an eclectic range of craft beers.

THE TIPPLE OF PIRATES is supposedly rum, but it's all beer in the pirate-themed brewpub Barba Roja, in the heart of a leisure park in the city of Escobar, some 50km (30 miles) from Buenos Aires. Escobar is known as the flower capital of Argentina and is a popular tourist destination, so opening up Barba Roja in 2001 was a sound business decision for founders Antonio and Vivian Mastroianni. Inside the brewpub the bold, swashbuckling décor – the serving staff wear pirate-style scarves on their heads – is a curious adjunct to the sight of copper-clad brewing vessels surrounding the bar. Yet, Barba Roja is definitely a serious beer-making concern, and far-sighted in that it poses the serious question: why shouldn't great beer be served in an environment where families come to relax and enjoy themselves?

The brews are a mixture of craft-brewing aesthetics with Raspberry Bock, an intensely fruity beer that is matured for 20 days with fresh raspberries, the rich stout Negra Fuerte, and the smoky-sweet Barrel-Aged Red Ale leading the charge; then there are pale lagers, some of which feature herbs or lemon and lime juice. Given that lime juice was an essential tonic at sea in the 18th century, the beers would surely have gone down very well with the men who roved the high seas at the time.

Buccaneer beer
Drinking beer is serious fun at the pirate themed brewpub

THE FACTS...

OWNER Antonio and Vivian Mastroianni

FOUNDED 2001

ADDRESS Ruta 25, N° 2567, Escobar, 1625 Buenos Aires

WEBSITE www.cerveceriabarbaroja.com.ar

PHILOSOPHY Craft beer brewed and served in a family atmosphere in a leisure park

TASTING NOTES

STRONG RED ALE WOOD-AGED ALE, 9% ABV
Chestnut-amber in colour, this strong, wood-aged beer offers up tempting aromas of smoke, roast barley, caramel sweetness, spice, and toffee.
FOOD PAIRING: Grab a slice of ripe stilton or a similar cheese.

NEGRA FUERTE DUNKEL, 4.5% ABV
In the glass it pours dark cola in colour beneath a soft white head of foam. Notes of roasted barley, sweet caramel, and slight chocolate combine with hints of treacle and liquorice.
FOOD PAIRING: Serve with a large slab of grilled steak and don't stint on the onions.

WINNER DOPPELBOCK, 4.8% ABV
This Doppelbock is weaker than others. In the glass it's dark chestnut, with a toasty, slightly smoky, sweetish nose. It's a mixture of toastiness, roast barley, coffee, and chocolate.
FOOD PAIRING: This has enough sweetness and toastiness for the Latin American spicy minced beef mash-up called picadillo.

BARBA ROJA STRONG RED ALE   **BARBA ROJA** NEGRA FUERTE   **BARBA ROJA** WINNER

BOLIVIA

KUSHAAV

www.cervezasgourmet.com.bo

THE BOLIVIAN CAPITAL of La Paz gained another microbrewery in 2012 when Alejandra Saavedra set up Kushaav; the city already had four brewing enterprises. Having taken courses in several countries, Saavedra was in a strong position to create a wide range of brews – the first beer created was the fruity Aleksandra golden ale. A strong porter called Coqueta then joined the family, and was later followed by the malty session ale, El Salar; the latter has locally grown quinoa added to the mix. Barley and hops are brought in from Germany and the US, and all the beers are bottle conditioned.

CHILE

TŰBINGER

www.tubinger.cl

GERMAN-BORN CHRISTOPH FLASKAMP moved to Chile in 1990. In reaction against what he felt were the poor beers of his adopted country, he spent a period of time honing his home-brewing skills before setting up Tübinger Brewery in 2007, south of Santiago. Ironically for a German brewer, he chose to focus on UK beer styles: his debut beers were a classically English brown ale, with a substantial amount of roast malt in the grist, and a pale ale – although this did use German hops. Since then he has celebrated his homeland's beer with the strong, dark doppelbock Tübinator.

SZOT

www.szot.cl

CHILE IS BY-AND-LARGE dominated by large multi-national lager brands, but the past few years have seen a small but noticeable band of microbreweries emerging. Szot is one such, set up by Californian Kevin Szot in 2006 after he and his family moved to Santiago, Chile. His initial aim was to focus on the kind of beers he'd enjoyed in the US, so he brewed a pale ale, a stout, and, rather unusually, a steam beer. As time went by these were joined by a strong ale, a double IPA, and a barley wine; the barley wine is intensely sweet with a strong blast of hoppy flavour. All the beers are bottle-conditioned.

SZOT BARLEY WINE

COLOMBIA

BOGOTÁ BEER

www.bogotabeercompany.com

COLD LAGER WITH LITTLE FLAVOUR is the tipple of choice for many Colombians, but beer is big in the country and the last few years have seen a growth in the thriving microbrewing scene. Founded in 2002, Bogotá Beer was one of the earliest to pick up on this trend and the company has gone from strength to strength since then, opening over a dozen outlets in Bogotá. As for the beers, they vividly portray an Anglo-American-German-Belgian influence, and include an IPA, a pale ale, a weiss, and a witbier.

COSTA RICA

CRAFT BREWING COMPANY

www.beer.cr

COSTA RICA'S ENTRY into the craft-brewing revolution was made when this 16-hl (10-barrel) brewhouse was opened by American expats Peter Gilman and Brandon Nappy in 2010. The brewmaster is Chris Derrick, whose CV includes a stint at US brewery Flying Dog (see p.158). The brewery is close to the city of Cartago but sends its beers across the country. Alongside its IPA, Tropical Golden Ale, and Red Ale, it makes an excellent wheat beer flavoured with the local sour-tasting fruit, cas.

CUBA

CERVECERIA BUCANERO

www.cervezacristal.com

CUBA'S MOST POPULAR BREWERY, Cerveceria Bucanero, is based in Holguin on the eastern side of Cuba. It opened in 1988 with aid from East Germany, but capitalism is well and truly in its system these days – it is now owned by global giant A-B InBev. Cristal is its best-selling beer, a thirst-quenching pale lager whose logo is plastered nationwide, while Max is a stronger (6.5% ABV), slightly darker brew that was introduced in 2006.

EL SALVADOR
BREW REVOLUTION
www.brewrevolution.com

ANDY AND NANELLE NEWBOM founded Brew Revolution in 2012 after they moved from San Francisco to the El Salvadoran surfing mecca of Playa El Tunco. Their philosophy is unashamedly craft beer-centric with a strong US influence. Mercurio IPA – a combination of IPA and the cane sugar and citrus flavours of El Salvador – and Nyx Black Ale, a black beer with coffee aromas, are just two of the brewery's beers. However, for their seasonal beers the Newboms make use of indigenous ingredients such as local honey and fruit in their attempt to make authentic El Salvadoran craft beer.

JAMAICA
DESNOES & GEDDES
www.jamaicadrinks.com

THINK JAMAICA and beer, think Red Stripe. This international lager has been brewed by Desnoes & Geddes since 1928, although it started off as an ale and only became a lager in 1938. It was one of the few beers James Bond was ever seen with, in the books *Dr No* and *The Man with the Golden Gun*. However, D&G – now owned by drinks company Diageo – are also known for their Dragon Stout, a rich sweet tropical stout, as well as a variety of Red Stripe-branded lagers flavoured with ginger, apple, or lime.

PERU
CERVEZA ARTESANAL DE TOMÁS
www.facebook.com/pages/Cerveza-Artesanal-De-Tomás-LIMA-PERU/337363640553

CERVEZA ARTESANAL DE TOMÁS is a Lima brewpub that was founded by Eduardo Tomás in 2006. It was the first of its kind and a brave move in a country where beer culture is rather one-dimensional. In spite of this, the brewery has prospered and now offers up to ten different beers. There's a definite Germanic influence on the lagered beers, while other beers include a porter with added nuts and

DESNOES & GEDDES DRAGON STOUT

carob, a stout with honey, and several weird and unusual brews. These include a green-coloured mint beer along with one flavoured with local pineapples – a fruity beer that Tomás suggests matching with seafood.

NORTON RATS PUB
www.nortonratspub.com

SITUATED OVERLOOKING the main square of the Peruvian city of Cusco, Norton Rats is a popular hangout for tourists, backpackers, and locals, who have been visiting it since 1997 in search of beer with more flavour than the usual chilled pale lagers. In 2012, the beer choice was increased when a microbrewery was set up and several new beers produced, including Norton Brown Ale, Norton Pale Ale, and Snortin' Norton Porter. There are also plans for seasonal and one-off ales.

TRINIDAD AND TOBAGO
CARIB
www.caribbrewery.com

REGULAR VISITORS to Trinidad and Tobago will be familiar with a cold glass of Carib. It's a pale golden lager – at 5.2% ABV it's stronger than most – that was originally launched in 1950. Its clever and powerful branding would have the rest of the world believe that life in the Caribbean is one long carnival. The brewery also produces other beers, including Royal Extra Stout, as well as contract-brewing for Guinness, Heineken, and Mackeson.

URUGUAY
MASTRA
www.mastra.com.uy

BREWING CRAFT BEER in a wine country like Uruguay is one thing, but selling it in a market that is aggressively patrolled by large breweries is another. Montevideo-based Mastra took on this challenge in 2007 with a laser-sharp focus on their branding and a determination to stick with three core beers. American Stout is as dark as a moonless night with assertive bitterness; Golden Extra Special is a strong English ale that uses German hops, while Strong Scotch Ale is a robust, fruity, slightly smoky iron brew of a beer.

ASIA & AUSTRALASIA

JAPAN

Contrary to popular belief, the traditional Japanese drink sake, which is made from rice, actually has more in common with beer than wine in terms of its production process, making Japan one of the oldest brewing nations in the world. European brewers took beer to Japan in the 1820s and for most of its recent brewing history the large Japanese brewers have produced lager-style beers, similar to those found in most parts of Europe: sweet-tasting, pale, and yellow, but tempered with the addition of rice. However, this all changed in 1987 when the national brewer Asahi (see p.242) introduced its Super Dry brand, made with highly attenuated yeast. It is crisp and dry with very little sweetness, and came to be regarded as a beer style in its own right.

For many years, Japan's brewing scene was dominated by large national brewers. It took a change in the law to end their stranglehold on the market; starting in 1994, commercial brewers were only required to brew 600hl (511 barrels), rather than 20,000hl (17,043 barrels), in order to obtain a licence. One of the initial licences granted was to Echigo (see p.236), Japan's first brewpub, which opened in February the following year.

From 1995 until 1999, over 175 breweries opened in Japan, but due to the influence of global economic crises, the production of beers from microbreweries fell. Many of the first wave of breweries to open bit the dust. However, recent years have seen a resurgence of craft brewing – the number of brewers is on the rise again and there are now more than 200; the country also has a thriving Craft Beer Association. If you're tempted to visit, one of the best places in Japan to enjoy outstanding craft beer is the Great Japan Beer Festival, which is held each April in Tokyo.

BAIRD BREWING

Enthused by Japan's microbrewing revolution in the 1990s, influenced by US craft beer can-do, and determined to use the best raw materials, Baird has become one of Japan's most celebrated craft breweries.

THE FACTS...

OWNER Bryan Baird

FOUNDED 2001

ADDRESS Baird Brewing Company, 9-3, Tadehara-cho, Numazu, Shizuoka, 410-0843

WEBSITE www.bairdbeer.com

PHILOSOPHY Balance plus complexity equals character

AMERICAN BRYAN BAIRD went to Japan in 1995 after finishing college, just around the time when the microbrewing boom was taking off in the country. He was a great fan of US craft beer, but also a passionate lover of Japanese culture. Disenchanted with his corporate job, he came up with the idea of setting up a brewery in his adopted homeland, where he'd also got married. He returned to the USA to take an intensive course run by the American Brewers Guild and gain experience working in a variety of breweries including Redhook in Seattle. In 2001, he and his wife Sayuri set up a brewpub in the port city of Numazu. Such was Baird's commitment to producing beers that were both balanced and complex that the word got out and people started making the trip to the Numazu Fishmarket Taproom. The brewery has since increased in size several times, while Bryan Baird has opened three other taprooms in the Tokyo area. The hops are whole flower, the barley is floor-malted, the fruits are fresh, and the local water has a billowing softness. All this makes for a striking selection of beers that include an IPA, a crisp, snappy lager, a bittersweet porter, plus seasonal beers, some of which make use of local yuzu fruit and freshly picked figs.

BAIRD BREWING ANGRY BOY BROWN ALE

BAIRD BREWING RISING SUN PALE ALE

BAIRD BREWING KUROFUNE PORTER

TASTING NOTES

ANGRY BOY BROWN ALE AMERICAN BROWN ALE, 6.8% ABV
Light chestnut in colour, there's a wisp of caramel, demerara sugar, faint orange, and vanilla on the nose, while within the full, chewy mouthfeel, there's a spicy, herbal presence leading off to a long fruity finish with a hint of spices.

FOOD PAIRING: Go Mexican with chicken fajitas; the spiciness of the beer won't stand for any bullying from the chillies used.

RISING SUN PALE ALE 5.3% ABV
In the glass, it's a shimmering dark gold, while on the nose, there is a sparkling array of orange citrus, some floral notes, and a background of malt graininess. The palate features citrus fruitiness, balanced with sweetness before its clean, dry finish.

FOOD PAIRING: Slap a Kobe beefburger under the grill, grab some onion relish, and let the three of them get on with each other. You'll be amazed.

KUROFUNE PORTER 6% ABV
As dark as midnight with mocha coffee, chocolate, liquorice, and vanilla. Smooth and creamy with complex flavour notes.

FOOD PAIRING: Delicious with seared scallops to complement the sweetness and chaperone the crunchy burnt bits.

ECHIGO

A change in brewing restrictions in Japan unleashed a torrent of microbrewing as a reaction against the climate of "dry" beer; Echigo was at the forefront and remains an important player in the world of Japanese craft brewing.

THE FACTS...

OWNER Uehara Shuzo

FOUNDED 1994

ADDRESS 3970 Fukui, Nishiura, Niigata City, Niigata 953-0076

WEBSITE www.echigo-beer.jp

PHILOSOPHY The aim is fresh, high-quality beer that is delicate but also full of flavour

WHEN THE JAPANESE AUTHORITIES lifted restrictions on brewing in 1994, there was a rush to set up microbreweries. First in the queue was Echigo, which was founded by the sake brewery Uehara Shuzo. Brewing and drinking began in its light and airy brewpub in 1994, in the city of Niigata on the north-west coast of Honshu Island. Despite the Japanese penchant for "dry" lagers, Echigo looked to craft breweries in the US for its inspiration – customers were more likely to find a pale ale, an amber, or a stout in their glass, than a standard lager with rice in the mix. Echigo Pilsner was the one concession to this aspect of the market, and it has since become one of the brewery's best sellers. As other breweries and brewpubs joined the fray, Echigo went from strength to strength and in 1999, opened another brewery that focused more on canned beers for the budget conscious; this allowed the original brewpub to concentrate on its small batch brewing. Given that Niigata is seen as the rice growing capital of Japan and home to the highly coveted Koshihikari strain, the brewery eventually produced a dry rice beer, Koshihikari Echigo Beer. Back at the brewpub though, the focus is on craft beer with the likes of Echigo 90 Days Stout and the limited release Brown Porter favoured among fans.

TASTING NOTES

STOUT 7% ABV

Midnight black with an espresso-coloured head, the nose pulsates with notes of coffee, chocolate, nuts, and a slight roastiness, while the palate has a creamy mouthfeel with toffee, chocolate, and milky coffee notes. The finish is bittersweet.

FOOD PAIRING: A dream with smoked fish. The strong flavours help to coax out a pleasing sweetness and saltiness.

BROWN PORTER 6% ABV

Sleek chestnut brown in colour, there's milk chocolate and mocha coffee on the nose, with roast notes in the background. In the mouth, there's more chocolate, a malty sweetness, and a creamy mouthfeel. This seasonal beer finishes dry and bitter.

FOOD PAIRING: Ideal with a fruit tart, such as raspberry, where the fruitiness would be superb with the chocolate flavours.

PILSNER 5% ABV

In the glass, it's dark yellow in colour, while the nose is slightly sweet and grassy with hints of grain in the background; crisp carbonation, a whisper of lemon, and a subdued grainy dryness lead to a quick finish.

FOOD PAIRING: A delicate beer, it would be ideal with sushi.

ECHIGO STOUT

ECHIGO BROWN PORTER

ECHIGO PILSNER

Stylish cans
Canned beers, once regarded as a sign of being down-market, are now favoured by many craft brewers

FUJIZAKURA HEIGHTS

Superb German-influenced craft beers are brewed and brought to life in the monumental shadow of Mount Fuji by a brewer who went all the way to Germany to learn his craft, and has since become a master.

THE FACTS...

OWNER Fuji Kanko Kaihatsu
FOUNDED 1997
ADDRESS 3633-1 Funatsu, Fujikawaguchiko-machi, Minami Tsuru-gun, Yamanashi 401-0301
WEBSITE www.fuji-net.co.jp/beer/
PHILOSOPHY Dedication and passion allied with traditional German brewing techniques

FUJIZAKURA HEIGHTS IS A SMALL BREWERY with an attached restaurant called Sylvans, an appropriate name for a place hidden away in a forest. The woodland is not the only thing that gives Fujizakura Heights' position such a magical aura – its hometown of Fujikawaguchiko is sited on the northern side of Mount Fuji and overshadowed by the dormant volcano; the escapist's paradise of Lake Kawaguchi is also close. Crowds flock to the area and when they've hiked, climbed, or mountain biked they are in need of intense refreshment, and brewmaster Miyashita Hiromichi is ready for them. He was tasked to start the brewery in 1997 and while he protested to his bosses that brewing was beyond his ken, they simply sent him off to learn about it, first with a German brewer in Japan and then to study the subject for six weeks in Germany.

All this work obviously paid off as Fujizakura Heights is especially noted for its spirited interpretations of German beer styles and has the awards to show for it. In the beginning, Hiromichi's employers merely wanted a Pils and Weizen, as German beer was all the rage for many of the microbreweries being set up. They then asked him to make a more specialist style, a Rauchbier, with the intention of getting drinkers to make a link between the beer and the scent of the trees around Sylvans. The accolades have continued to roll in. As well as the all-year-round trio, Hiromichi oversees small batches of other German styles including a bock, dunkelweizen, smoked weizen, rauchbock, weizenbock, chocolate wheat, Oktoberfest märzen, and Oktoberfest weizen. All that early training was time well spent.

TASTING NOTES

RAUCH SMOKED BEER, 5.5% ABV
Dark amber in colour, resting beneath a thick collar of off-white foam, the smoke flavour of Rauch is delicate on the nose, with a hint of woodsmoke rising from the valley below. On the palate, this beer is an elegant mixture of smokiness and caramel with a fruity sweetness in the background. The finish is quick.

FOOD PAIRING: Rauch works deliciously with a platter of smoked sausages and some freshly cured ham. Let the fireworks begin!

WEIZEN WHEAT BEER, 5.5% ABV
Ripe banana and vanilla ice cream notes swirl off the nose of this pale gold, slightly hazy classic riff on a Bavarian wheat beer. The palate has a soft, slightly creamy character with more banana sweetness plus an edge of palate sourness that magnifies its refreshing qualities.

FOOD PAIRING: Try a glass of Weizen and sashimi (squid and prawn, perhaps, with soy sauce and ground ginger on the side); the light acidity and brisk carbonation of the beer will tease out appetizing hints of the ocean.

DOPPELBOCK 8% ABV
Springtime sees the annual release of this dark and dangerously drinkable malt-driven spirituous treat. The nose is nutty, toasty, earthy, and has alcoholic sweetness – a character that is replicated on the palate before its clean, boozy, slightly sweet finish.

FOOD PAIRING: Even in spring, the cold still lingers on the slopes of Mount Fuji, so a rich beef or venison stew with a glass of Doppelbock is a gastronomic treat with which to keep the cold at bay.

INSPIRED BY A NUMBER OF US BREWERS, SOME JAPANESE BREWERIES, SUCH AS YO-HO (SEE P.241), ARE PUTTING GREAT BEERS INTO CANS

EACH YEAR AT THE YOKOHAMA BEER FESTIVAL, THOUSANDS OF BEER LOVERS RAISE THEIR GLASSES AND CELEBRATE THE JOYS OF CRAFT BEER

ISE KADOYA

Narihiro Suzuki's family used to serve rice dumplings to religious pilgrims, but since 1997 it's the devout of the craft beer world that have been turning up in Ise City in search of beery blessings.

THE FACTS...

OWNER Narihiro Suzuki

FOUNDED 1997

ADDRESS 6-428 Shinkyu, Ise City, Mie 516-0017

WEBSITE www.isekadoya.com

PHILOSOPHY Small is beautiful when it comes to beer-making

THE FAMILY OF ISE KADOYA'S FOUNDER and owner Narihiro Suzuki have been trading in Ise City since the late 16th century, when they supplied religious pilgrims with rice dumplings called mochi. But in 1997, Suzuki oversaw the conversion of some of the family's storage warehouses into a restaurant, brewery, and beer shop, all of which go under the name Biyagura. Initially they produced a stout, a weizen, and an English pale ale, commonplace microbrewery beers. Then in 1999, on the suggestion of visiting beer writer Michael Jackson, the latter was changed to a Cascade-hopped American pale ale and the awards began to fly in. The brewery now produces five regular beers, plus a series of seasonals and one-offs that have the feel of a grand tour around the world beer scene. One brew might be a rye ale, another a weizenbock, while Rendaizi Spice has coriander, nutmeg, and cinnamon alongside persimmon in the mix. Suzuki takes pride in describing the brewery as a micro, believing that by being small it can pay close attention to the brewing process. Uniquely for Japanese breweries, brewmaster Masakazu Nakanishi uses an open-style fermentation tank, with the aim of producing a smoother, fuller-bodied beer.

ISE KADOYA LAMBIC STYLE WHITE PEACH

ISE KADOYA STOUT

Best of both
An American-style IPA with a Japanese twist awaits inside the bottle

TASTING NOTES

LAMBIC STYLE WHITE PEACH FRUIT BEER, 5% ABV
Not a real lambic, but there is a hint of sourness about this hazy, golden creation. The tangy, acidic, sour-sweet, peachy tastes transport the drinker to Belgium's Senne Valley.
FOOD PAIRING: It works well with fruit pie, such as peach – the spritz in the beer cuts through the sweetness.

STOUT 5% ABV
Tarmac black with a tan-white collar of foam on top. Notes of coffee, dark chocolate, and roast grain engage in a whirl of aromatics on the nose, while the mouthfeel is smooth and creamy as milky coffee, leading to a dry, bittersweet finish.
FOOD PAIRING: Pair with grilled oysters, udon noodles, and pickled vegetables to set off fireworks in the mouth.

SINTO BEER AMERICAN PALE ALE, 5% ABV
There is a glow of orange amber in a glass of Sinto, with a subtle tingle of citrus on the nose and a background of grassy hop, while the palate has more citrus, a soft graininess, and a bittersweet finish.
FOOD PAIRING: Try with chopped pork stir-fry topped with kimchi (fermented vegetables) and rice noodles.

ISE KADOYA SINTO BEER

YO-HO

Like many breweries, Yo-ho started off wanting to stand out from the crowd. They have achieved this by brewing audaciously flavoured ales in unique can-only packaging, which have caught the imagination of beer-lovers.

THE FACTS...

OWNER Hoshino Resorts
FOUNDED 1996
ADDRESS 2148 Nagakura, Karuizawa, Nagano 389-0111
WEBSITE www.yonasato.com
PHILOSOPHY Provide a variety of beers; make people happy

YO-HO (KNOWN AS YONA YONA IN JAPANESE) is the biggest craft brewery in Japan – its beers are distributed widely and are a constant presence at specialist beer bars such as Popeye in Tokyo. The company is based in the Nagano Prefecture and the beer is brewed several miles away in Saku City. Apart from their American-influenced, bold, colourful flavours, Yo-ho is unique in that the beer is sold only in cans, although some bars serve it by hand pump. Canning the beer dates from the start of the brewery, which was founded by leisure company Hoshino Resorts in 1996. The idea was to encourage people to buy the beer for home consumption, to make it easier for supermarkets to stock the beers, and for environmental reasons. Brewmaster Toshiyuki Ishii, who joined the company in 2001 after several years of working at Stone Brewing in San Diego, put Yo-ho on the map. Using his Californian experience he made the brewery's first US-influenced barley wine and created Tokyo Black after the owners decided they wanted a beer to rival Guinness. The current brewmaster is Masafumi Morita. His robust porter took Bronze at The Brewing Industry International Awards in 2012, and he is currently planning a series of barrel-aged beers, using Japanese whisky barrels.

TASTING NOTES

YONA YONA ALE AMERICAN PALE ALE, 5.5% ABV
Sunshine gold in a glass, the nose pulsates with tropical and citrus fruit. The palate has tropical fruit, a restrained sweetness and grainy background, finishing with a crisp dryness.
FOOD PAIRING: The fruitiness lifts the flavour of lamb, while the crisp dryness will cleanse the palate.

AOONI IPA, 7% ABV
Coppery or orange-yellow in colour, there is, a blast of sweet citrus, with richer caramel notes. In the mouth, there is grapefruit with some sweetness, peppery spice, and a whisper of nuttiness. The finish starts off juicy before becoming dry.
FOOD PAIRING: Pizza or pasta are the way to go with this IPA as the hop flavours match the herby nature of the dishes.

TOKYO BLACK ROBUST PORTER, 5% ABV
First brewed in 2005, this beer is black with dark chestnut tints. It offers a sweet siren call of caramel, vanilla, mocha, chocolate, and a hint of liquorice, which is echoed on the palate.
FOOD PAIRING: Would work well with a platter of soft cheese such as Camembert, Brie, or goat's cheese.

Eye candy
Yo-ho beers, which are only available in cans, stand out from the crowd with their pleasing designs

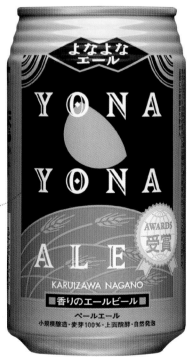

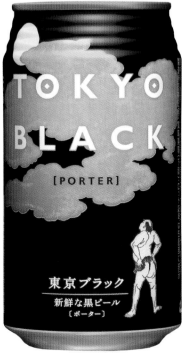

YO-HO YONA YONA ALE   **YO-HO** AOONI   **YO-HO** TOKYO BLACK

ASAHI BREWERIES

www.asahibeer.com

THE TOP DOG in the Japanese brewing industry began in 1889 as the Osaka Beer Brewing Co – Asahi Beer was produced three years later. It wasn't until 1989, however, that Asahi Breweries emerged with its own separate identity, while 1996 famously saw it responsible for its first dry beer. Those with a yearning for something different from a company that not only brews beer but owns wine, whisky, and soft drinks holdings often plump for Asahi Black, a good interpretation of a black lager.

BAEREN BIER

www.baerenbier.com

GERMAN-STYLE BEER is big at Baeren Bier, a small brewery set up in 2001 in Morioka, the capital of the Iwate Prefecture. Using equipment shipped over from Germany – some of it a century old – Baeren produces an appetizing range that includes a dortmunder/helles called Classic, a pilsner, and a weizen, plus occasional beers such as a pale ale and milk stout. Uniquely, Baeren possesses a "cool ship" – an open vessel used for cooling wort – which is often used in the production of lambic, although no beer of that style is planned here.

BAYERN MEISTER BIER

www.bmbier.com

STEPHAN RAGER moved to Japan from his homeland of Germany in 1996 to work in a brewery. However, the desire to start up his own business became overwhelming and he began brewing in 2004 amid the hills below Mount Fuji. Rager sources malt, hops, and yeast from Bavaria and as you might expect, concentrates on his homeland's beer styles. His two most popular beers are the clean-tasting Prinz Pils and Edelweiss wheat beer; he also makes a weizenbock plus special brews several times a year.

COEDO

www.coedobrewery.com

SWEET POTATOES are a speciality of the Tokyo dormitory city of Kawagoe and are widely used to flavour ice cream and coffee in the area. Coedo has been based in the city since it was formed in 1996 – though its old brewery is now a restaurant – and unsurprisingly

ASAHI BREWERIES BLACK

BAEREN CLASSIC

COEDO SHIKKOKU

makes use of the root vegetable for its reddish lager Beniaka. This sweet potato beer was challenging when first brewed but with the help of German brewmasters it's become a mighty beer. Coedo also brews a pilsner, a weizen, and a dark beer called Shikkoku.

GINGA KOGEN

www.gingakogenbeer.com

BUSINESSMAN ISAO NAKAMURA formed Ginga Kogen in the town of Sawauchi in 1996 with the aim of helping its economic development. Located in Iwate Prefecture to the north-east of Honshu Island, the area receives the highest annual snowfall in Japan, which is perhaps why the brewery focuses on making Bavarian-style beers, as the climate is similar to Bavaria. Its main beer is an unfiltered hefeweizen but there are also several American-style beers. The brewery's restaurant and bar is the perfect place to watch snow fall and study its beers.

HELIOS IWATEKURA

www.helios-syuzo.co.jp

THERE ARE ONLY two breweries on Okinawa; one of them is the massive Orion, while the other is this much more modest outfit that first started producing beer in 1998 – though it is part of a distillery that began in 1961. Its flagship beer is Goya Best, a lager that has goya, or bitter melon, added to the mix. The result is a refreshing beer with an appetizing bitterness. A pale ale, porter, and weizen are also made.

HIDA TAKAYAMA

www.hidatakayamabeer.co.jp

ESTABLISHED IN 1996, and one of the longer established craft breweries in Japan, Hida Takayama's stand-alone brewery – there is no tap or restaurant – is located in central Japan in a region known as Japan's Alps. Grab a glass of rich, dark brown-red, seasonally brewed Belgian Abbey-style Karumina (10% ABV) on a cold winter's day and heaven awaits; there are plenty for the rest of the year as well including a pale ale, pilsner, and ESB.

HIDEJI

www.hideji-beer.jp

HIDEJI'S BOTTLE LABELS have a colourful and cartoonish style that attracts the eye. The beer inside is equally attractive, with the

brewery, which was set up in 1996, offering up a pleasing selection of different beers. These include a US-influenced pale ale, a Germanic pilsner and Belgian wheat beer. Every month Hideji produces a special beer, while winter is the time when the dark creamy 7% Shuji Stout is brewed. Home for Hideji is the attractive coastal area of Nobeoka City on the southern island of Kyushu.

HITACHINO NEST

www.hitachinonest.com

LONG-ESTABLISHED SAKE manufacturer Kiuchi rolled out the Hitachino Nest brand of beers in 1996 with what it called "a hint of our traditional sake brewing method" – Japanese Classic Ale is matured in sake casks. Based in the Ibaraki Prefecture, in an urbanized area close to Tokyo, the brewery produces an eclectic selection of beers, with White Ale perhaps the best known and most garlanded of these. Influenced by the Japanese love for Hoegaarden, it has a similar spicy and refreshing profile, though the inclusion of orange juice gives it a unique flavour.

KINSHACHI

www.kinshachi.jp

KINSHACHI BEGAN BREWING IN 1996, a craft beer arm of the Morita Shuzo company, which also happens to make sake, miso, and soy sauce. Several variations on a German beer theme were initially brewed, but 2005 saw the successful launch of Nagoya Red Miso Lager. The accolades accorded to the beer inspired other such eclectic creations, including a beer with black miso and another with Japanese green tea added to the mix.

KIRIN BREWERY

www.kirin.com

THE KIRIN IS A MYTHICAL CREATURE that always appears on the beer labels of this Yokohama-based brewery. It's supposed to bring luck, which some might argue it has done ever since Kirin was formed in 1907 when two of the first breweries in Japan merged after the country opened up to the west. Since then, through earthquake, war, and corporate shenanigans, Kirin has held its head high. It's best known for its crisp and clean-tasting signature beer Kirin Ichiban Shibori, which was first brewed in 1990; Ichiban means "first" and "best", and the beer is brewed with 100 per cent malt.

HITACHINO NEST JAPANESE CLASSIC ALE

KIRIN KIRIN BEER

MINAMI SHINSYU

www.ms-beer.co.jp

THE COMPACT CITY OF KOMAGANE sits in the middle of the so-called Japanese Alps, surrounded by snowy peaks – a Shangri-La of sorts where the beers that Minami Shinsyu brews make for a welcome tonic after a day in the mountains. The brewery has been based here since its formation in 1996, and beers such as its Amber Ale, Dunkel Weizen, and the more esoteric Apple Hop can be found at its Brewery restaurant along with excellent food – beers can be bought at the brewery.

MINOH AJI

www.minoh-beer.jp

DRINKS STORE OWNER MASAI OSHITA set up Minoh in 1997 and promptly got his two daughters on board. They are now in charge and oversee a thriving, multi-award-winning business that has its home in Minoh City, just south of Osaka. It was one of the first Japanese craft breweries to produce a double IPA: W-IPA is 9% ABV and has a positive smack of Cascade hops on the nose. Pale Ale, Imperial Stout, and Weizen are also among the regular beers brewed by the company.

NASU KOHGEN

www.nasukohgenbeer.co.jp

AS LOCATIONS GO the setting for this brewery and its restaurant is pretty impressive. Turn off the motorway north of Tokyo, near the town of Nasu, and you will find the brewery in the middle of dense woodland. The packaging of the beers is classy and they are not cheap, but both drinkers and beer judges agree on the merits of the beers, such as its Scottish Ale and Stout. The seasonal Nine-Tailed Fox barley wine is a cult beer and various vintages can be found in Tokyo's craft beer bars.

ORION

www.orionbeer.co.jp

THE ISLAND OF OKINAWA has been home to Orion since 1957. German-style lagers were its forte at the beginning, but it then decided to make its lagers more palatable for the occupying American forces by making them lighter and paler in colour and success started to come. The beer is produced using fresh spring water drawn from behind the brewery and Hallertauer hops from Germany, while the malt is carefully selected from the best European and Australian varieties. Orion's produce was initially confined to Okinawa, but after an agreement with Asahi they are now more widely distributed throughout the mainland. The brewery's best-selling beer is Premium Draft Beer.

OTARU

www.otarubeer.com.jp

THERE ARE ONLY TWO German nationals living in the port of Otaru in the north of Japan and one of them is brewmaster Johannes Braun. Born into a Bavarian family that has been brewing since the 17th century, and a graduate of Scotland's Heriot-Watt University where he studied whisky distilling, he was offered a job with Otaru when it opened in 1996. Braun applies the traditional German rules of beer-making. He uses organic ingredients such as high-grade barley, wheat, and hops imported from Germany and Otaru's clear water to make authentic German brews. Under his care, Otaru brews an exemplary trio of regulars – Pilsener, Dunkel, and Weiss – as well as German-styled seasonals such as Rauchbier.

OZENO YUKIDOKE

www.ryujin.jp

AS IS COMMON with some microbreweries that sprang up in the mid-1990s, Ozeno Yukidoke's parent company makes sake; it branched out into beer in 1997. The beers produced in the city of Tatebayashi have an American craft beer aesthetic, without opting for the extreme sensibility. This results in a portfolio that includes a West Coast-style IPA that was first brewed in 2005 and is ideal with sushi, plus a Brown Weizen, a Stout, and a big hitter of a barley wine named Heavy Heavy.

SANKT GALLEN

www.sanktgallenbrewery.com

WHILE EVERYONE ELSE is pushing the hop envelope and looking for the lost chord of bitterness, Sankt Gallen, based in the Atsugi province of Kanagawa Prefecture, seems to have made a virtue of sweetness with beers. These include its rich Imperial Chocolate Stout, a variety of beers flavoured with pineapple, cinnamon, and apple, as well as sweet, but strong ales aimed at customers on St Valentine's Day. However, don't be

MINOH AJI MINOH BEER

deceived, this well-regarded brewery close to Yokohama can hop and rock with the best of them, as Yokohama XPA demonstrates. Put together, all of this makes Sankt Gallen an intriguing brewery.

SAPPORO

www.sapporobeer.jp

SAPPORO IS ONE OF THE "BIG FIVE" Japanese breweries and one of the oldest, having been founded in the 1870s, as Japan opened out to the west and German brewmasters started travelling there to set up businesses. Even though the company started life in the city of Sapporo on the northerly island of Hokkaido, it now has five breweries throughout the country and also owns Sleeman in Canada, while the Sapporo Beer Museum in Sapporo is a popular tourist attraction. Its three most well-known beers are the all-malt premium lager Yebisu, Sapporo Draft, and Sleeman Cream Ale.

SHIGA KOGEN

www.tamamura-honten.co.jp

THE COMPANY TAMAMURA HONTEN has been making sake since the early 19th century, but it wasn't until 2004 that it decided to open a brewery as well. Based in the town of Yudanaka in the Nagano region, the brewery, Shiga Kogen, is very much on the craft brewing scene as its collaboration with Nøgne Ø (see p.135), oak-ageing of its Saison, and a beer made with freshly picked hops suggest. Meanwhile its House IPA features a tremendous burst of crispness and citrussiness.

SHONAN

www.kumazawa.jp

BEACH BUMS AND SURF DUDES flock to the Shonan coastal region about an hour from Tokyo in search of fresh air and relaxation outside the city. The chances are that after a day chasing waves, yachting, and windsurfing, a cool glass of Shonan Liebe or Pilsner goes down as a treat. The Chigasaki-based brewery only started making beer in 1996, though its parent company, Kumazawa, had been a sake brewer since 1872. The beer is made using the purest water from an aquifer that comes from the Tanzawa mountain range to the north, reputedly taking 70 years to travel through the aquifer to the well. Beers such as Weizenbock Bitter, Ruby, and Liebe (pale,

SHIGA KOGEN HOUSE IPA

SHONAN WEIZENBOCK

amber, and dark), as well as other seasonal beers, have been winning awards since their early days. As well as the refreshing lagered beers, Shonan's seasonal beers have featured the current crop of fashionable New World hops, such as Nelson Sauvin.

SUNTORY

www.suntory.com

EVEN THOUGH it has long been known for its whisky, Suntory is one of the big five of Japanese brewing, having made beer since the 1960s. IPAs and weizenbocks are notable by their absence with the company producing a raft of low-alcohol, low-carb beers. Its Premium Malt is 100% malt and very palatable. In Japan, high taxes are imposed on drinks using malt as a raw ingredient, which has spawned the "third beer" category where the likes of pea or soy protein have gone into the mash. Suntory stopped making *happoshu* or low-malt beers in 2012.

SWAN LAKE

www.swanlake.co.jp

THE AWARDS HAVE BEEN SHOWERED on Swan Lake, an accomplished craft brewery that was set up in 1997. Located in the beautiful mountainous countryside of the Niigata Prefecture, where there is also a Swan Lake bar and restaurant, the brewery makes use of locally grown ingredients and pure mountain spring water. Some of the treasures it produces include a ravishing Imperial Stout, a well-balanced IPA with plenty of tropical fruit notes, and its Samurai Barley Wine, which stands up well to ageing.

T.Y. HARBOR BREWERY

www.tyharborbrewing.co.jp

OTIS REDDING WOULD HAVE ENJOYED hanging out at this waterfront brewery and restaurant. He could have sat on the dock of the bay watching the tide roll away, with beer at hand. T.Y. Harbor opened in 1997 and was modelled on similar establishments on the US West Coast. It remains Tokyo's only independent microbrewery and the highly accomplished beers possess a strong US craft brewing influence – the Amber, Pale Ale, Barley Wine, and IPA are all aromatic and bold. The restaurant also serves up suitable diner food.

AUSTRALIA

Drinkers in the UK and on the Continent might be forgiven for thinking that Australia's favourite drink is Foster's, thanks to the company's colourful advertising campaigns. But it isn't. Once upon a time, suited businessmen planned to put the beer on just about every bar possible from London to Berlin. But the "Foster's-ization" of Western Europe didn't happen, and it never happened in Australia either. Instead, these days the country is gaining a reputation for its craft brewing, and many beer drinkers worldwide are taking an interest.

Many look to long-time favourite, Cooper's (see pp.248–249) of Adelaide, which has been producing some world-class bottle-conditioned beers for more than 100 years. But small is beautiful, too, and there is an increasing number of new brewers wanting to have their moment in the full glare of the midday sun. As local brewers travelled the world, they came to experience beers that they wanted to emulate when they returned home. This growth in interest was followed by a new generation of bar and off-licence owners who realized that selling a wide range that included both locally brewed beers and those from overseas would be good for business. The number of microbreweries is now well over one hundred, even though many have to survive on very small levels of production. Australia, which once had a reputation for only serving ice-cold lagers, has taken craft brewing to its heart – it has fallen under the spell of US-style IPAs, English stouts, Belgian wheat beers, and Czech pilsners. Brewers are producing not only wild beers, sour beers, and those that have been wood-aged, but also imperial stouts made with Belgian yeasts, saisons, and pale ales.

JAMES BOAG'S

Ever since James Boag set up his eponymous brewery in Launceston, owners have come and gone – reflecting the ups and downs of the Australian brewing industry – but Boag's beers still refresh and revive Tasmanian beer lovers.

THE FACTS...

OWNER Lion Breweries

FOUNDED 1883

ADDRESS 39 William Street, Launceston, Tasmania 7250

WEBSITE www.boags.com.au

PHILOSOPHY Tasmania: the only place it's possible

THE BREWING WORLD IS ONE THAT has rarely stood still. Families come and go, companies are bought, sold, changed, or closed. Those with the longest pedigree are often the ones that have had the most chequered careers. You could argue that this has been the way with James Boag's, and yet its beers remain at the heart and soul of Tasmanian brewing culture. Queen Victoria was on the throne when James Boag and his son, also called James, bought the already established Esk Brewery in Launceston in 1883. Although they kept the name Esk Brewery, the company became more usually known as Boag's Brewery, as it is known to this day. The Boag family were part of the company until 1976 when George Boag, the grandson of

James Boag II, retired, although Cascade had bought the brewery in 1922.

Fast forward to the early 1990s and American merchant banker, Philip Adkins, became chief executive and a major shareholder. It was during his time that James Boag's Premium Lager was launched, a beer that would become the brewery's flagship brew. Adkins famously chose to pick a fight with the beer writer Michael Jackson, when he criticized the coldness and blandness of Australian beers, though he had praised Premium Lager. The merry-go-round of owners turned again in 2000 when San Miguel took over. Subsequently in 2007 the current owners, Lion Breweries, stepped into the frame. Today, even though the brewery focuses on a range of lagers notable for their refreshment rather than their complexity, its honey porter and an English-style pale ale are widely acclaimed. Boag's Centre for Beer Lovers is based at Launceston's historic Tamar Hotel and features a museum, while brewery tours are a popular tourist excursion for visitors to the city.

JAMES BOAG'S
DRAUGHT

JAMES BOAG'S
PREMIUM LAGER

JAMES BOAG'S
WIZARD SMITH'S ALE

TASTING NOTES

DRAUGHT   PALE LAGER, 4.7% ABV

Clean and refreshing, this amber-gold lager has hints of lemon citrus on the nose, a crisp carbonation on the palate, and a medium-soft mouthfeel with hints of caramel before a quick finish that features a whisper of citrus.

FOOD PAIRING: It's got to be a pork bap with a little touch of apple sauce – the beer's crispness elevates a mere snack into something much grander.

PREMIUM LAGER   PALE LAGER, 5% ABV

The aroma of this golden lager is a waft of lemon caught on a gentle breeze, while the palate tingles with a gentle lemon citrus character, an appetizing tanginess, and a hint of white pepper; the long finish is bitter.

FOOD PAIRING: Put some prawns on the barbecue, dole out helpings of a crispy green salad, and you're on fire.

WIZARD SMITH'S ALE   ENGLISH PALE ALE, 5% ABV

Named after a former employee who saved stranded brewery horses in the great flood of 1929, this amber brew boasts an earthy, grainy nose, a creamy mouthfeel, caramel and citrus notes, and a longish dry finish.

FOOD PAIRING: Go spicy and pair this with a chicken korma – watch the carbonation cut through the creamy sauce, and the caramel and citrus counterpoint the curry's sweetness.

COOPERS BREWERY

The South Australia city of Adelaide has been home to Coopers since 1862. The brewery is still family-owned and produces a scintillating range of world-beating beers, including its famous Sparkling Ale.

HISTORY, HERITAGE, FAMILY VALUES – Adelaide-based Coopers has them all. Their first brew was made in 1862 when a Yorkshire-born immigrant, Thomas Cooper, brewed a beer for his sick wife. Unlike other "colonial" beers of the time, there was no sugar in his brew, only malt, hops, yeast, and water. Coopers ales quickly became a success and spread through the new state of South Australia. Now Coopers are the largest Australian-owned brewery and Cooper family members remain at the helm. In 2001 the company moved a short distance from the site they'd occupied in Adelaide since 1881, to a new $40 million brewery in the suburb of Regency Park. You could argue that there is a contrarian spirit to Coopers. After all, Australia is the land of the ice-cold lager served in a frosted glass, but they remain best known for a Sparkling Ale that is brash, breezy, and hoppy – an Australian ale that has become world-famous and is the direct descendant of the beer that Thomas Cooper made for his wife all those years ago. However, the company does have a sound business head – Crown Gold lager has been brewed since 1968, and Coopers' zesty, sprightly Premium Lager is a favourable alternative to those drinkers who might not like ale, but do prefer a lager with some character. Other beers in the portfolio include a roasty-toasty stout that competes with Guinness in Australia's bars, Pale Ale, Mild Ale, and the sumptuous and luxurious Vintage Ale, which ages well.

THE FACTS...

OWNER Coopers Brewery Ltd

FOUNDED 1862

ADDRESS 461 South Road, Regency Park, South Australia, 5010

WEBSITE www.coopers.com.au

PHILOSOPHY From humble beginnings to the largest Australian-owned brewery

COOPERS BREWERY BEST EXTRA STOUT

COOPERS BREWERY DARK ALE

COOPERS BREWERY SPARKLING ALE

COOPERS BREWERY ORIGINAL PALE ALE

Metamorphosis
*First brewed in 1998,
the bottle-conditioned ale
will change as it ages*

COOPERS BREWERY EXTRA STRONG VINTAGE ALE

TASTING NOTES

BEST EXTRA STOUT DRY STOUT, 6.3% ABV
This beer pours a very dark chestnut brown with an espresso-coloured head; there's mocha coffee, milky coffee, and milk chocolate on the nose, while in the mouth, it's reminiscent of bitter milky coffee with plenty of vanilla and dark biscuity flavours. This is a beer for Sambuca lovers.

FOOD PAIRING: Make it casual with thick slices of rare roast beef and horseradish in fresh granary bread or take it to the end of the meal with bittersweet desserts such as tiramisu.

DARK ALE BROWN ALE, 4.5% ABV
The beer is amber-brown, topped with a tight collar of cappuccino foam that fades away to release roast, nutty, and caramel notes. It's a generous mouthful of flavour for its relatively low strength, with toffee, demerara sugar, and chocolate notes, before finishing with a light bitterness.

FOOD PAIRING: Serve with glazed barbeque ribs and the beer's roasty, caramel notes will wrap themselves tightly around the sweet, spicy, smoky meat.

SPARKLING ALE AUSTRALIAN PALE ALE, 5.8% ABV
Pale gold in colour, the nose is aromatic, with hints of dried fruit and ripe peach. In the mouth, it's herbal, slightly spicy, and sparky on the tongue, while a biscuity, grainy dryness provides a backbone for the finish. Eminently thirst-quenching.

FOOD PAIRING: A plate of oysters on the shell with just a dash of Tabasco will create a magnificent floor show of flavour in your mouth.

ORIGINAL PALE ALE GOLDEN ALE, 4.5% ABV
Prickly carbonation makes this honey-coloured pale ale a lively little chap on the palate. The aroma is faint lemon while on the palate it is bittersweet, with hints of citrus, and leads to a quick but dry finish. A pleasing summer's day refresher.

FOOD PAIRING: Refreshment is the key aim of this beer, but its brisk bouquet of bubbles would make it a natural partner for fried food such as fish and chips.

EXTRA STRONG VINTAGE ALE 7.5% ABV
Chestnut brown in colour with rich fruitcake, hop resins, and faint citrus on the nose. Depending on the age, there could be notes of toffee, caramel, roast grain, fruit jelly, and Orange Muscat on the palate, while the finish is dry and bitter.

FOOD PAIRING: Sweet, creamy puddings, such as strawberry shortcake, work well with the Vintage's roastiness and dark maltiness, cutting through the creaminess of the dessert and adding another taste dimension.

HOLGATE BREWHOUSE

Paul and Natasha Holgate travelled around the USA and Europe in the late 1990s and returned bursting with the desire to emulate the craft beer breweries they saw and enjoyed on their journey – thus, Holgate Brewhouse was born.

THE FACTS...

OWNER Paul and Natasha Holgate

FOUNDED 1999

ADDRESS 79 High Street Woodend, Victoria 3442

WEBSITE www.holgatebrewhouse.com

PHILOSOPHY Full-flavoured cask beers and lagers that are brewed true to style

HOME FOR THE HOLGATE BREWHOUSE is the late 19th-century redbrick Keatings Hotel in the town of Woodend, which once welcomed travellers on their way from Melbourne to go prospecting in the Bendigo goldfields. Now it's not only a brewhouse but also a bar, restaurant, and hotel, that instead of gold-diggers welcomes travellers in search of Holgate's award-winning beers. The original inspiration for taking up life in the company of barley and hops was a journey that Paul Holgate and his wife Natasha took through the USA and Europe – they were utterly bowled over by the quality and range of the beers that they encountered. Once back home, the couple ditched their corporate careers and began brewing in 1999; three years later they took over the running of the hotel. It's a common enough story: beer and food lovers in a country where beer is relatively one-dimensional go travelling, discover taste and flavour, and want to make it their life. There are hundreds of brewers throughout the world who have had that epiphany; however, one of the things that marks out Paul Holgate is the fact that he serves his ESB and cask-conditioned Porter on hand pump – presumably a reflection of his family's original Mancunian background.

His range also includes his take on pale ale, a pilsner, which contains lots of Saaz hops but is brewed in a Dortmunder style, and an American IPA. Special one-offs include a double IPA, Belgian-style witbier and an annual Easter beer that is rather special and is notably different every year. In 2011, Beelzebub's Jewels was a Belgian-style quadrupel that had been aged in Pinot Noir barrels. Thank goodness for beer epiphanies.

HOLGATE BREWHOUSE
ESB

HOLGATE BREWHOUSE
MT MACEDON ALE

HOLGATE BREWHOUSE
PILSNER

TASTING NOTES

ESB ENGLISH BITTER, 5% ABV
Despite its name, this is more of a best bitter than an ESB in the classic English sense. Light amber in colour, it has an accomplished mixture of citrus hop and grainy biscuitiness on the nose, followed by light caramel and citrus notes on the palate and a dry bitter finish.

FOOD PAIRING: Delicious with tapas – the sweet and spice of grilled chorizo is perfect with the malty sweetness and citrus fruit of the beer.

MT MACEDON ALE AMERICAN PALE ALE, 4.5% ABV
Honey-gold in colour, this polished pale ale has a suggestion of tropical fruit on the nose along with a more rigorous touch of hop resin. There is more tropical fruit in the mouth, a grainy sweetness, and a balance of bitterness in the finish.

FOOD PAIRING: Bitterness, fruitiness, malty sweetness with a bowl of chilli con carne – what's not to like?

PILSNER 5.1% ABV
The spelling is Bohemian (and Saaz hops are used), but this is more of a Bavarian-style pilsner with a slight spicy hop character, a whisper of graininess, and bitterness in the finish. Bohemia meets Bavaria in Woodend.

FOOD PAIRING: Pilsner is a light and delicate beer that is overwhelmed by strongly flavoured dishes; seafood goes well with it and fried calamari would be even better as the quenching bitterness will cut through the oiliness.

LITTLE BREWING

Award-winning home-brewer Warwick Little took the plunge into the commercial world in 2007. His range of Belgian- and US-influenced beers has tickled and tantalized the palates of the beer drinkers of New South Wales.

THE FACTS...

OWNER Warwick and Kylie Little

FOUNDED 2007

ADDRESS Unit 1, 58 Uralla Road, Port Macquarie, New South Wales 2444

WEBSITE www.thelittlebrewingcompany.com.au

PHILOSOPHY Beers brewed without compromise and true to style

LITTLE BREWING
WICKED ELF PALE ALE

WHAT GOES THROUGH THE MIND of a home-brewer when a batch of freshly made beer goes right, when it tastes as good or even better than the beer bought in the bar or supermarket? Most will look forward to the next brew, while some will start thinking of moving up onto the next level and beginning commercial brewing. The latter is the option that home-brewer Warwick Little took at the end of 2006 when, along with his wife Kylie, he started setting up brewing kit in the coastal city of Port Macquarie. A few months later in July 2007, the beers of Little Brewing were on sale and the dream that may have driven Little through his years of home-brewing finally became a reality. Not all home-brewers make it, but Little, who had won awards for his home-brews, has thrived in the competitive world of craft brewing. As well as his home-brewing prowess, perhaps it also helped that he has a university degree in wine science, winery laboratory experience and, on a more metaphysical level, maybe it was something to do with the fact that

his ancestors had been in the English brewing and pub trade from the 18th century until the 1970s. His selection of beers is released under the Wicked Elf and Mad Abbot range, with the latter being a series of Belgian Trappist-inspired beers such as a dubbel and a tripel. As for the regulars, Belgium, Bohemia, and the US are the influences with a witbier, pale ale, and pilsner being produced. Seasonal specials include a kölsch and a porter. These beers have been amply rewarded, but it's ironic that until 2011 Little Brewing's beers were unavailable in their hometown due to all the bars and pubs being tied to larger breweries. Port Macquarie's loss is Melbourne, Sydney, and Brisbane's gain.

TASTING NOTES

WICKED ELF PALE ALE AMERICAN PALE ALE, 5.4% ABV
Deep amber in colour, the Cyrano de Bergerac-sized nose of this pale ale hums with big floral and citrus notes and a juicy caramel balance. There's an equally succulent burst of citrus and malt sweetness on the palate before a bitter finish.

FOOD PAIRING: Try it with red meat or full flavoured game, such as mallard or even hare; hotly spiced Thai or Indian dishes also collaborate well.

MAD ABBOT TRIPEL BELGIAN TRIPEL, 9.5% ABV
You'd swear this beer had been crafted by holy hands, such is its closeness to the classic Trappist pale strong beer. The fragrant nose features lychee, peach, a biscuity sweetness and alcohol, with similar notes on the palate plus a champagne-like softness before its long spirituous, bitter, and dry finish.

FOOD PAIRING: Serve chilled as an apéritif or wait until the end of the meal and accompany with a pungently ripe soft cheese such as Stinking Bishop.

WICKED ELF PORTER PORTER, 6.2% ABV
Talk about contradictions: it's midnight in the glass, while morning aromas of espresso and chocolate lift themselves onto the nose. The mouthfeel is rich and luscious, smooth and soothing, with more chocolate and coffee notes, all held in place by a robust earthiness, before it finishes dry and bitter.

FOOD PAIRING: Try this beer with beef casserole and it will just melt into the dish.

LITTLE BREWING
MAD ABBOT TRIPEL

LITTLE BREWING
WICKED ELF PORTER

LITTLE CREATURES

When three friends got together to form a brewery in 2000, ice-cold lager was the norm, but they had a notion that their US-influenced, hoppy pale ale might just be successful. How right they were.

THE FACTS...

OWNER Lion Breweries

FOUNDED 2000

ADDRESS 40 Mews Road, Fremantle, Western Australia, 6160

WEBSITE www.littlecreatures.com.au

PHILOSOPHY To create great hop-driven pale ale

LITTLE CREATURES WAS FOUNDED IN 2000. It was the collective brainchild of Howard Cearns, Nic Trimboli, and Phil Sexton. The new brewery was set up in the Western Australian city of Fremantle in an old waterfront building that had once been a crocodile farm. Alongside the brewery, which fans are encouraged to visit, there is an on-site bar and restaurant. Cearns, who had worked in the creative design side of the brewing industry, came up with the brewery name, citing the hobbits or little creatures that drifted from pub to pub in *The Lord of the Rings*. Sexton, on the other hand, was a master brewer who had created Bridgeport IPA in the US and founded Matilda Bay (see p.256),

which had later been bought by Lion Nathan. Eager for a second bite at the brewing cherry, he got to work and produced what would become the brewery's signature beer, Pale Ale. This was an American-influenced pale ale that didn't stint on the hops. It was a revelation, given that the first wave of the Australian microbrewing revolution had peaked and ice-cold lager still remained the dominant beer. Other beers followed, including Pilsner and Rogers Beer – apparently named after a couple of men called Roger who developed it – while Single Batch is a regular limited release, which could be anything from the brewery's take on an old classic style to something quite different. In 2012, it was announced that Lion Breweries had bought Little Creatures but they promised that little would be changed. At the same time, plans were announced that a second Little Creatures brewery would be built in the city of Geelong in the state of Victoria. Little Creatures is not so little these days.

LITTLE CREATURES
BRIGHT ALE

LITTLE CREATURES
PALE ALE

LITTLE CREATURES
ROGERS BEER

TASTING NOTES

BRIGHT ALE GOLDEN ALE, 4.5% ABV
Bright is the right description for this straw-coloured refresher – it gleams gold in the glass and has a quenching, bittersweet character that makes it ideal as a sunny summer's day drink in the garden.
FOOD PAIRING: Go Asian and cook up a serving of pad thai and wait for the bittersweetness of the beer to lift the bright colours of the dish.

PALE ALE AMERICAN PALE ALE, 5.2% ABV
The beer that announced the arrival of Little Creatures is a gold-honey colour, while the nose flutters with notes of grapefruit, biscuity sweetness, and orange. Take a swig and enjoy tropical fruit, a medium mouthfeel, and a bitterness that hangs around in the finish.
FOOD PAIRING: Roast a chicken and note how the beer lifts and adds to the sweetness of the meat, while sage and onion stuffing will find a comfortable partner in the tropical fruitiness of the beer.

ROGERS BEER ENGLISH PALE ALE, 3.8% ABV
For a beer that's comparatively low in alcohol, this dark amber session all-rounder packs a lot of flavour into the glass: toffee, caramel, some passionfruit, a crisp mouthfeel, and a sturdy bitter finish.
FOOD PAIRING: For a traditional feel, try this with a steak and kidney pie – the beer's toffee and caramel notes will provide an appetizing contrast to the meat.

MALT SHOVEL

Malt Shovel might be part and parcel of the gigantic Lion Breweries empire, but its craft brewing sensibilities are kept intact and thrive under the guidance of the legendary master brewer Chuck Hahn and his James Squire beers.

THE FACTS...

OWNER Lion Breweries
FOUNDED 1998
ADDRESS 99-101 Pyrmont Bridge Road, Camperdown, Sydney, New South Wales, 2050
WEBSITE www.maltshovel.com.au
PHILOSOPHY Dedicated to quality

AFTER BEING CAUGHT STEALING CHICKENS, James Squire was transported to Australia. After all, this was 1785 when all manner of small transgressions were severely punished, but we should give thanks for small mercies – without Squire's exit from his homeland, his name wouldn't be adorning the labels of Malt Shovel's beers. As well as being a chicken thief, Squire is also known as the first person to brew on the Australian continent, which is why Malt Shovel has looked to him for inspiration. These days, under the more up-to-date guidance of Chuck Hahn, who is widely admired throughout the brewing industry, drinkers have good reason to think that brewing has come on since the days

of Squire. After years with Molson Coors and Steinlager, US-born Hahn started his own eponymous brewery in the late 1980s until Lion Nathan bought it in the following decade. The corporation continued with the Hahn Brewery but also set up Malt Shovel in 1998, which brewed the James Squire range – to all intents and purposes this was the company's craft brewery arm. The brewery's home is part of an old stable block in the Camperdown suburb of Sydney.

Hahn is head brewer of both businesses, but whatever the intricacies of ownership, Malt Shovel's James Squire range features highly accomplished beers. They are supplied to the four James Squire-branded brewpubs that can be found in Sydney, Perth, and Melbourne, where small batches of seasonal beer are produced. And if James Squire were alive today one would hope that he would enjoy his namesake beer, though you'd have to keep an eye on the chickens if he came to visit!

MALT SHOVEL THE CHANCER

MALT SHOVEL NINE TALES

MALT SHOVEL FOUR 'WIVES'

TASTING NOTES

THE CHANCER GOLDEN ALE, 4.5% ABV
This honey-gold coloured ale sparkles in the glass, with subdued notes of citrus fruit on the nose. It is sprightly and sparky with citrus lemon in the mouth, with hints of tropical fruit and a grainy sweetness before the quenching finish.

FOOD PAIRING: A lightly flavoured beer demands an equally nimble, fleet-of-foot dish, so put sea bass under the grill and taste how divinely it goes with this beer.

NINE TALES AMBER ALE, 5% ABV
This copper-coloured ale is a blend of three malts and three hops grown in Tasmania. It has a toasty, slightly nutty nose, while the palate is a smooth assembly of toffee and caramel sweetness balanced by an easy-going bitterness. The finish is dry and offers a hint of nuttiness.

FOOD PAIRING: The toasty, nutty notes match and complement the char and sea-fresh sweetness of seared scallops served on the half-shell accompanied by sweet, roasted squash purée.

FOUR 'WIVES' PILSENER, 5% ABV
Named in honour of James Squire's wife and three mistresses, Four 'Wives' contains Saaz hops from both the Czech Republic and New Zealand, which produce a spicy, floral bouquet on the nose. In the mouth it's crispy and subtly spicy with a hint of lemon, all leading to a brisk bitter finish.

FOOD PAIRING: What could be more compatible than a plate of juicy, meaty, salty bratwurst and a glass of Four 'Wives'?

BILLABONG BREWERY

www.billabongbrewing.com.au

HOME FOR BILLABONG is the Perth suburb of Myaree where Alan Proctor began brewing in 1993. He initially focused on the "brew on premise" market, where anyone could come and brew their own beer and take it home. This still continues, but the brewery also entered the commercial market in 2006 with the award-winning 4 Hop Ale, which features a quartet of hops that are added at eight different stages. It is also noted for its selection of gluten-free beers, such as Blonde.

BLUETONGUE

www.bluetongue.com.au

BLUETONGUE WAS STARTED by four businessmen in 2003 in the wine region of Hunter Valley in a suburb of Newcastle (it has since moved to the town of Warnervale). Now owned by the Foster's Group, a subsidiary of SABMiller, it produces four regular brands, including its "craft" range duo Traditional Pilsener – which has plenty of tropical fruit on the nose – and an alcoholic Ginger Beer. Back in 2006, it famously hired Paris Hilton for the launch of its now defunct low-carb Bondi Blonde brand.

BOOTLEG

www.bootlegbrewery.com.au

TOURISTS SEEKING A BREAK from trailing around vineyards in the Margaret River region often fetch up at Bootleg's bar and restaurant, which is part of the Bootleg brewing complex. Having started brewing in 1994 with a single Bitter Beer, Bootleg now produces a range of award-winning beers under the watchful eye of head brewer Michael Brookes, who joined in 1998, initially working as a bartender. Popular beers include the full-bodied brown ale Raging Bull, the crisp, citrussy Settler's Pale Ale, and an English-style bitter named Toms Amber Ale.

BRIDGE ROAD BREWERS

www.bridgeroadbrewers.com.au

BEN KRAUS OPENED BRIDGE ROAD in 2005, setting up the brewing kit in an old coach house at the back of his parents' hotel in the

BILLABONG BLONDE

BRIDGE ROAD CHESTNUT PILSNER

scenic Victoria town of Beechworth. The main beer he produces is Beechworth Pale Ale, a zesty, refreshing American-style pale ale, though he also brews a Bavarian-influenced weisse and a pilsner flavoured with chestnuts; his attractively packaged "Chevalier" range of beers includes a citrussy Saison and a spicy Bière de Garde.

BRIGHT

www.brightbrewery.com.au

THERE USED TO BE A BRIGHT BREWERY in the town of the same name, but it folded in the middle of World War I. Fast-forward to the start of 2005 when two local couples had the bright idea of resurrecting it. Beer was first brewed elsewhere, but a year later a microbrewery was installed and the ale flowed. The likes of the aromatic Hellfire Amber Ale and the rich, robust Staircase Porter can either be enjoyed at the onsite bar or in cafés, bars, and restaurants as far away as Melbourne.

CARLTON DRAUGHT

www.carltondraught.com.au

CARLTON DRAUGHT is one of Australia's best-selling mainstream lagers. It was first brewed in 1956 at the Darwin brewery, owned by what was then Carlton & United Breweries. Consolidation after consolidation has followed and the beer is now brewed in Abbotsford, a suburb of Melbourne. The company has also changed its name to Carlton & United Beverages and is now a subsidiary of SABMiller. It is pale in colour, 4.6% ABV (at one time it was 5%), is served as cold as a winter's day in Siberia, and is moderate in its bitterness.

CASCADE

www.cascadebreweryco.com.au

CASCADE IS THE OLDEST working brewery in Australia, having been set up in South Hobart in 1832 by Englishman Peter Degraves. It is also one of the most picturesque breweries in the land, castle-like and solidly built with Mount Wellington posing in the background. Fire badly damaged it in 1967 but it was carefully renovated and remains an important stage on Tasmania's tourist trail. Now part of SABMiller, it's known for its mainstream Cascade Premium Lager, though it dips its toes into the craft beer pool with speciality brands such as First Harvest Ale and produces its own Cascade Stout.

CROWN

www.thecrowncompany.com

THIS IS A PREMIUM LAGER made by SABMiller subsidiary Carlton & United Beverages and brewed at its Melbourne Abbotsford site. It was reportedly first brewed in 1919 and only served to visiting foreign dignitaries. It wasn't until 1954 that Crown became available to the wider public in honour of Queen Elizabeth II's first visit to Australia. It has since become one of the best-selling lagers in the country, and is noted for its iconic thin-necked bottle-shape. Since 2008, the brewery has aimed its annual one-off Crown Ambassador release at the luxury beer market.

FERAL BREWING

www.feralbrewing.com.au

YOU CAN DRINK WELL in the Western Australia region of Swan Valley, where the long-established wine-makers have now been joined by several microbreweries, including Feral. Set up in 2002, the brewery shares its space with a bar and restaurant, where the bold beers of head brewer Brendan Varis can be tasted. The signature beer is a spicy, juicy, fruity Belgian-style wheat beer called Feral White, though its American-style IPA Hop Hog, Smoked Porter, and powerful barley wine Razorback mean there is plenty to enthuse over at the tap.

GAGE ROADS

www.gageroads.com.au

PETER NOLIN AND BILL HOEDEMAKER originally worked for craft beer pioneers, the Sail & Anchor brewpub but left it in 2002. Three years later, Gage Roads in the Perth suburb of Palmyra started producing beer. Beers hitting the road throughout Western Australia and further afield include a northern Germany-style lager, the IPA Sleeping Giant, and the fragrant Atomic Pale Ale. As well as its main brands, Gage Roads likes to brew limited release one-offs – in 2013, they brewed a dry-hopped Strong Ale for Australia Day.

GRAND RIDGE BREWERY

www.grand-ridge.com.au

MIRBOO NORTH IS A SMALL TOWN in the state of Victoria, which is where Grand Ridge embraced the art and science of brewing in the late 1980s under a previous owner and different name. Current owner Eric Walters oversees a bright and colourful range of craft beers including its signature beer Brewers Pilsener. However, Grand Ridge's accomplished range also includes a barley wine, stout, and classic Australian bitter. In 2012 the brewery won 11 medals at the Australian International Beer Awards.

HAHN

www.hahn.com.au

CHARLES "CHUCK" HAHN set up his eponymous brewery on an old factory site in a Sydney suburb in 1986 after spending several years brewing Steinlager in New Zealand. Hahn Premium was an immediate success, but an economic downturn in the early 1990s eventually led to Lion Nathan stepping in to buy the business. Hahn's beers are now produced at Tooheys (see p.257), while Hahn himself is at the helm at the company's "craft" brewery Malt Shovel (see p.253). The beers brewed are mainstream lagers, with Premium Light one of the best-selling light beers in Australia.

KNAPPSTEIN

www.knappstein.com.au

THOSE WHO SAY the grape and the grain shouldn't mix haven't tried Knappstein's fragrant, fruity, full-bodied Reserve Lager. It's the only beer brewed at the Knappstein winery in the South Australia town of Clare, which is plum in the middle of the Clare Valley wine region. The beer has been made since 2006 when Lion Nathan bought the Knappstein winery. There had previously been a brewery on the site until 1916 and so Nathan succeeded in bringing the tradition back to its old home.

LORD NELSON BREWERY HOTEL

www.lordnelsonbrewery.com

THE LORD NELSON claims a couple of historical firsts – it is Sydney's oldest licensed hotel and is one of the longest established Australian brewpubs, with brewing having started in 1987. English-style ales are made at the back of the bar with six regulars on tap, although seasonal beers are also produced. Although the emphasis is on pale ales, Old Admiral is a full-bodied old ale that will cure the homesickness of any passing beer-loving pom.

LORD NELSON OLD ADMIRAL

MATILDA BAY

www.matildabay.com.au

WHEN PHIL SEXTON STARTED brewing beer for Fremantle's Sail & Anchor pub in 1984, he was a pioneer and the tasty craft beers he produced included the rich dark lager Dogbolter and refreshing Redback wheat beer – the first of its style to be brewed in Australia. Nowadays, the brewery is owned by Carlton & United Beverages and located in a Melbourne suburb, with mainstream brands, such as its Bohemian Pilsner brewed at Cascade, while the so-called "garage brewery" in Port Melbourne caters to the more adventurous beer lover.

MOO BREW

www.moobrew.com.au

STYLISHLY SHAPED BOTTLES that hint at the connoisseurship of the wine drinker and labels especially designed by artist John Kelly give the products of Moo Brew an obvious cachet. It also helps that Moo's head brewer Owen Johnston is fabulously adept at making beer. Based on a winery in gorgeous countryside outside Hobart, Tasmania, Johnston oversees a sleek selection of beers including a spicy Bavarian-style hefeweizen, an elegant pilsner, a light Belgian pale ale, an American dark ale, and an aromatic American-style pale ale, plus regular specials of which the Imperial Stout is one of the most eagerly awaited.

MOUNTAIN GOAT

www.goatbeer.com.au

FRIENDS DAVE BONIGHTON and Cam Hines started Mountain Goat in 1997 with what is still their signature beer, Hightail Ale – a fruity complex ale that has won plenty of awards. The beers were contract-brewed at first, but eventually the two persistent pals raised the money and opened their own brewery. Now based in the Melbourne suburb of Richmond, Mountain Goat also brews a selection of one-off batches that can be found at the brewery-based Goat Bar, which opens every Friday evening.

MURRAY'S

www.murraysbrewingco.com.au

MURRAY'S KICKED OFF brewing in 2003, located at an iconic hotel that inspired the famous Aussie country song, The Pub With No Beer. Rapid growth and demand for their eclectic beers saw a move to Port Stephens in the Hunter Valley region in 2009, where the brewery was joined by a restaurant, bar, and winery. Head brewer Shawn Sherlock produces a stimulating selection of boldly flavoured beers including a US-UK crossover Angry Man pale ale, a refreshing wheat beer, a fruity lager, and other more random extreme beers including a Belgian-style imperial stout.

PURE BLONDE

www.pureblonde.com.au

PURE BLONDE is one of the best-selling low-carb beers in Australia. Brewed by Carlton & United Beverages, it was launched in 2004 and quickly became a favourite among the more health-conscious who wanted to enjoy a beer, but were also keen to cut down on the calories. According to its makers, its USP is a longer brewing time that breaks down more natural sugars than usual. The end result is a beer with 70% less carbohydrate than a standard full-strength version.

REDOAK

www.redoak.com.au

WHETHER IT'S A HEFEWEIZEN flavoured with blackberry, an oatmeal stout, a Bavarian pilsner or the much awarded raspberry-bomb Framboise Froment, Redoak brews a beer for every occasion. It was set up in Sydney in 2004 by David Hollyoak, who made his first home-brew ginger beer at 14. His elegant and inventive interpretations of some of the world's great beer styles are best explored at the brewery's Boutique Beer Café where beer- and food-matching dinners and beer classes are regular events.

SCHARER'S

www.scharers.com.au

SMALL IS BEAUTIFUL FOR SCHARER'S, which only produces two beers: a bock and a Bavarian-style lager. Inspired by German brewers to make high-quality natural beers, publican Geoff Scharer built a microbrewery at the historic George IV inn in the New South Wales town of Picton in 1987. He sold the business in 2006 with the stipulation that the recipes wouldn't be changed. The new owners have stuck to that promise and the beers are now also available at the Australian Hotel in the Rocks area of Sydney. Sadly, Geoff Scharer died in 2012, but he is remembered as an Australian craft beer pioneer.

MURRAY'S ANGRY MAN

SOUTH AUSTRALIA BREWING

www.lionco.com.au

THIS ADELAIDE-LOCATED BREWERY first swung into action in 1859 with West End Draught, which today is one of the best-selling beers in South Australia. As with many beers that have a tradition reaching back into the colonial era, what probably started off as an ale is now a generic pale lager. The brewery is currently owned by Lion Nathan Company and has two sites, one of which is devoted to making the Southwark brand of beers. Southwark Old Stout, a rich, roasty dark beer that was launched in 1984, is made here.

STONE & WOOD

www.stoneandwood.com.au

BYRON BAY IS A BREEZY BEACHSIDE town north of Sydney with gorgeous beaches that encourage an alternative surfer mentality among the locals. Three former Matilda Bay veterans and a local publican established Stone & Wood here in 2008. They brew a quartet of beers, including a sprightly, thirst-quenching lager that is ideal after an afternoon spent riding waves, a deep red brew named Jasper Ale, a golden, cloudy Pacific Ale, and an intriguing limited release interpretation of a Stein lager where hot rocks are added to the brew. Pacific Ale is slightly unusual in that it is unfiltered, which gives it its cloudy colour and means that the flavour that is usually lost through the filtering process is preserved. It is also unpasteurized so that it has a crisp fresh taste that pasteurized beers do not always have.

SUNSHINE COAST

www.sunshinecoastbrewery.com

THE SUN HAS CERTAINLY SHONE for Sunshine Coast Brewery since it opened on Australia Day in 1998. Located in a suburb of Maroochydore on the Queensland Sunshine Coast, the brewery has picked up a hatful of awards for well-crafted beers, including the crowd-pleasing Summer Ale. This bright mid-strength beer has a tropical fruit hop aroma with flavours of passion fruit, peach, and melon. More European-influenced beers such as Hefeweizen, Czech Mate Pilsner, and Glasshouse Rauch are also produced. Until 2012 the brewery had a tap in Kunda Park, but this has closed and now beer can be bought directly from the brewery.

TOOHEYS

www.lionco.com.au

THE TOOHEY BROTHERS moved from Melbourne to Sydney in the 1860s and started brewing at the end of the decade. Tooheys Old Black Ale was one of their debutants and it continues to be made today under the name of Tooheys Old. By the start of the 20th century, Tooheys had moved to the Surry Hills suburb of Sydney. They later moved to the Lidcombe area of the city, where their beer is still being brewed today, though it is now under the ownership of Lion. One of their bestsellers is Tooheys New, which was actually launched in 1931 and marked a sea-change for the brewery, as it was the first of many lager brands to be brewed by the company. Tooheys Extra Dry, a crisp, dry lager is another popular beer brewed and widely sold by the company today.

VICTORIA BITTER

www.victoriabitter.com.au

VICTORIA BITTER, or VB as it is commonly known, was first brewed at the start of the 20th century when the name was probably more correctly used than it is now. It started off as a bitter but it is actually now a lager, although the original name remains. Owned by Carlton & United Beverages, it's one of the best-selling beers in the country and brewed at its owner's Melbourne plant. Powerful TV advertising from the 1960s onwards helped to make the brand popular throughout the country. Back in 2009, its ABV was lowered from 4.9% to 4.6%, a decision that was reversed in 2012.

WIG & PEN

www.wigandpen.com.au

HOMESICK BEER-LOVING BRITS on a visit to the Australian capital usually make a beeline for this British-style cosy traditional brewpub where cask-conditioned beers are served with the aid of hand pumps. Beer has been brewed at the Wig & Pen in Canberra since 1994 and today it brews ten regular beers as well as popular one-off batches. Alongside the real ales can be found such delights as a sprightly, thirst-quenching pilsner, a spicy hefeweizen, and one-offs such as Beetroot Berlinerweiss. They also produce a low-alchohol beer called Mister Natural, which takes its name from an Australian rock song. Wig & Pen was named the best small brewery in Australia at the 2012 Australian International Beer Awards.

STONE AND WOOD PACIFIC ALE

IMPORTANT ASIAN &
AUSTRALASIAN NATIONS

European-style beers have been brewed across most countries in Asia and Australasia since the late 1800s. However, few would have predicted the spectacular growth in consumption that has taken place in recent years. Across the region, many countries are now regarded as offering international brewing companies a great opportunity for expansion, as the more established markets in Europe and North and South America have reached maturity.

Unsurprisingly, China is by far the biggest market, with consumption now topping more than 50 billion litres (305 million barrels) of beer a year. The majority of this is produced by large multi-nationals, which are able to distribute throughout the whole country and around the world. Will Chinese consumers follow the trend that seems to have gripped the rest of the planet, including neighbouring Japan, and turn to their local craft brewers for exciting, innovative new beers? Only time will tell.

For most of the last century, New Zealand's brewing scene was dominated by two large brewing companies: DB and Lion. However, thanks to consumer demand there is now a fast-growing number of small breweries setting up and many exciting and award-winning beers being produced. The craft-brewing scene is also developing in India, with many of the new wave of brewpubs looking to the US not just for inspiration but for capital, too. And while Asia is home to its own international brewers – San Miguel, Asia Pacific, and Thailand's Singha – there are an increasing number of innovative, often German-inspired, brewpubs opening as well, across Singapore, Cambodia, Vietnam, Laos, and South Korea. Worth seeking out is Sri Lanka's well-renowned Lion Stout – a highly drinkable bottle-conditioned stout.

EMERSON'S

Time spent in Edinburgh sampling the malty delights of Scottish beer gave the 18-year-old Richard Emerson an antipathy towards the homogeneous blandness of the New Zealand beer scene, which led him to set up his own brewery.

THE FACTS...

OWNER Lion Breweries
FOUNDED 1992
ADDRESS Emerson Brewing Company, 14 Wickliffe Street, Dunedin 9016
WEBSITE www.emersons.co.nz
PHILOSOPHY To produce fresh, naturally carbonated, living beers full of natural flavour

EMERSON'S LONDON PORTER

EMERSON'S 1812

THE TOWN OF DUNEDIN IN NEW ZEALAND is known as the "Edinburgh of the south", the irony of which could not have been lost on Richard Emerson after he had accompanied his biochemist father to the Scottish capital in the 1980s. It was here that he developed a liking for full-malt beers, a taste not found in the flabby, bland beers of his homeland. Two years after returning home in 1990, he set up his eponymous brewery. The first brew, Emerson's London Porter, was unleashed at the start of 1993 to great acclaim. Success meant that the brewery swiftly outgrew its original site, settling into its current home, an industrial estate, in 2005. Its clean, cool lines of stainless steel might not have the romance of an old Trappist cloister or a brick-built tower brewery in the English Midlands, but the beers that Richard Emerson still oversees have a character and strength of flavour that make them some of the best-loved in the country. Opinions and emotions were mixed when in November 2012 it was announced that Lion Breweries had bought the brewery. However, Richard Emerson and his team are to remain in control. Whatever the future, Emerson's is guaranteed a place in the pantheon of New Zealand's craft beer heroes.

TASTING NOTES

LONDON PORTER 4.9% ABV
This is a sleek chestnut brown beast with a roasty, toasty nose balanced by a hint of sweetness, with flavours of mocha coffee, milk chocolate, roasted coffee beans, and a creamy mouthfeel.
FOOD PAIRING: The dark, smooth flavours of the Porter are a perfect match for a braised rack of lamb.

1812 PALE ALE, 4.9% ABV
A classic pale ale that became a benchmark for those that followed. Amber in colour with an orangey, citrus character and rich malt notes, and a long dry finish.
FOOD PAIRING: Fire up the barbecue, slather a chicken in lemon juice, start grilling, and watch how the citrussy notes lift the sweetness while the rich malt matches the char of the meat.

PILSNER 4.4% ABV
One of the first organic beers produced in the country. Organic malt is brought in from overseas, while Riwaka comes from the hop-growing Nelson region. With a blast of citrus and passion fruit, the palate balances malt sweetness and crisp dryness.
FOOD PAIRING: The light fruity character of the Pilsner dictates a delicate dish, something like calamari or grilled prawns.

EMERSON'S PILSNER

MOA

Moa draws on the wine-making skills of its home territory, the Marlborough region of New Zealand, to produce a series of elegantly flavoured beers that are at home both at the bar and on the dining table.

THE FACTS...

OWNER The Moa Group
FOUNDED 2003
ADDRESS Moa Brewing Company, Jacksons Road RD3, Blenheim, Marlborough
WEBSITE www.moabeer.com
PHILOSOPHY Wine-making techniques are used to produce an elegant range of bottle-conditioned beers

Wired tight
A muselet, or wire cage, adds a touch of practical glamour to the bottle – it stops the pressured beer forcing the cork out

MOA BLANC

MOA ORIGINAL

MOA BREAKFAST

MOA'S FOUNDER, JOSH SCOTT, is based in the wine country of the Marlborough region and comes from a family of well-known wine-makers. Yet it was the grain rather than the grape that first caught his imagination. After he started making beer as a teenager, he continued to hone his craft over the years at various breweries before taking the plunge and setting up Moa in 2003. However, he didn't completely turn his back on viniculture – Moa's beers have become a byword for elegance and flavour by applying the techniques learnt from Scott's family to brewing. This means that barrel ageing and bottle fermentation and conditioning (similar to the way champagne is produced) is at the core of Moa's brewing philosophy. Locally grown hops are favoured, while the water used in the beer comes from a natural spring that flows beneath the brewery. The beer is packaged in a selection of elegantly shaped bottles ranging from 12 fl oz (330ml) up to 50 fl oz (1.5l) magnum. All this preparation and attention to detail have not gone unnoticed: Moa's beers have won a lot of awards. As a result, as Scott has happily admitted, the beers are not cheap, but they can be enjoyed like wine, alongside fine food.

TASTING NOTES

BLANC GERMAN WHEAT BEER, 5% ABV
This is a German-style wheat beer, with 65% of wheat in the mash. There are banana, vanilla, and citrus notes, while in the mouth it is creamy and comforting, offering up hints of banana, spice, and citrus. Moa recommends it be served at 4°C (39°F).
FOOD PAIRING: With its creamy texture, brisk carbonation, and luminous fruit notes, a meaty, slightly oily fish such as grilled salmon would make the perfect partner.

ORIGINAL PILSNER, 5% ABV
Nelson Sauvin hops help to produce a bold, colourful tropical fruitiness with sweet biscuit-like notes. On the palate it's smooth with tropical fruit notes and a refreshing dry finish.
FOOD PAIRING: The bright colours and flavours of Asian cuisine are heavenly with this beer, perhaps a Thai hot and sour soup.

BREAKFAST FRUIT LAGER, 5.5% ABV
This is a lager-style beer that includes cherries and malted wheat. The nose has a sharp yet subdued hint of cherry along with whispers of cut apple. On the palate Breakfast is sprightly and champagne-like in its fullness, and gives an appetizing sense of refreshment.
FOOD PAIRING: Its champagne-like sprightliness and fruitiness will work with crème brûlée, teasing out the vanilla notes.

RENAISSANCE

Californian Andy Deuchars came to New Zealand to learn how to make wine, but the call of craft beer was too much for him and his brother-in-law Brian Thiel and so Renaissance's exemplary beers were brought into the world.

THE FACTS...

OWNER Renaissance Brewing Company

FOUNDED 2005

ADDRESS Renaissance Brewing, 1 Dodson Street, Blenheim 7240, Marlborough

WEBSITE www.renaissancebrewing.co.nz

PHILOSOPHY To make beers that rival our grape-based cousins

BROTHERS-IN-LAW ANDY DEUCHARS and Brian Thiel also became brothers-in-beer when the two Californians founded Renaissance in 2005. The pair were ideal partners. Thiel had trained as a motor mechanic, which made him invaluable in dealing with the nuts and bolts of getting a brewery up and running, while Deuchars had already brewed on the US West Coast with Anderson Valley (see p.183) before coming out to New Zealand with the aim of training as a wine maker. However, the lure of brewing was too strong and wine's loss was beer's gain. The two of them set up in the historic old Grove Mill in Blenheim. The Mill is the oldest commercial building in Blenheim and has a colourful past – it has also been home to an ice cream factory, malt house, and two wineries. Given that the drinkers of New Zealand generally plumped for pale lager-style beers, Renaissance took a different approach on its debut and wowed the world of Kiwi craft beer with an eclectic ale-orientated portfolio featuring such Old World classics as pale ale, Scotch ale, and porter. This approach certainly paid them dividends as the awards began to roll in. However, lager drinkers have not been forgotten and are well served by the brewery's Paradox, a fruity, tangy pilsner that bursts with citrus and tropical fruit notes courtesy of the Riwaka hop. In 2008, Søren Eriksen joined as an assistant brewer and along with Deuchars helped to develop a range of limited edition seasonal beers under the title of the Enlightenment range. In 2012, this included a black rye IPA and a wheat IPA. Eriksen is in the unusual position of not only being a Renaissance man but also using his employer's kit for his own beers that are sold under the name 8 Wired (see p.262).

TASTING NOTES

RENAISSANCE
VOYAGER

RENAISSANCE
CRAFTSMAN

RENAISSANCE
STONECUTTER

VOYAGER INDIA PALE ALE, 6% ABV
Dark orange in colour, this IPA contains a blend of New Zealand and English hops, which work together to produce a big hitter of a nose with resiny hop and tangy grapefruit. On the palate, grapefruit and a honeyed sweet maltiness combine before the long bitter finish.

FOOD PAIRING: How about fish and chips? The hop bitterness cuts through the oiliness of the dish while the citrus notes bring out the juiciness and sweetness of the fish.

CRAFTSMAN CHOCOLATE OATMEAL STOUT, 4.9% ABV
Deep-flavoured stout with a rich aroma of milk chocolate on the nose. In the mouth, it's silky and soothing, buoyant with coffee, chocolate, and roast notes, plus hop earthiness as a balance before leading to a long soulful finish.

FOOD PAIRING: Chocolate beer with a chocolate dessert perhaps, but a much better relationship is formed when it contrasts with a raspberry or strawberry tart.

STONECUTTER SCOTCH ALE, 7% ABV
Dark amber in colour, this intriguing beast offers a fusion of toffee, caramel, chocolate, dark fruit, and a whisper of smokiness on both the nose and the palate. The finish is dry and appetizing. Nine varieties of malted barley are used in the mash.

FOOD PAIRING: This rich-flavoured ale is a natural to be served alongside roast beef, where its dark brooding presence will lift the flavour of the meat.

8 WIRED

www.8wired.co.nz

SØREN ERIKSEN was working as a biochemist in Perth, Australia, when he received his beer epiphany courtesy of the beers of Little Creatures (see p.252). Home-brewing beckoned first and then he landed a job at Renaissance Brewing (see p.261) in Blenheim. Since 2009 he has been brewing big-flavoured, hop-happy beers under the 8 Wired name. Using New Zealand hops and inspired by the US craft beer scene, beers such as Hopwired I.P.A and Saison Sauvin have won him many brewing awards.

EPIC

www.epicbeer.com

EPIC IS AN AUCKLAND-BASED microbrewery whose beers are brewed under contract at Steam Brewing, where founder Luke Nicholas was once head brewer. Formed in 2006, Epic is known as one of the leading stars in the New Zealand craft-brewing firmament, with its imperial IPA Hop Zombie much sought after. Brewing collaborations have also taken place with the likes of Dogfish Head (see pp.154–155) and Thornbridge (see p.41).

GALBRAITH'S BREWING COMPANY

www.alehouse.co.nz

A FORMER LIBRARY has been home to this Auckland-based brewpub since 1995, when Keith Galbraith started brewing the kind of cask-conditioned beers he'd enjoyed on a visit to the UK. With help from the then brewer at Larkins, Bob Hudson, Galbraith built up a strong reputation for its real ales. Hand pumps are in evidence at the pub, but the brewery also produces a Bohemian lager and Resurrection, a strong Trappist-style beer.

GOOD GEORGE

www.goodgeorge.co.nz

GOOD GEORGE started brewing in the Hamilton suburb of Frankton in 2012. It's a compact brewpub based in a former church, originally called the Church of St George, hence its name. Former Thornbridge (UK) brewer Kelly Ryan is the brewmaster and his beers include an amber, an IPA with German and New Zealand hops, and a spiced beer with peppery native bush herbs and orange zest. He has also started a barrel-ageing programme.

HARRINGTON'S BREWERIES

www.harringtonsbreweries.co.nz

CHRISTCHURCH'S LARGEST BREWERY has been making beer since 1991, when John Harrington set up the operation on the site of the old Wards Brewery. Still owned by the Harrington family, the brewery produces a broad portfolio of beers including several different styles of lagered beers, plus a porter, stout, bitter, and a hefeweizen.

MAC'S

www.macs.co.nz

FORMER ALL-BLACK TERRY MCCASHIN kicked off the New Zealand microbrewing revolution in 1981 when he set up his own brewery. In 2000, he sold the brands to Lion, who now brew them in Nelson and Wellington. Despite coming under the umbrella of the massive drinks group, Mac's beers remain popular with beer lovers, especially the Belgian-style wheat beer Great White and the fragrant and fruity Hop Rocker Pilsener.

MONTEITH'S

www.monteiths.co.nz

THE BREWERY CAME INTO BEING IN 1868 in the West Coast town of Greymouth, and it is now owned by DB Breweries. In 2001, DB decided to close the brewery stating it to be outdated and inefficient, but such was the outcry that it was reopened within days. Nowadays the original brewery is used mainly for Monteith's Brewer's Series beers, such as the Barrel Aged Porter, while the more regular beers are brewed at DB Breweries sites in Auckland and Timaru.

MUSSEL INN

www.musselinn.co.nz

ONEKAKA IS A COLOURFUL COMMUNITY located in the beautiful and remote area of Golden Bay on the north-western tip of South Island. It's an ideal home for the idiosyncratic joys of the Mussel Inn, where beer has been brewed since 1995 (they also make cider and soft drinks). Its most famous beer is Captain Cooker Manuka Beer, which contains freshly picked tips off the manuka tree, along with New Zealand organic hops. Other beers produced include the Golden Goose lager and a powerful Belgian-style beer Monkey Puzzle.

8 WIRED HOPWIRED I.P.A.

SHAKESPEARE HOTEL & BREWERY

www.shakespearehotel.co.nz

AUCKLAND IS HOME to the late-Victorian Shakespeare Hotel & Brewery, where former owner Peter Barraclough set up the first brewpub in New Zealand in 1986. The brewing kit is squeezed into a space behind the bar, and this is where veteran craft brewer Ben Middlemiss is regularly brought in to weave his magic with beers such as the succulent pale ale Dogberry and a spicy Belgian-style wheat beer White Lady.

STEAM BREWING

www.steambrewing.co.nz

THE OTAHUHU SUBURB OF AUCKLAND is home to Steam Brewing, which started brewing in 1995. Initially it brewed beers for the Cock & Bull brewpub in East Tamaki, but in 2004 the company increased in size when it bought Auckland Breweries and then supplied the Cock & Bull chain of pubs. The pubs were sold in 2012 and the beers discontinued but Steam is now a leading contract brewery, whose clients include Epic and Croucher.

STEINLAGER

www.steinlager.com

IN 1958 THE MINISTER OF FINANCE Arnold Nordmeyer, concerned about the amount of beer imports flooding into New Zealand, challenged national brewers to create a lager that could hold its own with the big European brands. The result was Lion Breweries' Steinecker. Steinlager, as it is now known, is a big player in the New Zealand brewing scene. Its range includes the crisp, tangy Classic and smooth, refreshing Pure.

THREE BOYS

www.threeboysbrewery.co.nz

RALPH BUNGARD originally wanted to make wine, but after studying in the UK – and drinking the ales – he returned home eager to set up a brewery. While working as a university lecturer, he started brewing and went full time with Three Boys in 2006. The beers are made in the Christchurch suburb of Woolston using malted barley mainly grown in the Canterbury area plus aromatic New Zealand hops. Beers include the spritzy Wheat and the rich, toasty Porter.

THE MUSSEL INN CAPTAIN COOKER MANUKA BEER

YEASTIE BOYS DIGITAL IPA

TUATARA BREWING

www.tuatarabrewing.co.nz

BACK IN 2002 when Carl Vasta began brewing on a farm in the hills north of Wellington, little did he know that 10 years later New Zealand Prime Minister John Key would drop in for a beer. Key also opened Tuatara's new operation in Paraparaumu, an impressive sign of the brewery's growth over a decade. A series of European- and US-style beers are brewed, including its vibrant India Pale Ale and a luscious Bohemian Pilsner.

THE TWISTED HOP

www.thetwistedhop.co.nz

THE TWISTED HOP is the tale of two Brits who emigrated to New Zealand separately in 2003 and began to miss their homeland's beers. Within 12 months Martin Bennett and Stephen Hardman had installed The Twisted Hop brewpub in the Lichfield Lanes part of Christchurch. Craft beer fans swooned over cask beers such as Golding Bitter and Hopback IPA. The 2011 earthquake damaged The Twisted Hop, but a new brewery and pub opened in 2012.

WIGRAM BREWING

www.wigrambrewing.co.nz

THE INFLUENCE OF THE HOME-BREWER on the New Zealand craft beer renaissance cannot be underestimated, as the example of Wigram founder Paul McGurk illustrates. After 10 years of full-mash hobby brewing, he set up Wigram in 2003 in the Christchurch suburb of the same name. Today McGurk produces an eclectic selection of beers including Propeller Lager, Mustang Pale Ale, Dakota Dark, Bitter, plus a Spruce Beer inspired by a beer Captain Cook had brewed in 1773.

YEASTIE BOYS

www.yeastieboys.co.nz

STU MCKINLAY AND SAM POSSENNISKIE set up the Yeastie Boys in 2008 in Wellington, though the beers are contract-brewed by Invercargill Brewery. As the name suggests, the duo bring a rock'n'roll sensibility to their beers with liberal use of aromatic New Zealand hops in beers such as their American-style porter Pot Kettle Black and the self-styled "aggressive wee beast" Digital IPA. The Yeastie Boys' adventurousness has not gone unnoticed and awards have been showered on them.

BEIJING YANJING

Beijing's brewery has grown hugely since it started in 1980 and it's now one of the top four brewing companies in China, employing thousands of people. It uses fresh mineral water from beneath the city to make its beers.

THE FACTS...

OWNER Beijing Yanjing Brewery Co

FOUNDED 1980

ADDRESS Shuanghe Road, Shunyi District, Beijing 101300

WEBSITE www.yanjing.com.cn

PHILOSOPHY To make the real taste of China

Beijing's best!
This popular beer is common in the Chinese capital and throughout the country

BEIJING YANJING YANJING BEER

BACK IN 1980 BEFORE Beijing Yanjing was founded, grabbing a beer in the Chinese capital wasn't always easy, even though the thirst for beer had been growing since the end of the 19th century. For the citizens of Beijing, finding beer for sale at the time was also something of an adventure. Word of mouth was a useful if slightly unpredictable tool, while sometimes those in search of beer would have the happy accident of stumbling on freshly delivered stock. This inconsistency of supply was probably a major factor in the decision to build a brewery that would administer to the specific beery needs of the Chinese capital's citizens. It has been a huge success, and over the three decades since its emergence into the world, Beijing Yanjing has grown into the fourth-largest brewery in China.

Beijing Yanjing epitomizes large, mass-production brewing. Although it sources its mineral water from 91m (300ft) below the Beijing Yanshan mountains, its main plant employs 20,000 people and covers an area of about 2sq km (1sq mile). Plus, as well as a raft of pale lagers and some fruit beers, it also produces some soft drinks.

However despite its size, there doesn't seem to be an end to its growth in sight, with the beer granted the accolade of "the taste of China". Even though it has Beijing in its title and is the best-selling brand of beer in the Chinese capital – it has 85 per cent of the Beijing market – the company also operates brewing plants in other parts of the country. What makes all this expansion so unique is that unlike its equally large competitors in the brewery industry, which have been bought up by the likes of Anheuser-Busch and SABMiller, Beijing Yanjing remains free from foreign ownership. Maybe that's why it's often served at Chinese state functions.

TASTING NOTES

YANJING BEER PALE LAGER, 5% ABV

Into the glass goes a stream of pale yellow lager with a brush of grainy sweetness on the nose. This is followed by a smooth, slightly creamy, rounded mouthfeel and a light tingle of malt-driven sweetness, before its swift finish.

FOOD PAIRING: Delicate, sweet-tasting seafood, such as stir-fried prawns, shrimp, or squid, are ideal company for a glass or two of this sweet, thirst-quenching beer.

GUANGZHOU ZHUJIANG

South China's best-selling beer, Zhujiang, is made in one of the largest breweries in the world. Known for its pale lagers, Guangzhou Zhujiang is also note-worthy for having produced one of the first ales in China.

THE FACTS...

OWNER Guangzhou Zhujiang Brewery Group

FOUNDED 1985

ADDRESS 118 Modiesha Avenue, East Xingang Road, Guangzhou 510308

WEBSITE www.zhujiangbeer.ca

PHILOSOPHY Using imported European raw materials and German yeast to make a crisp family of beers

GUANGZHOU ZHUJIANG BEGAN LIFE in the mid-1980s, just as China was starting to open out to the world. One of the new businesses eager to explore what had up until then been a sealed system was the brewing group Interbrew (now known as Anheuser-Busch InBev), who helped with the set-up. Their involvement deepened in 2002, when they bought 25 per cent of the brewery's shares.

Guangzhou Zhujiang is based in the city of Guangzhou, formerly known as Canton, which lies on the Pearl River delta, at what is regarded as one of the largest brewery sites in the world; the word Zhujiang translates literally as "Pearl River". The partnership with the multi-national Anheuser-Busch InBev has helped to make the brewery's debut beer, the light and crisp pale lager Zhujiang – pronounced "joo jung" – beer the best-selling brand in South China; it is also exported to the US, UK, France, and Australia. The size of the brewery plant is also helpful in making the brand widely available – it is estimated that nearly 50,000 bottles of the brewery's beers are produced every hour.

For the raw materials used in the beer, fresh water is drawn from a source beneath the brewery, hops come from the Czech Republic, while the barley is grown in Canada. As is the tradition for brewing in China, and Japan, rice is also added to the mix, and fermentation is with a German yeast strain. Cantonese cuisine has an excellent reputation and the brewery is not shy in suggesting beer and food matches for many of the province's dishes, such as wonton soup and steamed scallops with ginger and garlic. Zhujiang also produces several other variations on the pale lager theme and claims to be one of the first Chinese breweries to produce a top-fermented ale.

GUANGZHOU ZHUJIANG
PEARL RIVER 12°

GUANGZHOU ZHUJIANG
GOLD LABEL

GUANGZHOU ZHUJIANG
ZHUJIANG BEER

TASTING NOTES

PEARL RIVER 12° PALE LAGER, 4.3% ABV

A golden beer that when poured into the glass has a shy nose with hints of lemon in the background. The mouthfeel is soft and mellow, with some malt sweetness and a brisk, crisp carbonation before it leads to a rapid finish.

FOOD PAIRING: Slurp your way through a bowl of noodles with beef in black bean sauce and you'll find this beer an ideal accompaniment.

GOLD LABEL PALE LAGER, 4.3% ABV

Refreshment on a hot summer's day is a great reason to quench your thirst on this clean-tasting, pale-gold coloured lager that is light-bodied and slightly sweet on the palate. The finish is quick with a subdued sweetness making a brief return.

FOOD PAIRING: Try a bowl of traditional Cantonese sweet and sour pork – the beer's carbonation and sweetness will blend well with the dish's sweet-sour character.

ZHUJIANG BEER PALE LAGER, 5.3% ABV

This beer is pale yellow-gold in colour beneath a thin, short-lived collar of snow-white foam. There are sweetish malt notes on the nose with a suggestion of sweet lemon; on the palate it is crisp, light, and refreshing leading to a dry but short finish.

FOOD PAIRING: The crisp cutting edge of the beer's carbonation makes it a perfect companion to fatty foods such as a plate of prawn dumplings or barbecued pork buns.

TSINGTAO

Founded by German colonists, Tsingtao is one of the oldest breweries in modern China. It has come through war and revolution and continues to refresh beer drinkers both in China and around the world.

THE FACTS...

OWNER Tsingtao Brewery Co
FOUNDED 1903
ADDRESS Hong Kong Road, Central 266071 Qingdao
WEBSITE www.tsingtao.com.cn
PHILOSOPHY Blending the finest raw materials with fresh spring water from Laoshan mountain to produce beers with a special appeal

BEER CAME TO CHINA at the end of the 19th century as the major European powers ploughed into the country and took advantage of what was then a fractured and weakened state. Inevitably, as Germany and Britain were some of the countries involved, brewing came along with the gunboats. Tsingtao was founded in 1903 by German colonists in the seaport of Qingdao, under the name of the Anglo-German Brewery; the first beers were served on the 22nd December 1904. The Germans left during World War I and a Japanese company, the Dai-Nippon Brewery, took over. Following World War II, the Japanese were forced out and after the Communist victory in 1949 the brewery was nationalized. This remained the state of affairs until the early part of the 1990s when the brewery was privatized. At one stage Anheuser-Busch owned 27 per cent of the company, which enabled it to produce Budweiser in China, but the company left in 2009 and in a twist of fate, Japan's Asahi is now the second-largest shareholder. Given the political ups and downs in China since 1949, it's a testament to the durability of Tsingtao that not only does it remain the second best-selling beer brand in the country, but it is also the beer most people around the world would mention if asked to name a Chinese beer – it is, after all, the fourth largest beer brand in the world. It is a survivor: not only did it survive the various occupying powers, but in the early years of Communist rule when the country was blockaded, local peasants were encouraged to grow hops and barley for the company. Now the barley is grown in Canada and Australia, although the hops are Chinese, as is the rice – a common adjunct in China's beers – while the water emerges from springs on the famous Laoshan mountain, reputedly one of the birthplaces of Taoism. Its main beer, Tsingtao, is a pale lager, while most of the other beers produced at the central brewery and other plants in China are variations on the same theme – although unfiltered, weaker, or stronger – but it does also produce a stout and a dark beer. The market for beer in China is massive and continues to grow. Given the challenges it saw off in the 20th century, Tsingtao's chances of remaining at the forefront of beer in years to come are good.

In demand drink
Beers from Tsingtao are some of China's most popular and widely recognized

TSINGTAO LAOSHAN

TSINGTAO TSINGTAO

TSINGTAO SHANSHUI

TSINGTAO AUGERTA 1903

Brew and far between
Dark beers, such as Premium Stout, are a rarity in China – most are pale and yellow

TSINGTAO PREMIUM STOUT

TASTING NOTES

LAOSHAN PALE LAGER, 4% ABV
This lager is pale sunshine in the glass with a whisper of grass and citrus fruit on the nose. In the mouth it's quick and swift, leaving traces of sweet grain and citrussy lemon before exiting with a quick, welcome farewell of bitterness.

FOOD PAIRING: This is a beer for a hot summer's day, served as cold as possible; pair it with chargrilled chicken with a squeeze of lemon juice on top.

TSINGTAO PALE LAGER, 4.8% ABV
Honeyed yellow in colour and with a slight hint of malt sweetness and lemon citrus on the nose, Tsingtao's signature beer is lightly carbonated and lightly brushes the palate with sweet graininess and a faint touch of lemon citrus before its crisp finish.

FOOD PAIRING: Pour a glass and grab a plate of seafood sushi; the two of them make an exemplary couple as the beer's sweetness contrasts with the sushi's mouth-watering juiciness and hint of the sea.

SHANSHUI PALE LAGER, 4% ABV
Very pale yellow in colour, this lager has a shy nose with some malt sweetness and citrus fruitiness whirling about in the background. On the palate it has a light, clean character with the brisk carbonation providing most of the sensory theatre. The finish is quick.

FOOD PAIRING: Go basic and serve with fish and chips – the brisk carbonation will scrub the palate clean ready for the next mouthful.

AUGERTA 1903 PREMIUM AMERICAN-STYLE LAGER, 4.7% ABV
Pale yellow in colour, this has a slight nose of grain and some sweetness. The mouthfeel is light to medium with hints of citrus, malt sweetness, and an edge of peppery bitterness that gives way to a dry finish.

FOOD PAIRING: Szechuan dry-fired beef is an ideal match, as the peppery bitterness and light carbonation of the beer will lift the spiciness of the beef and add an extra element of flavour.

PREMIUM STOUT EXPORT STOUT, 7.5% ABV
A rare dark beer from China, this is the colour of cola when poured, while the nose offers up milky chocolate, caramel, liquorice, and some toasted grain. The palate has cold coffee, liquorice, a creamy mouthfeel, some roast notes, and a dry finish.

FOOD PAIRING: This should work well with the spicy notes of Szechuan-style chicken with a side helping of satay sauce.

CAMBODIA

KHMER

www.cambodiabeer.com.kh

THE LARGEST INDEPENDENT brewer in Cambodia, Khmer has invested heavily in new technology in recent years. It produces a very drinkable 5% ABV US-style lager that is light with hints of sweetness but not much hop. The beer is a perfect refresher at the end of a hot and humid day. Cambodia Lager is sold in bottles, cans, and on draught, and is best enjoyed well chilled.

KINGDOM

www.kingdombreweries.com

CAMBODIA MIGHT NOT HAVE much of a reputation either as a classic beer destination or as a country with an established brewing heritage, but Kingdom wants to change all that. The brewery opened in 2010 and it says it wants to establish itself as a craft brewer of German-style beers. The brewery is currently importing its hops and malt from Germany and the Czech Republic. Kingdom produces a pilsner-style beer and a dark lager.

INDIA

ARBOR BREWING COMPANY

www.facebook.com/arborbrewindia

DRINKERS IN BANGALORE can now enjoy US craft beers in a local brewpub thanks to investment by the Arbor Brewery in Michigan. The US company is working with University of Michigan graduate Gaurav Sikka, who is originally from Bangalore. While studying in the US, Sikka developed a taste for Arbor's beers and wanted to bring them to his hometown. The US recipes are being given an Indian twist – Arbor's Strawberry Blonde beer has now become a Mango Blonde.

BIERE CLUB

www.thebiereclub.com/brews.html

BANGALORE IS DEVELOPING quite a reputation as a home to Indian brewpubs, and the Biere Club was one of the first to open up in the city. A range of ales, lagers, stouts, and wheat beers are produced, drawing inspiration from UK and US brewing traditions. The range includes an intense stout, which is flavoured with coffee, and a zesty, orange-laced wheat beer.

DOOLALLY

www.doolally.in

NEW LAWS IN INDIA now make it much easier for entrepreneurs to open up brewpubs, and Doolally is Pune's first. The brewery produces small batches of craft beer for sale in its stylish bar and says it is on a mission to show that Indian beers can have taste. Its range includes rye, wheat, and dunkel-style lagers, all of which are Bavarian in style.

INDEPENDENCE

www.independencebrewco.com/

THE SPIRIT OF THE US craft-brewing revolution is now sweeping across India. Another of the new start-ups in Bangalore, Independence, was set up by Avanish Vellanki and Shailendra Bist with the help of legendary Californian brewer Greg Koch, co-founder of Stone Brewing (see pp.178–179). Their mission is "Independence from boring beers". The range includes a Belgian-style wheat, a saison, a dubbel and a tripel. The UK-influenced ales include a wholesome porter and a brown.

ROCKMAN

www.rockmangroup.com/beerisland

GERMAN BREWING TECHNOLOGY is at the heart of Rockman's Beer Island brewpub and leisure complex in Gurgaon, about 19 miles (30km) south of New Delhi, in one of the wealthiest parts of India. Two gleaming kettles stand proud in the Bavarian bar where German-style wheat, dark, and pale lager beers are produced following German purity laws. The associated Keg & Barrels restaurant has curious, comfortable, and cosy barrel-shaped seating areas.

TOIT

www.toit.in

CRAFT BREWERS LOVE TO USE local ingredients, so it's no surprise that Toit's brewers use basmati rice to make its blonde beer. The rest of the beer range is inspired by some of the best beer styles in Belgium, and includes an orange and spiced wheat ale.

The smart brewpub in Bangalore was founded in 2010 by three good friends, Sibi Venkataraju, Arun George, and Mukesh Tolani, who love to recommend food pairings to accompany their beers.

UNITED BREWERIES

www.theubgroup.com

HISTORICALLY, WHEREVER THE BRITISH civil service and army went, beer followed. The company's first breweries were based in southern India but can now be found across the region. United Breweries' best-known beer is Kingfisher, a crisp, lager-style beer, with some hints of sweetness. Kingfisher is exported around the world and is brewed under licence by Shepherd Neame in the UK, where it has proved to be a hit in Indian restaurants.

LAOS

LAO

www.beerlao.la

LAO BREWING COMPANY'S BEERLAO, a pale 5% ABV lager, is its best-selling beer. The beer, which is made with a mixture of local rice and imported malt, is the country's leading brand. The company, which is part-owned by Carlsberg, would now like to roll out this success internationally. The company also make a 6.5% ABV dark beer and a premium version of its pale lager, which uses Sapphire aroma hops and has a hint of tangerine.

MONGOLIA

KHAN BRÄU

www.khanbrau.net

KHAN BRÄU IS A POPULAR, UPMARKET German-style brewpub that opened in 1996, in the bustling, cosmopolitan capital city of Ulaanbaatar, in central north Mongolia. The beers are also sold in a chain of restaurants across the city as well as in its own beer garden. The range comprises a pretty standard list of German brews including a pale lager, a wheat, and a dark. Popular with overseas tourists, the locals have also got a taste for the beers. What sets Khan Bräu apart from other native beers is the fact that they are made without using additives. It has been a huge success.

SINGAPORE

ASIA PACIFIC

www.tigerbeer.com

WIDELY AVAILABLE ACROSS Asia, Asia Pacific's most famous beer is Tiger, a lager-style beer that is best served well chilled. The beer was first brewed in the 1930s and gained some notoriety when the author Anthony Burgess used its advertising slogan "Time for a Tiger" as the title of his first novel in his Malayan trilogy *The Long Day Wanes*. The company also makes an interesting 8% ABV stout, ABC Extra Stout.

ARCHIPELAGO

www.archipelagobrewery.com

WHEN IT OPENED IN 1931, Archipelago Brewery specialized in German-inspired beers. But times have changed, and now a southern hemisphere twist has been given to many of its beers – aromatic New Zealand hops have added mango and passion fruit flavour to its take on a Czech lager. And in the spirit of craft collaboration, the brewery has worked with local beer blogger Daniel Goh to create a one-off Oktoberfest beer – a Vienna-style red lager called Red October.

SOUTH KOREA

OKTOBERFEST

www.oktoberfest.co.kr

ONE OF SEOUL'S FIRST BREWPUBS, Oktoberfest opened in 2002, its German-style beers appealing not just to the tourists who visit South Korea, but to many locals who have spent time working in Germany. The brewery was founded by Bang Ho-kwon and Michael Paik, who met in 1997 in Munich, where they developed a taste for lager-style beers. The bar's most popular beer is its spicy wheat beer.

SRI LANKA

LION

www.heinekeninternational.com

ONE OF ASIA'S MOST FAMOUS BEERS is brewed on the island of Sri Lanka. The bottle-conditioned Lion Stout, produced by Lion Brewery, is as dark as a tropical night and full

ASIA PACIFIC TIGER

BOON RAWD SINGHA

of swirling fig and molasses flavours, with the bittersweet caress of freshly brewed coffee. Full of dark rum and wine flavours, it has a long warming finish. The brewery, which was founded in 1881, is now owned by Heineken.

THAILAND

BOON RAWD

www.boonrawd.co.th

FIRST COMES THE HEAT, then the humidity, and then you hear the noise of the traffic. Welcome to Bangkok, one of Asia's vibrant beating hearts. Not far from the city is Boon Rawd Brewery, a family-owned company, where Singha is brewed. This marvellous full-bodied lager-style beer has a bold hop character. A perfect thirst-quencher, it's great with the salty-sweetness of Thai food.

TAWANDANG

www.tawandang.com

BANGKOK HAS TWO German-inspired brewpubs owned by Tawandang Brewery, and another can be found in Singapore. But rather than try and recreate a German-style bar, the company says it is creating a true modern Asian atmosphere. The bright and breezy entertainment is full of Eastern promise. As for the beers, there are several well-made, easy-drinking beers: a golden lager, a malty, aromatic weizen, and a sweet, dark reddish-brown dunkel.

VIETNAM

LOUISIANE BREWHOUSE

www.louisianebrewhouse.com.vn

THE LOUISIANE BREWHOUSE is flying the flag for microbrewers in the bustling seaside resort of Nha Trang in Vietnam, where eastern and western cultures collide. The malts used come from Australia and the hops are flown in from New Zealand to make its pilsner and dark lager. There is also a witbier and a red ale. The ginger ale is flavoured with locally grown ginger and lemongrass. The local water is purified and refined with the aim of recreating the brewing water from well-known beer-making locations such as Burton-on-Trent in the UK.

SOUTH AFRICA

Although a lot of beer is consumed in South Africa, most of it is produced by one company. South African Breweries (SABMiller) – one of the world's largest brewing companies – dominates the beer market and brews the vast majority of beers that South Africans drink while cooking steaks on the braai or down in roadside shebeens. Its brands include Castle, Lion, and Carling Black Label, and they can be found almost everywhere.

Despite this, there is a small, exciting craft beer scene and talented brewers to be found. Craft brewing kicked off in 1983 when Lex Mitchell set up in Knysna in the Eastern Cape. Lex had left SABMiller to set up a boat-building business on the picturesque Knysna lagoon, but carried on brewing at home for his own pleasure – soon his hobby turned into a microbrewing business (see p.275). And as other beer-loving South Africans have travelled overseas and experienced different beer styles, they have returned with a taste for Belgian, German, UK, and US beers. These diverse influences are now reflected in the portfolios of the new brewers setting up. Both Boston Breweries' (see p.273) founder Chris Barnard and Moritz Kallmeyer of Drayman's Brewery (see p.274) were inspired by beers they had encountered while travelling in Europe. Although these brewers may be relatively few in number, they are well worth seeking out. Beers from the country's band of craft brewers can be tried at one of the local festivals

BOSTON BREWERIES

After sampling European beers, Chris Barnard was disappointed with beers he found at home. He taught himself to brew and set up his own brewery to ensure that Cape Town beer lovers had something that tickled their palates.

THE FACTS...

OWNER Chris Barnard

FOUNDED 2000

ADDRESS 48 Carlisle Street, Paarden Eiland, Cape Town, Western Cape 7405

WEBSITE www.bostonbreweries.co.za

PHILOSOPHY Hand-crafted beers with plenty of flavour

SAM ADAMS IS CONSPICUOUS by its absence at Boston Breweries in Cape Town, which was set up by Chris Barnard in 2000. Despite the name, it's nothing to do with the craft beer behemoth over the Atlantic in the US; instead it comes from a time when Barnard was brewing in a vacant space in a local factory that just happened to be called the Boston Bag Company. At the time, he was still refining his home-brewing and was giving away excess beer to the workers, who were then selling it to the local bar. The phone rang one day and it was a bar owner, who liked what he had been sold and wanted to know when he would be getting more beer from the Boston Bag Company's factory, or "Boston beer" as he termed it – by a happy accident the name of the brewery emerged.

Prior to all this, like many young people in South Africa, Barnard had gone travelling around Europe and enjoyed drinking the different beers he found there. When he returned home, the beer scene seemed flat in comparison. Home-brewing beckoned and after taking a fact-finding trip around Bavaria he decided to do something about it; by September 2000 Boston Breweries was a reality. It's a busy brewery, for as well as producing its own beers, Boston also contract-brews for several smaller concerns, such as Jack Black (see p.279). Given the period Barnard spent researching brewing in Bavaria, it's no surprise to discover that he focuses on cold-fermenting beers, with his debut beer, Premium Lager, being one of the bestsellers. There's also a 10% ABV bock style and a weiss amongst the beers, though changes have been rung with a pumpkin beer that is now brewed seasonally.

TASTING NOTES

LOADED CANON ALE DOPPELBOCK, 10% ABV
A lot of malt goes into this amber-red monster of a beer and there's a rich, ripe sense of restrained sweetness, alcohol, and aromatic hop on the nose. It's equally rich on the palate with a deep fruity overtone, caramel sprinkles, and some smoke, before it descends into a lasting, lustful finish.

FOOD PAIRING: A beer to be enjoyed on its own before bed, or with a hunk of well-matured West Country cheddar cheese.

BOSTON PREMIUM LAGER PALE LAGER, 4% ABV
Dark gold in the glass with a light and frisky nose of sweet grain and grassy, floral notes in the background. The mouthfeel is light- to medium-bodied with a crispness that is followed by a bittersweet finish with hints of grain that add an appetizing dryness.

FOOD PAIRING: Pair this with shellfish all the way, such as large grilled prawns – the crisp, bitter tones of the beer will draw out the food's innate sweetness.

JOHNNY GOLD WEISS BEER, 5% ABV
This Bavarian-style weissbier is hazy gold in the glass with classic banana notes on the nose. In the mouth it's soft and slightly acidic, which livens up the palate, while cloves, vanilla, and banana notes lead the way towards a quick fruity finish.

FOOD PAIRING: Put another boerewors sausage on the braai and pour a glass of this weiss – it's a match made in heaven.

BOSTON BREWERIES
LOADED CANON ALE

BOSTON BREWERIES
BOSTON PREMIUM LAGER

BOSTON BREWERIES
JOHNNY GOLD

DRAYMAN'S

Brewing had always been a passion of Moritz Kallmeyer, and in 1997 he finally achieved his dream by setting up Drayman's Brewery. He continues to delight Pretoria beer-lovers with his range of German-influenced beers.

THE FACTS...

OWNER Moritz Kallmeyer

FOUNDED 1997

ADDRESS 222 Dykor Road, Silverton, Pretoria, Gauteng, 0127

WEBSITE www.draymans.com

PHILOSOPHY To share and expand the spirit of fellowship and enjoyment of great beer

THE STORY OF this Pretoria-based brewery is the story of the brewing passion and endless search for perfection by its founder and brewer, Moritz Kallmeyer. He made traditional African maize beer and fruit wines while he was at school, but the beer epiphany really hit him in college when he tried his hand at home-brewing. Out in the world of work as an exercise therapist he continued to hone his brewing expertise and finally realized that it was time to make a go of it as a career. However, this was the mid-1990s and South Africa's microbrewing renaissance had yet to occur. Finally, in 1996 he landed his first brewing job at a brewpub in Pretoria and even though the enterprise failed he was not deterred – a year later he started Drayman's. The brewery was initially housed in the garage of his home before he moved into a former cowshed on the family farm. In 2000, he bought a house in the Silverton district of Pretoria, converted it into a brewery, and has been there ever since. The interior features a colourful mural of what looks like a traditional brewery – copper kettles and barrels in Bavaria – so it's no surprise to learn that Germanic brewing traditions are a big influence on his beers. The portfolio includes an alt, weiss, rauch, and a kölsch (but no pils). However, with a nod to England he also produces the seasonal Merlin's Mild and Goblin's Bitter, which use a yeast strain descended from one originally used by Whitbread Brewery. He has also branched out to distilling his own whisky.

TASTING NOTES

BERGHOF KÖLSCH, 4% ABV

Pale gold in colour, this kölsch-style beer has a hint of malt sweetness and freshly cut grass on the nose. The palate is light to medium and has a restrained sweetness before finishing with a gentle bitterness.

FOOD PAIRING: The delicacy of the beer will be overwhelmed by strongly flavoured dishes, so try it with a frittata and watch how its carbonation lifts the flavour.

EMPEROR INDIA PALE ALE 4% ABV

In direct contrast to the big booming alcoholic IPAs of modern breweries, this amber-coloured beer is session-strength with quiet notes of citrus on the nose and an adept balance between malt sweetness and more citrus on the palate. The finish is bittersweet.

FOOD PAIRING: Big IPAs work well with spicy food, but this one needs a little tenderness. Try it with a Greek salad and watch the beer's bittersweetness play off the feta's saltiness.

DRAYMAN'S BERGHOF

DRAYMAN'S EMPEROR INDIA PALE ALE

MITCHELL'S

South Africa's first microbrewery has a history dating back as far as 1983. Although the founder, Lex Mitchell, sold the brewery in 1989, it still maintains his high standards of brewing and produces a tempting range of beers.

LEX MITCHELL WAS a very astute man. Back in 1983, South African microbreweries were virtually unheard of, but Mitchell went against the grain and set up Mitchell's in the Western Cape town of Knysna. A former employee of South African Breweries (as SABMiller was then called), he clearly knew what he was doing, and his business prospered; in 1989 it was bought by UK brewing group Scottish & Newcastle. Several owners have come and gone since – Scottish & Newcastle was snapped up by Heineken in 2008 – but the brewery now has South African owners and continues to thrive. Even though Lex Mitchell is no longer with the brewery he founded, one thread of consistency since the early days is the brewmaster Dave McRae, who has been with the company since 1985 and is now one of the owners. There's a decidedly British feel to the beers that McRae has looked after over the years, including the rich and creamy Raven stout, which is classed as a milk stout, and Bosun's

Bitter, a 3.6% ABV English bitter that was the brewery's second beer, launched in 1983. There are other influences though: Forester's is a light lager, while Millwood is a blend of Forester's and Bosun's Bitter. The latter beer apparently came about when the brewery found out that local drinkers were blending the beer together in their homes and bars and so decided to produce their own version. The survival and thriving nature of this brewery, which is the second largest in the country, is a tribute to Lex Mitchell's foresight all those years ago. The man himself is now brewing with a new local microbrewery called Bridge Street.

THE FACTS...

OWNER Dave McRae, Coen Bezuidenhout, Dennis Finch, Dave Wright

FOUNDED 1983

ADDRESS Mitchell's Brewing, 3 Arend Street, Knysna 6570

WEBSITE www.mitchellsbrewery.com

PHILOSOPHY Completely natural beers, made with 100 per cent barley, water, hops, and yeast and containing no artificial preservatives or chemicals

TASTING NOTES

RAVEN MILK STOUT, 5% ABV
Black in the glass beneath a beige collar of foam, this stout offers up notes of demerara sugar and ground coffee beans on the nose, while in the mouth it is full-bodied, roasty, sweetish, and gently bitter. The finish is long and dry with hints of smoke.

FOOD PAIRING: It's a no-brainer to pair this bittersweet stout with oysters, such as those found in the brewery's local river.

90 SHILLING SCOTCH ALE, 5% ABV
This beer is light amber in colour while the nose has spicy fruitcake and caramel notes. The palate is defiantly malt-driven, with caramel, cinnamon, and dried fruit flavours, a full-bodied mouthfeel, and a lingering bittersweet finish.

FOOD PAIRING: The aromatic, full-bodied feel of the beer means that it can stand up to spicy dishes – how about a chicken satay with the beer, which will add another layer of flavour and also cut through the sauce?

OLD WOBBLY STRONG LAGER, 7% ABV
Even though the name suggests an English strong ale, this gold-coloured beer is deemed to be a strong lager by the brewery – it's got a honeyed, sweetish nose, while on the palate it's spirituous, fruity, and bittersweet before it finishes dry and sweetly bitter.

FOOD PAIRING: The alcohol and malty sweetness makes this a beer that would be bold and bracing alongside a colourful dish: chicken, stir-fried with basil, oregano, and garlic, served on top of polenta, might just do the job.

MITCHELL'S RAVEN   **MITCHELL'S** 90 SHILLING   **MITCHELL'S** OLD WOBBLY

SHONGWENI

When Englishman Stuart Robson opened the Shongweni Brewery in South Africa, he wanted to introduce the complexities of bottle-conditioned beer to drinkers who were more used to ice-cold lagers.

THE FACTS...

OWNER Brian Stewart

FOUNDED 2006

ADDRESS Robson's, Estate B13 Kassier Rd, Shongweni Valley, KwaZulu-Natal

WEBSITE www.shongwenibrewery.com

PHILOSOPHY Hand-crafted beer that uses only the finest ingredients, natural processes, and no artificial additives

STARTING UP A MICROBREWERY in South Africa is one thing, but making life even more interesting by bottle conditioning the beers is another – after all, South Africa's beer culture largely revolves around Arctic-cold lagers, and ale is often regarded to be "warm and flat beer". There's also another barrier to making a success of such an enterprise: in South Africa there is a restrictive on-trade pub and bar situation. Although pubs are not "tied" to a particular brewery in the same sense as they often are in the UK, many of them receive much of their chilling or fridge equipment from either the country's biggest brewer SABMiller or a subsidiary. This then makes it difficult for them to stock alternative products, as there is no equivalent of the "guest beer" concept.

So there were plenty of challenges for English expatriate Stuart Robson when he set up Shongweni in 2006 in the Valley of 1,000 Hills, close to the KwaZulu-Natal city of Durban. A keen home-brewer from the age of 16, he had travelled through Europe and been bowled over by the beers he'd encountered, especially the *bières de garde* of northern France. He had also achieved two college degrees in biological sciences, so was familiar with the way that commercial brewing works. As soon as he decided that brewing was for him, he took a Brewlab course in the north of England and spent some time working at various UK breweries. He then moved to the southern hemisphere where, together with his South African wife, Sherene, he set about educating the local beer palate. The two of them made an ideal team: Robson with the brewing knowledge, Sherene with a business background; she has been instrumental in the management of the brewery and in ensuring that the beer is well marketed and sold.

The brewery's portfolio of beers reflected Robson's appreciation of world beer styles, including the likes of Wheat Beer, West Coast Pale Ale, and the brewery's first beer, Durban Pale Ale, which was inspired by the IPAs sent to India in the 19th century. According to Robson, the port of Durban was an essential stop for these IPA-carrying ships and legend has it that local soldiers were prone to helping themselves to supplies. The brewery also produces several fruit beers, including mango, pineapple, and strawberry, which are all made using only locally grown fruit. And last but not least, there is also the brewery's best-selling beer, East Coast Ale, which is a South African-inspired beer that Robson has said "is unashamedly pitched directly at the lager drinkers. It's a golden ale in style but served at temperatures more associated with pilsners. It has been great for us to introduce people to the range of beers without there being too much of an initial leap in their minds. Once hooked by the taste of a craft beer, customers try our other beers and many then introduce their own friends to the beers".

Robson's passion and dedication helped Shongweni build up a strong reputation for its beers and they are now exported to various countries around the world, including the UK. The majority of the beers are bottled, but there are also some draught products, including Robson's Pilsner and Durban Brunne; there is also a specially made beer called Cowbell that is sold exclusively in a brasserie in Durban. In 2012, change came when the Robsons sold the brewery and moved back to the UK. The current owner is Brian Stewart, who had been a home-brewer for 25 years, and he now runs the brewery with his two sons Gary and Donn. Despite this change, the Shongweni Brewery has continued to go from strength to strength with an exciting range of craft beers.

TASTING NOTES

BLACK CHERRY LAGER 4% ABV

Amber in colour, this fruit-flavoured draught-dispensed lager has cherry notes on the nose, a brisk, crisp carbonation on the palate, and a sweetish centre with hints of cherry, before finishing dry and slightly fruity.

FOOD PAIRING: A great thirst-quencher on a summer's day, this is also ideal with roasted duck.

ROBSON'S PILSNER 4% ABV

The pilsner is a crisp golden lagered beer with a fresh, spicy mouthfeel thanks to the use of Czech Saaz hops. It's golden in colour and has slight hints of honey on the nose, while the finish is crisp and bittersweet. It is served on draught.

FOOD PAIRING: It's crisp enough to stand up to spice, so would be ideal with chilli chicken wings.

DURBAN BLONDE GOLDEN ALE, 5% ABV

As the name suggests, this draught beer is the colour of sunlight and it's ideal easy-drinking for a hot day. It's crisp on the palate, slightly honeyed, and features some hints of orange, before it finishes dry and bittersweet.

FOOD PAIRING: Great if quaffed in a beach bar, but also ideal for a braai on which succulent beefburgers or Mozambican prawns are grilling.

WEST COAST ALE

AMERICAN PALE ALE, 5% ABV

Light amber in colour, this pale ale has a rich nose of grain, hop spiciness, and hints of mocha coffee. On the palate, there is a mash-up of light chocolate, a slight roastiness, plus a zing of citrus fruit, before it finishes with a lingering bittersweet character.

FOOD PAIRING: The beer has a richness of malt-derived flavours plus hop-driven spiciness – chuck some spare ribs on the braai and get ready to rumble.

EAST COAST ALE

GOLDEN ALE, 4% ABV

Gold-amber in colour with tropical fruit – that could be pineapple – on the nose. The palate has more of the tropical fruit character, with a crisp and refreshing carbonation leading to a dry finish with more tropical fruit returning.

FOOD PAIRING: Fire up the braai and chuck some boerewors sausages on – you will discover that the fruitiness and crispness of the beer make the perfect companions.

DURBAN PALE ALE 5.7% ABV

This is dark gold in colour with tantalizing orange notes on the nose and an undercurrent of caramel. It has a full-bodied mouthfeel with a pleasing contrast between caramel sweetness and deep citrus notes; the finish is dry and slightly fruity.

FOOD PAIRING: South Africa's national dish is bobotie, a spicy, fruity stew – grab a glass of this strong pale ale, which will cut through the sauce and spice and refresh the mouth.

Balancing act
A complex balance of biscuity malt and spicy hops is achieved by an 8-week conditioning period

SHONGWENI WEST COAST ALE

SHONGWENI EAST COAST ALE

SHONGWENI DURBAN PALE ALE

BIERWERK AFRIKAN ALES

www.bierwerk.com

DANISH-BORN Christian Skovdal Andersen is the brains behind this "gypsy" brewery, which first started brewing at Boston Breweries in Cape Town and then moved over to Camelthorn in Namibia. Andersen, who previously brewed in Denmark with Ølfabrikken, is inspired by the diversity of local ingredients and what he sees as the potential for craft beer in the continent. Two beers are made: a dark, oaky bittersweet imperial stout and a British-style bitter using only South African-grown raw ingredients.

BIRKENHEAD

www.walkerbayestate.com

WINE AND BEER CO-EXIST very happily on the Walker Bay Estate in Stanford on the Western Cape. This is prime wine country, but since 1998 it's also been the home of Birkenhead, one of the earlier craft beer-makers to appear in South Africa. Its signature beer is a crisp, refreshing, bittersweet Premium Lager, but it also makes Honey Blonde Ale and the fearsomely flavoursome Black Snake – this is a mash-up of brandy with the brewery's Chocolate Malt Stout and Honey Blonde Ale. It's 10% ABV and allegedly as dangerous as a black mamba!

CLARENS

www.clarensbrewery.co.za

ARTISTS AND TOURISTS make their way to the beautiful Free State village of Clarens where home-brewer Stephan Meyer set up his brewery in 2006 (the brewery's beer festival is an annual fixture for beer lovers as well). There's a definite English influence to his regular beers with the Blonde being a light golden ale, English Ale featuring nutty and caramel notes, and the stout going full out for a creamy, roasty, toasty mouthfeel. Production of the beers is divided between bottle and keg, which is sold at the brewery tap.

DEVIL'S PEAK

www.devilspeakbrewing.co.za

DEVIL'S PEAK is the one of the mountains that overlooks Cape Town and it was at its base in 2010 that the eponymous brewery was set up by US-exile Greg Crum, along with a couple of local business partners. A long-time home-brewer, he had a hankering for the eclectic beers of the US – especially the West Coast – and realized that in order to make them available he had to make them himself. If you want a saison, imperial stout, or a well-hopped IPA then he is your man. As for the future, don't be surprised to see Crum having a go at a Flemish red or a smoked porter. This devil won't peak anytime soon.

THE DOG AND FIG

www.diybeer.co.za/micro-brewery/the-dog-and-fig-brewery

THERE'S AN ELEMENT of derring-do about The Dog and Fig Brewery. Founded in 2008 by a bunch of friends, it firmly nails its colours to the mast of craft brewing. Its portfolio of beers includes a traditional-style copper-hued Alternatiewe Alt, a feisty Wicked Weiss, and their homage to local traditions, Boisterous Buchu, which is described as an aromatic ale that fuses together the cultures of ancient Africa and colonial Europe. It's a small operation, based on the Klein Afrika farm outside the town of Parys in the Free State. Crystal clear water for the brewery comes from a pure source from deep within this ancient meteorite impact zone.

GILROY'S

www.gilroybeers.co.za

STEVE GILROY USED TO BE in a band, but in 2000 he opened a restaurant with an attached microbrewery in Johannesburg and immediately began to gain accolades for his beers – some call him the guru of the microbrewing movement. In 2008 he moved to his current home in the popular tourist attraction of Ngwenya Glass Village in the town of Muldersdrift and the beers continue to flow. Four beers are brewed, including Serious Dark Ale, a strong, warming amber ale that pulsates with rich nutty and roast notes. Live music and brewery tours led by Steve himself are part of the attraction of visiting this lively brewpub, which combines good food and beer with a warm Irish welcome.

HOPS HOLLOW

www.hopshollow.com

YOU'LL FIND THIS SMALL BREWERY, restaurant, and country house high up on the Long Tom Pass in the Mpumalanga province. It was here that the original owners Theo and Sarie de Beer began brewing in 2001, with Willie and

BIRKENHEAD PREMIUM LAGER

Magdaleen Botha taking over the establishment in 2008 and continuing the good brewing work. A quartet of beers is produced, with the emphasis on European styles. Diggers Draught is a kölsch-inspired ale made using imported German winter wheat malt. Like all Hops Hollow beers it is made using the pure soft mountain water that is local to the area. Blacksmith's Brew is a Belgian witbier style after the Belgian "Hoegaarden Witbier"; Mac's Porter is a deep dark ruby colour with flavours of mocha and chocolate and has been described as "hooligan juice" for its aphrodisiacal powers! Old Bull Bitter remains firmly rooted in the English tradition, using Styrian Goldings leaf hops imported from the UK and the original Whitbread yeast strain.

JACK BLACK

www.jackblackbeer.com

THIS US-INFLUENCED microbrewery is not named after the comedy actor Jack Black, but after a New York pre-Prohibition brewer. The brewery was set up in 2007 and is based in Cape Town – the beers are brewed under contract at Boston Breweries – and the pre-Prohibition theme is well and truly celebrated with its flagship Reserve Classic Lager, which looks back to the rich all-malt beers of Prohibition, albeit with Saaz and the South African hop Southern Promise. A pilsner, pale ale, and amber ale are also produced.

NAPIER

www.napierbrewery.co.za

IT'S A FAMILIAR STORY. A group of friends are fed up with big brewers' beers and get together to make their own. Mark Humphrey, Craigan Miller, and Allan Smith did exactly that when they started Napier Brewery in 2007 and it proved to be a wise move. Based in the Western Cape, Napier is a thriving artisanal brewery that looks to both British and German brewing traditions for its inspirations. It's very hands-on: its Old Charlie Stout is a robust dark beer, whose roasted barley is hand-kilned at the brewery.

NOTTINGHAM ROAD

www.nottsbrewery.co.za

HOME FOR ONE of the most successful South African microbreweries, Nottingham Road, is in the grounds of an elegant hotel and conference centre in the KwaZulu-Natal Midlands. The brewery was founded in 1996

and it is fortunate in that it is able to brew its beers with water from its own artesian well, adding just malt and hops – there are no adjuncts here. Beers range from the low-alcohol (3% ABV) Tiddly Toad Lager to the rich, roasty, and strong Pickled Pig Porter, which is also used to make the brewery's beer cheese.

SAGGY STONE

www.saggystone.co.za

SAGGY STONE IS UP IN THE MOUNTAINS near the town of Robertson, which is known for its wine tourism. Based on a family farm, the pub and restaurant came first and then the brothers Adrian and Phillip Robinson decided to make their own beer as well. They brew two regular beers with pure mountain water, one of which is uniquely based on the Californian common beer, called California Steam. The other is Stone Draught, while Big Red Ale is a seasonal speciality.

THREE SKULLS BREW WORKS

www.threeskulls.co.za

AS THE NAME MIGHT SUGGEST, Three Skulls Brew Works is not a conventional brewery. Based in a suburb of Johannesburg, and launched at the Clarens Beer Festival in 2012, there's a real sense of adventure about the beers the three friends – one of whom spent several years honing his craft at SABMiller – make. US hops are sought after and used with relish in the American pale ale, while mango and lavender go into one wheat beer, and peach and rosemary end up in another. This is craft beer South African style!

TRIGGERFISH

www.triggerfishbrewing.co.za

TRIGGERFISH BREWERY was founded in 2011 and is housed in a former dynamite factory in the Western Cape town of Somerset West. One-time home-brewer Eric van Heerden, who honed his talent in the US for a year, is the founder and owner. Unsurprisingly, given his sojourn in the US, his beers are an explosive combination of bright, expressive hopping – such as the American amber ale Roman Red and American pale ale Ocean Potion – and extreme, high-alcohol imperial dark beers. The brewery has a tasting room where the beers are served with pulled pork sandwiches and spicy wings.

TRIGGERFISH ROMAN RED

NAMIBIA

Namibia is one of the largest beer markets in the Southern African region, and many of its beers have ties with or are influenced by German traditions. But German-style beer is not the only thing on offer. Some locals drink oshikundu, or ontaku, a traditional Namibian drink made from fermented millet. It is brewed and consumed very quickly. The millet flour is mixed with a small quantity of boiling water – enough to make the mash – and then it is left to ferment for 24 hours or so. Some extra water and sugar might be added to complete the brew. Across Namibia and Africa as a whole, millet or sorghum beers are often made, and they are considered to be a food as much as a drink as they are a valuable source of carbohydrates, vitamins, and minerals.

Namibia has a number of notable breweries – some are relatively small but others, such as Namibia Breweries, produce brands such as Windhoek and Hansa, which are exported worldwide. Camelthorn brewery (see facing page) – named symbolically for a native African tree that can survive in drought-stricken conditions – was set up in 2009 by former Californian microbrewery employee Jörg Finkeldey. This start-up was one of the first in Namibia for decades, and its highly commended beers are proving that when it comes to craft brewing, Namibia is hot on the heels of its South African neighbours.

CAMELTHORN

When Jörg Finkeldey set up his brewery in 2009 he wanted to introduce the craft beer revolution to Namibia. So far so good – despite tough trading conditions, he has made Camelthorn into a byword for great craft beer.

THE FACTS...

OWNER Jörg Finkeldey

FOUNDED 2009

ADDRESS 76 Nickelstreet (Unit 2), Windhoek

WEBSITE www.camelthornbrewing.com

PHILOSOPHY To bring great craft beer to Namibia

THE CRAFT BREWING REVOLUTION finally arrived in Namibia in 2009, when Jörg Finkeldey founded Camelthorn in Windhoek, where the country's other brewery, the much larger Namibian Breweries (see pp.282–283), is based. Finkeldey was no beer novice; he had first brewed in 1992 in a Californian microbrewery and after that had earned his living travelling around the world designing and selling brewing equipment. He returned home with his family in 2006 and for the next three years planned his brewing enterprise, which he symbolically named after a hardy Namibian tree that is able to thrive in drought-hit areas. At the time he said: "The early brewing pioneers resemble the resilience of the Camelthorn, and we shall continue this quest for endurance and survival". Unsurprisingly, given the dominant influence of German brewing techniques in Namibia, Finkeldey's beers mostly went in this direction. One example is the German-style Weizen, which was designed by award-winning German brewer Michael Plank. However, Finkeldey then turned to an old brewing friend when producing Red, an American ale, while Red Dune Rooibos was made using leaves from the rooibos tree. In a region where big lager brands rule the roost, it's a tough trading world for Camelthorn, and like many a small Belgian brewery Finkeldey exports a fair amount of his beers. Next-door neighbour South Africa is an important market, and the brewery also contract-brews for the "gypsy" brewery Bierwerk Afrikan Ales (see p.278). Nothing is certain in the world of brewing, especially in the David and Goliath situation of Namibia's beer world, but Finkeldey is surviving and picking up plaudits for his beers – he obviously chose the name of his brewery wisely.

CAMELTHORN RED

CAMELTHORN BOKBEER

CAMELTHORN WEIZEN

TASTING NOTES

RED AMBER ALE, 4.5% ABV

Light amber in colour, the nose has a waft of juicy citrus, cut grass, and undertones of caramel, while the palate is bittersweet, grainy, citrussy, and grassy before it finishes dry with an appetizing bitterness at the finish.

FOOD PAIRING: The spicy and fruity hop aromatics, crisp carbonation, and bitterness will help this beer deal with a spicy dish such as green chicken curry.

BOKBEER WEIZENBOCK, 7% ABV

This dark chestnut, strong wheat beer has a spicy, malt-sweet, caramel nose, while on the palate it's crisp, well carbonated, and medium-bodied with caramel, banana, and a whisper of cloves. The finish lingers with hints of banana fruitiness.

FOOD PAIRING: This is a strong-flavoured beer, but the brisk carbonation helps to cut through rich sauces and bring out the sweetness and flavour in a venison stew or similar.

WEIZEN BAVARIAN HEFEWEIZEN, 4.5% ABV

This amber-orange wheat beer has a crisp, appetizing bite on the palate; malt sweetness, banana friskiness, and hints of clove provide the bright, colourful notes, while there's a satisfying hint of tartness in the finish.

FOOD PAIRING Try this with a grilled chicken salad as the crisp carbonation can draw out the sweetness of the meat, while the light acidity and tartness of the beer means it will get along famously with any dressing.

NAMIBIA BREWERIES

German colonists brewed the first beers in what is now called Namibia, and even though they were kicked out nearly a century ago, their brewing legacy lives on through a fine group of lagers made by Namibia Breweries.

THE FACTS...

OWNER Ohlthaver List Group
FOUNDED 1920
ADDRESS Iscor Street, Northern Industrial, Windhoek
WEBSITE www.nambrew.com
PHILOSOPHY Beers made with a strict adherence to the *Reinheitsgebot*

NAMIBIA BREWERIES
HANSA DRAUGHT

THE STORY OF NAMIBIA BREWERIES is the story of Namibia's colonial past and its emergence into statehood in 1990. Prior to World War I, the German empire ruled the country, a consequence of the so-called "Scramble for Africa" in the 19th century. One of the by-products of the country's hegemony was the formation of four breweries in 1904 – German settlers initially had beers imported from Europe, but the crippling costs made brewing beer in the country the preferable option. In 1920, after Germany's defeat and expulsion from the country, two businessmen, Carl List and Hermann Ohlthaver, brought the four breweries together to become South West Breweries, which was based in Windhoek. It is still based there today – the company's brewery in Swakopmund closed in 2005.

Throughout the decades that followed, the beers produced by the company were brewed in accordance with the German purity laws, or *Reinheitsgebot* (see p.52), of 1516 – a practice that continues today – malted barley is also brought in from Germany, as are the hops. There was one more name change to come: in 1990 when Namibia finally gained independence the company became known as Namibia Breweries.

Given the use of the *Reinheitsgebot*, it comes as no surprise to discover that the beers brewed are all lager styles varying in strength from 4–7% ABV, although its Windhoek Lager (first brewed in 1920) is one of the country's well-known and favourite beers; it is also exported abroad. Other brands produced by the company include Hansa Pilsener, Tafel Lager, and the strong Urbock, which is brewed once a year and released during the winter. The Namibians and their South African neighbours are not the only ones to enjoy the products of this brewery. In 2008, the sweet, citrussy Windhoek Lager, the bittersweet Windhoek Draught, and lightly bitter Tafel Lager all won Gold Medals at a prestigious brewing competition in Berlin, a sign that keeping to the *Reinheitsgebot* down through the years still seems like a good idea.

The brewery is committed to ensuring that beer drinkers get the most from their beer: the Namibia Breweries website contains instructions for how to pour the perfect pint, and provides a number of recipes for budding chefs who want to use their beer to great culinary effect.

Pure at heart
German influences are still evident in the beers

NAMIBIA BREWERIES
WINDHOEK LIGHT

NAMIBIA BREWERIES
TAFEL LAGER

Champion brews
Winning medals at a prestigious German beer competition adds to the prestige of these Reinheitsgebot brewed beers

NAMIBIA BREWERIES
WINDHOEK LAGER

NAMIBIA BREWERIES
WINDHOEK DRAUGHT

TASTING NOTES

HANSA DRAUGHT PALE LAGER, 4% ABV
Sunlit gold in colour with a slight hint of fruitiness and sweet graininess on the nose, Hansa Draught is a beer for refreshment. This uncomplicated beer, whose flavour profile is subtly sweet on the palate, gives a short, sharp shock of bitterness in the finish.

FOOD PAIRING: Seafood is the natural choice to enjoy with such a beer, perhaps some grilled prawns with just a drizzle of zingy lemon juice over them.

WINDHOEK LIGHT PALE LAGER, 2.4% ABV
Light by name, light by nature. This beer is straw in colour with a gentle breeze of malt sweetness on the nose, followed by a mixture of similar sweetness and then a hushed bitterness in the finish. It has a crisp and refreshing mouthfeel.

FOOD PAIRING: Despite its adherence to the light beer style, this has a surprising amount of flavour and might just make the ideal companion to a plate of juicy, salty bratwurst.

TAFEL LAGER 4% ABV
Tafel Lager gleams pale gold in the glass, sitting beneath a fluffy white head of foam. The aroma is shy, with sweetness and a hint of grain. In the mouth, there are delicate hints of sweetness and crisp carbonation, and a light bitter finish.

FOOD PAIRING: This is ideal for refreshment on a hot summer's day, but it would also be an ideal partner for a roast dinner.

WINDHOEK LAGER 4% ABV
A long-established favourite, this clear golden lager has a hint of grainy sweetness and lemon citrus on the nose, while the palate sees further light sweetness, a mineral-like dryness, slight lemon, and a soft bitter finish.

FOOD PAIRING: Once again, the beer's carbonation and crispness is key to the kind of dish it's matched with; grilled salmon should see the beer cut through the oiliness and lift the flavour of the fish.

WINDHOEK DRAUGHT PALE LAGER, 4% ABV
Pristine gold with a snowy white head of foam. The nose is grainy with slight floral notes in the background. The mouthfeel is light to medium and has a hint of fruit and grainy sweetness. The finish is bittersweet.

FOOD PAIRING: Spicy food will work well with the crispness of Draught, so why not try with a chilli con carne?

LEGEND HAS IT THAT THE GODS TAUGHT AFRICANS TO BREW. TODAY, CRAFT
BREWERS LOOK TO MODERN TECHNOLOGY RATHER THAN MYSTICISM

A CHILLED WHEAT BEER, AS FOUND AT CAMELTHORN BREWERY (SEE P.283), PROVIDES WELCOME RELIEF FROM THE PARCHING HEAT OF THE AFRICAN SUN

GLOSSARY

abbey ale Belgian family of strong, fruity beers either produced or inspired by monastery brewers.

ABV Alcohol by volume, expressed as a percentage. A measure of the strength of a beer.

adjuncts Strictly speaking, anything added to the brewing process other than barley, hops, yeast, and water. More usually refers to unmalted grains such as rice, barley, oats, and maize, added to increase alcohol content and lighten flavour.

ale A beer made with ale yeasts. Styles include golden ale, brown ale, mild, and bitter.

ale yeasts Yeasts used in traditional top-fermenting ales, originating from recycled yeast skimmed from the surface of the last batch. They ferment at room temperature.

alt, altbier German style of beer similar to British bitter or pale ale, especially associated with Düsseldorf.

aromatic hops A term used to distinguish the floral and fruitier hops, such as Cascade and Goldings, that are used to impart additional flavours and aromas to beer. Aromatic hops are usually added later in the boil than bittering hops to maintain the subtlety of their attributes.

barley wine An extra-strong style of ale, originally English, but now produced by many US brewers.

Berliner Weisse A pale, top-fermented wheat beer from northern Germany.

bière de garde "Keeping beer" traditional to northern France. Brewed in winter and spring, then bottled and stored to be drunk later in the year by thirsty farmhands. The style is now brewed year-round in several brewing nations.

bitter, best bitter English beer style, usually designating a well-hopped ale. Best bitter usually refers to stronger variants of the beer.

bittering hops Hop varieties such as Chinook and Fuggles that are rich in chemical compounds that result in the bitter taste sensation in beer and are used to balance the sweetness of malt. As distinct from aromatic hops.

blond, blonde A mainly French and Belgian term for a golden beer.

bock A German term for a strong beer – formerly seasonal, but not any more. Several variations include the even-stronger doppelbock and urbock, made in the original 13th-century style. *See also eisbock.*

bottle conditioning The process by which beers are bottled with live yeast and sometimes fermentable sugars, extending storage life and allowing flavour and effervescence to develop further over time.

bottom fermenting Term used to describe yeasts of the Saccharomyces carlsbergensis strain that are used to make lager. During lagering (storage), the yeast sinks to the bottom of the brew, producing a clean-tasting beer.

brettanomyces A semi-wild genus of yeast used in lambic beers and some porters and stouts. Provides a distinctive aroma and flavour.

brew kettle The vessel in which the wort is boiled with hops to combine their flavours, usually for about 90 minutes.

brewpub A bar or restaurant with its own small brewery on the premises.

broyhan Top-fermented pale wheat beer created in Germany in 1526.

burton union A system of fermentation in galleries of linked casks, in which a stable yeast culture develops over time. Introduced in the 19th century in the brewing town of Burton-on-Trent in England.

carbonation Carbonation is the cause of effervescence in beer, and is generated by the metabolic action of yeast or by the artificial introduction of pressurized gas.

cask conditioning, cask ale The practice of bringing draught beer to maturity in the cask, in the conditioning room of a brewery or in the cellar of a pub. Times range from a week to a year or more.

c-hops Term used for hops with a very high aromatic potential, which convey especially grapefruit and resiny flavours. They are known by this term because many have names beginning with C (Cascade, Chinook, Cluster, Centennial, for example), but it also encompasses Amarillo and Simcoe.

contract brewing Commercial arrangement in which the creator of a beer contracts to have it produced at a brewery with spare capacity.

coolship A large, shallow, open vessel used for cooling wort. Today, they are primarily used by brewers wanting to ferment beer using wild airborne yeasts.

copper Alternative name for the brew kettle. Many copper kettles survive, but today a greater number are made from stainless steel.

curaçao A small, bitter orange grown in the former Dutch colony of Curaçao in the Caribbean. The dried peel is used in some Belgian wheat beers, most notably Hoegaarden.

decoction A process in which some of the wort is removed from the mash tun, heated to a higher temperature, then returned to the brew. It helps produce complex caramel flavours and clearer beers.

doppelbock *see bock.*

dortmunder Pale golden, full-bodied, bottom-fermented beer from Dortmund in Germany.

double, dubbel A Belgian abbey ale, stronger than a pilsner but less so than a triple or trippel.

dry hopping The addition of hops to the finished brew to enhance its aroma and flavour.

dunkel, dunkler bock Dunkel means "dark" in German, and the term most readily applies to dark lagers though it can also be applied to dark wheat beers. A dunkler bock is a bock-strength dark lager.

eisbock The strongest type of bock, lagered in ice-cold cellars, with frozen water crystals filtered off to increase the strength of the beer.

ester, estery An ester is a natural chemical compound that imparts fruity and spicy flavours (banana, strawberry, clove). Consequently, estery is a tasting note associated with some beers.

export Term often used for a premium beer, except in Germany, however, where it indicates a Dortmunder-style beer.

extreme beers Term originating in the US to describe a wide range of beer styles that are extraordinary in some way. Unusual ingredients, wild yeast fermentation, bourbon-keg ageing, or very high alcohol content might earn a beer the title "extreme".

fermentation The conversion of malt sugars to alcohol and CO2 by the action of yeast.

feistbeer German term for any beer that is traditionally brewed for a festival. Sometimes it refers to märzen and Oktoberfest styles, both strong variants of Vienna lager.

gose Distinctively salty style of wheat beer native to Leipzig.

grist Ground malt (or other grains) which, along with warm water, forms the basis of wort.

gueuze, geuze A blend of young and old lambic beers, blended to produce a sparkling, refreshing beer.

head The foam that forms on top of a beer when it is poured.

hefeweizen German term for wheat beer with yeast sediment. "Hefe" is a German word for yeast.

hell, helles German term designating a pale-coloured beer.

hops Hop flowers – in dried, pellet, or resinous form – are added to beer to give flavour, aroma, and a bitterness to complement the sweetness of malt. *See also aromatic hops, bittering hops, and noble hops.*

hop back A sieve-like vessel through which a brew is filtered. Its purpose is either to remove hop petals, or, when pre-filled with fresh hops, to add more flavour to the brew.

imperial stout Extra-strong stout made for export; the name stems from the beer's popularity with the Russian Imperial court.

IPA India pale ale; a robust and heavily-hopped beer that was originally made to withstand the rigours of export by sea to India from Britain. Now also produced by several other brewing nations.

kellerbier "Cellar beer" in German; usually an unfiltered lager, hoppy and only lightly carbonated.

kölsch Light style of top-fermenting golden ale first brewed in and around the city of Cologne (Köln).

kriek A Belgian lambic in which macerated cherries are fermented, giving a tart, fruity flavour.

lace, lacing Pattern of foam left clinging to the sides of the glass.

lactic, lactic acid An acid that imparts a sour flavour to beer, produced when lactobacilli metabolize sugars. A tasting note for some beers.

lactobacillus A family of bacteria, usually benign, that convert sugars to lactic acid. The resulting sourness defines certain styles, such as Berliner weisse.

lager Family of bottom-fermented beer styles. Examples range from black beers such as schwarzbier to the more familiar golden pilsner.

lambic Designates beers fermented by wild, airborne yeasts in small, rural breweries in the Payottenland region of Belgium.

late hopping The technique of adding hops to the brew kettle in the final minutes of boiling, so imparting pronounced hop flavours.

lees Yeast deposits resulting from secondary fermentation in the bottle.

malt Barley or other grains that have undergone a process of controlled germination, which is arrested at a point when the seed contains high concentrations of starches. After drying, kilning, or roasting, the malt may be made into grist for brewing.

maltings A facility in which the grain is steeped in water, allowed partially to germinate, and then dried.

märzen Originally a German style of medium-strong beer brewed in March (März in German) and matured until September or October. These days, the style of beer may be brewed and drunk year-round.

mash The mixture created when the grist is steeped in hot water. The mashing process breaks down grain starches into fermentable sugars.

mash bill A US term for the proportion of different grains used in the mash.

méthode champenoise, méthode traditionelle A form of bottle conditioning that follows the method for creating Champagne. A secondary fermentation is achieved in the bottle by adding yeast and fermentable sugars. Beers made with this method are usually produced in Champagne-style bottles and the beer can usually mature for several years.

microbrewery Generic term for small breweries founded from the 1970s onwards producing relatively small quantities of beer. The US Brewers Association defines the term as a brewery that produces less than 15,000 barrels of beer per year.

mild A lightly-hopped and thus mild-tasting ale, usually of modest alcoholic strength. Traditionally associated with the industrial regions of Wales and the English midlands.

milk stout A sweet stout made with unfermentable lactose sugars, derived from milk, that sweeten the beer's final taste.

münchner (Munich dunkel) A German style of dark lager that was developed in Munich.

noble hops Term used specifically for a group of four traditional aromatic varieties of hops that are low in bitterness: Hallertau, Žatec (or Saaz), Tettnanger, and Spalter.

nonic glass A classic style of smooth-sided beer glass, typically made in half-pint and pint sizes. It is characterized by a bulge in its profile that aids grip.

northwest hops Refers to the Pacific Northwest of the US – the country's main hop-growing region. Cluster hops were traditionally grown here, but now many other, especially aromatic, varieties are grown too.

oatmeal stout A revived style, popular in the US, brewed with up to 5 per cent oats.

Oktoberfest A two-week beer festival held in the Bavarian city of Munich in Germany.

original gravity A measure of density of wort. High density indicates abundant fermentable sugars. The more sugar, the stronger the resulting beer will be.

oud bruin "Old brown"; a Flanders-style beer with a lengthy ageing period of up to a year.

pale ale A style of beer that originated in the UK, characterized by the use of pale malts. It mostly applies to bottled beers.

pasteurization Heat treatment process applied to beer to maintain its stability during storage. Arguably, pasteurization deadens the flavour of beer marginally.

pilsner, pils A popular style of golden lager pioneered in the Czech town of Plzeň, or Pilsen.

Plato (°) Often used in central Europe – Czech and Slovak brewers often produce and name 10° and 12° versions of their beers. Similar to original gravity, it is not a measure of strength but indicates the ratio of fermentable sugars to water.

porter A family of very dark beers characterized by dark chocolate malt flavours and assertive hop bitterness.

priming The addition of sugar to a beer before bottling to encourage carbonation.

rauchbier A German style of lager made from malt that has been smoked over beechwood fires. The beer is a Franconian speciality.

reinheitsgebot The German beer purity law of 1516; now superceded by updated legislation but still a guiding principle in German beer making. Under its ruling, beers must not contain anything but water, yeast, malt, and hops.

saison Originally a Belgian beer style; a dry, strongish ale, traditionally brewed in winter for drinking in summer. These days, the style can be produced year-round, and it is usually bottle-conditioned.

schwarzbier "Black beer" in German. A dark, opaque style of lager.

seasonal beers Beers made for limited periods of sale, usually to suit climatic conditions at a given point of the year (such as märzens and saisons), or to celebrate a holiday or commemorate a historical event – a festbier for Oktoberfest, for example.

session beer Term describing an easy-drinking beer that is relatively low in alcohol and thus suitable for drinking in quantity.

sour ales, sour beer Originating in Flanders, these ales typically undergo ageing for between 18 months and two years in oak tuns, during which they gain a sharply thirst-quenching acetic character.

stein A traditional German tankard, made either of glass or ceramic (stein translates as "stone").

stout A dark style of beer, usually top-fermenting, that is made with highly roasted grain.

tap, taproom On-site bar or pub that serves a brewery's products direct to visiting drinkers.

top fermenting Descriptive of all ale yeasts of the Saccharomyces cerevisiae strain, which produce a thick foam at the top of the fermentation tank.

tun A vessel in which the mash is steeped.

triple, tripel, trippel Traditionally the strongest Belgian abbey ale; though there are now quadruples to

exceed them. In more general use, it denotes a very strong ale.

trub The sediment left at the bottom of the fermenter after fermentation has occurred, though it can come from other vessels. It primarily contains hop remnants and dead yeast.

urbock *see bock.*

urtype "Original type" in German; term used to emphasize that a beer is an authentic example of an established style.

Vienna lager Bronze-to-red lager with a sweetish malt aroma and flavour. Pioneered by Austrian brewer Anton Dreher.

weiss, weisse "White" in German, denoting a wheat beer.

weizenbier German generic term for wheat beer.

wheat beer Beer containing a high level of malted wheat. Usually top-fermented and often bottle-conditioned. Pale and cloudy with suspended yeast particles, creamy-textured and sweetish.

wild beer Beer that has been spontaneously fermented by wild yeasts, through being left exposed to the elements for a period of time. The classic example is Belgian lambic.

wit, witbier "White", "white beer" in Belgian: wheat beer.

wort An infusion containing fermentable sugars that is produced by the mashing process. The wort is filtered, boiled, and cooled before yeast is added to initiate the process of fermentation.

yeast A large family of unicellular fungal organisms, certain species of which are active agents in brewing and baking.

Yorkshire squares Square fermenting vessels associated with traditional brewing in the English county of Yorkshire. They are said to produce a remarkably well-balanced beer between sweet maltiness and yeasty sourness.

INDEX

PICTURE CREDITS

The publisher would like to thank the following for their kind permission to reproduce their photographs:

Key: a-above; b-below/bottom; c-centre; f-far; l-left; r-right; t-top

4–5: © Cath Harries. 6: © Cath Harries. 8: © SABMiller (bl). 9: SABMiller (br, tl); © Cerveceros de Espana (tr). 10: © The Pike Brewing Company. 11: © The Pike Brewing Company (tl, tr). © CAMRA (bl). Courtesy of John Holl & Jack McAuliffe (br) 12: Courtesy Orange County Archives (tr). © Anchor Brewing (cr). Courtesy of John Holl & Jack McAuliffe (bl) 14: © Cath Harries cl, cb, tr). 15: © Cath Harries (tr, br). 22: © CAMRA (bl). 23: © www.craftbeerassociation.jp (bl). Angela Pfeiffenberger-Stacey (br). 24-25: © Cath Harries (bc). 57: © Cath Harries. 100: © Cath Harries. 101: SABMiller. 113: Kreativ Fotografering / Jonas Ankersand (all). 124: Tino Gerbaldo (all). 152: Courtesy of Brooklyn Brewery (all). 171: © studioschulz.com (all). 173: Russian River Brewing Company (all). 178: © studioschulz.com (tl). 214: Stéphane Daoust (c). 229: © Erica Colombo (tl). 230: Piano&Piano, Santiago-Chile (l). 232: SABMiller (bl,r); © www. craftbeerassociation.jp (tl,cr).233: www. craftbeerassociation.jp (tr). 239: © www.craftbeerassociation.jp. 270: SABMiller (l). 271: SABMiller (tr).

Dorling Kindersley would also like to thank all the breweries that took part in the book who kindly supplied us with beer and brewery images.

All other images © Dorling Kindersley For further information see: www. dkimages.com

ABOUT THE AUTHORS

Tim Hampson is a journalist and writer who for many years has travelled the world in pursuit of the perfect beer. His published works include *The Beer Book* (DK), *Eyewitness Companion Beer* (DK), *Great Beers* (DK), *101 Beer Days Out*, *London's Riverside Pubs*, *London's Best Pubs*, *London's Best Style Bars*, *Room at the Inn*, *The Oxford Companion to Beer*, and *1001 Beers You Must Try Before You Die*. He writes the news for *What's Brewing* newspaper and his work has been published in many periodicals including the *Telegraph, Guardian, Drinks International,* and *American Brewer*. He is a regular broadcaster on beer and pubs, is a judge at beer competitions around the world, and is currently chairman of the British Guild of Beer Writers.

Stan Hieronymus is an expert on US beer culture and a man of many questions. Dan Carey of New Glarus Brewing (see p.167) likened Stan to the television detective Columbo, saying, "You are leaving, then there is always one more question." Stan has shared the answers he collected in hundreds of magazine articles about beer, contributed to numerous books, and written seven books of his own, including *For the Love of Hops* and *Brew Like a Monk*. He has won numerous awards, including USA Beer Writer of the Year, but particularly treasures a Southwest Book Award for *Frank Applegate of Santa Fe: Artist and Preservationist*, co-written with his wife, Daria Labinsky, who deserves all the credit for that one. He thanks her and their daughter, Sierra, every day for letting him ramble about asking questions.

Sylvia Kopp is an independent beer sommelier and journalist based in Berlin, Germany. She is a jury member at the World Beer Cup (USA) and the European Beer Star (Munich, Germany), holds lectures and seminars about beer, and hosts tastings and beer dinners for consumers and professional audiences. For German food magazines like *Effilee, essen & trinken,* and *Der Feinschmecker* she writes reports about beers and brewers. She is also co-author of the international beer guide *1001 Beers You Must Try Before You Die*.

Adrian Tierney-Jones is an award-winning journalist and author specializing in beer, pubs, and travel, whose work appears in the UK's *Daily Telegraph, Beer Magazine, Sunday Times Travel Magazine,* the *Publican Morning Advertiser,* and *All About Beer* amongst many others. His books include *Great British Pubs, The Big Book of Beer,* and *1001 Beers You Must Try Before You Die*; he has contributed to several other books including *The Oxford Companion to Beer*. He is chief European judge for the World Beer Awards and a passionate talker about beer, whether to a crowded hall or friends in his local pub.

ACKNOWLEDGMENTS

TIM HAMPSON'S ACKNOWLEDGMENTS

In an era when beer is made and acclaimed worldwide it is impossible for a book of this depth, breadth, and quality to be the work of one person. In my quest to find the perfect beer, I had to enlist the help of other beer travellers who are fellow students of the astonishing, joyful diversity of brewing. Adrian Tierney-Jones is mobilizing the English language to find original ways of describing the vivid creations brewers can create from the apparently simple ingredients of malt, hops, yeast, and water. His rock and roll eloquence is bringing beer to a new audience. Stan Hieronymus has been criss-crossing the US for many years and is an articulate eyewitness to the world's most exciting brewing nation. There are no shades of mediocrity in his electrifying prose and his savant-like knowledge of brewing in the US is unrivalled. Sylvia Kopp writes better about beer in her second language than most people can do in their first. She is on a mission to tell the world about beer, its myriad flavours, and its benefits to our health. She has also convinced me that Germany can compete on the craft beer stage. Thanks too should go to the beer writers Carsten Berthelsens and Conrad Seidl for their wise council on the merits of including some of the brewers. Finally there are many unsung heroes at Dorling Kindersley who helped make this book happen. However, without one it would probably have never seen the light of day. The project's editor Becky Shackleton pushed, cajoled, and skillfully guided us all through the book's schedule with humour, tact, and immense professionalism.

PUBLISHER'S ACKNOWLEDGMENTS
Proofreader Fiona Wild
Indexer Bill Johncocks
Picture researcher Jenny Faithful

Dorling Kindersley would also like to thank:
All the breweries that took part in the book, many of which provided us with logos and bottle and brewery imagery.

Charles and Rose Finkel, founders of the **Pike Brewing Company**, Seattle, who kindly gave us so much of their time and expertise and allowed us to use images from their excellent Pike Micro Brewery Museum – one of the largest archives of beer-related items in the world.

Charles Guerrier and Ryouji Oda from **The Japan Craft Beer Association**, who went above and beyond to help us source so many excellent images.

Cath Harries for giving us access to her large and outstanding collection of brewing and beer images.

Stephanie Mountifield from **SABMiller**, Neil Walker from **CAMRA**, and John Holl and Jack McAuliffe for providing us with images; John Sadler for picture research; Jack Anderson for modelling.